THE SOUTH CHINA SEA DISPUTE

ISEAS – Yusof Ishak Institute (formerly the Institute of Southeast Asian Studies) was established as an autonomous organization in 1968. It is a regional centre dedicated to the study of socio-political, security and economic trends and developments in Southeast Asia and its wider geostrategic and economic environment.

The Institute's research programmes are the Regional Economic Studies (RES, including ASEAN and APEC), Regional Strategic and Political Studies (RSPS), and Regional Social and Cultural Studies (RSCS).

ISEAS Publishing, an established academic press, has issued more than 2,000 books and journals. It is the largest scholarly publisher of research about Southeast Asia from within the region. ISEAS Publications works with many other academic and trade publishers and distributors to disseminate important research and analyses from and about Southeast Asia to the rest of the world.

THE SOUTH CHINA SEA DISPUTE
NAVIGATING DIPLOMATIC AND STRATEGIC TENSIONS

Edited by
Ian Storey and
Lin Cheng-yi

ISEAS YUSOF ISHAK INSTITUTE

First published in Singapore in 2016 by
ISEAS Publishing
30 Heng Mui Keng Terrace
Singapore 119614
E-mail: publish@iseas.edu.sg
Website: http://bookshop.iseas.edu.sg

The responsibility for facts and opinions in this publication rests exclusively with the authors and their interpretations do not necessarily reflect the views or the policy of the publisher or its supporters.

ISEAS Library Cataloguing-in-Publication Data

The South China Sea Dispute : Navigating Diplomatic and Strategic Tensions / edited by Ian Storey and Cheng-Yi Lin.
1. South China Sea—International status.
2. Territorial waters—South China Sea.
3. South China Sea—Claims.
4. South China Sea—Strategic aspects.
5. China—Foreign relations—Southeast Asia.
6. Southeast Asia—Foreign relations—China.
7. United States—Foreign relations—Southeast Asia.
8. Southeast Asia—Foreign relations—United States.
I. Storey, Ian.
II. Lin, Cheng-yi.
KZA1692 S722   December 2015

ISBN 978-981-4695-55-8 (soft cover)
ISBN 978-981-4695-56-5 (E-book PDF)

Cover Photo: CSIS Asia Maritime Transparency Initiative/DigitalGlobe.

Typeset by International Typesetters Pte Ltd
Printed in Singapore by Markono Print Media Pte Ltd

CONTENTS

ABOUT THE CONTRIBUTORS

Alice D. Ba is Associate Professor of Political Science and International Relations at the University of Delaware, Dewark. Her research focuses on the politics of regionalism in East Asia and the Asia Pacific, especially ASEAN; Southeast Asia's relations with China, the United States and Japan; and comparative questions of regime building and institutional change. The author of *(Re)Negotiating East and Southeast Asia: Region, Regionalism, and the Association of Southeast Asian Nations* (2009), Professor Ba also co-edited *Contending Perspectives on Global Governance: Coherence Contestation and World Order* (2005). Her articles have appeared in *Asian Survey, Contemporary Southeast Asia, International Relations of the Asia-Pacific* and *Pacific Review.* Her recent chapters and articles include "Power Bumps on the Way to Community: Asia's Competing Security Logics" (2014); "Is China Leading: China, Southeast Asia, and East Asian Integration" (2014); and "The Association of Southeast Asian Nations: Between Internal and External Legitimacy" (2013). A research associate of the ASEAN Studies Center at American University in Washington, D.C., Professor Ba also serves on the editorial boards of *Australian Journal of International Affairs, Journal of Current Southeast Asian Affairs* and Routledge's Comparative Asian Politics series.

Aileen San Pablo-Baviera is a Professor at the Asian Center, University of the Philippines and editor-in-chief of *Asian Politics & Policy.* She is also a Visiting Professor at the University of Malaya where she teaches at the Asia-Europe Institute. Her teaching and research specializations include contemporary China and International Relations (specifically Southeast Asia–China relations, Asia-Pacific security, the South China Sea maritime and territorial disputes and regional integration). Her recent publications include "Changing Dynamics in Philippines–China–US Relations: Impact of the South China Sea Disputes" (2014); "An ASEAN Perspective on the South China Sea: China–ASEAN Collision or China–US Hegemonic

Competition" (2014); "Territorial and Maritime Jurisdiction Disputes in East Asia: Comparing Bilateral and Multilateral Approaches" (2013); and "Accommodation with Hedging: Southeast Asia's Changing Perspectives toward China" (2010). Professor Baviera has held visiting fellowships and lectured at various institutions in Australia, China, Japan, India, Malaysia, Singapore, Taiwan and the United States. She is an active member of the Philippine Association for Chinese Studies and the National Research Council of the Philippines, as well as founding president of the recently established Asia Pacific Pathways to Progress Foundation.

Hoang Anh Tuan is Vietnam's ambassador to the Republic of Indonesia. He was formerly Director-General of the Institute for Foreign Policy and Strategic Studies at the Diplomatic Academy of Vietnam (DAV) in Hanoi. He is also co-founder of the Southeast Asia Roundtable, Washington, D.C. He served as Minister Counselor at the Embassy of Vietnam in Washington D.C. from March 2007 to September 2010. Before that, he held various research positions at DAV, including the director of research. Dr Hoang obtained his undergraduate degree at the College of Foreign Affairs, Hanoi and his Master's and PhD from the Fletcher School of Law and Diplomacy, Tufts University. He has been a visiting fellow at various research institutions, including the Institute of International Peace Research, Norway; the Nordic Institute of Asian Studies, Denmark; the Institute of Southeast Asian Studies, Singapore; and Uppsala University, Sweden. He has published extensively on politics and security in East Asia and the foreign policies of Vietnam, China and the United States.

Anne Hsiu-An Hsiao is an Associate Research Fellow at the Institute of International Relations (IIR), National Chengchi University in Taiwan. She received her PhD in Law from the London School of Economics and Political Science (LSE) in the United Kingdom. Her research interests include theory and development of international law; international law issues related to cross-straits relations; dispute settlement and conflict management of territorial disputes, especially in the South and East China Seas. Before joining IIR, Professor Hsiao served on Taiwan's National Security Council and at the Taiwan Foundation for Democracy (TFD).

Li Mingjiang is an Associate Professor at the S. Rajaratnam School of International Studies (RSIS), Nanyang Technological University, Singapore. He is also the Coordinator of the China Programme at RSIS. He received his PhD in Political Science from Boston University. His research interests include China's diplomatic history, Sino–U.S. relations, Asia-Pacific security, and domestic sources of Chinese foreign policy. He is the author (including editor and co-editor) of twelve books. His recent co-edited volumes include *China's Power and Asian Security* (2014) and *New Dynamics in US–China Relations: Contending for the Asia Pacific* (2014). He has published articles in *Global Governance, Cold War History, Journal of Contemporary China, The Chinese Journal of International Politics, China: An International Journal, China Security, Harvard Asia Quarterly, Security Challenges* and *The International Spectator*. Dr Li frequently participates in various track-two events on East Asian regional security.

Cheng-yi Lin is a Research Fellow at the Institute of European and American Studies, Academia Sinica, Taiwan. He received his PhD in Foreign Affairs from the University of Virginia in 1987. He has conducted extensive studies on Sino–American relations and Taiwan's national security policy. His articles have been published in *American Foreign Policy Interests, Asian Affairs, Asian Survey, China Quarterly, Issues & Studies, Journal of Northeast Asian Studies* and *Korean Journal of Defense Analysis*. He co-edited *Rise of China: Beijing's Strategies and Implications for the Asia-Pacific* (2009) and *The Future of United States, China, and Taiwan Relations* (2011). He was Director of the Institute of European and American Studies at Academia Sinica (1998–2003), Director of the Institute of International Relations at National Chengchi University (2004–5), and Executive Director of the Center for Asia-Pacific Area Studies at Academia Sinica (2009–12).

Elina Noor is Director, Foreign Policy and Security Studies, Institute of Strategic and International Studies (ISIS) Malaysia. She was previously a key team member of the Brookings Institution's Project on U.S. Relations with the Islamic World in its formative years post-September 11, 2001 and researched on weapons of mass destruction terrorism prior at the Center for Nonproliferation Studies, Monterey Institute of International Studies in Washington, D.C. Her policy interests include U.S.–Malaysia relations, cyber warfare and security, radicalization and terrorism, and major power relations. Her commentaries have appeared in local and foreign media, including the *New Straits Times, BFM*, the *New York Times* and *Al-Jazeera*. Ms Noor read law at Oxford University and earned her Blue playing ice hockey there. She obtained an LLM in Public International Law from the London School of Economics and Political Science (LSE), graduating with distinction at the top of her class. A recipient of the

Perdana (Malaysian Prime Minister's) Fellowship, she also holds a Master's degree in Security Studies from Georgetown University where she was a Women in International Security Scholar. She has been honoured twice by *Marie Claire Malaysia* magazine as a Woman of Style and Substance, and by *The Malaysian Women's Weekly* as one of its 2011 Great Women of Our Time.

Denny Roy is a Senior Fellow at the East-West Center, Honolulu, Hawaii where he focuses on international security issues in the Asia-Pacific region. Prior to joining the East-West Center in 2007, Dr Roy worked at the Asia-Pacific Center for Security Studies in Honolulu, the Naval Postgraduate School in Monterey, the Strategic and Defence Studies Centre at the Australian National University in Canberra, the National University of Singapore, and Brigham Young University in Utah. He obtained his PhD in Political Science from the University of Chicago in 1991. His articles have appeared in *International Security, Survival, Asian Survey, Security Dialogue, Contemporary Southeast Asia, Armed Forces & Society* and *Issues & Studies*. His books include *The North Korea Crisis and Regional Responses* (co-editor, 2015); *Return of the Dragon: Rising China and Regional Security* (2013); *The Pacific War and Its Political Legacies* (2009); *Taiwan: A Political History* (2003); and *China's Foreign Relations* (1998).

Yoichiro Sato holds a B.A. (Law) from Keio University, a Master's degree (International Studies) from the University of South Carolina, and PhD (Political Science) from the University of Hawaii. He is currently a Professor at Ritsumeikan Asia Pacific University (APU) and is the Director of the Democracy Promotion Center. Before joining APU, he was an Associate Professor at the U.S. Department of Defense's Asia-Pacific Center for Security Studies, Honolulu, where he taught mid-rank military and diplomatic officers. He has also taught at Auckland University in New Zealand, Kansai Gaidai Hawaii College and the University of Hawaii. His main research areas include Japanese foreign policy, Asia-Pacific security and political economy, maritime security and fisheries issues. His major works include *The U.S.–Japan Security Alliance: Regional Multilateralism* (co-editor, 2011); *Norms, Interests, and Power in Japanese Foreign Policy* (co-editor, 2008); and *The Rise of China and International Security: America and Asia Respond* (co-editor, 2008). He has appeared in international media, including *Time Magazine*, Bloomberg Television, MSNBC, National Public Radio, *Defense News, New Zealand Herald,*

TVNZ (New Zealand), Radio Australia, *Agence France-Presse* (France), the *Strait Times* (Singapore), and Al Jazeera.

Clive Schofield is Professor and Director of Research at the Australian Centre for Ocean Resource and Security (ANCORS) at the University of Wollongong (UOW). He is also the Leader of the Sustaining Coastal and Marine Zones research theme within the UOW Global Challenges Program. He is an Australian Research Council (ARC) Future Fellowship and is a former ARC QEII Fellow. He holds a PhD (Geography) from the University of Durham in the United Kingdom and an LLM from the University of British Columbia, Canada. Professor Schofield's research interests relate to international boundaries and particularly maritime boundary delimitation and marine jurisdictional issues. He has published over 200 scholarly publications including twenty-two books and monographs (including edited works) on these issues as well as geo-technical aspects of the law of the sea and maritime security. He serves as an International Hydrographic Office (IHO)-nominated Observer on the Advisory Board on the Law of the Sea (ABLOS). He has also been involved in the peaceful settlement of boundary disputes, through the provision of advice and research support to governments engaged in boundary negotiations and in cases before the International Court of Justice and has been appointed as a Peacebuilding Adviser on behalf of the United Nations and the World Bank.

Yann-huei Song is currently a Research Fellow at the Institute of European and American Studies, Academia Sinica, Taiwan. He is also an Adjunct Professor at the School of Law, Soochow University in Taipei, Taiwan. Professor Song received his PhD in International Relations from Kent State University, Ohio and LLM and JSD from the School of Law (Boalt Hall), University of California, Berkeley. He has broad academic interests covering ocean law and policy studies, maritime security and sovereignty and maritime disputes in the East and South China Seas. Professor Song is a member of the editorial boards of *Ocean Development and International Law* and *Chinese (Taiwan) Yearbook of International Law and Affairs*. He is the co-editor of *Major Law and Policy Issues in the South China Sea: American and European Perspectives* (2014). His recent articles include "Legal Status of Taipei Island under the United Nations Convention on the Law of the Sea", *Korean Journal of International and Comparative Law* (2015) and "The Impact of the Law of the Sea Convention on Conflict and

Conflict Management in the South China Sea", *The International Journal of Ocean Development and International Law* (co-author, 2013).

Ian Storey is a Senior Fellow at the ISEAS – Yusof Ishak Institute, Singapore. He specializes in Asian security issues, with a focus on Southeast Asia. At the Institute, he is the editor of the peer review academic journal, *Contemporary Southeast Asia*. His research interests include Southeast Asia's relations with China, the United States and Japan, maritime security in the Asia Pacific (especially the South China Sea dispute), China's foreign and defence policies and the roles and interests of Asian countries in the Arctic. Prior to joining the Institute, he held academic positions at the U.S. Defense Department's Asia-Pacific Center for Security Studies in Honolulu, Hawaii, and at Deakin University, Melbourne, Australia. He received his PhD from the City University of Hong Kong and his Master's degree from the International University of Japan. He is the author of *Southeast Asia and the Rise of China: The Search for Security* (2011). Dr Storey has published articles in *Asia Policy, Asian Affairs, Asian Security, China Brief, Contemporary Southeast Asia, Harvard Asia Quarterly, Naval War College Review, Parameters, Political Science, Terrorism Monitor* and *Jane's Intelligence Review.* His opinion pieces have appeared in the *Straits Times,* the *Wall Street Journal* and the *South China Morning Post,* and he is regularly interviewed by the international media.

1

INTRODUCTION

Ian Storey and Cheng-yi Lin

Between early May and mid-July 2014 the state-owned China National Offshore Oil Corporation (CNOOC) deployed its largest and most modern oil rig, Hai Yang Shi You-981 (HYSY-981), into Vietnam's claimed exclusive economic zone (EEZ). CNOOC's action not only sparked a major crisis in Sino–Vietnamese relations, but also arguably raised tensions in the South China Sea to their highest point since the dispute first came to prominence in the late 1980s. The HYSY-981 Incident also reinforced negative trends which have dimmed the prospects of a negotiated settlement of the dispute and highlighted the limited effectiveness of attempts to more effectively manage the conflict both by the Southeast Asian claimants (Vietnam, the Philippines, Malaysia and Brunei) and China on a bilateral basis, and by the Association of Southeast Asian Nations (ASEAN) and the People's Republic of China (PRC) using a multilateral approach.

Together with the Sino–Japanese confrontation over sovereignty of the Senkaku/Diaoyu Islands in the East China Sea, the South China Sea dispute currently sits at the top of Asia's security agenda. Due to rising levels of nationalism over ownership of the disputed atolls, more strident assertions of sovereignty by the various claimants, growing competition over maritime resources, worsening geopolitical rivalries among the Great Powers and the rapid modernization of regional armed forces, maritime disputes are likely to remain the most important potential areas of conflict in Asia for the foreseeable future.

This Introduction provides an overview of the central aspects of the South China Sea dispute and is divided into seven sections. After this introductory section, the second part focuses on the geopolitical significance of the South China Sea and how the problem has increasingly become an area of contention between China and the United States. The third part identifies the reasons why tensions have been rising over the past several years. Part four looks at how the absence of political will among the claimants stands in the way of a legal or negotiated settlement. The fifth section examines how ASEAN and China have attempted to better manage the dispute with mixed success. Part six assesses why a continuation of the status quo could endanger the peace, stability and prosperity of the Asia-Pacific region and beyond. The final section provides a brief introduction to the rest of the chapters in this volume.

THE GEOPOLITICAL SIGNIFICANCE OF THE SOUTH CHINA SEA DISPUTE

At the heart of the South China Sea dispute is the question of who exercises legitimate ownership over hundreds of small islands, atolls and reefs. The PRC — and the Republic of China (ROC) or Taiwan — assert sovereignty over virtually all of these geographical features based on claims of discovery and historical usage dating back to the 2nd century BC. China's (and Taiwan's) historical claims in the South China Sea are represented on official maps by a discontinuous U-shaped line — generally referred to as the "nine-dash line map" even though PRC maps denote ten dashes and ROC maps eleven — which encompasses more than 80 per cent of the sea. There are two major archipelagos within the line: the Paracel Islands and the Spratly Islands.[1] In 1974, China evicted South Vietnamese troops from the western half of the Paracels, but Hanoi still maintains a sovereignty claim. Further south, the PRC/Taiwan and Vietnam claim ownership of all the Spratly Islands while Malaysia, the Philippines and Brunei claim parts of the group.[2] Since the Second World War, all of the claimants except Brunei have occupied atolls in the Spratlys: Taiwan occupies two, China eight, Malaysia five, the Philippines nine and Vietnam more than twenty.

Due to their small size, the majority of features in the Spratlys do not have any intrinsic value in themselves. Indeed, according to the 1982 United Nations Convention on the Law of the Sea (UNCLOS), many of the Spratly features should really be classed as rocks — and thus restricted to a 12 nautical miles (nm) territorial sea — or low-tide elevations which are incapable of generating either a territorial sea or a 200 nm EEZ. Those features which meet the UNCLOS criteria of an island — a naturally formed area of land, surrounded by water and above water at high tide and which can sustain human habitation — can generate both a territorial sea and an EEZ, and this allows their owners to harvest the lucrative bounty of the seas, such as fisheries, hydrocarbons and minerals. The living and non-living resources in the South China Sea are not insignificant. By some estimates 10 per cent of the global catch is made in the South China Sea,[3] and as a source of protein for hundreds of millions of people in Southeast Asia, its regional significance cannot be overstated. Regarding oil and gas, the scale of hydrocarbon resources in the South China Sea is difficult to determine with any certitude, mainly because the territorial disputes have prevented energy companies from conducting comprehensive surveys. As a result, all estimates are somewhat — perhaps even highly and occasionally widely — speculative. Chinese estimates are at the high end of the scale, usually between 100–200 billion barrels of oil (bbo) and oil equivalent. In 2012, for instance, CNOOC estimated that the South China Sea held 125 bbo and 500 trillion cubic feet (tcf) of gas in undiscovered resources.[4] U.S. and Russian estimates are much lower. In 2010, the U.S. Geographical Survey estimated the South China Sea might contain 5–22 bbo and 70–290 tcf of gas in undiscovered resources — though its estimate did not cover the entire sea.[5] Russia's Research Institute of Geology and Foreign Countries projects a modest 6 bbo of which 70 per cent is gas.[6] Absent a resolution of the dispute or the political will to jointly explore for resources, the true extent of hydrocarbons in the South China Sea will remain unknown and, more importantly, the oil and gas will stay locked under the seabed. Nevertheless, the *perception* that the South China Sea is rich in energy resources continues to act as a powerful driver of the dispute.

Important though sovereignty and maritime resources are, the significance of the South China Sea dispute transcends these issues for three main reasons: the geographical location of the atolls; the basis of China's claims; and the increasingly important role the dispute plays in the geopolitics of the Asia-Pacific region.

Located at the crossroads of South, Southeast and Northeast Asia, the South China Sea occupies a critical geographical position. The sea lanes that pass through it provide the shortest route between the Pacific and Indian Oceans and function as vital arteries of world trade and energy shipments. Detailed statistics on shipping movements through the sea are not available, but it is estimated that more than 100,000 vessels transit through the Straits of Malacca, Sunda and Lombok-Makassar every year, or more than half the world's annual merchant fleet tonnage[7] (by comparison, in 2013, 16,596 ships passed through the Suez Canal and 12,045 through the Panama Canal).[8] The U.S. Pacific Command estimates that US$5.3 trillion worth of goods passes through the South China Sea per annum.[9] The South China Sea sea lanes are particularly important to the economic powerhouses of Northeast Asia — China, Japan and South Korea — which are heavily dependent on energy imports from the Middle East and Africa. The U.S. Energy Information Agency estimated that in 2011, approximately 15.2 million barrels of crude oil per day passed through the Straits of Malacca (almost one third of the global oil trade) and 6 tcf of Liquefied Natural Gas (LNG) through the South China Sea (over half of global LNG trade).[10]

Conflict or even instability in the South China Sea could, therefore, threaten the free flow of maritime commerce with serious repercussions for the global economy. As Singapore's Defence Minister Ng Eng Heng warned in 2014, "It's completely artificial to think that there are somehow firewalls between trade and security. At some point, [the dispute] may impact trade and our real economies."[11] And as Australia's Defence Minister, David Johnson, cautioned at the 2014 Shangri-La Dialogue,

> Continuing confrontations such as those we are seeing in the South China Sea pose a clear threat to the collective good of all nations in the region. Any breakdown in security through miscalculation or actions that run contrary to the general principles of international law and the free flow of goods and services through our region would be catastrophic for all of our nations.[12]

While all countries in the region have a strongly vested interest in maintaining stability and secure sea lanes, as noted later, an accidental military clash at sea could put this collective interest at risk.

How the dispute is resolved has important implications for international legal norms, perhaps even the post-war international order. UNCLOS is often referred to as the "constitution of the seas", and as of 2014, 166 parties had ratified it, including all of the South China Sea claimants except Taiwan which is not a member of the UN. As noted, China indicates its claims in the South China Sea using a nine-dash line. In a protest note following a joint submission by Vietnam and Malaysia in 2009 to the UN body tasked with examining outer continental shelf claims, China declared it had "indisputable sovereignty over the islands in the South China Sea and the adjacent waters, and enjoys sovereign rights and jurisdiction over the relevant waters as well as the seabed and subsoil thereof".[13] Attached to the protest note was a map showing the nine-dash line, the first time China had officially lodged it with an international organization. The Chinese government, however, has studiously avoided clarifying what the line actually means. This has given rise to four possible interpretations:[14] first, China is claiming sovereignty over all of the features within the line and the 12 nm territorial seas and 200 nm EEZs generated by the atolls; second, China is claiming the area inside the line as its "historical waters"; third, China claims the area inside the line as an EEZ and continental shelf generated by the Paracel and Spratly Islands; fourth, China claims sovereignty of the islands, EEZs and continental shelves generated by those features as well as "historical rights" to maritime resources inside the nine-dash line.

While the first interpretation is comparable to the territorial and jurisdictional claims of the Southeast Asian claimants, the second, third and fourth interpretations are more problematic as few non-Chinese legal experts believe they are compatible with UNCLOS. Increasingly, however, through its actions and the views of Chinese legal scholars, it is the fourth interpretation that seems to be emerging as China's official position. In 2013, for instance Gao Zhiguo, China's judge on the International Tribunal on the Law of the Sea (ITLOS) — the dispute resolution mechanism established under UNCLOS — and Bing Bing Jia argued in an American law journal that the nine-dash line was "synonymous with a claim of sovereignty over the island groups that always belonged to China and with an additional Chinese claim of historical rights of fishing, navigation, and other marine activities (including the exploitation of resources, mineral or otherwise) on the islands and in the adjacent waters".[15] Due to the problematic nature of the nine-dash line map, a number of countries have called on China to clarify precisely what it is claiming and how those claims are consistent with UNCLOS. Several countries have concluded that China's ultimate aim is to enforce its claims within the nine-dash line, and thereby achieve dominance within it. Indeed the U.S. Department of State has expressed concern at the "incremental effort by China to assert control over the area contained in the so-called 'nine-dash line'".[16] And according to Philippine Foreign Secretary Albert del Rosario in 2014, China's aim is to "unilaterally impose its so-called nine-dash line as a basis for claiming sovereignty over the whole of the South China Sea" and that if Beijing is successful it will become a "Chinese lake".[17] Japanese Prime Minister Shinzo Abe has also warned against the South China Sea becoming a "Chinese lake".[18] China takes a very different view. According to Yun Sun, some Chinese legal experts have argued that since China's "historical rights" predate UNCLOS, "it cannot retroactively be applied to supersede China's sovereignty, sovereign rights and maritime administrative rights formed throughout history".[19] When a state accedes to UNCLOS, any prior claims to "historical rights" are extinguished. But as the former Prime Minister of Singapore, the late Lee Kuan Yew, predicted in 2014, "A rising China is seeking to assert its sea boundary claims. It is naïve to believe that a strong China will accept the conventional definition of what parts of the sea around it are under its jurisdiction."[20]

The third reason why the South China Sea dispute is significant is that increasingly it has become an issue of dissension between the United States and China. America is not a party to the South China Sea dispute but because of its extensive economic, political and strategic interests in Asia it is a significant stakeholder. America's official line is that it does not take a position on competing territorial claims, opposes the use of force or coercion to resolve the dispute and supports a negotiated settlement in accordance with international law. When tensions began to rise in 2007–8, senior U.S. officials began to express concern at "coercive diplomacy" but without naming China specifically — though it was clear to all which country was being referred to.[21] The July 2010 meeting of the ASEAN Regional Forum (ARF) marked a turning point when then Secretary of State Hillary Clinton declared that the South China Sea was "pivotal" to regional security and that America had a "national interest in freedom of navigation, open access to Asia's maritime commons, and respect for international law in the South China Sea".[22] Since then, U.S. officials have continued to stress America's national interests in the South China Sea, but their criticism of China's behaviour has become more explicit. In August 2012, for instance, the State Department expressed concern at China's actions at Scarborough Shoal and over the upgrading of the administrative status of Sansha City.[23] In February 2014, senior U.S. officials directly blamed China for fuelling tensions, criticized fishing regulations introduced by the authorities on Hainan Island in January, warned Beijing against establishing an Air Defence Identification Zone (ADIZ) over the South China Sea (such as the one the Chinese government established over parts of the East China Sea in November 2013), backed the Philippines' legal arbitration at the UN, and for the first time explicitly challenged the legality of the nine-dash line.[24] In May, the State Department described the deployment of HYSY-981 as "provocative", "destabilizing" and "aggressive".[25] America has also openly criticized

China for undermining international norms through its actions in the South (and East) China Sea. For example, it described China's attempts to block the resupply of Filipino Marines on Second Thomas Shoal in the Spratlys in March 2014 as "inconsistent" with freedom of navigation, while William J. Burns, Deputy Secretary of State, has highlighted how the South China Sea dispute is handled "reveals whether the threat of force or the rule of law will govern disputes and whether the same rules will apply to big and small countries alike".[26] In a speech delivered in June 2014, Danny Russel, Assistant Secretary of State Bureau of East Asian and Pacific Affairs, opined that China should hold itself to "a high standard of behavior" and not "wilfully disregard diplomatic and other peaceful ways of dealing with disagreements" in favour of "economic and physical coercion" which is "destabilizing and dangerous".[27]

China has rejected these criticisms, and its state-run media has regularly rebuked America for "meddling" in the dispute, exaggerating threats to freedom of navigation and using the dispute as a pretext to "pivot" or "rebalance" to Asia. Chinese officials have also accused Washington of hypocrisy for criticizing China for not abiding by UNCLOS when America has yet to ratify the agreement.[28] China has also challenged the U.S. position that it is a neutral party due to its capacity-building support for some of the Southeast Asian claimants, particularly the Philippines and Vietnam. When the U.S. proposed a freeze on building activities in the South China Sea in August 2014, Chinese officials promptly rejected it as interference, said they could do whatever they wanted on the disputed atolls and announced the construction of five lighthouses in the Paracels.[29]

Differences of opinion between the United States and China over military surveillance activities in the EEZ of a coastal state has been a long-standing area of disagreement between the two countries, and one which has become conflated with the South China Sea dispute. While the U.S. regards such activities as a freedom of navigation right permissible under UNCLOS, China views them as provocative and illegal, despite the fact that China itself gathers military intelligence in the EEZ of foreign states, as it did off Hawaii in July 2014 during U.S.-led Rim of the Pacific multilateral naval exercises (in which the Chinese Navy itself participated) and again a few months later when the U.S. Navy conducted exercises off Guam.[30] As China has beefed up its naval presence on Hainan Island, the U.S. has stepped up its surveillance activities — especially of Chinese submarines — in the South China Sea bringing the armed forces of both countries into closer proximity. An incident on 19 August 2014 in which a Chinese fighter jet intercepted a U.S. P-8 Poseidon surveillance aircraft in international airspace near Hainan led to mutual recriminations: the U.S. accused the Chinese pilot of dangerous and unprofessional behaviour, while China charged America with undermining regional stability and called on it to end its surveillance missions, a call Washington rejected. Such encounters raise the risk of a U.S.–China military clash and further complicate the South China Sea dispute.

RISING TENSIONS IN THE SOUTH CHINA SEA

Over the past few decades, tensions in the South China Sea have been cyclical. China's behaviour has been the key variable, though of course the actions of the other claimants have also been a contributory factor. But as the most powerful actor, it is China that has set the tone for the dispute. Thus in the early 1990s tensions began to rise when China became more assertive in trying to uphold its claims, but eased considerably in the first half of the 2000s when Beijing adopted a more accommodating stance as part of its so-called "Charm Offensive" in Southeast Asia.[31] Since 2007–8, tensions have once again been on the upswing and, as most analysts would agree — including the majority in this volume — the primary reason is renewed Chinese assertiveness.

Buoyed by its sustained economic growth, China's confidence on the world stage has been steadily growing, and the 2008 Beijing Olympics was widely seen as a key indicator of the country's emergence as a Great Power. China's confidence was bolstered during the 2008–9 Global Financial Crisis, from which it emerged essentially unscathed. With America distracted by the economic crisis and preoccupied with its military interventions in Iraq and Afghanistan, China saw an opportunity to press home its claims. The rapid modernization of China's navy, together with the expansion of its civilian maritime enforcement agencies, provided Beijing with the means to expand its presence in the South China Sea and apply coercive pressure on the Southeast Asian claimants, especially the Philippines and Vietnam. China's growing thirst for energy resources and food security also provided an additional driver for the government to press its "historic rights" within the nine-dash line.

China's new leadership under President Xi Jinping has bolstered the country's new-found confidence and assertive posture in the South China Sea. The Xi government's message to its Asian neighbours is that while China remains committed to "peaceful development" it has no intention of compromising its sovereignty claims and will respond firmly to countries that challenge those claims.[32] Moreover, under Xi, China's policy in the South China Sea has become increasingly centralized, coordinated and proactive. The deployment of HYSY-981 in May 2014 provided a good illustration of this greater policy coherence: the presence of a large flotilla of civilian maritime patrol vessels, warships and fishing trawlers to act as a protective cordon around HYSY-981 suggested a high degree of inter-agency cooperation, and it is likely that the decision to send the rig was taken at the highest levels of the Chinese government given the inevitable negative reactions from Vietnam and other regional states.

Beijing denies all blame for rising tensions in the South China Sea and insists that responsibility lies with the Southeast Asian claimants, especially Vietnam and the Philippines, as well as the United States and Japan. A common theme in the Chinese narrative is that Beijing exercises "restraint and patience" in the South China Sea.[33] Over the past few years, Chinese media commentaries have repeatedly accused the Philippines and Vietnam of "plundering" China's resources in the South China Sea and raising tensions through their "aggressive actions".[34] President Xi's assertion during the HYSY-981 crisis that "We will never stir up trouble, but will react in the necessary way to the provocations of countries involved" was typical in that it put the onus for rising tensions on the other claimants.[35]

The leaders of the Philippines and Vietnam have, however, laid the blame for rising tensions firmly at China's door. Philippine Foreign Secretary Del Rosario has been a particularly sharp critic of China, accusing it of raising tensions due to its "excessive and expansive" maritime claims and "aggressive patterns of behaviour" that threaten regional peace and stability.[36] Philippine President President Benigno Aquino has even drawn parallels between China's behaviour in the South China Sea and Nazi Germany's in Europe in the 1930s.[37] At his keynote speech at the Shangri-La Dialogue in 2013, Vietnamese Prime Minister Nguyen Tan Dung criticized China's behaviour without directly naming the country; but during the HYSY-981 crisis, the gloves came off, and Dung declared China's deployment of the oil rig posed a threat to "peace, stability, security, safety and freedom of navigation, cooperation and development in the region and the world".[38] Dung and Aquino reiterated this missive at a joint meeting a few weeks after the drilling rig had entered Vietnam's waters.[39] The Philippines and Vietnam's fellow ASEAN members have been more circumspect in their comments, but most have been troubled by China's actions.

China's attempts to push its claims have damaged its international image and created anxiety across the region. A poll conducted in mid-2014, for instance, found that in the Philippines 93 per cent of respondents were concerned about conflict with China, 85 per cent in Japan, 84 per cent in Vietnam and 66 per cent in Malaysia — even in China, 62 per cent of respondents were concerned.[40] And yet Beijing seems prepared to absorb the reputational costs and press on with its assertive policy confident that the Southeast Asian claimants will avoid confrontation with China for three reasons. First, as they become more economically dependent on China the costs of challenging its claims rise.[41] Second, they cannot match China's naval capabilities, even collectively. Third, the United States will not intervene militarily on their behalf because it does not take a position on competing sovereignty claims and because a war with China over the atolls is not in its national interests. The Chinese leadership must also have taken note of the Obama administration's more cautious foreign policy and reluctance to employ military power in response to international hotspots such as Syria, Iraq and Ukraine during 2013–14. As China feels that time is ultimately on its side, there seems little prospect of it adopting a more accommodating posture.

ROADBLOCKS TO A RESOLUTION

Disputes among nations are seldom insoluble. However, resolving interstate problems requires agreement among the conflicting parties on what the nature of the problem is, and whether it should be addressed through direct negotiations or through legal arbitration. Solutions can be expedited when the parties are prepared to offer concessions and reach compromises. Unfortunately these conditions render the South China Sea dispute particularly intractable. Defining the nature of the dispute is problematic because China's nine-dash line is, as noted earlier, ambiguous and seemingly incompatible with UNCLOS. Because most of the claimants were once victims of Western or Japanese colonialism, sovereignty is a highly senstive issue and governments must endeavour to uphold the country's sovereignty claims or else be perceived by nationalists — and the other claimants — as being weak. None of the claimants have engaged in serious bilateral discussions and legal avenues are currently closed — at least on the sovereignty issue — because Beijing eschews legal arbitration.

The International Court of Justice (ICJ) at The Hague is the only international body that could make a ruling on the ultimate sovereignty of the Paracel and Spratly Islands. Maritime disputes involving non-sovereignty issues can be adjudicated by ITLOS. Cases brought before the ICJ on matters of sovereignty require the consent of all parties. While the Philippines has indicated that it would be prepared to submit its claims to the Spratlys to the ICJ, none of the other Southeast Asian claimants have done so. Most importantly, China does not, as a matter of principle, submit its border, sovereignty or maritime boundary disputes to international legal arbitration, including the ICJ and ITLOS. China's refusal to consider legal arbitration for the South China Sea dispute is predicated on two factors: severe domestic repercussions should the judicial body rule against China; and the suspicion that Western-created institutions are biased against China.

Because China refuses to give its consent, the ICJ cannot adjudicate the South China Sea dispute. How about ITLOS? In 2006, China excluded itself from compulsory arbitration procedures on matters concerning sea boundary delimitations, historic bays and titles and military activities. However, this did not prevent the Philippines from unilaterally challenging the legality of China's expansive claims in the South China Sea at ITLOS in January 2013. The Philippines requested ITLOS to issue an award that, *inter alia*, declares China's maritime claims based on its nine-dash line to be contrary to UNCLOS and therefore invalid.[42] China refused to participate in the proceedings on the grounds that ITLOS did not have jurisdiction.[43] Nevertheless, the case is proceeding and an Arbitral Tribunal is currently assessing the Philippine submission. If the Tribunal accepts jurisdiction, a ruling — which will be legally binding but not enforceable — is expected in 2016. A favourable ruling for Manila would provide it with a legal and a moral victory, narrow the scope of the dispute to sovereignty of the atolls, benefit the other claimants and put the onus on China to provide legal justification for its claims. How China will respond to an unfavourable ruling remains to be seen.

The UN encourages countries with disputes to resolve them through bilateral or multilateral negotiations and only revert to legal arbitration when the parties are deadlocked. It would therefore be preferable for the claimants to settle among themselves the question of sovereignty, maritime boundaries and resource rights. For a host of reasons, however, arriving at a negotiated settlement is fraught with difficulties. The Paracels is a bilateral dispute between China and Vietnam; however, Beijing does not recognize that a dispute exists and refuses to discuss the sovereignty question with Hanoi (much as Japan does not recognize a dispute with China over the Senkaku/Diaoyu Islands and South Korea with Japan over the Dokdo/ Takashima Reef). And while Beijing accepts that there is a dispute over the Spratlys, it regards it as a bilateral problem that can only be resolved between China and each of the Southeast Asian claimants on a one-on-one basis (and not between the four Southeast Asian countries as a group and China). Since the early 1990s China has successfully resolved many of its sovereignty disputes through bilateral negotiations, but for the South China Sea this approach has found little support among the Southeast Asian countries due to asymmetries in power: the Southeast Asian claimants are concerned that an economically and militarily strong China would be able to pressure them into accepting unfavourable terms. Other problems stand in the way of a negotiated settlement too. Over the past few years nearly all of the claimants have attempted to strengthen their sovereignty and jurisdictional claims through national legislation, submissions to the UN and acts of administration. Together with rising nationalist fervour over sovereignty of the islands, this has made it harder for governments to make concessions or reach compromises. An additional complication to a negotiated settlement is that it would be nearly impossible for Taiwan to participate in talks concerning sovereignty of the islands because, in accordance with the One China policy which Beijing demands as a condition of diplomatic relations, none of the other parties recognize it as a sovereign state.

Setting aside the sovereignty issue in favour of joint development is a third possible option to resolve the dispute. In the late 1970s, Chinese Premier Deng Xiaoping asserted that while sovereignty of the South China Sea atolls belonged to China, the claimants should shelve the dispute and engage in joint development. This formula has been repeated many times by China's leaders, most recently by President Xi in 2013.[44] Yet China has never explained in detail how joint development would work, nor suggested a framework to operationalize it. In 2011, the Philippines proposed transforming the South China Sea into a "Zone of Peace, Freedom, Friendship and Cooperation" (ZoPFF/C) by enclosing the Spratlys, demilitarizing the islands and establishing a joint agency to manage seabed resources and fisheries — essentially a roadmap for Deng's proposal. China, however, dismissed the idea out of hand, and none of the Philippines' ASEAN partners supported it. As a result, the ZoPFF/C failed to gain momentum.

THE ASEAN–CHINA CONFLICT
MANAGEMENT PROCESS

As all parties to the South China Sea dispute have been acutely aware of the roadblocks in the way of a negotiated settlement, since the end of the Cold War the focus of discussions has been on how the conflict can be better managed. Because peace and stability in the South China Sea is fundamental to Southeast Asia's security, ASEAN has taken the lead in proposing a series of initiatives aimed at reducing tensions and building trust among the claimant countries. After more than twenty years of talks and agreements, however, the results have been fairly disappointing.

ASEAN's first public statement on the problem was the 1992 ASEAN Declaration on the South China Sea, also known as the Manila Declaration.[45] The Declaration was issued in response to rising tensions in the sea as the various claimants moved to bolster their claims. In order to position itself as a neutral party, ASEAN's 1992 Declaration did not apportion blame for increased tensions but called on all parties to resolve their disputes peacefully, renounce the use of force, exercise "self-restraint", negotiate cooperative confidence building measures (CBMs) and draw up a "code of international conduct". It was not until 1999, however, that Beijing finally indicated that it was ready to begin talks with ASEAN about such a code, by which time the dispute had become a serious source of friction between China and Vietnam and China and the Philippines. Following two years of discussions, in November 2002, ASEAN and China issued the Declaration on the Conduct of Parties in the South China Sea (DoC).[46] The one-page agreement built on the Manila Declaration — as well as the work of the South China Sea workshops hosted by Indonesia between 1991 and 2002 — and called on the parties to resolve their disputes peacefully, exercise self-restraint and implement CBMs — but unlike the 1992 Declaration it proscribed the occupation of unoccupied features. Although it was widely hailed as a major breakthrough at the time, the DoC had significant weaknesses: it was non-binding, did not specify which activities contravened the self-restraint clause and Taiwan was not a party to the agreement. Moreover, although ASEAN and China established a senior officials meeting and joint working group to operationalize the DoC, it was not until July 2011 — against a backdrop of surging tensions — that the two sides agreed on a set of implementation guidelines. Talks on designing cooperative CBMs began in early 2012 but it was not until mid-2013 that China finally consented to start discussions on a binding Code of Conduct for the South China Sea (CoC) which the DoC calls for and which ASEAN hopes will "promote trust and confidence, prevent incidents, and manage incidents should they occur" and thus create a "conducive environment of the eventual resolution of the disputes".[47] Those discussions began in September 2013 and continued during 2014. At the time of writing it is difficult to speculate when the CoC will be signed, mainly because the two sides have different timeframes: while ASEAN leaders have repeatedly called for expedited talks leading to the "early conclusion" of the CoC, China has indicated that it is in "no rush".

RISKS AND DANGERS

There is unlikely to be a breakthrough, either political or legal, in the South China Sea dispute for the foreseeable future. This being the case, what are the risks and dangers inherent in a continuation of the status quo?

Few observers envisage a major war in the South China Sea involving large-scale naval battles, air strikes and amphibious landings. As noted earlier, all of the parties to the dispute, and indeed all members of the international community, have a common interest in the maintenance of peace and stability in the South China Sea and ensuring the free flow of maritime trade. As the Vietnamese Prime Minister Nguyen Tan Dung cautioned in 2013, "A single irresponsible action or instigation of conflict could well lead to the interruption of these huge trade flows, with unforeseeable consequences not only to regional economies but also to the entire world."[48] Among the claimants, China possesses the strongest armed forces and could, in theory, "resolve" the problem by force. The reputational costs to China would, however, be very costly: cutting the Gordian Knot would completely undermine China's "peaceful development" thesis, cause irreparable damage to its relations with Southeast Asian countries, and push them into closer alignment with the United States. None of these outcomes would be in China's interests, and would outweigh any gains to be made from access to resources.

But while a major war is an unlikely scenario, conflict cannot, of course, be ruled out. As in the East China Sea, the main risk in the South China Sea is that a skirmish on the water involving patrol boats, warships, fishing trawlers, survey vessels or oil rigs sparks a military clash that quickly escalates into an unplanned and dangerous crisis in which lives are lost. As U.S. Defense Secretary Chuck Hagel warned at the ASEAN Defence Ministers' Meeting-Plus (ADMM-Plus) in August 2013, "Actions at sea to advance territorial claims do no strengthen any party's legal claim. Instead they increase the risk of confrontation, undermine regional stability and dim the prospects for diplomacy."[49] This risk of tensions turning into conflict is heightened due to the relative absence in Asia of effective crisis prevention and de-escalation mechanisms of the kind negotiated by the United States and some of its allies with the Soviet Union during the Cold War, such as hotlines and Incidents at Sea agreements.

The South China Sea Dispute: Navigating Strategic Tensions

This edited volume is composed of thirteen chapters which were originally presented at the "Workshop on the South China Sea Dispute: Political and Security Implications for the Region's Future" in 2012 organized by the Center for Asia-Pacific Area Studies of Academia Sinica and the East-West Center in Hawaii, but which have been thoroughly updated since that event.

In Chapter 2, "Untangling a Complex Web: Understanding Competing Maritime Claims in the South China Sea", Clive Schofield sets the geographical scene by investigating competing claims to maritime jurisdictions and how the opacity of some of those claims not only stand in the way of a negotiated settlement but also joint development of resources.

In Chapter 3, "China Debates the South China Sea Dispute", Mingjiang Li reviews the on-going debates within the PRC on what approach it should take to the dispute and how best to uphold its sovereignty and jurisdictional claims. In the following chapter, "Taiwan's Evolving Policy towards the South China Sea Dispute, 1992–2016", Anne Hsiu-an Hsiao and Cheng-yi Lin explain Taiwan's evolutionary policy approach towards the South China Sea issue under Presidents Lee Teng-hui, Chen Shui-bian and Ma Ying-jeou and then examine the current opportunities and challenges for Taiwan in the context of improving cross-straits relations.

The next two chapters are devoted to Southeast Asian countries and the role of ASEAN. In Chapter 5, "The South China Sea: Primary Contradictions in China–Southeast Asia Relations", Alice D. Ba situates the issue within the overall context of Southeast Asia's relations with China, how the concerned parties have tried to manage the problem in the past, the costs of increased politicization of the dispute since 2008 and the enormous challenges for ASEAN as it faces growing U.S–China rivalry in

Southeast Asia centered on the maritime dispute. In Chapter 6, "Rising Tensions in the South China Sea: Southeast Asian Responses", Ian Storey traces the highs and lows of the ASEAN–China conflict management process before going on to examine the perceptions of, and policy responses to, the regional hotspot by each of the ten ASEAN members.

The next three chapters focus on individual Southeast Asian claimants. Aileen S.P. Baviera in Chapter 7, "The Philippines and the South China Sea Dispute: Security Interests and Perspectives", looks at Manila's maritime claims and the factors which have contributed to the "deteriorating security seascape" of Sino–Philippine relations and how, in response, the Philippines has relied on diplomacy and, more recently, international legal arbitration to protect its claims. In Chapter 8, "A Vietnamese Perspective on the South China Sea Dispute", Hoang Anh Tuan argues that China's increased assertiveness has raised the prospect of conflict, facilitated America's "pivot" to Asia and not only damaged China's regional relationships and image but also its long-term economic prospects and leadership aspirations. Elina Noor, in Chapter 9, "The South China Sea Dispute: Options for Malaysia", assesses the country's energy and geopolitical interests in the South China Sea, its cautious approach to the dispute and its options for mitigating the problem, both bilaterally with China and in concert with its ASEAN partners.

The next three contributions assess the interests, roles and policies of the United States and Japan. In Chapter 10, "The United States and the South China Sea: Front Line of Hegemonic Tension?", Denny Roy adopts a geopolitical perspective and argues that because China's policy in the South China Sea challenges major U.S. interests in the Asia-Pacific region, the dispute is likely to exacerbate Sino–U.S. rivalry and may herald the beginning of a turbulent hegemonic transition. In the following chapter, "The South China Sea Dispute in U.S.–ASEAN Relations", Yann-huei Song posits that as tensions have risen, the dispute has become an increasingly salient issue in America's relations with ASEAN and has served to promote closer ties between the United States and its friends and allies in Southeast Asia: in short, that Washington has actually benefitted from renewed Chinese assertiveness. In the final chapter, "Japan and the South China Sea Dispute: A Stakeholder's Perspective", Yoichiro Sato considers how events in the South China Sea have paralleled those in the East China Sea, and why Tokyo believes that Beijing's policies in the maritime domain pose a threat to its national interests in Asia. The volume ends with a concluding chapter.

Notes

This chapter draws in part from Ian Storey, "Discordes en mer de Chine méridionale: les eaux troubles du Sud-Est asiatique" [Disputes in the South China Sea: Troubled Southeast Asian Waters] which first appeared in *Politique étrangère* 79, no. 3 (Fall 2014): 35–47. It is reproduced here with the kind permission of the publishers.

1. China also claims sovereignty over the Pratas Islands group (occupied by Taiwan), Macclesfield Bank and Scarborough Shoal.
2. In fact Brunei has never made a formal claim on Louisa Reef which lies inside its EEZ. Ian Storey, "Brunei's Contested Sea Border with China", in *China and Its Borders: Twenty Neighbors in Asia,* edited by Bruce Elleman, Stephen Kotkin and Clive Schofield (New York: M.E. Sharpe, 2012), pp. 37–46.
3. See UNEP/GEF South China Sea Project website, available at <http://www.unepscs.org/>.
4. "The South China Sea", U.S. Energy Information Administration, 7 February 2013, available at <http://www.eia.gov/countries/regions-topics.cfm?fips=SCS>.
5. "Assessment of Undiscovered Oil and Gas Resources of Southeast Asia, 2010", U.S Geographical Survey Fact Sheet 2010–3015 (June 2010), available at <http://pubs.usgs.gov/fs/2010/3015/pdf/FS10-3015.pdf>.
6. Clive Schofield, Ian Townsend-Gault, Hasjim Djalal, Ian Storey, Meredith Miller and Tim Cook, *From Disputed Waters to Seas of Opportunity: Overcoming Barriers to Maritime Cooperation in East and Southeast Asia* (Washington, D.C.: National Bureau of Asian Research, July 2011), p. 12.
7. "The South China Sea", U.S. Energy Information Administration, op. cit.
8. See the Suez Canal Authority, available at <http://www.suezcanal.gov.eg/sc.aspx?show=13#> and the Panama Canal Authority, available at <http://www.pancanal.com/eng/index.html>.
9. "Press Briefing by NSA for Strategic Communications Ben Rhodes and Admiral Robert Willard, U.S. Pacific Command", The White House, Office of the Press Secretary, 13 November 2011, available at <http://www.whitehouse.gov/the-press-office/2011/11/13/press-briefing-nsa-strategic-communications-ben-rhodes-and-admiral-rober>.
10. "The South China Sea", U.S. Energy Information Administration, op. cit.
11. "South China Sea Disputes May Disrupt Trade in Asia", *Straits Times*, 5 June 2014.
12. "Managing Strategic Tensions", Senator David Johnson, Minister for Defence, Australia, Shangri-La Dialogue, 31 May 2014, available at <https://www.iiss.org/en/events/shangri%20la%20dialogue/archive/2014-c20c/plenary-3-bce0/senator-david-johnston-4254>.
13. See <http://www.un.org/depts/los/clcs_new/submissions_files/mysvnm33_09/chn_2009re_mys_vnm_e.pdf>.

14. Duong Danh Huy, "China's U-Shaped Line in the South China Sea", *Asia Sentinel*, 19 September 2012, available at <http://www.asiasentinel.com/politics/chinas-u-shaped-line-in-the-south-china-sea/>.

15. Zhiguo Gao and Bing Bing Jia, "The Nine-Dash Line in the South China Sea: History, Status, and Implications", *The American Journal of International Law* 107, no. 95 (2013): 108.

16. Danny Russel, Assistant Secretary of State Bureau of East Asian and Pacific Affairs, U.S. Department of State, Before the House Committee on Foreign Affairs Subcommittee on Asia and the Pacific, 5 February 2014; William J. Burns, Deputy Secretary of State, Keynote Address at the Asia Society of Policy Institute Launch, New York, 8 April 2014.

17. "PH Repivots Defense Links to US", *Philippine Daily Inquirer*, 26 March 2014.

18. Shinzo Abe, "Asia's Democratic Security Diamond", *Project Syndicate*, 27 December 2012, available at <http://www.project-syndicate.org/commentary/a-strategic-alliance-for-japan-and-india-by-shinzo-abe>.

19. Yun Sun, "China's New Calculations in the South China Sea", *Asia-Pacific Bulletin* (East-West Center), 10 June 2014, available at <http://www.eastwestcenter.org/sites/default/files/private/apb_267_0.pdf>.

20. Lee Kuan Yew, "Past Key to Understanding China's Territorial Claims", *Straits Times*, 29 March 2014.

21. International Institute for Strategic Studies, speech as delivered by Secretary of Defense Robert M. Gates, Singapore, 31 May 2008, available at <http://www.defenselink.mil/speeches/speech.aspx?speechid=1253>.

22. Hillary Rodham Clinton, Remarks at Press Availability, Hanoi, Vietnam, 23 July 2010, available at <http://m.state.gov/md145095.htm>.

23. Press Statement, Patrick Ventrell, Acting Deputy Spokesperson, Office of Press Relations, Washington, D.C., 3 August 2012.

24. "Territorial Claims: US Asia-Pacific Commander Lauds Manila's Approach", *Today* [Singapore], 6 February 2014; "U.S. Could Change Military Posture If China Expands Air Defense Zone", Kyodo, 1 February 2014. According to Danny Russel, "Any use of the 'nine dash line' by China to claim maritime rights not based on claimed land features would be inconsistent with international law." Danny Russel, Assistant Secretary of State Bureau of East Asian and Pacific Affairs, U.S. Department of State, Before the House Committee on Foreign Affairs Subcommittee on Asia and the Pacific, 5 February 2014.

25. Jen Psaki, Spokesperson, Daily Press Briefing, U.S. Department of State, Washington, D.C., 6 May 2014; 20 June 2014.

26. Marie Harf, Deputy Spokesperson, Daily Press Briefing, U.S. Department of State, Washington, D.C., 31 March 2014; William J. Burns, Deputy Secretary of State, Keynote Address at the Asia Society of Policy Institute Launch, New York, 8 April 2014.

27. "The Future of U.S.–China Relations", Testimony, Daniel R. Russel, Assistant Secretary, Testimony Before the Senate Foreign Relations Committee, Washington, D.C., 25 June 2014.

28. "Beijing 'Consistent' on S. China Sea: FM", *China Daily*, 1 March 2012; "Xinhua Accuses Clinton of 'Meddling' in S. China Sea Row", *Straits Times*, 15 July 2012; "Clearing the Sea of Troubles", *China Daily*, 4 May 2013.

29. "China to Build Lighthouses on 5 Isles in Defiance of US Calls", Reuters, 7 August 2014.

30. "Chinese Spy Ship Lurks Around U.S.-led Pacific Naval Drills", *Washington Post*, 21 July 2014; "Chinese Ship Spies on Valiant Shield, and that's OK with US", *Stars and Stripes*, 22 September 2014.

31. See Chapter 3 in Ian Storey, *Southeast Asia and the Rise of China: The Search for Security* (Abingdon, Oxon.: Routledge, 2011), pp. 64–98.

32. "Xi Vows Peaceful Development While Not Waiving Legitimate Rights", Xinhua News Agency, 29 January 2013.

33. "China Military Warns of Confrontation Over Seas", Reuters, 21 April 2012; "Better to be Safe than Sorry", *China Daily*, 30 July 2012.

34. "Vietnam Underestimates China's Will to Protect Sovereignty", *Global Times*, 11 December 2012; Liu Qiang, "Beijing sees Manila as a Troublemaker", *Straits Times*, 13 May 2014.

35. "Xi says China Won't Stir Trouble in South China Sea", Reuters, 31 May 2014.

36. "Philippines, U.S. Begin War Games Focusing on Maritime Threats", Reuters, 5 May 2014.

37. "Philippine Leader Sounds Alarm on China", *New York Times*, 4 February 2014.

38. "Vietnam Won't Trade Sovereignty for 'False Friendship': PM", *Thanhn Nien*, 23 May 2014.

39. "Hanoi, Manila Urge World to Condemn China's Actions", *Today* [Singapore], 22 May 2014.

40. "Asian Nations' Fears of War Elevated as China Flexes Muscle, Study Finds", *Wall Street Journal*, 14 July 2014.

41. Bonnie Glaser and Deep Pal, "Is China's Charm Offensive Dead?", *China Brief* 14, issue 15 (31 July 2014), available at <http://www.jamestown.org/single/?tx_ttnews%5Btt_news%5D=42691&no_cache=1#.VES-VrX2P5o>.

42. Notification and Statement of Claim, Department of Foreign Affairs, Manila, 22 January 2013, available at <http://www.dfa.gov.ph/>.

43. "China Rejects Philippines' Arbitral Request: FM", Xinhua News Agency, 19 February 2013.

44. M. Taylor Fravel, "Xi Jinping's Overlooked Revelation on China's Maritime Disputes", *The Diplomat*, 13 August 2013, available at <http://thediplomat.com/2013/08/xi-jinpings-overlooked-revelation-on-chinas-maritime-disputes/>.

45. "ASEAN Declaration on the South China Sea, Manila", 22 July 1992, available at <http://www.asean.org/3634.htm>.

46. "Declaration on the Conduct of Parties in the South China Sea", 4 November 2002, available at <http://www.asean.org/asean/external-relations/china/item/ declaration-on-the-conduct-of-parties-in-the-south-china-sea>.

47. Chairman's Statement on the Post Ministerial Conference (PMC) 10+1 Sessions, Naypyitaw, Myanmar, 9–10 August 2014.

48. "Building Strategic Trust for Peace, Cooperation and Prosperity in the Asia Pacific Region: Nguyen Tan Dung", Shangri-La Dialogue 2013, Keynote Address, 1 June 2013, available at <http://www.iiss.org/en/events/shangri%20 la%20dialogue/archive/shangri-la-dialogue-2013-c890/opening-remarks-and-keynote-address-2f46/keynote-address-d176>.

49. "Hagel Warns Ministers over Territorial Tensions", *Straits Times*, 30 August 2013.

2

UNTANGLING A COMPLEX WEB: UNDERSTANDING COMPETING MARITIME CLAIMS IN THE SOUTH CHINA SEA

Clive Schofield

This chapter outlines and analyses the competing claims to maritime jurisdiction made in the South China Sea. As the title suggests, this is not a straightforward task. Indeed, the South China Sea is perhaps the world's most contested maritime space, characterized by complex coastal geography, numerous sovereignty disputes over islands featuring multiple claimants, excessive and controversial claims to baselines, conflicting and overlapping maritime claims to and controversial submissions regarding extended continental shelf rights.

The chapter begins with an overview of the geographical setting of the South China Sea before moving on to address the competing claims to maritime space that exist within the Sea. The latter section covers issues related to baselines as well as broad unilateral and supposedly historic-based maritime claims. Existing maritime boundary delimitation agreements and joint maritime arrangements are reviewed before the implications of fresh developments — particularly the extended continental shelf submissions and the reactions they provoked — are examined with a view to untangling and at least partially clarifying a most complex web of conflicting maritime claims.[1]

GEOGRAPHICAL CONTEXT

The South China Sea (together with the Gulf of Thailand) represents an extensive semi-enclosed sea located between the southern coasts of China and Taiwan to the north, the mainland coasts of Southeast Asia to the west, and the archipelagic island groups of the Philippines, Borneo and Indonesia to the east and south. It encompasses an area of approximately three million square kilometres (equivalent to around 874,660 square nautical miles (nm)).[2]

In total, ten states (or entities) border the South China Sea: Brunei, Cambodia, China, Indonesia, Malaysia, the Philippines, Singapore, Taiwan, Thailand and Vietnam.[3] Among these coastal states, six can be regarded as claimants in the sense that they claim sovereignty over all or some of the disputed islands and related insular features together with their associated maritime spaces. These are: Brunei, China, Malaysia, the Philippines, Taiwan and Vietnam. This is not, however, to suggest that the other littoral states do not advance maritime jurisdictional claims in the South China Sea — some of which, indeed, overlap with those made by neighbouring coastal states — just that territorial sovereignty over the disputed South China Sea islands is not an issue. By way of example, Indonesia's maritime claims in the southwestern South China Sea overlap with those of other littoral states, notably Malaysia and Vietnam, and are, moreover, also likely to overlap with the claims of whichever state or states is ultimately determined to hold sovereignty over the disputed Spratly Islands.[4] In this context, it is also notable that Indonesia's maritime claims in this area cut into parts of the South China Sea that lie within China's nine-dash line (see below).

That the South China Sea is a semi-enclosed sea bordered by multiple states has both geospatial and legal implications. From a geographical perspective, the South China Sea's near encirclement by coastal states has the inevitable consequence that their maritime claims converge, thereby enhancing the potential for overlapping maritime claims and disputes in the absence of agreement on the delimitation of maritime boundaries or, alternatively, some form of joint management mechanism. That said, the broad dimensions of the South China Sea mean that 200 nm maritime claims from opposing mainland and main island coastlines do not overlap, potentially leading to the existence of a large pocket or "donut hole" of high seas in the central South China Sea.

This maritime jurisdictional picture is, however, complicated by the existence in the South China Sea of multiple groups of islands and other features. These island groups comprise hundreds of generally small islands, islets, rocks, reefs, low-tide elevations and submerged features. As can be seen from Figure 2.1, the key island groups in the South China Sea are (clockwise from the northwest): the Paracel Islands,[5] the Pratas Islands,[6] Scarborough Shoal[7] and Macclesfield Bank,[8] the Spratly Islands[9] and the Natuna Islands.[10] With the exception of the Natuna Islands, which are under undisputed Indonesian sovereignty, all of these island groups are subject to some form of sovereignty dispute and all play a role with respect to competing claims to maritime jurisdiction.

The international legal implications of the South China Sea's status as a semi-enclosed sea arise from the specific provisions in the United Nations Convention on the Law of the Sea (UNCLOS) that deal with such bodies of water.[11] In this context it is important to note that all of the South China Sea littoral states, with the exception of Cambodia, are parties to the Convention.[12] Taiwan, a non-UN member, is also a non-party to the Convention. Article 123 of UNCLOS deals specifically with cooperation between states bordering enclosed and semi-enclosed seas and provides that such states "should cooperate with each other in the exercise of their rights and in the performance of their duties" under the Convention.[13] With this objective in mind, UNCLOS stipulates that the littoral states of a semi-enclosed sea "shall endeavour" to coordinate on the management, conservation, exploration and exploitation of the living resources of the sea; to coordinate regarding their shared obligations under the Convention to the protection and preservation of the marine environment; and, to coordinate with respect to marine scientific research including undertaking joint programmes of scientific research where appropriate.[14] Those South China Sea states which are parties to UNCLOS are therefore under an obligation to cooperate with one another as outlined in Article 123. However, the Convention is silent on how such cooperation and coordination among states bordering enclosed and semi-enclosed seas should be conducted. In the case of the South China Sea, such measures are few and far between.

FIGURE 2.1
Competing Maritime Claims in the South China Sea

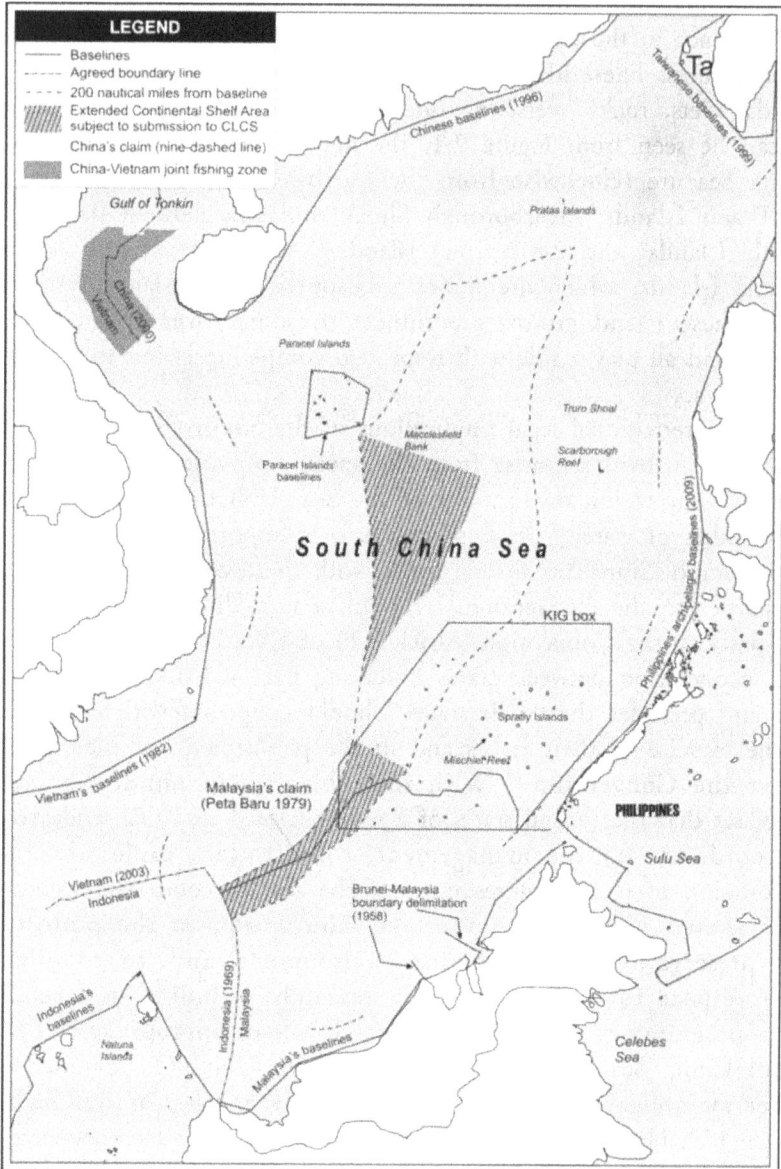

Source: Adapted from Clive Schofield, Ian Townsend-Gault, Hasjim Djalal, Ian Storey, Meredith Miller and Tim Cook, "From Disputed Waters to Seas of Opportunity: Overcoming Barriers to Cooperation in East and Southeast Asia", *National Bureau of Asian Research (NBR), Special Report* 30 (Seattle: NBR, July 2011), p. 5.

COMPETING CLAIMS TO MARITIME JURISDICTION

Baselines

Claims to maritime jurisdiction depend on sovereignty over land territory in keeping with the long-standing legal maxim that "the land dominates the sea".[15] The "edge" or limit of the land, and thus the starting line for the measurement of a coastal state's maritime claims, is provided by baselines defined along its coasts. The default scenario is that coastal states possess "normal" baselines coincident with "the low-water line along the coast as marked on large-scale charts officially recognized by the coastal State".[16] Such normal baselines represent the predominant type of baseline worldwide though they are by no means the only type of baseline provided for under UNCLOS.[17] In the context of the South China Sea, normal baselines are especially relevant to maritime claims generated from islands (see below). The provisions of Article 6 of UNCLOS dealing with reefs are also pertinent here.

Among the alternatives to normal baselines, straight baselines and archipelagic baselines, governed by Articles 7 and 47 of the Convention respectively, are especially relevant to the South China Sea. Article 7 offers the opportunity for coastal states to depart from normal, low-water line, baselines along selected parts of their coastlines "where the coastline is deeply indented and cut into, or if there is a fringe of islands along the coast in its immediate vicinity". The objective of Article 7 is to cater for especially complex coastal geography.[18] Unfortunately, Article 7 includes no indication as to the depth or frequency of such deep indentations or cuts into the coastline needed for a particular stretch of coastline to qualify for the application of straight baselines or, alternatively, how many, how close to one another and how far offshore fringing islands need to be.[19]

Certain South China Sea littoral states have taken the view that their coastlines are complex enough to justify the application of straight baselines along large parts of their coastal fronts. In particular, China (and Taiwan) and Vietnam have defined extensive systems of straight baselines along large sections of their coasts. It is highly questionable whether the coastlines in question are either sufficiently deeply indented or cut into or feature a suitable fringe of islands sufficiently close to the coast to justify their being fronted by a system of straight baselines. This is especially the case given that the International Court of Justice (ICJ), as expressed in its decision in the Qatar/Bahrain Case, has stated unequivocally that the method of straight baselines in accordance with UNCLOS "must be applied restrictively".[20] Accordingly, these claims to straight baselines have been heavily criticized and been subject to international protests, notably by the United States.[21]

For its part, Malaysia did not formally claim straight baselines until 2006, even though they could be inferred from official Malaysian maps dating from 1979.[22] Further, although Malaysia's Baselines of Maritime Zones Act 2006 does not contain coordinates for Malaysia's straight baselines,[23] some of its straight baselines are illustrated in the maps contained in its joint extended continental shelf submission with Vietnam.[24]

Two archipelagic states also border the South China Sea: Indonesia and the Philippines. Both have defined archipelagic baselines in keeping with Article 47 of UNCLOS which provides a significantly more stringent series of tests than does Article 7 concerning straight baselines.[25] Indonesia has a long association with the archipelagic concept, having claimed archipelagic baselines since 1960, and played a vital role in its eventual acceptance by the international community and incorporation into UNCLOS. Indonesia has subsequently extensively revised and refined its claims, notably through legislation dating from 1996 and regulations of 2002 and 2008.[26] The latest version of Indonesia's archipelagic baselines was deposited with the UN Secretary General on 11 March 2009, accompanied by a map illustrating the baselines, consisting of 195 points.[27]

The Philippines' claim to baselines, first made in 1961, was, prior to their recent amendment, at variance with the terms of UNCLOS. In particular, the Philippines claimed straight baselines enclosing internal waters rather than archipelagic baselines enclosing archipelagic waters and also included a segment 141 nm in length as compared to the 125 nm limit provided by Article 47(2) of UNCLOS.[28] In 2009, however, the Philippines revised its baselines and brought them into line with UNCLOS.[29] Consequently the main archipelago of the Philippines has a system of archipelagic baselines defined around it with outlying islands, such as Scarborough Shoal and a number of features among the Spratly Islands group over which the Philippines claims sovereignty, being referred to as being "regime of islands".[30] That said, the maritime claims of the Philippines remain problematic thanks to its claim to the Philippines Treaty Limits, of which more later.

Maritime Zones

UNCLOS has gained widespread international recognition and at the time of writing there were 166 parties to it.[31] For parties to the Convention it provides the binding legal framework governing maritime jurisdictional claims and the delimitation of maritime boundaries between national maritime zones. Indeed, those parts of the Convention dealing with maritime claims and maritime boundary delimitation can be considered declaratory of customary international law.[32] As previously noted, all of the South China Sea littorals with the exception of Cambodia and Taiwan are parties to UNCLOS.

UNCLOS offers a clear spatial framework for defining the limits to national claims to maritime jurisdiction. It is perhaps easy to forget quite what a major step forward this represented. Previous efforts aimed at codifying the international law of the sea had tended to flounder on this issue, especially concerning the breadth of the territorial sea. UNCLOS represented a breakthrough. Accordingly, landward of a coastal state's baselines lie either its land territory — including the inter-tidal foreshore landward of normal low-water line baselines — or internal waters.[33] Under UNCLOS, agreement was reached on 12 nm as the maximum extent of the territorial sea.[34] UNCLOS also provides for a contiguous zone out to 24 nm from relevant baselines.[35] Additionally, and significantly, the concept of the exclusive economic zone (EEZ) out to a limit of 200 nm was introduced.[36] Concerning the continental shelf, complex criteria are contained in Article 76 whereby the outer limits of the continental shelf may be determined, in partnership with a scientific and technical body established through the Convention, namely the United Nations Commission on the Limits of the Continental Shelf (CLCS or the Commission).[37]

Claims to 12 nm territorial seas and 200 nm EEZs are commonplace among the South China Sea littoral states. It is also the case that a number of those countries have made full or preliminary submissions to the CLCS concerning so-called "extended continental shelf" rights, that is, to seabed areas seawards of their claimed 200 nm limits (see below).

Insular Status and Claims to Maritime Jurisdiction

A critical issue in the South China Sea context is the capacity of the disputed insular features to generate extensive claims to maritime jurisdiction. In keeping with the Regime of Islands, as provided by Article 121 of UNCLOS, an island consists of "a naturally formed area of land, surrounded by water, which is above water at high tide".[38] In principle such features are to be treated just as any other land territory and therefore generate the full suite of maritime claims.[39] However, UNCLOS Article 121(3) states that "Rocks which cannot sustain human habitation or an economic life of their own shall have no exclusive economic zone or continental shelf."

This distinction between islands capable of generating extended claims to maritime jurisdiction and a disadvantaged subcategory of island, that is, the "rock", has significant implications in terms of potential maritime claims. If an island had no maritime neighbours within 400 nm, it could generate 125,664 sq. nm (431,014 km²) of territorial sea, EEZ and continental shelf rights. In stark contrast, if deemed a mere "rock" incapable of generating EEZ and continental shelf rights, only a territorial sea of 452 sq. nm (1,550 km²) can be claimed.[40] At the time of writing, no conclusive means has emerged by which to conclusively distinguish between islands capable of generating extended maritime claims (that is, to EEZ and continental shelf rights) and mere "rocks" which cannot.

That said, there is arguably an increasingly clear trend for small islands, especially those that are sparsely inhabited or uninhabited and located far offshore, to be awarded a much reduced capacity to generate maritime claims and to influence the course of maritime boundaries. Although state practice remains somewhat mixed on this issue, this trend has become increasingly clear and is particularly pronounced in the rulings of international courts and tribunals.[41]

Low-tide elevations, which are submerged at high tide but are above water at low tide, have a severely restricted role in respect of maritime zones. This is significant in the South China Sea context as many of the features that make up the Spratly Islands group for example are, in fact, low-tide elevations. Such features are incapable of generating maritime claims in their own right and may only be used as base points for the measurement of such claims if located wholly or partially within the breadth of the territorial sea measured from the normal baseline of a state's mainland or island coasts.[42] It is of note, for example with respect to Louisa Reef, that it remains unclear whether low-tide elevations constitute territory as such and therefore it remains open to question whether they can be subject to a claim to sovereignty.[43] Entirely subsurface features, such as Macclesfield Bank, have no capacity to generate claims to maritime jurisdiction. This has not, however, prevented numerous such features in the Spratlys from being occupied. Additionally, where artificial islands, installations or structures have been constructed, as has occurred in the South China Sea, these man-made features are covered by Article 60 of UNCLOS which is explicit in stating that they "do not possess the status of islands", have no territorial sea of their own and do not affect the delimitation of the territorial sea, the EEZ or the continental shelf.

Unilateral Claims

In common with the general practice of coastal states worldwide, many of the South China Sea states have advanced broad, ambit claims to maritime jurisdictional zones. However, several of the claimant states have been more specific regarding the spatial limits of at least some of their maritime claims. For example, in 1979 Malaysia issued the *Peta Baru* (New Map), a map that shows the limits of the country's unilateral territorial sea and continental shelf claims.[44] For its part, the Philippines has unilaterally defined an area termed the Kalayaan Island Group (KIG) but this claim does not, it seems, represent either a claim to the maritime spaces within this defined space, but rather represents a means to assert claims to sovereignty over the eight Spratly features that fall within it (see below).[45] This interpretation is supported by the fact that, as noted above, the Philippines' baselines revision of 2009 leaves the South China Sea islands claimed by the Philippines outside the country's archipelagic baselines, instead dealing with them under the "regime of islands", that is, in a manner consistent with UNCLOS.[46] For its part, Brunei has, through the publication of a series of maps in 1988, defined a rectangular maritime claim extending into the South China Sea.[47] More recently, in 2010, Indonesia defined its "forward position" in terms of its maritime claims through the publication of an official map.[48] The map shows that Indonesia's EEZ claims extend well to the north and east of its existing continental shelf boundary lines with both Malaysia and Vietnam.

Historic Claims

The South China Sea is also host to maritime claims apparently based on historic factors. These are distinct from the historical elements to claims to sovereignty over territory, that is, the disputed islands of the South China Sea. A notable example is the Philippines' claims to rights within its so-called Treaty Limits or "box" defined by several late nineteenth- and early twentieth-century treaties.[49] For a considerable period, the Philippines claimed territorial sea rights within the Treaty Limits box, and thus out to 285 nm at its furthest extent from the Philippine baselines[50] — claims that were clearly incompatible with UNCLOS. The United States and other countries have protested the Philippines' claims.[51] As mentioned above the Philippines amended its baselines legislation in 2009.[52] In a subsequent decision of 16 July 2011, the Supreme Court of the Philippines was explicit in stating that "The breadth of the territorial sea *shall be measured from archipelagic baselines* drawn in accordance with article 47 [of UNCLOS]",[53] indicating abandonment on the part of the Philippines of its former claim to territorial waters jurisdiction over the entirety of the marine area between its baselines and the Treaty Limits. This conclusion is underscored by the May 2014 delimitation of an EEZ between Indonesia and the Philippines which cuts through the southeastern corner of the so-called Philippines box.[54]

The apparently historical claims that have provoked the most attention and controversy in the South China Sea are those of China, especially with respect to its (in)famous nine-dash line claim. The claim (if it can be termed as such), remains opaque. An eleven-dash line developed from the 1930s and appeared on a map issued in 1947 by the Republic of China. This claim was subsequently adopted by the PRC in 1949, albeit with two dashes removed and the dashes shown being made shorter and somewhat differently located, from the early 1950s.[55] These dashed lines are frequently joined up to form a so-called "U-shaped line" although it is worth noting that official Chinese sources consistently show a discontinuous line. The meaning of the nine-dash line is, however, uncertain. It remains unclear whether the dashed line represents a claim to sovereignty over the territory (that is, the disputed islands) within it, is indicative of a unilateral claim to a maritime boundary, or represents a claim to the maritime spaces within the dashes, whether as historic waters or another type of maritime zone. For example, Zhiguo Gao and Bing Bing Jia encompass a range of interpretations in addressing this issue when they assert that the nine-dash line

> has become synonymous with a claim of sovereignty over the island groups that always belonged to China and with an additional Chinese claim of historical rights of fishing, navigation, and other marine activities (including the exploration and exploitation of resources, mineral or otherwise) on the islands and in the adjacent waters.[56]

The authors go on to suggest that the nine-dash line has a "residual function" as potential maritime boundaries.[57] The fact that China included a map showing the nine-dash line in its protest notes with respect to the extended continental shelf submissions of Vietnam alone, and Malaysia and Vietnam jointly, has served to heighten regional concerns over this apparently historically-inspired claim potentially relevant not only to the disputed islands of the South China Sea but also their surrounding maritime spaces.[58] It is worth noting that the issue of the validity of China's nine-dash line claim has been raised by the Philippines in its arbitration with China in accordance with Annex VII of UNCLOS.[59]

Agreed Maritime Boundaries and Joint Arrangements

Contrary to perceptions that the South China Sea is primarily an arena of disputes, incremental progress has been achieved in terms of maritime boundary delimitation. Examples include China and Vietnam's 2000 agreement on maritime boundary delimitation through the Gulf of Tonkin/Beibu Gulf,[60] the Indonesia–Vietnam continental shelf boundary of 2003[61] and Indonesia and Singapore's territorial sea boundary agreements of 1973 and 2009.[62] Additionally, Brunei and Malaysia inherited territorial sea boundaries from the United Kingdom[63] and also appear to have clarified their maritime boundary issues through a 16 March 2009 Exchange of Letters.[64]

The South China Sea also features multiple provisional arrangements of a practical nature in lieu or in addition to maritime boundary agreements. Such joint development mechanisms have been established between Malaysia and Thailand (agreed in principle in 1979[65] and implemented from 1990) concerning seabed energy resources, between Malaysia and Vietnam, also related to seabed hydrocarbons exploration and development in 1992,[66] and between China and Vietnam in 2000 concerning joint fishing activities as part of their above-mentioned maritime boundary treaty.[67]

Extended Continental Shelf Submissions and Their Implications

In 2009, in common with many coastal states around the world, a number of the South China Sea states made submissions to the CLCS. In particular, submissions were made by Vietnam alone and Malaysia and Vietnam jointly.[68] These submissions are significant because they relate to areas seaward of the 200 nm limit from these states' mainland coasts. The implication of these submissions is that, as far as Malaysia and Vietnam are concerned, the disputed islands of the South China Sea are incapable of generating full 200 nm EEZ and continental shelf rights. This is significant because if the disputed islands are in fact islands capable of claiming EEZ rights, then any high seas pocket in the central South China Sea as a consequence of 200 nm claims as measured from mainland and main island coastlines disappears. Under this scenario, no extended continental shelf would, in fact, exist in the South China Sea.[69]

The exchanges between the South China Sea states prompted by the extended continental shelf submissions are also valuable in that, to an extent, they serve to clarify the positions of some of the claimants as well as highlight differences between them. It is, however, worth emphasizing that the CLCS has a scientific and technical role rather than a legal one. That is, the CLCS lacks the mandate to address areas subject to a sovereignty dispute or to assess the merits of competing claims to overlapping areas of extended continental shelf. Furthermore, the Commission's recommendations are also specifically without prejudice to the delimitation of maritime boundaries.[70]

The extended continental shelf submissions of Malaysia and Vietnam provoked protests from China which, in turn, prompted counter-protests that also generated responses from Beijing. Indeed, Beijing issued near-identical protest notes including, as noted above, maps showing its nine-dash line, stating that China has "indisputable sovereignty over the islands in the South China Sea", and that, consequently, Malaysia and Vietnam's joint submission "seriously infringed China's sovereignty".[71] Malaysia and Vietnam countered that their submissions "constitute legitimate undertakings" in the implementation of its obligations as a party to UNCLOS.[72] Vietnam further stated that the Paracel Islands and Spratly Islands "are parts of Vietnam" over which it has "indisputable sovereignty".[73]

Subsequently, communications have also been directed to the UN Secretary General by Indonesia[74] and the Philippines,[75] both protesting the nine-dash line, with the latter's note also generating a vigorous response from Beijing.[76] The Chinese response, dated 14 April 2011, to the note from the Philippines is especially intriguing as China stated that "China's Nansha [Spratly] Islands is fully entitled to Territorial Sea, EEZ, and Continental Shelf".[77]

It is also worth noting that further submissions relating to extended continental shelf rights can be anticipated. The Philippines, having made a partial submission, in respect of the Benham Rise region located to the east of the Island of Luzon, left the door open to making a further submission, potentially in relation to parts of the South China Sea.[78] Similarly, China made a submission of preliminary information in 2009 relating to areas of continental shelf beyond 200 nm from its baselines in the East China Sea but reserved its right to make further submissions on the outer limits of its continental shelf "in other sea areas", a reference that could presage a Chinese submission in respect to parts of the central South China Sea.[79] China subsequently made a submission to the CLCS on 14 December 2012 which served to replace its earlier preliminary submission.[80] While this submission was again restricted in geographical scope to the East China Sea, it was specifically stated to be a partial one and "without prejudice to any future submission by China on delineation of the outer limits of the continental shelf in ECS and other sea areas", leaving the way open for a potential future Chinese submission with respect to the South China Sea.[81] Moreover, Brunei has also made a preliminary submission which can be anticipated to become a full submission in due course though this has yet to eventuate despite the fact that Brunei's 2009 submission of preliminary information indicated that this would occur "within 12 months".[82]

Implications and Prospects

Arguably the extended continental shelf submission process has shed some light on the previously opaque claims of some of the parties to the South China Sea islands disputes. It is also the case, however, that key differences between the parties have been highlighted. For example, Malaysia and Vietnam have defined their EEZ limits in the South China Sea and have strongly implied that they regard the disputed islands as being incapable of generating EEZ and continental shelf rights.

In contrast, China has included depictions of the nine-dash line in its official communications with the UN Secretary General. While attention was focused on China's inclusion of its nine-dash line map with its protest notes, the language used in the Chinese protests is potentially instructive. In particular, China's *note verbale* in response to the above-mentioned submissions of Malaysia and Vietnam, states that China having "sovereignty" over waters "adjacent" to the disputed South China Sea islands and "sovereign rights" over "relevant waters as well as the seabed and subsoil thereof". This, together with its statement that it not only claims sovereignty over the disputed South China Sea islands, but that the islands are capable of generating the full suite of claims to maritime jurisdiction, is potentially significant. This language is, arguably, consistent with claims to territorial sea, EEZ and continental shelf rights made from the disputed islands, as opposed to a claim to historic waters or similar within the nine-dash line.[83]

Unfortunately, it is not possible to be entirely definitive on this point as China's claim remains less than explicit. Indeed, the counterpoint to the apparently enhanced degree of clarity with respect to China's territorial and maritime claims in the South China Sea, as well as their increasing alleged consistency with UNCLOS, is provided by a number of incidents that have occurred between China's maritime surveillance and enforcement agencies and those of other South China Sea littoral states. Such actions have included enforcement activities related to fisheries jurisdiction, for example with respect to waters that Indonesia considers to form part of its EEZ,[84] as well as interventions to disrupt oil and gas survey and exploration activities conducted by the Philippines and Vietnam in their respective coastal waters.[85] Additionally, in June 2012 the China National Offshore Oil Corporation (CNOOC) issued tenders for oil concessions in close proximity to the Vietnamese coastline, yet just within the nine-dash line.[86] This action was followed up in May–July 2014 with the deployment by China of an oil rig and undertaking of exploratory drilling activities in an area to the southwest of the Paracel Islands, leading to clashes between rival vessels and a distinct ratcheting up in regional tensions.[87] These acts of administration and enforcement activities also suggest a claim to maritime jurisdiction to the spaces semi-defined by the nine-dash line and therefore appear to be at odds with suggestions that China's claims are increasingly in keeping with UNCLOS. It is also abundantly clear that China's view is distinctly at odds with the position adopted by Malaysia and Vietnam, throwing their differences into sharp relief. The enactment, from 1 January 2013, of new regulations on the part of the People's Congress of Hainan Province in southern China apparently providing for the inspection, detention or expulsion of foreign vessels in waters under its jurisdiction, potentially encompassing the waters within the nine-dash line, only served to deepen suspicions.[88]

Ultimately, there is a limit to how far the complex and conflicting web of South China Sea claims and counter-claims can be disentangled as some of the claims remain obstinately and seemingly intentionally opaque. Without a clear understanding as to which of the South China Sea littoral states claims what, both in terms of territorial sovereignty over islands and in respect of maritime space, as well as on what legal basis, it is difficult, if not impossible, to envisage a resolution of the multifaceted South China Sea disputes. Moreover, in the absence of a clear understanding of the scope of claims to maritime jurisdiction and thus the dimensions of maritime areas subject to overlapping maritime claims, discussions on joint development in the South China Sea, whether on a bilateral or multilateral basis, are likely to be stillborn.[89] It remains to be seen whether the — at the time of writing — ongoing arbitration proceedings between the Philippines and China will assist in clarifying a number of the most vexed outstanding questions directly relevant to the South China Sea dispute, notably the exact nature and legal validity of China's nine-dash line claim and concerning the regime of islands as it applies to certain South China Sea insular features.

Notes

1. This chapter builds on the author's earlier contributions, notably Clive Schofield, "Dangerous Ground: A Geopolitical Overview of the South China Sea", in *The South China Sea: Towards a Cooperative Management Regime*, edited by Sam Bateman and Ralf Emmers (London: Routledge, 2009), pp. 7–25; and, Clive Schofield, "What's At Stake in the South China Sea?: Geographical and Geopolitical Considerations", in *Beyond Territorial Disputes in the South China Sea: Legal Frameworks for the Joint Development of Hydrocarbon Resources*, edited by Robert Beckman, Clive Schofield, Ian Townsend-Gault, Tara Davenport and Leonardo Bernard (Cheltenham, UK: Edward Elgar Publishers, 2013), pp. 11–46.

2. This figure is provided by Hasjim Djalal who suggests that the southern limit of the South China Sea to be 1° North parallel of latitude. It should be noted, however, that the International Hydrographic Organization (IHO) definition is more extensive, stretching from the Strait of Taiwan in the north to Lucipara Point on the east coast of Sumatra at around the 3° South parallel of latitude. See Hasjim Djalal, "South China Sea Island Disputes", in *Security Flashpoints: Oil, Islands, Sea Access and Military Confrontation*, edited by Myron H. Nordquist and John Norton Moore (The Hague: Martinus Nijhoff Publishers, 1998), pp. 109–33. See also, International Hydrographic Organization (IHO), *Limits of Oceans and Seas*, 3rd ed., Special Publication no. 23 (Monte Carlo: IHO, 1953), p. 30.

3. This chapter will predominantly concentrate on territorial and maritime jurisdictional issues in the South China Sea proper, rather than those related to the Gulf of Thailand. For an analysis of maritime claims in the Gulf of Thailand, see Clive Schofield and May Tan-Mullins, "Claims, Conflicts and

Cooperation in the Gulf of Thailand", *Ocean Yearbook*, vol. 22 (Leiden/ Boston: Martinus Nijhoff, 2008), pp. 75–116.

4. See I.M. Andi Arsana and Clive Schofield, "Indonesia's 'Invisible' Border with China", in *Beijing's Power and China's Borders: Twenty Neighbors in Asia*, edited by Bruce A. Elleman, Stephen Kotkin and Clive H. Schofield (New York: M.E. Sharpe Publishers, 2012), pp. 60–79.

5. The Paracel Islands comprise around 130 islands, predominantly divided between the Crescent and Amphritite groups. See United Kingdom Hydrographic Office (UKHO), *China Sea Pilot*, vol. 1, 8th ed., Admiralty Sailing Directions (Taunton, UK: UKHO, 2010), pp. 75–78.

6. Ibid., p. 78.

7. Scarborough Shoal is described in the relevant British Admiralty Sailing Directions (Pilot) as being "steep-to on all sides and consists of a narrow belt of coral enclosing a lagoon of clear blue water". While the reef and associated lagoon are extensive, the majority of the feature is submerged at high tide. South Rock, at 3 m high, is the "tallest rock" located at the southeast extremity of the reef. See United Kingdom Hydrographic Office (UKHO), *China Sea Pilot*, vol. 2, 9th ed., Admiralty Sailing Directions (Taunton, UK: UKHO, 2010), p. 74.

8. An entirely submerged feature described as a "below-water atoll" with numerous patches at its edge with a least depth of less than 20 m and a least depth of 9.1 m for a detached shoal towards the centre of the Bank. See UKHO, *China Sea Pilot*, vol. 1, op. cit., pp. 68–69.

9. Estimates regarding the number of features comprising the Spratly Islands vary considerably but most fall within the 150–180 range. See, for example, Daniel J. Dzurek, "The Spratly Islands: Who's On First?", *Maritime Briefing* 2, no. 1 (1996): 1. See also Schofield, "Dangerous Ground", op. cit., pp. 9–10.

10. Comprising an extensive group of islands in the southwestern South China Sea. See UKHO, *China Sea Pilot*, vol. 2, op. cit., pp. 78–86.

11. United Nations, *United Nations Convention on the Law of the Sea*, Publication no. E97.V10 (New York, NY: United Nations, 1983). See 1833 UNTS 3, opened for signature on 10 December 1982, Montego Bay, Jamaica (entered into force on 16 November 1994), available at <http://www.un.org/Depts/los/convention_agreements/convention_overview_convention.htm>.

12. Cambodia signed the Convention on 1 July 1983 but has yet to become a party to it. For dates of the signatures, ratifications and accessions of the South China Sea states to UNCLOS, see

> United Nations, Status of the United Nations Convention on the Law of the Sea, of the Agreement relating to the implementation of Part XI of the Convention and of the Agreement for the implementation of the Convention

relating to the conservation and management of straddling fish stocks and highly migratory fish stocks.

(New York: United Nations, updated to 7 August 2013), available at <http://www.un.org/Depts/los/reference_files/status2010.pdf>.

13. UNCLOS, Article 123.
14. Ibid.
15. See, for example, Prosper Weil, *The Law of Maritime Delimitation: Reflections* (Cambridge: Grotius, 1989), p. 50.
16. Ibid, Article 5.
17. See J.R. Victor Prescott and Clive H. Schofield, *The Maritime Political Boundaries of the World* (Leiden/Boston: Martinus Nijhoff Publishers, 2005), pp. 94–97.
18. For example where the configuration of the coastline is "highly irregular". See International Hydrographic Organization (IHO) (with the International Oceanographic Commission and the International Association of Geodesy), *A Manual on Technical Aspects of the United Nations Convention on the Law of the Sea, 1982*, 4th ed., Special Publication no. 51 (Monaco: IHO, 2006), Chapter 4, p. 6. See also, United Nations, *Baselines: An Examination of the Relevant Provisions of the United Nations Convention on the Law of the Sea* (New York: Office for Ocean Affairs and the Law of the Sea, United Nations, 1989).
19. The U.S. Department of State has published its own guidelines on the proper definition of straight baselines. These Guidelines offer a useful, if arguably conservative, interpretation of the application of Article 7 of UNCLOS but, as the study itself states, "do not have international standing as benchmarks against which all such systems should be measured". See United States Department of State, "Developing Standard Guidelines for Evaluating Straight Baselines", *Limits in the Seas*, no. 106 (Washington, D.C.: Bureau of Oceans and International Environmental and Scientific Affairs, 31 August 1987).
20. *Case Concerning Maritime Delimitation and Territorial Questions between Qatar and Bahrain* (Qatar v. Bahrain) (Merits) [2001], ICJ Rep. 40, paragraph 212, available at <http://www.icj-cij.org/docket/files/87/7027.pdf>.
21. See in particular the critical analyses of the straight baselines claims of China, Taiwan and Vietnam available in the U.S. Department of State's *Limits in the Seas* series, available at <http://www.state.gov/e/oes/ocns/opa/c16065.htm>. See also J. Ashley Roach and Robert Smith, *United States Responses to Excessive Maritime Claims*, 3rd ed. (The Hague: Martinus Nijhoff Publishers, 2012).
22. Notably from the *Peta Baru* of 1979. See the *Peta Menunjukkan Sempadan Perairan dan Pelantar Benua Malaysia* [Map Showing the Territorial Waters and Continental Shelf Boundaries of Malaysia], often referred to as the *Peta*

Baru [New Map], was published by the Malaysian Directorate of National Mapping in two sheets, 21 December 1979

23. Vivian L. Forbes, "The Territorial Sea Datum of Malaysia", *MIMA Bulletin* 14, no. 4 (2007): 7–8.

24. Joint Submission to the Commission on the Limits of the Continental Shelf pursuant to Article 76, paragraph 8 of the United Nations Convention on the Law of the Sea 1982 in respect of the southern part of the South China Sea, Executive Summary, 6 May 2009, available at <http://www.un.org/Depts/los/clcs_new/submissions_files/submission_mysvnm_33_2009.htm>.

25. Article 47(1) provides that an archipelagic state may draw baselines joining "the outermost points of the outermost islands and drying reefs of the archipelago" but goes on to provide five key conditions for the construction of a valid system of archipelagic baselines. These are that the claimant state's "main islands" must be included within the archipelagic baseline system; that the ratio of water to land within the baselines must be between 1:1 and 9:1; that the length of any single baseline segment must not exceed 125 nm; that no more than 3 per cent of the total number of baseline segments enclosing an archipelago may exceed 100 nm; and, that such baselines "shall not depart to any appreciable extent from the general configuration of the archipelago". See UNCLOS, Article 47. For analysis of claims to archipelagic baselines and archipelagic waters, see Martin B. Tsamenyi, Clive H. Schofield and Ben Milligan, "Navigation through Archipelagos: Current State Practice", in *Freedom of the Seas, Passage Rights and the 1982 Law of the Sea Convention*, edited by Myron H. Nordquist, Tommy B. Koh and John Norton Moore (The Hague: Martinus Nijhoff, 2008), pp. 413–54.

26. See Clive H. Schofield and Andi Arsana, "Closing the Loop: Indonesia's Revised Archipelagic Baselines System", *Australian Journal of Marine and Ocean Affairs* 1, no. 2 (2009): 57–62.

27. For maritime zone notification and a complete list of the coordinates, see <http://www.un.org/Depts/los/LEGISLATIONANDTREATIES/STATEFILES/IDN.htm>.

28. See Republic Act No. 3046, An Act to Define the Baselines of the Territorial Sea of the Philippines, of 17 June 1961, subsequently amended by Republic Act No. 5446, An Act to Amend Section One of the Republic Act Numbered Three Hundred and Forty Six Entitled "An Act to Define the Baselines of the Territorial Sea of the Philippines", of 18 September 1968, available at <http://www.un.org/Depts/los/LEGISLATIONANDTREATIES/STATEFILES/PHL.htm>. See also, Tsamenyi, Schofield and Milligan, "Navigation through Archipelagos", op. cit., pp. 442–45.

29. See Republic Act No. 9522, An Act to Amend Certain Provisions of Republic Act No. 3046, As Amended by Republic Act No. 5446, To Define

the Archipelagic Baselines of the Philippines, and for Other Purposes, 10 March 2009. See *Law of the Sea Bulletin* 70 (2000): 32.
30. Ibid.
31. Comprising 165 states plus the European Community. See "Status of the United Nations Convention on the Law of the Sea", op. cit.
32. See Roach and Smith, *Excessive Maritime Claims*, op. cit., pp. 4–5.
33. Internal waters lie landwards of straight baselines (UNCLOS, Article 7), landward of river closing lines (UNCLOS, Article 9), bat closing lines (UNCLOS, Article 10) and within ports (UNCLOS, Article 11). UNCLOS Article 8 provides that where internal waters have been created through the construction of a system of straight baselines, "which had not previously been considered as such, a right of innocent passage as provided in this Convention shall exist in those waters".
34. UNCLOS, Article 3 provides that "Every State has the right to establish the breadth of the territorial sea up to a limit not exceeding 12 nautical miles", measured from baselines determined in accordance with the Convention. Article 4 further states that "the outer limit of the territorial sea is the line every point of which is at a distance from the nearest point of the baseline equal to the breadth of the territorial sea".
35. UNCLOS, Article 33.
36. UNCLOS, Articles 55–75. In particular, Article 57 of UNCLOS provides that the EEZ "shall not extend beyond 200 nautical miles from the baselines from which the breadth of the territorial sea is measured". As most coastal states claim a 12 nm territorial sea, the actual breadth of the EEZ is usually 188 nm seaward of territorial sea limits.
37. See Commission on the Limits of the Continental Shelf website, available at <http://www.un.org/Depts/los/clcs_new/clcs_home.htm>.
38. UNCLOS, Article 121(1).
39. UNCLOS, Article 121(2).
40. For the sake of this theoretical calculation, the features in question are assumed to have no land area.
41. See, for example, Clive H. Schofield, "Islands or Rocks: Is that the Real Question?: The Treatment of Islands in the Delimitation of Maritime Boundaries", in *The Law of the Sea Convention: US Accession and Globalization*, edited by Myron H. Nordquist, John Norton Moore, Alfred H.A. Soons and Hak–So Kim (Leiden/Boston: Martinus Nijhoff, 2012), pp. 339–40.
42. UNCLOS, Article 13(1).
43. See *Case Concerning Maritime Delimitation and Territorial Questions between Qatar and Bahrain* (Qatar v. Bahrain) (Merits) [2001], ICJ Rep. 40 paragraphs 205–6, available at <http://www.icj-cij.org/docket/files/87/7027.pdf>; *Case Concerning Sovereignty over Pedra Branca/Pulau Batu Puteh, Middle Rocks*

and South Ledge (Malaysia/Singapore), Judgment of 23 May 2008, paragraphs 295–96, available at <www.icj-cij.org/docket/files/130/14492.pdf>; Robert Beckman and Clive H. Schofield, "Moving Beyond Disputes over Island Sovereignty: ICJ Decision Sets Stage for Maritime Boundary Delimitation in the Singapore Strait", *Ocean Development and International Law* 40 (2009): 4.

44. The *Peta Baru*, op. cit.

45. See Lowell Bautista and Clive Schofield, "Philippine–China Border Relations: Cautious Engagement Amid Tensions", in Elleman, Kotkin and Schofield, *Beijing's Power and China's Borders*, op. cit., p. 242.

46. See Republic Act No. 9522, op. cit.

47. Maps Showing Continental Shelf of Brunei Darussalam (1988); and Maps Showing Fishery Limits of Brunei Darussalam (1988). Also of note is the Map Showing Territorial Waters of Brunei Darussalam (1987). See Ian Storey, "Brunei's Contested Sea Border with China", in Elleman, Kotkin and Schofield, *Beijing's Power and China's Borders*, op. cit., pp. 36–45. See also Renate Haller-Trost, "The Brunei–Malaysia Dispute over Territorial and Maritime Claims in International Law", *Maritime Briefing* 1, no. 3 (1994): 4–5.

48. Bakosurtanal, *Map of the Republic of Indonesia* (Cibinong: Bakosurtanal, 2010).

49. Specifically, the *Treaty of Peace between the United States and Spain*, signed in Paris, 10 December 1898, T.S. No. 343 (Treaty of Paris); the *Treaty between Spain and the United States for the Cession of Outlying Islands for the Philippines*, signed at Washington, 7 November 1900, T.S. No. 345 (Cessation Treaty); and the *Convention between the United States and Great Britain Delimiting the Philippine Archipelago and the State of Borneo*, signed at Washington, 2 January 1930, T.S. No. 856 (Treaty of Washington). See, for example, Lowell Bautista and Clive Schofield, "Philippine–China Border Relations: Cautious Engagement Amid Tensions", in Elleman, Kotkin and Schofield, *Beijing's Power and China's Borders*, op. cit., pp. 234–49.

50. In accordance with Republic Act No. 3046 of 17 June 1961. See also, Prescott and Schofield, *The Maritime Political Boundaries of the World*, op. cit., p. 452.

51. See Tsamenyi, Schofield and Milligan, "Navigation through Archipelagos", op. cit., pp. 134–38.

52. See Republic Act No. 9522, op. cit.

53. *Prof. Merlin M. Magallona, et al. v. Hon. Eduardo Ermita, in his capacity as Executive Secretary, et al.* G.R. No. 187167, 16 July 2011, *en banc* (Carpio, J.), available at <http://sc.judiciary.gov.ph/jurisprudence/2011/august2011/187167.html> (emphasis in original). See also, United States

Department of State, "Philippines: Archipelagic and Other Maritime Claims and Boundaries", *Limits in the Seas*, no. 142, 15 September 2014 (Washington, D.C.: Office of Ocean and Polar Affairs, Bureau of Oceans and International Environmental and Scientific Affairs, U.S. Department of State, 2014), p. 5, available at <http://www.state.gov/documents/organization/231914.pdf>.

54. "Agreement between the Government of the Republic of the Philippines and the Republic of Indonesia concerning the Delimitation of the Exclusive Economic Zone Boundary", 23 May 2014, available at <http://www.gov.ph/2014/05/23/agreement-between-the-government-of-the-republic-of-the-philippines-and-the-government-of-the-republic-indonesia-concerning-the-delimitation-of-the-exclusive-economic-zone-boundary/>.

55. See, for example, Li Jinming and Li Dexia, "The Dotted Line on the Chinese Map of the South China Sea: A Note", *Ocean Development and International Law* 34 (2003): 287; Zou Keyuan, "The Chinese Traditional Maritime Boundary Line in the South China Sea and Its Legal Consequences for the Resolution of the Dispute over the Spratly Islands", *International Journal of Marine and Coastal Law* 14 (1997): 52; and Kuan-Hsiung Wang, "The ROC's Maritime Claims and Practices with Special Reference to the South China Sea", *Ocean Development and International Law* 41 (2010): 237–52.

56. Zhiguo Gao and Bing Bing Jia, "The Nine Dash Line in the South China Sea: History, Status and Implications", *American Journal of International Law* 107 (2013): 108.

57. Ibid.

58. Note from the Permanent Mission of the People's Republic of China addressed to the Secretary General of the United Nations, CML/17/2009, 7 May 2009, available at <http://www.un.org/Depts/los/clcs_new/submissions_files/mysvnm33_09/chn_2009re_mys_vnm_e.pdf>. See also, Note from the Permanent Mission of the People's Republic of China addressed to the Secretary General of the United Nations, CML/18/2009, 7 May 2009, available at <http://www.un.org/depts/los/clcs_new/submissions_files/vnm37_09/chn_2009re_vnm.pdf>.

59. See the "Notification and Statement of Claims" of the Philippines of 22 January 2013, available from the Department of Foreign Affairs of the Republic of the Philippines, available at <www.dfa.gov.ph>. Despite the fact that China returned the Philippines notification and has indicated that it will not participate in any arbitration arising from the action of the Philippines, nonetheless an Arbitration Tribunal has been established and Rules of Procedure adopted with the Permanent Court of Arbitration acting as Registry for the case. See the website of the Permanent Court of Arbitration, available at <http://www.pca-cpa.org/showpage.asp?pag_id=1529>.

60. Agreement between the Socialist Republic of Vietnam and the People's Republic of China on the Delimitation of the Territorial Sea, Exclusive Economic Zone and Continental Shelf between the Two Countries in the Tonkin Gulf, 25 December 2000 (entry into force on 30 June 2004). See "People's Republic of China–Vietnam", *International Maritime Boundaries*, vol. V, edited by David A. Colson and Robert W. Smith (Leiden: Martinus Nijhoff, 2005), pp. 3,745–58. See also, Nguyen Hong Thao, "Maritime Delimitation and Fishery Cooperation in the Tonkin Gulf", *Ocean Development and International Law* 36 (2005): 25–44.

61. Agreement between the Government of the Socialist Republic of Vietnam and the Government of the Republic of Indonesia concerning the Delimitation of the Continental Shelf Boundary, 26 June 2003 (entry into force on 29 May 2007). See "Agreement between the Government of the Socialist Republic of Vietnam and the Republic of Indonesia concerning the Delimitation of the Continental Shelf Boundary", *International Maritime Boundaries*, vol. VI, edited by David A. Colson and Robert W. Smith (Leiden: Martinus Nijhoff, 2011), pp. 4,301–15.

62. Agreement Stipulating the Territorial Sea Boundary Lines between Indonesia and the Republic of Singapore in the Strait of Singapore, 25 March 1973 (entry into force on 29 August 1974). See, The Geographer, U.S. Department of State, "Territorial Sea Boundary: Indonesia–Singapore", *Limits in the Seas*, no. 60 (Washington, D.C.: The Geographer, U.S. Department of State, 11 November 1974). See also, Ministry of Foreign Affairs, Indonesia, "The Signing of the Treaty Between the Republic of Indonesia and the Republic of Singapore Relating to the Delimitation of the Territorial Seas in the Western Part of the Strait of Singapore", Press Release Jakarta, 10 March 2009, available at <http://www.deplu.go.id/_layouts/mobile/PortalDetail-PressReleaseLike.aspx?l=en&ItemId=c148acb8-88c6-4e24-9dd3-352ec9cd90c2>.

63. The territorial sea boundaries between Brunei and Malaysia were defined in 1958 out to the 100 fathom isobath through two British Orders in Council. See *International Maritime Boundaries*, vol. I, op. cit. pp. 924–28.

64. See Storey, "Brunei's Contested Sea Border with China", op. cit., pp. 39–41. It is also notable that Brunei's submission of preliminary information to the CLCS further states that maritime boundaries between Brunei and Malaysia have been delimited by virtue of the 1958 Orders in the Council and "an Exchange of Letters dated 16 March 2009" which served to delimit territorial sea, EEZ and continental shelf rights "to a distance of 200 nautical miles". See "Brunei-Darussalam's Preliminary Submission concerning the Outer Limits of Its Continental Shelf", 12 May 2009, available at <http://www.un.org/Depts/los/clcs_new/commission_preliminary.htm>.

65. Memorandum of Understanding between the Kingdom of Thailand and [the Republic of] Malaysia on the Establishment of a Joint Authority for the Exploitation of the Resources of the Sea-Bed in a Defined Area of the Continental Shelf of the Two Countries in the Gulf of Thailand, 21 February 1979. See *International Maritime Boundaries*, vol. I, op. cit., pp. 1,107–10, 123; see also, <http://www.un.org/Depts/los/LEGISLATIONANDTREATIES/PDFFILES/TREATIES/THA-MYS1979CS.PDF>.

66. Memorandum of Understanding between Malaysia and the Socialist Republic of Vietnam for the Exploration and Exploitation of Petroleum in a Defined Area of the Continental Shelf Involving the Two Countries was signed on 5 June 1992 and entered into force on 4 June 1993. See *International Maritime Boundaries*, vol. III, op. cit., pp. 2,335–44.

67. Agreement on Fishery Co-operation in the Tonkin Gulf between the Government of the People's Republic of China and the Government of the Socialist Republic of Vietnam, 25 December 2000. See Nguyen Hong Thao, "Maritime Delimitation and Fishery Cooperation", op. cit.

68. Joint Submission to the Commission on the Limits of the Continental Shelf pursuant to Article 76, paragraph 8 of the United Nations Convention on the Law of the Sea 1982 in respect of the southern part of the South China Sea, Executive Summary, 6 May 2009, available at <http://www.un.org/Depts/los/clcs_new/submissions_files/submission_mysvnm_33_2009.htm>; and, Submission to the Commission on the Limits of the Continental Shelf pursuant to Article 76, paragraph 8 of the United Nations Convention on the Law of the Sea 1982, Partial Submission in Respect of Vietnam's Extended Continental Shelf: North Area (VNM-N), Executive Summary, 7 May 2009, available at <http://www.un.org/Depts/los/clcs_new/submissions_files/mysvnm33_09/chn_2009re_mys_vnm_e.pdf>. See also, Andi Arsana and Clive Schofield, "Adding Further Complexity?: Extended Continental Shelf Submissions in East and Southeast Asia", *Maritime Energy Resources in Asia: Legal Regimes and Cooperation*, edited by Clive Schofield, National Bureau of Asian Research Special Report no. 37 (Seattle: National Bureau of Asian Research, February 2012), pp. 35–59.

69. Sam Bateman and Clive H. Schofield, "Outer Shelf Claims in the South China Sea: New Dimension to Old Disputes", *RSIS Commentary* 65/2009 (Singapore: S. Rajaratnam School of International Studies, 1 July 2009), available at <http://www.rsis.edu.sg/publications/Perspective/RSIS0652009.pdf>.

70. Article 76(10) of UNCLOS explicitly provides that "[t]he provisions of this article are without prejudice to the question of delimitation of the continental shelf between States with opposite or adjacent coasts". See also, Annex II of UNCLOS and the Rules of Procedure of the Commission on the Limits of the Continental Shelf. The current version of the Rules is contained in

Doc. CLCS/40/Rev.1 of 17 April 2008, available at <http://www.un.org/Depts/los/clcs_new/commission_documents.htm#Rules%20of%20Procedure>.

71. See Note from the Permanent Mission of the People's Republic of China addressed to the Secretary General of the United Nations, CML/17/2009, 7 May 2009, available at <http://www.un.org/Depts/los/clcs_new/submissions_files/submission_mysvnm_33_2009.htm>; see also an English language translation of China's reaction to Vietnam's submission, available at <http://www.un.org/depts/los/clcs_new/submissions_files/vnm37_09/chn_2009re_vnm.pdf>.

72. See Note from the Permanent Mission of Malaysia to the United Nations to the Secretary General of the United Nations, HA 24/09, 20 May 2009; and, Note from the Permanent Mission of the Socialist Republic of Vietnam to the United Nations to the Secretary General of the United Nations, 86/HC-2009, 8 May 2009, available at <http://www.un.org/Depts/los/clcs_new/submissions_files/submission_mysvnm_33_2009.htm>; and, <http://www.un.org/depts/los/clcs_new/submissions_files/vnm37_09/vnm_re_chn_2009re_vnm.pdf>.

73. Note from the Permanent Mission of the Socialist Republic of Vietnam to the United Nations to the Secretary General of the United Nations, No. 86/HC-2009, 8 May 2009, available at <http://www.un.org/Depts/los/clcs_new/submissions_files/vnm37_09/vnm_re_chn_2009re_vnm.pdf>.

74. See Note from the Permanent Mission of Indonesian to the United Nations to the Secretary General of the United Nations, No. 840/POL-703/VII/10, 8 July 2010, available at <http://www.un.org/Depts/los/clcs_new/submissions_files/mysvnm33_09/idn_2010re_mys_vnm_e.pdf>.

75. See Note from the Permanent Mission of the Republic of the Philippines to the United Nations to the Secretary General of the United Nations, No. 000228, 5 April 2011, available at <http://www.un.org/Depts/los/clcs_new/submissions_files/mysvnm33_09/phl_re_chn_2011.pdf>.

76. See Note from the Permanent Mission of the People's Republic of China to the United Nations to the Secretary General of the United Nations, CML/8/2011, 14 April 2011, available at <http://www.un.org/Depts/los/clcs_new/submissions_files/mysvnm33_09/chn_2011_re_phl_e.pdf>.

77. Ibid.

78. The Philippines specifically reserved its rights to make "other submissions in the future". See Executive Summary, "A Partial Submission of Data and Information on the Outer Limits of the Continental Shelf of the Republic of the Philippines Pursuant to Article 76(8) of the United Nations Convention on the Law of the Sea", available at <http://www.un.org/Depts/los/clcs_new/submissions_files/submission_phl_22_2009>, p. 12.

79. "Preliminary Information Indicative of the Outer Limits of the Continental Shelf Beyond 200 Nautical Miles of the People's Republic of China

[translation]", 11 May 2009, available at <http://www.un.org/depts/los/clcs_new/submissions_files/preliminary/chn2009preliminaryinformation_english.pdf>, p. 5.

80. "Submission by the People's Republic of China Concerning the Outer Limits of the Continental Shelf Beyond 200 Nautical Miles in Part of the East China Sea", 14 December 2012, available at <http://www.un.org/Depts/los/clcs_new/submissions_files/submission_chn_63_2012.htm>.

81. Ibid., p. 2.

82. See "Brunei-Darussalam's Preliminary Submission concerning the Outer Limits of Its Continental Shelf", op. cit., p. 7.

83. Robert Beckman and Clive Schofield, "Defining EEZ Claims from Islands: A Potential South China Sea Change", *The International Journal of Marine and Coastal Law* 29 (2014): 203–4.

84. Arsana and Schofield, "Indonesia's 'Invisible' Border with China", op. cit., pp. 67–70.

85. Regarding incidents between China and the Philippines see, for example, Jim Gomez, "Philippine Sends Warplanes Near Disputed Islands", *Associated Press*, 3 March 2011, available at <http://www.businessweek.com/ap/financialnews/D9LNT87G0.htm>; and, Jerome Aning and Norman Bordadora, "China Snubs PH Protest: Aquino to Send 'Spratlys Expert' to Beijing", *Philippine Daily Inquirer*, 3 May 2011. See also Bautista and Schofield, "Philippine–China Border Relations", op. cit., p. 244. Concerning incidents between China and Vietnam see, for example, Daniel Ten Kate, "South China Sea Oil Rush Risks Clashes as U.S. Emboldens Vietnam on Claims", *Bloomberg*, 27 May 2011, available at <http://www.bloomberg.com/news/2011-05-26/s-china-sea-oil-rush-risks-clashes-as-u-s-emboldens-vietnam.html>; "VN Condemns Chinese Intrusion", *Viet Nam News*, 28 May 2011, available at <http://english.vietnamnet.vn/en/politics/8839/vn-condemns-chinese-intrusion.html>; and, "China Reprimands Vietnam Over Offshore Oil Exploration", Reuters, 28 May 2011, available at <http://af.reuters.com/article/energyOilNews/idAFL3E7GS07E20110528>.

86. See China National Offshore Oil Corporation (CNOOC), "Notification of Part of Open Blocks in Waters under Jurisdiction of the People's Republic of China Available for Foreign Cooperation in the Year of 2012", 23 June 2012, available at <http://en.cnooc.com.cn/data/html/news/2012-06-23/english/322127.html>.

87. See, for example, Brian Spegele, Vu Trong Khanh and Josephine Cuneta, "Vietnam, Philippines Incidents Raise Sea Tensions", *Wall Street Journal*, 7 May 2014, available at <http://online.wsj.com/news/articles/SB10001424052702304431104579547241211054588>; and, Kate Hodal, "Despite Oil Rig Removal, China and Vietnam Row Still Simmers", *The Guardian*, 18 July 2014, available at <http://www.theguardian.com/world/2014/jul/17/oil-rig-china-vietnam-row-south-china-sea>.

88. Entitled "Regulations for the Management of Coastal Border Security and Public Order in Hainan Province". See M. Taylor Fravel, "Hainan's New Maritime Regulations: A Preliminary Analysis", *The Diplomat*, 1 December 2012, available at <http://thediplomat.com/china-power/hainans-new-maritime-regulations-a-preliminary-analysis/>. Despite initial controversy, it appears that these regulations are designed to have more limited applicability to waters around Hainan Island. See M. Taylor Fravel, "Hainan's New Maritime Regulations: An Update", *The Diplomat*, 3 January 2013, available at <http://thediplomat.com/china-power/hainans-new-maritime-regulations-an-update/>.

89. See Beckman and Schofield, "Defining EEZ Claims from Islands: A Potential South China Sea Change", op. cit.

3

CHINA DEBATES THE SOUTH CHINA SEA DISPUTE

Mingjiang Li[1]

The past few years have witnessed dramatic developments in the South China Sea dispute. In 2009, submissions to the United Nations Commission on the Limits of the Continental Shelf (CLCS) outlining extended continental shelf claims by several of the claimant countries created a round of diplomatic tussles. In particular, the People's Republic of China's (PRC) submission of its nine-dash line map of the South China Sea in a protest note to the CLCS sparked strong opposition from the other claimants. The diplomatic contentions at the ASEAN Regional Forum (ARF) in July 2010 in Hanoi — particularly between U.S. and Chinese officials — raised tensions to their highest level in over a decade. In the first half of 2011, a series of incidents, including Beijing's heavy-handed actions against Philippine and Vietnamese fishery and energy exploration activities, further strained relations with Hanoi and Manila. The Sino–Philippine standoff over Scarborough Shoal in 2012 raised tensions several notches higher, and led the Philippines to pursue closer relations with the United States and Japan, while the deployment of the Chinese oil rig Hai Yang Shi You-981 (HYSY-981) into waters near the Paracel Islands in May–July 2014 created a two-month crisis between Hanoi and Beijing.

As a result of the diplomatic and strategic repercussions of Beijing's actions in the South China Sea, Chinese policymakers and analysts have been forced to reassess the country's existing policy and future options.

This chapter examines China's South China Sea debate since 2009. It seeks to provide an analysis of three aspects of this debate: the various schools of thought that have emerged regarding what China's response should be; policy proposals regarding how China should respond to the changing dynamics; and areas of consensus and disagreement. It places the debate within the context of China's official position on the South China Sea. In doing so, we can derive a better understand of Beijing's future policy in the South China Sea.

Four main themes have emerged in China's debate. First, in contrast to widespread foreign criticism of China for its growing assertiveness, the predominant view among Chinese analysts is that rising tensions are mainly attributable to collusion between the United States and certain Southeast Asian claimants, particularly Vietnam and the Philippines. Second, it has frequently been proposed that China should be more proactive in the South China Sea rather than merely reactive to the actions of the other parties. It has been suggested that China can achieve this goal by taking initiatives in three areas: accelerating exploitation of living and non-living resources; restricting U.S. involvement; and exercising more flexibility in dealing multilaterally with the other parties, especially over non-traditional security challenges in the South China Sea. Third, the majority of Chinese analysts and officials believe that the disputes have led to a deterioration in the country's regional security environment. Fourth, it appears that there is an emerging consensus in China that the government should adopt a more balanced policy that takes into consideration the country's regional strategic objectives, territorial sovereignty, maritime interests and domestic opinions.

The debate over the South China Sea has often been framed as one between hardliners and moderates.[2] This chapter contends that there is, in fact, an important middle-of-the-road school of thought that advocates tougher policies to better protect Chinese interests but which eschews confrontation with the other claimants and external powers such as the United States and Japan. Based on these findings, this chapter concludes that Beijing is likely to practise a policy of non-confrontational assertiveness in the South China Sea for the foreseeable future.

CHINESE VIEWS ON RISING TENSIONS IN THE SOUTH CHINA SEA

Generally speaking, there are three schools of thought regarding the reasons for rising tensions. First, numerous pundits outside of China contend that it is Beijing's reversion to a more assertive posture that has fuelled rising tensions since 2007–8.[3] This view is widely accepted by the international media and many foreign observers and officials. Second, a minority group of international observers have argued that China has, in the main, simply reacted to the actions of the other claimants; actions that Beijing views as inimical to its own interests.[4] The debate within China itself reveals a third view, one that exposes strong perceptual differences between China and the outside world: that Southeast Asian states have colluded with the United States against Beijing, and that this collusion is the root cause of rising tensions in the South China Sea.[5]

Chinese analysts often argue that the primary reason for the uptick in tensions is Washington's "return to Asia".[6] Many Chinese are convinced that America's main objective is to pursue a policy of "soft containment" against the PRC, meaning engaging with China politically and economically while at the same time trying to limit China's growing influence. Rear Admiral (retired) Yang Yi's view well expresses rising anti-American sentiment in China. Yang has accused the United States of "exacerbating its time-honoured containment policy against China: on the one hand, it [Washington] wants China to play a role in regional security issues. On the other hand, it is engaging in an increasingly tight encirclement of China and constantly challenging China's core interests."[7] Supporters of this view also argue that as part of this strategy Washington is providing support to countries that have territorial disputes with China, emboldening them in the process.[8] They note that the increasing involvement of America in the South China Sea dispute has also been instigated by regional states such as Vietnam and the Philippines.[9] Various official statements seem to corroborate this line of interpretation.[10]

According to an article in the *People's Daily*, three major factors have contributed to renewed tensions. First, regional states have intensified efforts to exploit maritime resources in the South China Sea, especially hydrocarbons. The second factor is America's strategic shift to East Asia, and that Washington has specifically utilized the South China Sea issue to maintain its predominant security position in the region, a policy that has been facilitated by several regional states' desire to internationalize the dispute. Third, the PRC's rising political, economic and military power has prompted regional countries to encourage America to increase its presence in Asia so as to balance China.[11] This latter point, which at least in part recognizes China as part of the problem, though not widely shared by Chinese analysts, is better understood by some Southeast Asia experts in China. According to Ma Yanbing, the rise of Chinese power, particularly naval power, has significantly contributed to Vietnam's anxiety, and that this has led Hanoi to pursue policies to safeguard its national interests before China becomes too powerful.[12] Some of Vietnam's neighbours share this anxiety.

Over the past few years, a frequently noted theme in the discourse over the South China Sea has been concern for freedom of navigation. In the view of some Chinese analysts, Washington has concocted the "myth" of freedom of navigation and used it as a tool to apply pressure on China. They argue that the United States has posited a false thesis about the threat to freedom of navigation in the South China Sea.[13] They believe that Washington is simply using freedom of navigation as a pretext to intervene in the dispute and as an excuse to "pivot" or rebalance its military forces towards Asia.[14] Many Chinese analysts believe that U.S. rhetoric about freedom of navigation is really about American insistence that it has the legal right to conduct military activities in China's 200 nautical miles (nm) exclusive economic zone (EEZ).[15] Liu Feitao, for instance, has noted that U.S. military surveillance activities in the EEZs of coastal states, including the PRC, pose a grave national security threat. The author declares that "the real freedom of navigation that the US wants to maintain is American freedom to militarily threaten other countries".[16] This view seems to reflect the official Chinese position as well. At the 2010 ARF, Foreign Minister Yang Jiechi countered U.S. Secretary of State Hillary Clinton's statement on the South China Sea by denying that freedom of navigation was under threat.[17] Since then, on many occasions Chinese Foreign Ministry spokespersons have suggested that Washington uses freedom of navigation as a ploy to further its strategic interests.[18]

CHARTING CHINA'S APPROACH

The Growth of Hardline Views

Without question, rising tensions between the PRC and the Southeast Asian claimants and other stakeholders have fuelled nationalist sentiment in China. Chinese netizens have constantly expressed extremely harsh views of the other claimants, particularly Vietnam, the Philippines and the United States. They have also criticized the Chinese government for its weak stance.[19] A letter to the *National Defence Times*, entitled "No Strike in the South China Sea Now, No Opportunity in the Future", reflects the hawkish view of a significant proportion of the Chinese public.[20] Since

2010, China's *Global Times*, a newspaper notorious for profiting from popular nationalism, has published many hardline articles and editorials on the South China Sea dispute. In one editorial — which attracted international attention — it warned:

> ... some of China's neighbouring countries have been exploiting China's mild diplomatic stance, making it their golden opportunity to expand their regional interests.... Currently, China's mainstream understanding is that it should first go through the general channels of negotiating with other countries to solve sea disputes. But if a situation turns ugly, some military action is necessary.... If these countries don't want to change their ways with China, they will need to prepare for the sounds of cannons. We need to be ready for that, as it may be the only way for the disputes in the sea to be resolved.[21]

The People's Liberation Army (PLA) has also taken a hardline stance towards the South China Sea dispute. Immediately after the diplomatic wrangling between Chinese and U.S. officials at the ARF in 2010, the PLA-Navy organized large-scale exercises in the South China Sea. PLA Chief of General Staff General Chen Bingde stressed that "(the military) should pay close attention to changes in the situation and tasks, and get well prepared for military conflicts."[22] Instead of customary individual fleet manoeuvres, the northern, southern and eastern fleets of the PLA-Navy conducted a major joint exercise during celebrations to mark the founding of the PLA on 1 August 2010. Xu Guangyu, a senior fellow at the China Arms Control and Disarmament Association, has suggested that the PLA response is a "strategic necessity".[23] Major-General Luo Yuan commented that "China is the victim in the South China Sea issue yet [it] has been tolerant. Regional claimant states should not continue to be pushy ... otherwise the consequences may be more serious than 'muscle flexing'."[24]

Calculated Moderation

Amid all the hawkish rhetoric and remarks, China has been cognizant of the negative impact developments in the South China Sea have had on its security relations in the region. The 2010 White Paper on China's Diplomacy,[25] published by the Chinese Ministry of Foreign Affairs (MFA), and the Asia-Pacific Blue Paper, published by the Chinese Academy of Social Sciences (CASS) in January 2011, suggest that China faced unprecedented security challenges in 2010.[26] A group of analysts at CASS also concluded that America's "return to Asia" had driven a wedge between China and its neighbours, adding new complexities and weakening political trust between them.[27] Nevertheless, many Chinese analysts remain sober-minded and continue to advocate a cautious approach to the South China Sea.

In early June 2011, several prominent Chinese think-tanks — including CASS, the Pacific Society of China, the China Foundation for International and Strategic Studies, Renmin University and the Shanghai Institute of International Studies — co-organized a forum on regional security issues. The overall tone of the forum, which was attended by prominent Chinese analysts, was drastically different from the hawkish and hardline positions described earlier. For instance, Liu Jiangyong, a security analyst at Tsinghua University, noted that China should attempt to reconcile its "low profile" (*tao guang yang hui*) by "doing something" (*you suo zuo wei*) in the South China Sea, namely pursuing long-term cooperation to prevent tensions from escalating.[28]

Notably, many Chinese analysts view the military option in the South China Sea as unrealistic and have rejected it outright. The Hainan-based scholar Wu Shicun, President of the National Institute for South China Sea Studies, stresses that China has to keep a balance between protecting its own rights and maintaining stability in the South China Sea in order to sustain a period of strategic opportunity for China's domestic development. He believes that the South China Sea problem can be resolved peacefully through negotiations on the basis of contemporary international maritime law, including UNCLOS.[29] Moreover, if China were tempted to use force to resolve the dispute, it risks falling into a US-laid trap. Indeed one Chinese scholar has surmised that U.S. intervention in the South China Sea could be part of a conspiracy to weaken China by forcing it into a protracted regional war. He argues that for this reason alone, China should be cautious. Furthermore, China still lags far behind the United States in comprehensive national power, especially in military power, and will need more time for domestic development. Thus, he concludes that it would be counter-productive for China to get involved in military conflict.[30] Another reason why China should reject the use of force is that it would divert its attention away from the Taiwan problem and the dispute over ownership of the Senkaku/Diaoyu Islands with Japan in the East China Sea. Accordingly, from a geopolitical point of view, China should continue to focus on Taiwan and Japan while seeking cooperative partnerships with Southeast Asian countries. As long as China has not resolved the Taiwan issue and the East China Sea dispute, it should avoid exacerbating tensions with Southeast Asian countries.[31]

Xue Li, a strategist at CASS, also reproves the use of force in the South China Sea, as it would be highly detrimental to China's image and regional relations. Military action by China would not only provoke international condemnation but also undermine its peaceful development thesis and hinder the country's economic development.[32] Most analysts have stressed, therefore, that China needs to continue emphasizing peaceful means to resolve the dispute, and engage with regional states to enhance mutual confidence. They urge China to work with claimant states to reduce tensions and achieve progress in negotiations lest the United States finds further excuses to intervene.[33]

Official Handling of the Disputes

At the official level, China firmly insists on the validity of its claims in the South China and has defended its assertive actions against other parties. At the same time, Beijing has also endeavoured to mend fences with the other claimant states. By and large, the official handling of the crises in the South China Sea over the past few years reflect the policies advocated by moderate scholars. The MFA has been the agency that has played the lead role in handling the South China Sea dispute, and it has always favoured a moderate policy.[34] When asked to comment on the above-mentioned *Global Times* editorial, for instance, the MFA spokesperson said that while the media has a right to comment, it should do so objectively and responsibly. The spokesperson then reiterated China's peaceful intentions and emphasized negotiations as the preferred means to stabilize the situation.[35] Her statement can be interpreted as disapproval of the *Global Times'* editorial.

The MFA has denied accusations that its policy on the South China Sea is weak. Spokesperson Zhang Yan, for instance, has defended China's policy on the grounds that foreign policy is supposed to serve the domestic goal of building a more prosperous society.[36] Zhang Jiuheng, the former Director-General of the Department for Asian Affairs at the MFA, was also defensive of the official policy: "The South China Sea issue is indeed very complicated. We need to acknowledge the existence of the dispute. ... no one wants to see tensions in the region. No one wants to see military conflict in the region."[37] In response to growing domestic calls for China to adopt a tougher stance in international affairs, in 2010 Dai Bingguo — a State Councillor and one of former President Hu Jintao's most influential foreign affairs advisers — argued that

> if we cannot properly handle our relations with the outside world, the development opportunity in the 20 years of the new century provided by overall international peace, overall stability in the relations among major powers, and the rapid development of new science and technology will likely be lost.[38]

The diplomatic clashes at the ARF in 2010 prompted Beijing to reassess its policy on the South China Sea, in particular in response to the more interventionist posture of the United States. In the autumn, China attempted to tamp down tensions in the South China Sea and the other disputants responded positively to its diplomatic overtures. In August, Vietnamese Deputy Defence Minister Nguyen Chi Vinh visited Beijing and reassured his hosts of Vietnam's commitment to peace and stability. He indicated that Vietnam would refrain from the following three actions: forging an alliance with other countries; allowing foreign bases in Vietnam; and developing relations with other countries targeted at a third country.[39] At the China–ASEAN Summit in October, Premier Wen Jiabao reaffirmed China's willingness to work with ASEAN members to implement the Declaration on the Conduct of Parties in the South China Sea (DoC). At the inaugural ASEAN Defence Ministers Meeting Plus (ADMM-Plus) in October 2010, Chinese Defence Minister Liang Guanglie emphasized China's strategic goal of peaceful development.[40] In October, Vice Foreign Minister Zhang Zhijun visited four ASEAN countries on a fact-finding trip. During a visit to Singapore in November, then Vice President Xi Jinping attempted to reassure regional states of China's peaceful intentions.

By the end of 2010, many observers expected a period of relative calm in the South China Sea as the parties were engaged in discussing implementation guidelines for the DoC. However, a series of actions undertaken by Chinese law enforcement agencies against Philippine and Vietnamese activities in the South China Sea led to a renewal of tensions from March to June 2011. In an attempt to de-escalate the situation, Beijing and Hanoi agreed to talk. In June 2011, Vietnam sent a special envoy to Beijing. The two sides agreed to resolve their dispute through negotiations, to refrain from taking actions that would escalate tensions, to oppose the intervention of third parties and to actively lead public opinion in their own countries.[41] In late August, Chinese and Vietnamese defence officials met in Beijing and discussed ways to reduce tensions in the South China Sea. Senior officials of the two countries met again in Hanoi in early September for the fifth round of the annual Sino–Vietnamese Steering Committee. The joint statement issued by the committee chairs — State Councillor Dai Bingguo and Deputy Prime Minister Nguyen Thien Nhan — was reconciliatory in tone, with both sides pledging to abide by the DoC.

After several months of negotiations, Beijing eventually agreed to the implementation guidelines at the China–ASEAN Foreign Ministers Meeting in July 2011. China pledged to work with the other claimant states to implement the DoC, proposed a seminar on freedom of navigation in the South China Sea and the establishment of three technical commissions on marine scientific research and environmental protection, safety of navigation and search and rescue, and tackling transnational threats.[42] An editorial in the *People's Daily* lauded the guidelines as

> conducive to peace and stability in the South China Sea and will be significant for the resolution of territorial disputes and the demarcation of parts of the South China Sea among relevant countries. This also indicates that China and ASEAN countries have the resolve, confidence, and capability to promote peace and stability in the South China Sea.[43]

The visit by the leader of the Communist Party of Vietnam, Nguyen Phu Trong, to China in October 2011 was particularly significant. During the visit, the two sides agreed to establish a telephone hotline to manage and defuse future crises. Both countries agreed to deepen military cooperation by continuing the strategic dialogue at the deputy defence minister level, working to establish direct phone communications between their national defence ministries, expanding exchanges of military officers, exploring the feasibility of conducting combined patrols along their land border, continuing the combined naval patrols in the Gulf of Tonkin and increasing naval port calls. In the agreement concerning the basic principles for resolving their maritime disputes, China and Vietnam pledged to seek a basic and long-term solution to their maritime disputes. Both sides agreed to actively discuss temporary solutions that would not affect the positions and claims of either side, including joint development. Both countries agreed to first address less conflict-prone tasks, including the demarcation and joint development in the southern area of the mouth of the Gulf of Tonkin, cooperation in marine environmental protection, marine research, search-and-rescue operations and disaster prevention and relief. China and Vietnam also agreed that their heads of border negotiation delegations hold regular meetings and establish a dedicated hotline for use in emergency situations.[44]

During Philippine President Benigno Aquino's visit to China in late August and early September 2011, both countries downplayed their dispute in the South China Sea. In a joint statement, the two sides agreed that maritime disputes should not affect their overall relationship, that all parties should observe the DoC and that the problem should be resolved through peaceful negotiations.[45] Accordingly, China and the Philippines focused on business and economic ties: 200 Philippine entrepreneurs accompanied Aquino, and during the trip various initiatives to promote closer economic ties were announced. Beijing and Manila vowed to increase the value of bilateral trade to $60 billion and the number of tourists to two million by 2016.[46]

At the November 2011 ASEAN–China Summit, Premier Wen said that China would continue to be a "good neighbour, good friend and good partner" of ASEAN. He stated that China was willing to work with the ASEAN countries towards a comprehensive implementation of the DoC. He added that China was also willing to discuss the drafting of a Conduct of Conduct for the South China Sea (CoC). Wen also vowed to increase Chinese aid and economic cooperation with ASEAN member states. He suggested sending more business groups to ASEAN to enhance trade and investment ties, the establishment of an exhibition centre for ASEAN products in Nanning and enhancing the land and maritime connections between China and Southeast Asia. Wen also pledged to provide $10 billion in loans (including $4 billion in preferential loans) for infrastructure development projects in ASEAN countries and a $475 million China–ASEAN maritime cooperation fund to support marine scientific research and environmental protection, maritime transport, navigation safety, search and rescue and measures to counter transnational threats.[47] At the East Asian Summit (EAS) in Bali, Wen reacted calmly when U.S. President Obama and other leaders raised maritime security concerns, including the South China Sea.[48] Instead, Wen reaffirmed China's commitment to freedom of navigation in the South China Sea, expressed a positive view of the DoC and reiterated China's official position of seeking a peaceful resolution of the dispute.[49]

Many observers would agree that Chinese maritime law enforcement agencies have become more assertive in protecting China's interests in the South China Sea. While this is certainly true, it is also worth noting that Chinese patrol vessels have exercised restraint. On 2 March 2011, after warning the Philippine-chartered survey ship *MV Veritas Voyager* in waters claimed by China near Reed Bank, the two Chinese patrol vessels immediately left the scene before Philippine aircraft and coast guard ships arrived.[50] And the Chinese vessels did not return to the scene to harass the ship again.

Incidents in which Chinese vessels cut the cables of Vietnamese survey ships in May and June 2011 reflect slight differences in the way the Chinese handled the two events. In the first case, the crew of the Chinese marine surveillance ship cut the cable of the Vietnamese survey vessel. In the second case, the Chinese adopted a more skilful tactic. According to a Chinese MFA spokesperson, Chinese fishing boats were chased away by armed Vietnamese ships, and while fleeing the nets of one of the Chinese boats became entangled with the cable of the Vietnamese exploration vessel. The Chinese fishing boat was dragged for more than an hour before it broke free. The second case, if Beijing's version of events is true, would indicate that China has attempted to be more skilful in avoiding direct confrontation with Vietnam. It was argued that not only the Vietnamese vessel was operating in the maritime zone claimed by China, but also that Beijing was trying to justify its cable-cutting act on the grounds that it was trying to save the Chinese fishermen and the fishing boat from danger.[51]

It should be noted that President Xi Jinping seems to favour a more assertive policy in the South China Sea disputes than his predecessors. Xi was already largely in charge of major foreign policy issues before the 18th Party Congress in November 2012. He took the lead in decision-making during the Scarborough Shoal Incident in April–September 2012. During that crisis, Chinese government vessels not only prevented Philippine vessels from arresting Chinese fishermen who were allegedly fishing illegally in the area but also took actual control of the shoal. In response to Manila's efforts to seek a legal ruling from the International Tribunal for the Law of the Sea (ITLOS) in January 2013 on the legality of the nine-dash line, Beijing has reduced political and diplomatic interactions with Manila, suspended financial aid and loans to the Philippines and discouraged Chinese companies from investing in the Philippines and Chinese tourists from visiting the country. Chinese Coast Guard vessels have also attempted to prevent Philippine vessels from providing supplies to Filipino Marines stationed on Second Thomas Shoal.

Moreover, in early May 2014, Beijing decided to deploy the HYSY-981 oil rig into waters near the Paracels which Vietnam also claims as its EEZ. Vietnam responded strongly to the deployment. Hanoi sent its own law enforcement vessels and fishing boats to the area in an attempt to force the Chinese to withdraw the oil rig. Vietnamese leaders allowed massive anti-China demonstrations to take place in Hanoi, Ho Chi Minh City and a number of other cities. Hanoi also staged a successful international public relations campaign to denounce China's assertiveness. Perhaps partly due to Vietnam's strong responses, Beijing decided to withdraw the oil rig one month ahead of schedule in July. During and after the crisis, Beijing and Hanoi conducted high-level talks with a view to maintaining stable relations and preventing future incidents from occurring.

In mid-2014, Beijing began to undertake unprecedented land reclamation activities and the construction of artificial islands at Fiery Cross Reef and other features under its control in the Spratlys. It is quite clear that China is determined to further consolidate its presence in the Spratlys by building logistical and even military facilities on these artificial islands. It remains to be seen how China will use its strengthened presence in the Spratlys.

While many of China's assertive actions in the South China Sea from 2009 to 2012 were partially due to the decentralized nature of decision-making and competition among various maritime agencies, it appears that Chinese behaviour in the dispute since Xi Jinping took over as the country's top leader has been the result of greater centralization in policy-making and improved national coordination. China's South China Sea policy increasingly reflects Xi's strong and nationalistic personality. China under Xi's leadership is likely to be more serious about protecting its perceived national interests in the maritime domain. On the other hand, it should be noted that Xi Jinping is also strongly interested in building stable and good relations with China's neighbours, largely in reaction to America's "rebalance" to Asia. This is clearly reflected in China's policy towards India, its proposals for a twenty-first century "Maritime Silk Road" and the initiation of the Asian Infrastructure Investment Bank. The Xi administration seems to be cognizant of the limits of China's heavy-handed approach to the South China Sea disputes. Beijing realizes that its policy in the disputes cannot be too confrontational, otherwise its strategic influence in East Asia may be significantly compromised. The emerging consensus in the Chinese foreign policy community that Beijing made a serious mistake in the decision to deploy HYSY-981 in May 2014 attests to this thinking.[52]

LOOKING TO THE FUTURE

China's debate over the South China Sea has raised important issues that will help shape the country's approach to the dispute in the future. Participants in this debate have posed five questions. First, should China regard the South China Sea as a core interest? Second, should China be more flexible in allowing multilateral institutions to get involved? Third, should China be more proactive in exploiting the resources in the South China Sea? Fourth, should China consider a more legalistic approach towards solving the dispute? Fifth, how should China react to America's more interventionist stand in the South China Sea?

The South China Sea as a Core Interest?

Since mid-2010, Chinese analysts have debated whether the South China Sea should be regarded as a core interest, a notion that China has used to describe its position on the Taiwan, Xinjiang and Tibet issues; Beijing has made clear that it will not tolerate any external interference on these matters. While some scholars have supported the idea, others have urged caution. For example, Han Xudong, a senior security analyst at China's National Defense University, does not support the idea of classifying the South China Sea as a core interest, pointing out that given the country's limited military capabilities, it is premature and counter-productive to publicize a broad list of China's core interests.[53] Da Wei, a U.S. analyst at the China Institute of Contemporary International Relations, has recommended that China maintain a "minimalist definition" of core interest. He contends that "when handling territorial disputes, many countries often adopt compromises such as exchanging [disputed] territories or recognizing the status quo". He reasons that "often, big powers may 'let go of' some disputed areas. This doesn't mean that such countries have forsaken their core interests."[54]

Peking University Professor Zhu Feng believes that China's rhetoric of core interest in relation to the South China Sea has been misinterpreted by the media in the United States and Japan. He argues that the Chinese leadership — including the President, Premier and Foreign Minister — have never referred to the South China Sea as a core interest. Zhu notes that the belief that China now regards the South China Sea as a core interest is a misunderstanding. He argues that Chinese officials have only used the phrase in the context that a resolution of the South China Sea dispute through peaceful means is a core interest.[55] Analysts at the

Institute of Asia-Pacific Studies at CASS similarly note that the core interest thesis has been blindly accepted by foreign observers, and that such remarks have never been made by senior officials.[56] Xue Li, an expert on China's international strategy at CASS, also notes that Chinese interests in the South China Sea are not core interests, but "important national interests". Xue further argues that while China's interests in the maritime domain are very important, the survival of the nation does not depend on them.[57]

It is clear that Chinese officials have never officially described the South China Sea as a core interest.[58] When asked whether Chinese officials had used the term "core interest" during his visit to China in March 2011, former U.S. Deputy Secretary of State James Steinberg noted that "I didn't come away from our visit there as a decision that they were now defining the South China Sea as a core interest."[59] Moreover, some Chinese analysts have lamented that the foreign media have ranked the South China Sea as on par with issues such as Taiwan and Tibet, thus raising the concerns of the United States and other regional states. They believe that U.S. Secretary of State Hillary Clinton's description of the South China Sea as a U.S. "national interest" at the 2010 ARF was a direct response to the Chinese rhetoric of "core interest".[60]

Despite the fact that prominent scholars in China have dismissed the idea of defining the South China Sea as a core interest, public opinion tends to favour the opposite. According to a survey conducted by the *People's Daily* in January 2011, 97 per cent of 4,300 respondents agreed that the South China Sea should be classed as China's "core interest".[61] At the official level, the Chinese government does not list the South China Sea as a core interest. The 2011 White Paper on China's peaceful development stipulates that China's core interests comprises six categories: national sovereignty; national security; territorial integrity; national re-unification; the stability of the national political system; and the promoting of economic growth and maintaining social stability.[62]

In September 2010, MFA spokesperson Jiang Yu was asked to confirm the authenticity of reports that China now regarded the South China Sea as a core interest. Her reply, however, was ambiguous:

> All countries have core interests. Issues concerning state sovereignty, territorial integrity, and fundamental development interests are all crucial for any country. China believes that the South China Sea issue only concerns the disputes in territorial sovereignty and maritime

interests of relevant countries. It is neither a problem between China and ASEAN nor a regional or international problem. Hence, the issue has to be resolved through friendly talks among relevant parties and peaceful means.[63]

Jiang's remarks indicate that while the South China Sea is a very important concern for Beijing, it cannot be put on par with Taiwan and Tibet for two reasons: first, because China openly acknowledges that the South China Sea is under dispute; and second, that China seems willing to settle the problem through negotiations with the other claimants. In short, while sovereignty of the South China Sea atolls is disputed, the sovereignty of Taiwan and Tibet are not.

Should China Adopt a More Multilateral Approach?

For many years, China has strongly resisted the "internationalization" of the South China Sea dispute — that is to say discussion of the problem at regional or international forums. It prefers to deal bilaterally with the other claimants, on a one-on-one basis. China has remained firm on this matter. For instance, in the process of negotiating the implementation guidelines for the DoC, China succeeded in persuading the ASEAN countries to omit words such as "multilateral" and "international" from the final document. Beijing regarded this as a successful outcome.[64] Initially, China was reluctant to sign the implementation guidelines with ASEAN as a group, preferring instead to conclude a deal with the four ASEAN claimants only.[65] China has also vetoed ASEAN's proposed adoption of a prior consultation mechanism before engaging with China on the South China Sea issue.[66]

In the course of the debate over the past few years, dissenting views on how China should handle the South China Sea have emerged. Renmin University academic Pang Zhongying has, for instance, openly argued that China's preference for bilateralism will cause problems for China. He has therefore advocated a multilateral approach involving ASEAN, the United States, Japan and the UN.[67] But Liu Zhongmin, a seasoned observer of the South China Sea, opposes Pang's idea. On the substantive issue of sovereignty over the islands and the demarcation of maritime zones, he insists that Beijing uphold the principle of bilateralism and stresses that the multilateral approach should be reserved for improving safety of navigation and addressing non-traditional security threats such as piracy.[68]

CASS scholar Zhang Yunling has argued that the current situation in the South China Sea has undergone significant changes, and that China should adopt a more flexible approach. He sees value in discussing concrete measures for the demarcation of EEZs in the South China Sea in accordance with UNCLOS. He also proposes that ASEAN play a coordinating role, for instance, on the issue of sea lane security. The relevant parties can discuss ways to distinguish areas that are under dispute from areas that are not. Rather than engage in unilateral exploitation of resources in disputed areas, the parties should explore the idea of joint development. To prevent conflict, the disputed islands and reefs should not be awarded EEZs.[69] Zhang's ideas deviate from China's official position.

Other scholars have proposed that traditional and non-traditional security issues in the South China Sea be addressed separately. On traditional security issues, such as territorial sovereignty, the parties are unlikely to reach a solution in the near term. It is better, therefore, for China to put aside these issues and push for cooperation in other areas, such as safety of navigation and environmental protection. Some Chinese scholars have suggested that the ARF would be the most appropriate venue to discuss these issues.[70] This line of reasoning would appear to be more palatable to China, because for over a decade it has been discussing confidence building measures and dispute management mechanisms with ASEAN as a group. These discussions led to the adoption of the DoC in 2002.

Coping with the United States

Over the past few years, many Chinese scholars have suggested that Beijing should give priority to responding to Washington's increased focus on the South China Sea. Liu Jianfei, an expert at the Central Party School, argues that Sino–U.S. coordination is the most important factor in managing the South China Sea issue. If Sino–U.S. coordination falters, regional states may try to exploit the rivalry between Washington and Beijing.[71] Jin Canrong, at Renmin University, supports this view. He argues that the competition between China and America for primacy in the Asia Pacific will intensify in the near future. Accordingly, Beijing needs to prioritize the establishment of a good working relationship with Washington. Jin argues that strengthening Sino–U.S. ties is more important that improving relations with the ASEAN claimants.[72]

As America has become more proactive in the South China Sea, the PRC has responded accordingly. Prior to the 2010 ARF meeting, Beijing suspected that Secretary of State Clinton might raise the issue, and urged U.S. officials not to do so.[73] When Clinton ignored this request, Chinese officials reacted angrily. Thereafter, Beijing continued to press Washington not to "interfere" in the dispute. In June 2011, for instance, before the Sino–U.S. Consultation on Asia-Pacific affairs in Honolulu, Chinese Deputy Foreign Minister Cui Tiankai urged the United States — as a non-claimant party — not to get involved in the South China Sea dispute. Without specifying, he warned that one particular country's behaviour was tantamount to "playing fire" and that the U.S. should be careful so as not to get "burned by this fire". Cui suggested that the United States should reflect on its policy options and choose one that would be more effective in managing regional problems and contribute to better relations among relevant regional states, and exercise caution in making statements and taking actions.[74]

At the ASEAN–China Summit in November 2011, Premier Wen Jiabao warned external forces not to get involved in the dispute. Instead, it should be resolved through peaceful negotiations among the claimant states.[75] Wen made these remarks prior to the EAS at which U.S. President Barrack Obama was expected to raise the South China Sea issue. In response to America's Asian rebalance, Chinese State Councillor Dai Bingguo noted that the Asia Pacific is different from other regions and proposed the following: "Things like what to be done, what not to be done, how to do it, and when to do it, have to be based on the actual situation and the valuable experiences that have been accumulated in the region, full coordination, the views of regional states and the comfort levels of all regional states."[76] Dai's statement suggests that China believes the United States has been too interventionist on the South China Sea issue.

China and Resource Exploitation

As tensions have risen in the South China Sea, some Chinese analysts have urged the government to be more proactive in exploring for resources, arguing that when it comes to harvesting maritime resources, China cannot always keep a "low profile" (*tao guang yang hui*) and should deter the other claimants from doing so.[77] Zeng Xingqiu, the Chief Geologist of Sinochem, a state-owned energy company, noted that China's effort to fully explore the geological conditions in the South China Sea has been obstructed by Vietnam. He suggested that China should be more hardline in its policy towards the South China Sea.[78] Wu Shicun contends that since the Southeast Asian claimants are not willing to participate in joint development, China should take the opportunity to unilaterally develop the energy resources in the South China Sea. He reasons that any further delay will weaken China's influence and increase the costs of protecting its interests in the Spratly Islands.[79] Another observer has noted China's financial and technological advantages over the claimants, and believes that if China could mobilize all its resources to drill for hydrocarbons in the Spratlys, the whole situation would be immediately reversed: "We don't need to beg those so-called 'claimant states' to join us for 'joint development' — they will scramble to us to discuss [it]."[80]

Even at the official level, various proposals have been put forward to develop the resources in the South China Sea. In 2009, General Zhang Li, the former Deputy Chief of General Staff of the PLA, suggested that China should build a runway and port on Mischief Reef so that Chinese aircraft could patrol the area to protect Chinese fishing activities and enforce the country's sovereignty claims in the Spratlys.[81] Also in 2009, a senior official from the Administration of Fishery and Fishing Harbour Supervision of the South China Sea proposed that China build fishery administration bases on features under China's occupation to better protect fishery resources in the South China Sea.[82] China's Fishery Administration vessels began regular patrols in the Spratlys in April 2010.

Energy resources are an important driving force behind China's activism in the South China Sea. In 2005, the Chinese Ministry of Land and Resources identified the sea as one of ten strategic energy zones, and made plans to accelerate efforts to exploit the deep water oil and gas reserves in the region. The China National Offshore Oil Corporation (CNOOC), as well as several scientific research institutes in China, have stepped up efforts to assess oil and gas reserves in the deep water areas of the South China Sea.[83] CNOOC plans to invest $29 billion before 2020 to establish 800 oil platforms in deep water areas. The company also plans to produce 250 million tons of crude oil in deep water areas by 2015 rising to 500 million tons by 2020. To meet these targets, CNOOC has increased research into developing new technologies.[84]

With advances in China's deep-water energy exploration technologies, together with its rapidly growing law enforcement capabilities,[85] these proposals may soon become reality. Gao Heng, a senior researcher at CASS, among others, has suggested that China should set up a state commission on maritime affairs.[86] A centralized system in managing the twenty-two agencies involved in China's maritime affairs will certainly help Beijing implement a more coherent policy in the South China Sea.

Clarifying the Nine-Dash Line?

The nine-dash line that appears on official maps of the South China Sea has caused confusion among outsiders as to what exactly Beijing is claiming. Some observers believe that China views the area within the line as its "historic waters".[87] Even in China there is a lack of clarity, as both the media and analysts have used imprecise terms to describe the country's maritime claims. From time to time, they have claimed that China is entitled to three million square kilometres of "water territory", "ocean territory", "maritime territory" or "territorial seas".[88] Apparently, the three million square kilometres includes approximately two million square kilometres of sea area within the nine-dash line. Although unclear of the exact terms of entitlement, the general public seems to believe that China enjoys exclusive rights in the South China Sea. By and large, this sentiment is more or less shared by a fairly large segment of the country's International Relations experts who are not specialists in maritime affairs.[89]

Some Chinese analysts have suggested that China needs to clarify its claim in the South China Sea. One analyst argued that "currently the biggest and most urgent challenge for China is how to interpret the nine-dotted line because the ambiguity associated with this line concerns ASEAN countries and other countries the most."[90] Professor Sun Zhe, at Tsinghua University, has noted that while the South China Sea is very important for China, it should recognize that the South China Sea is not China's internal lake, for much of it is international waters. He cautions China against being perceived by the rest of the world as attempting to exercise control over the South China Sea.[91]

China's official position is that it "possesses indisputable sovereignty over the islands in the South China Sea and the adjacent waters, and it enjoys sovereign rights and jurisdiction over the relevant waters as well as the seabed and subsoil thereof".[92] More recently, Chinese officials have described the South China Sea as "jurisdictional waters", in which China exercises "jurisdictional rights". For example, in September 2011, in response to a question regarding a joint India–Vietnam oil exploration project in the South China Sea, an MFA spokesman stated:

> The oil and gas exploration activities of any foreign company in China's jurisdictional waters, without the permission of China, are illegal and invalid. We hope that relevant foreign companies will not participate in those oil and gas exploration activities and not get involved in the South China Sea dispute.[93]

A Legal Approach?

Despite the fact that the Chinese government has openly and formally ruled out the option of submitting the South China Sea dispute to international arbitration, some Chinese scholars have suggested that Beijing should consider a legal approach. Veteran Chinese maritime lawyer Liu Nanlai at CASS suggests that there are three main options for a resolution of the South China Sea dispute: war, political negotiations and international legal arbitration. He argues that force is not an option for China, and that even though political negotiations are currently China's favoured approach, in the future it may need to consider legal arbitration. Accordingly, China should begin feasibility studies to prepare for international arbitration.[94] Li Jinming, another veteran expert on the South China Sea, concurs, noting that China may not be able to refuse international arbitration indefinitely because the longer the dispute continues, the more disadvantaged China will be. He recommends, therefore, that China start preparing now by accumulating sufficient evidence to justify its claims in the South China Sea.[95] However, the use of legal arbitration as a way to resolve the dispute has always been a minority view in China. The Chinese government's refusal to participate in a UN arbitral tribunal called for by the Philippines in January 2013, indicates that China is still not prepared to pursue conflict resolution in the South China Sea dispute through legal means.

CONCLUSION

Heightened tensions in the South China Sea have sparked debate in China. The policy proposals presented by Chinese analysts reflect a diverse range of opinions in four main aspects: the origins of the tensions; a review of China's existing policies; the strategic dimensions of the South China Sea dispute; and what China's future policies should be.

Within China there is consensus on the root cause of the current set of problems in the South China Sea: the failure of regional states to respect China's interests and their collusion with external powers to undermine those interests. This consensus strongly suggests that China is unlikely to fundamentally change its policy towards the South China Sea. The logic is that if China is in the right, a major policy overhaul is unnecessary. Pressure for a tougher stance comes from popular nationalists rather than the academic community.

Rising popular nationalism, the modernization of the PLA and the expansion of the country's civilian maritime law enforcement agencies will continue to spur Chinese expansionism in the South China Sea. As a result, skirmishes at sea with the other claimants could become a more common occurrence. At the same time, however, China will not pursue a policy of confrontation in the South China Sea for three reasons: first, it wants to maintain good relations with Southeast Asian countries; second, it is cognizant that an aggressive policy would push ASEAN members closer to the United States; and third, because China needs to maintain stability along its periphery so that it can focus on economic development and domestic stability. Beijing understands, therefore, that it cannot allow tensions to spin out of control. China's handling of the disputes since 2009 attests to this strategic thinking. The combination of non-confrontation and assertiveness is likely to characterize China's behaviour in the South China Sea for the foreseeable future. And while other countries may discern a disconnect between rhetorical reassurances and China's heavy-handedness towards the other claimants, Beijing will refrain from confrontation in the South China Sea. Under the right conditions, China will not hesitate to exercise damage control by mending fences with the relevant parties in ways that are acceptable to the Chinese people.

Notes

1. An earlier version of this chapter appeared as Mingjiang Li, "Chinese Debates of South China Sea Policy: Implications for Future Developments", RSIS Working Paper 239 (17 May 2012).
2. Sarah Raine, "Beijing's South China Sea Debate", *Survival* 53, no. 5 (2011): 69–88.
3. See for instance, Li Mingjiang, "Reconciling Assertiveness and Cooperation? China's Changing Approach to the South China Sea Dispute", *Security Challenges* 6, no. 2 (Winter 2010): 49–68; Michael D. Swaine, "Perceptions of an Assertive China", *China Leadership Monitor*, no. 32 (2010); Ian Storey, "China's Missteps in Southeast Asia: Less Charm, More Offensive", *China Brief* 10, issue 25 (17 December 2010); Raine, "Beijing's South China Sea Debate", op. cit.; and Edward Wong, "China Navy Reaches Far, Unsettling the Region", *New York Times*, 14 June 2011.
4. Michael D. Swaine and M. Taylor Fravel, "China's Assertive Behavior — Part Two: The Maritime Periphery", *China Leadership Monitor*, no. 35 (2011).
5. Ji Peijuan, "Zhongguo xu jiasu kaifa nanhai" [China Needs to Accelerate Development in the South China Sea], *National Defense Times*, 29 June 2011.

6. Author's interviews with over ten leading Chinese scholars in Beijing and Shanghai, May–June 2011.

7. Yang Yi, "Shi zhongguo fanying guodu, haishi meiguo wuduan zhizhe?" [Is China Overreaction Or Is the U.S. Accusing Groundlessly?], *PLA Daily*, 13 August 2010.

8. Wang Xi, "Zhongguo zai nanhai qiaomiao fanji meiguo 'ruan e zhi'" [China Smartly Fights Back at American "Soft Containment"], *National Defense Times*, 5 August 2011.

9. Ji, "Zhongguo xu jiasu kaifa nanhai", op. cit.

10. See for instance, Foreign Ministry spokespersons' comments on 21 September 2010, available at <http://www.fmprc.gov.cn/chn/gxh/tyb/fyrbt/jzhsl/t761090. htm>, and 14 October 2010, available at <http://www.fmprc.gov.cn/chn/gxh/ tyb/fyrbt/jzhsl/t754554.htm>.

11. Ding Gang, "Nanhai wenti yuanhe hui bei chaore" [Why the South China Sea Issue Has Become So Hot], *People's Daily*, 2 August 2011.

12. Zhou Biao and Jiao Dongyu, "Nanhai boyi xiayibu" [The Next Step in the South China Sea Game], *National Defense Times*, 17 August 2011.

13. The U.S. government has made numerous statements emphasizing the critical importance of freedom of navigation in the South China Sea in the past few years. See for instance, "Tiny Island in South China Sea is Stirring Up Tensions", *USA Today*, 7 December 2012.

14. Li Xiaokun, "Navigation in South China Sea 'Not a Problem'", *China Daily*, 23 October 2010.

15. Zhang Jie et al., "Mei qiang tui nanhai wenti guojihua, yang jiechi qi bo xi lali 'wailun'" [U.S. Forcefully Pushes Internationalization of South China Sea Issue, Yang Jiechi Uses Seven Arguments to Counter Hillary's "Incorrect Points"], *Dongfang Zaobao*, 26 July 2010.

16. Liu Feitao, "Shui shuo nanhai buneng ziyou hangxing?" [Who says there is No Freedom of Navigation in the South China Sea?], *National Defense Times*, 12 November 2010.

17. "Yang Jiechi Makes Seven Points to Refute Hillary's Remarks on the South China Sea", available at <http://news.ifeng.com/mainland/detail_2010_ 07/25/1828213_0.shtml>.

18. Chinese Ministry of Foreign Affairs press briefings, available at <http://www. fmprc.gov.cn/chn/gxh/tyb/fyrbt/jzhsl/t834597.htm>.

19. Author's interviews with China-based analysts during 2011–12.

20. Long Siqi, "Nanhai zai bu da, jiu meiyou jihui le" [No Strike in the South China Sea Now, No Opportunity in the Future], *National Defense Times*, 3 October 2011.

21. "Don't Take Peaceful Approach for Granted", *Global Times*, 25 October 2011, available at <http://www.globaltimes.cn/NEWS/tabid/99/ID/680694/Dont-take-peaceful-approach-for-granted.aspx>.

22. "Chinese Military told to keep Close Eye on Situation", *People's Daily*, 30 July 2010, available at <http://english.people.com.cn/90001/90776/90785/7086388.html>.

23. "Show of Force in PLA South China Sea Drill", *South China Morning Post*, 30 July 2010.

24. Luo Yuan, "Zhongguo zai nanhai wenti shang yijing yi ren zai ren" [China Has Tolerated Time and Again in the South China Sea Issue], *National Defense Times*, 20 June 2011.

25. "Zhongguo waijiaobu fabu waijiao baipishu; zhongguo zheng mianlin kongqian tiaozhan" [Chinese Ministry of Foreign Affairs Publicizes White Paper on Diplomacy; China Faces Unprecedented Challenges], available at <http://www.sinonet.org/news/china/2011-01-11/117984.html>.

26. Li Xiangyang, eds., *Blue Book of Asia-Pacific 2010* (Beijing: Social Sciences Press, 2011).

27. Zhang Jie et al., "Zhoubian anquan xingshi si da bianhua yu zhongguo duice" [Four Changes in Regional Security Situation and China's Responses], *Shijie Zhishi* [World Knowledge], issue 2 (2011): 14–21.

28. Shang Hao, "Nanhai you cheng redian, zhongguo ying ruhe yingdui?" [South China Sea Becomes a Hotspot Again, How Should China Respond?], *Huaxia Shibao* [China Times], 6 June 2011.

29. Ji, "Zhongguo xu jiasu kaifa nanhai", op. cit.

30. Zhuang Liwei, "Nan zhongguo hai duice ying fucong zhanlue daju" [South China Sea Policy Should Follow the Overall Strategic Situation], *Dongfang Zaobao* [Oriental Morning Post], 18 March 2009.

31. Yuan Huajie, "Nanhai fengbo pinqi, zhongguo shishi 'liang jian'" [Tensions in the South China Sea Rise, China to Show Sword at the Right Moment], *CASS Bulletin* (19 March 2009).

32. Tu Fei and Xu Xin, "Zhongguo ying jianli guojia haishi weiyuanhui bao nanhai" [China Should Set Up a State Maritime Commission to Protect the South China Sea], *National Defense Times*, 7 October 2011.

33. Zhang et al., "Mei qiang tui nanhai wenti guojihua, yang jiechi qi bo xi lali 'wailun'", op. cit.

34. The Chinese Ministry of Foreign Affairs plays the coordinating role in handling the South China Sea dispute. Author's interviews with senior officials at the ministry in July 2012.

35. Chinese Ministry of Foreign Affairs press briefing, 25 October 2011, available at <http://news.xinhuanet.com/world/2011-10/25/c_111123305_2.htm>.

36. Shang, "Nanhai you cheng redian, zhongguo ying ruhe yingdui?", op. cit.

37. Deng Yajun, "Xin ba guo lianjun tumou guafen nanhai" [New Group of Eight Countries Plotting to Divide the South China Sea], *National Defense Times*, 3 August 2011.

38. Dai Bingguo, "Jianchi zou heping fazhan daolu" [Stick to a Peaceful Development Road], *People's Daily*, 13 December 2010.

39. "Yuenan guofangbu fubuzhang fang hua, cheng yong bu yu mei jiecheng junshi tongmeng" [Vietnamese Deputy Defence Minister Visits China, Vowing Not to Forge Military Alliance with U.S.], *Sohu.com*, 26 August, 2010, available at <http://news.sohu.com/20100826/n274480021.shtml>.

40. "China's Relation with US, ASEAN Eased in ADMM Plus", available at <http://www.wantchinatimes.com/news-subclass-cnt.aspx?id=20101013000060&cid=1301>.

41. Ministry of Foreign Affairs of the People's Republic of China, available at <http://www.fmprc.gov.cn/chn/gxh/tyb/fyrbt/jzhsl/t834597.htm>.

42. "Zhongguo dongmeng jiu luoshi nanhai ge fang xingwei xuanyan dacheng gongshi" [China and ASEAN Reach Consensus on Implementation of the DOC], *Global Times*, 20 July 2011, available at <http://world.huanqiu.com/roll/2011-07/1835028.html>. China organized a workshop on freedom of navigation in the South China Sea in Haikou in December 2011.

43. Wang Muke, "Zhongguo, nanhai hezuo de jiji tuidong zhe" [China: An Active Promoter of Cooperation in the South China Sea], *People's Daily*, 2 August 2011.

44. "Guangyu zhidao jiejue zhongguo he yuenan haishang wenti jiben yuanze xieyi" [An Agreement on Basic Principles Guiding the Settlement of Maritime Issues Between China and Vietnam], Xinhua News Agency, 12 October 2011, available at <http://news.xinhuanet.com/english2010/china/2011-10/12/c_131185606.htm>.

45. Ministry of Foreign Affairs of the People's Republic of China, available at <http://www.fmprc.gov.cn/chn/pds/gjhdq/gj/yz/1206_9/1207/t854349.htm>.

46. "Ajinuo fanghua huanhe zhong fei jinzhang guanxi" [Aquino Visits China, Alleviating Tense Sino–Philippine Relations], Xinhua News Agency, 1 September 2011, available at <http://news.xinhuanet.com/world/2011-09/01/c_121941388_3.htm>.

47. "China Pledges to be 'Good Friend'", *Straits Times*, 19 November 2011; "Zhongguo zongli wen jiabao: fandui waibu shili jieru nanhai" [Chinese Premier Wen Jiabao: China Opposes the Involvement of External Forces in the South China Sea], *Lianhe Zaobao*, 19 November 2011.

48. "Asia Finds Voice in Test of Wills with China", *Sydney Morning Herald*, 22 November 2011, available at <http://www.smh.com.au/opinion/politics/asia-finds-voice-in-test-of-wills-with-china-20111121-1nqzi.html>.

49. "Wen Jiabao jiu nanhai wenti chanming zhong fang lichang" [Wen Jiao States China's Positions on the South China Sea], Xinhua News Agency, 19 November 2011, available at <http://news.xinhuanet.com/2011-11/19/c_111180192.htm?prolongation=1>.

50. "ASEAN, China Hardening Positions on Overlapping Claims in South China Sea", *China Post*, 31 May 2011, available at <http://www.chinapost.com.tw/commentary/the-china-post/special-to-the-china-post/2011/05/31/304386/ASEAN-China.htm>.

51. Ministry of Foreign Affairs of the People's Republic of China, 9 June 2011, available at <http://www.fmprc.gov.cn/chn/gxh/mtb/fyrbt/dhdw/t829297. htm>.

52. Author's interviews with over twenty government-affiliated analysts and officials in China from June to October 2014.

53. "Han Xudong: bu yi mingshi 'guojia hexin liyi'" [Han Xudong: Not Wise to Clearly List "National Core Interest"], *Huanqiu Shibao* [Global Times], 3 August 2010.

54. "Da Wei: zhongguo weishenme yao xuanshi hexin liyi?" [Da Wei: Why Should China Declare Core interests?], *Huanqiu Shibao* [Global Times], 27 July 2010.

55. Author's interview with Zhu Feng, Beijing, May 2011.

56. Zhang et al., "Zhoubian anquan xingshi si da bianhua yu zhongguo duice", op. cit.

57. Tu and Xu, "Zhongguo ying jianli guojia haishi weiyuanhui bao nanhai", op. cit.

58. See Michael D. Swaine, "China's Assertive Behavior Part One: On 'Core Interests'", *China Leadership Monitor*, no. 34 (2011), available at <http://carnegieendowment.org/2010/11/15/china-s-assertive-behavior-part-one-on-core-interests/20tq>.

59. Yoichi Kato, "Interview with James Steinberg: U.S. Leadership Restored in 10 years After 9/11", *Asahi Shimbun*, 24 September 2011, available at <https://ajw.asahi.com/article/views/opinion/AJ2011092111598>.

60. Author's interviews with scholars at CASS in Beijing and at SIIS in Shanghai, June 2011.

61. Edward Wong, "China Hedges Over Whether South China Sea is a 'Core Interest' Worth War", *New York Times*, 30 March 2011.

62. The Information Office of the State Council, *China's Peaceful Development*, September 2011, available at <http://english.gov.cn/official/2011-09/06/content_1941354.htm>.

63. Chinese Foreign Ministry, 21 September 2011, available at <http://www.fmprc.gov.cn/chn/gxh/tyb/fyrbt/jzhsl/t754554.htm>.

64. Zhong Feiteng et al., "Nanhai ce: jieshi quan yu haiquan yi ge buneng shao" [South China Sea Policy: Not One Less for Interpretation Rights and Maritime Rights], *Huaxia Shibao*, 8 August 2011.

65. Author's interviews with ASEAN officials, ASEAN Secretariat, Jakarta, June 2011.

66. Author's interviews with Thai and Indonesian diplomats in Hainan, December 2011.

67. "Pang Zhongying: nanhai wenti, bufang huan ge silu" [Pang Zhongying: The South China Sea Issue, How About a New Mindset?], *Huanqiu Shibao* [Global Times], 5 August 2010.

68. Liu Zhongmin, "Nanhai wenti, buneng jiandan tan duobian" [South China Sea Issue: Not to Simply Consider Multilateralism], *National Defense Times*, 11 August 2010.

69. Zhou and Jiao, "Nanhai boyi xiayibu", op. cit.

70. Zhong et al., "Nanhai ce: jieshi quan yu haiquan yi ge buneng shao", op. cit.

71. Zhou and Jiao, "Nanhai boyi xiayibu", op. cit. The notion of Sino–U.S. coordination has not been fully explained. Most probably it means China and the U.S. discussing and positively handling their differences on the South China Sea issue.

72. Shang, "Nanhai you cheng redian, zhongguo ying ruhe yingdui?", op. cit.

73. Zhang et al., "Mei qiang tui nanhai wenti guojihua, yang jiechi qi bo xi lali 'wailun'", op. cit.

74. Deputy Foreign Minister Cui Tiankai's news briefing on 22 June 2011, available at <http://www.mfa.gov.cn/chn/gxh/tyb/wjbxw/t832915.htm>.

75. "Wen Jiabao jiu nanhai wenti chanming zhongfang lichang" [Wen Jiabao Explains China's Positions on the South China Sea], 20 November 2011, available at <http://www.fmprc.gov.cn/mfa_chn/ziliao_611306/zt_611380/ywzt_611452/2011nzt_611454/wjbdyldrhy_611516/t879057.shtml>.

76. "Dai Bingguo: zai yatai zuo shenme, zenme zuo yao zhaogu dajia de shushi du" [Dai Bingguo: What to Do and How to Do have to be Based on the Comfort Level of All Regional States], Xinhua News Agency, 22 November 2011, available at <http://news.china.com/domestic/945/20111122/16880700.html>.

77. Zhang et al., "Mei qiang tui nanhai wenti guojihua, yang jiechi qi bo xi lali 'wailun'", op. cit.

78. Shang, "Nanhai you cheng redian, zhongguo ying ruhe yingdui?", op. cit.

79. Ji, "Zhongguo xu jiasu kaifa nanhai", op. cit.

80. Yang Xiyu, "Nanhai wenti zhong de san ge cengci maodun" [The Three-layer Conflicts in the South China Sea Issue], *Jingji Guancha Bao* [Economic Observation Newspaper], 20 June 2011.

81. "Jiefangjun yuan fu zong canmouzhang jianyi zai nansha jian jichang he gangkou" [Former PLA Deputy Chief of Staff Suggests Building Airport and Port at Spratlys], 21 June 2009, available at <http://news.ifeng.com/mainland/200906/0621_17_1211801.shtml>.

82. "China Charts Course toward Secure South China Sea", *China Daily*, 1 July 2009.

83. "Nanhai bei liewei guojia shi da youqi zhanlue xuanqu zhi yi" [South China Sea Identified as One of the Ten Strategic Oil and Gas Reserve Areas], *Jingji Cankao Bao* [Economic Reference Newspaper], 5 April 2009.

84. Zhou Shouwei, "Nan zhongguo hai shenshui kaifa de tiaozhan yu jiyu" [Challenges and Opportunities for Deep Water Exploitation in the South China Sea], *Gao keji yu canyehua* [High Technology and Industrialization] (December 2008): 20–23.

85. Russell Hsiao, "China Intensifies Maritime Surveillance Missions", *China Brief* 11, issue 10 (3 June 2011).
86. Tu and Xu, "Zhongguo ying jianli guojia haishi weiyuanhui bao nanhai", op. cit.
87. Nguyen Hong Thao and Ramses Amer, "A New Legal Arrangement for the South China Sea?", *Ocean Development & International Law* 40, issue 4 (2009): 333–49.
88. Wang Qian, "China to Dive into Mapping Seabed", *China Daily*, 14 September 2011; Wang Xinjun, "China One Step Closer to Developing Aircraft Carrier", *China Daily*, 1 August 2011; "Refitting Aircraft Carrier Not to Change Naval Strategy", *China Daily*, 27 July 2011; Zhang Zixuan, "Cultural Relics Discovered Under Sea", *China Daily*, 17 May 2011.
89. Author's interviews with over fifty Chinese scholars since 2009.
90. Zhong et al., "Nanhai ce: jieshi quan yu haiquan yi ge buneng shao", op. cit.
91. Zhang et al., "Mei qiang tui nanhai wenti guojihua, yang jiechi qi bo xi lali 'wailun'", op. cit.
92. See for instance, "Zhongguo dui nanhai zhu dao ji qi fujin haiyu yongyou wukezhengbian de zhuquan" [China Owns Indisputable Sovereignty over South China Sea Islands and Their Adjacent Waters], Chinese Ministry of Foreign Affairs press briefing, 14 April, 2011, available at <http://news.xinhuanet.com/mil/2011-04/14/c_121306073.htm>.
93. Chinese Foreign Ministry, 22 September 2011, available at <http://www.fmprc.gov.cn/chn/gxh/tyb/fyrbt/t861266.htm>.
94. Nie Xiushi, "Wo yuan xuezhe biaoshi: falv caijue huo ke jiejue nanhai wenti" [CASS Scholar: Legal Adjudication May Solve the South China Sea Problem], *CASS Bulletin*, 23 April 2009.
95. Zhang et al., "Mei qiang tui nanhai wenti guojihua, yang jiechi qi bo xi lali 'wailun'", op. cit

4

TAIWAN'S EVOLVING POLICY TOWARDS THE SOUTH CHINA SEA DISPUTE, 1992–2016

Anne Hsiu-an Hsiao and Cheng-yi Lin

The Republic of China (ROC) or Taiwan was the first country to claim sovereignty over the Pratas Islands (Tungsha Islands), Macclesfield Bank (Chungsha Islands), the Paracel Islands (Shisha Islands) and the Spratly Islands (Nansha Islands) in the South China Sea after Japan's withdrawal from the islands at the end of the Second World War. In November 1946, the ROC government moved to "restore" the South China Sea atolls to Chinese sovereignty.[1] On 1 December 1947, the ROC Ministry of the Interior renamed those islands and formally transferred their administration from Guangdong Province to the Hainan Special Region. In 1948, the ROC government published an official map which showed the four archipelagos within the so-called "U-shaped" line.[2] The ROC's control over the Paracel and Spratly Islands was challenged by France and the Philippines in 1947 and 1949, and was disrupted between May 1950 and July 1956 due to the Nationalist government's (Kuomintang or KMT) defeat in the Chinese Civil War. However, the KMT re-established a garrison on Itu Aba (Taiping Island) in July 1956 and the ROC on Taiwan has controlled the island ever since. Apart from Itu Aba, Taiwan also controls Ban Than Reef (Zhongzhou Reef), approximately 5 km from Itu Aba as well as the Pratas Islands (Tungsha Islands).

Despite being a claimant in the South China Sea, Taiwan's position as a party to the territorial dispute has been undermined due to Southeast Asian countries adherence to Beijing's "One China" policy. It has even been argued that Taiwan — which is not recognized as a sovereign state by the majority of countries — "has no juridical standing to make any claims to any territory".[3] Inevitably, the "China factor" plays a role in Taiwan's policy considerations towards the South China Sea dispute. When cross-straits relations are cordial, Taiwan and mainland China (the People's Republic of China, PRC) tend to develop a shared dedication to promoting territorial claims on behalf of "China". When relations deteriorate, however, cross-straits coordination over the South China Sea breaks down and Taiwan tends to become more concerned about the security threat posed by the PRC and therefore adopts a more conciliatory policy towards the Southeast Asian claimants in order to balance Beijing.[4] This view has been borne out by developments after the mid-1990s. Before the 1996 Taiwan Straits Crisis, Taiwan reportedly offered tacit support to the PRC during the latter's clash with Vietnam at Johnson Reef in the Spratlys in 1988. In addition, during the 1990s participants from the PRC and Taiwan cooperated at the Indonesian Workshops on Managing Potential Conflicts in the South China Sea (hereinafter, the South China Sea Workshops).[5] In contrast, between the 1996 crisis and the election of President Ma Ying-jeou in May 2008, there was scarcely any policy coordination between Taiwan and the PRC over the South China Sea. In some cases, domestic factors such as Taiwan's party politics and bureaucratic coordination, or its attempts to improve relations with the Southeast Asian claimants to break the island's diplomatic isolation, also affected Taiwan's policy towards the South China Sea.

This chapter compares Taiwan's policy towards the South China Sea under three successive presidents between 1992 up until January 2016. President Lee Teng-hui (1988–2000) established a legal mechanism to strengthen Taiwan's claims in the South China Sea during the 1990s, but in 1999 took the dramatic step of replacing marine forces stationed on Itu Aba with coast guard personnel. His successor, President Chen Shui-bian (2000–8), tried to promote Taiwan's role as a party to the South China Sea dispute by controversially ordering the construction of an airstrip on Itu Aba during his second term. Chen's successor — President Ma Ying-jeou (May 2008–present) — has endeavoured to foster an environment conducive to cross-straits energy and other functional cooperation in the South China Sea. The chapter provides an overview of the main policy developments in relation to the South China Sea under each president, and examines how the "China factor" and the state of cross-straits relations have influenced the rationales for those major policy decisions as well as their outcomes. It concludes that cross-straits relations continue to pose complicated challenges to Taiwan's South China Sea policy, despite the significant easing of tensions between Taipei and Beijing in recent years.

PRESIDENT LEE'S SOUTH CHINA SEA POLICY AND DECISION TO REPLACE MARINES WITH COAST GUARD PERSONNEL ON ITU ABA IN 1999

Prior to the 1990s, Taiwan's policy towards the South China Sea dispute had been largely reactive and limited to issuing declarations or protests reiterating its territorial claims. However, in the early 1990s this approach began to change as competition among the other claimants over ownership of the islands and access to natural resources intensified. In 1992, President Lee Teng-hui established an inter-agency task force at the deputy ministerial level for the South China Sea, with the minister of the interior as its chairman, to formulate a more coherent policy.[6] In addition, Taiwan declared a 4,000-metre prohibited sea/air zone and a 6,000-metre restricted sea/air zone around the Pratas Islands and Itu Aba to demonstrate its sovereignty and administrative control[7] in reaction to reports that the PRC was building an air base on the Paracel Islands and that other claimants were also planning to construct airstrips on the atolls they occupied.[8] As a result of the task force's deliberations, in 1993 the Ministry of the Interior under the Executive Yuan adopted "Policy Guidelines for the South China Sea".[9] The prologue to the guidelines states:

> On the basis of history, geography, international law and the facts, the Spratly Islands, the Paracel Islands, Macclesfield Bank and the Pratas Islands have always been a part of the inherent territory of the Republic of China... The South China Sea area within the historic water limit is the maritime area under the jurisdiction of the Republic of China, in which the Republic of China possesses all rights and interests.

Article 2 of the guidelines sets out the following five goals: first, safeguard ROC sovereignty over the islands in the South China Sea; second, strengthen the development and management of the South China Sea; third, promote cooperation among the littoral states; fourth, achieve a peaceful resolution of the disputes; and fifth, protect the marine environment. Following the promulgation of the guidelines, the government frequently expressed Taiwan's willingness to temporarily set aside the sovereignty dispute and cooperate with the other claimants to develop the resources in the South China Sea, and to participate in regional dialogues related to the dispute. In 1995, President Lee proposed the establishment of a multilateral South China Sea Development Company with funds of US$10 billion, with the profits from its activities used to support infrastructure development in the ASEAN countries.[10]

In April 1994, Taiwan dispatched marine police boats to Itu Aba to protect Taiwanese fishing boats from pirate attacks. A second patrol was scheduled to take place the following year, but it was cancelled due to rising tensions in the Spratlys between the PRC and the Philippines over the former's occupation of Mischief Reef in early 1995. The cancellation of the mission was criticized by some observers in Taiwan and also exposed the continued lack of bureaucratic coordination.[11] As a result, the government decided to set up an inter-ministerial task force to handle future crises in the South China Sea. In January 1998, the government promulgated the Law of the Republic of China on the Territorial Sea and the Contiguous Zone as well as the Law of the Republic of China on the Exclusive Economic Zone and Continental Shelf.[12] In February 1999, the government published the first batch of territorial sea baselines for Taiwan and its associated islets, the Pratas Islands and Scarborough Shoal (*Huangyan Dao*) in Macclesfield Bank. The declaration stated that the baselines for the Spratlys would be announced at a later date, though the Paracels were not mentioned. This omission was probably deliberate due to escalating tensions over the Spratlys and China's *de facto* control of the Paracels.[13]

Between 1988 and 1995, Taiwan's relations with the PRC improved. In April 1993, the two sides held formal talks in Singapore for the first time in decades. The talks were held on the basis that both sides recognized that there is only "One China", though their interpretations of that differed (the so-called "1992 consensus").[14] However, cross-straits relations rapidly deteriorated after President Lee's visit to the United States in June 1995 and China's live missile tests in waters adjacent to Taiwan in July 1995 and March 1996. In July 1999, Lee announced that cross-straits relations should henceforth be characterized as "state-to-state" or at least "special state-to-state".[15] Beijing responded angrily with verbal attacks and military intimidation.[16] However, a further crisis was averted after a devastating earthquake occurred in Taiwan on 21 September 1999, which resulted in an outpouring of international sympathy.

In November 1999, the government announced that it intended to create a coast guard personnel from which would replace the garrison of marines on Pratas Islands and Itu Aba. This took many observers by surprise given that the situation in the South China Sea was still volatile following renewed tensions between China and the Philippines over the upgrade of structures on Mischief Reef in November 1998. The deliberations on switching the garrison had begun in March 1999, and after seven meetings the decision was made on a division of labour between the Ministry of National Defense (MND) and the newly-created Coast Guard Administration (CGA). Defense Minister Tang Fei subsequently submitted the proposal to President Lee Teng-hui and Secretary General of the National Security Council Ying Tsung-wen for final approval, apparently bypassing the cabinet.[17]

Tang Fei had admitted that Taiwan was incapable of effectively defending the islands it administered and that it would also be more appropriate to let coast guard personnel handle civilian and jurisdictional issues such as fishing disputes. According to Tang, the CGA "would be less controversial in performing missions like cracking down on maritime smuggling and stowaways, as well as environmental protection".[18] His remarks partly explained why the government wanted to create the CGA to garrison the Spratlys and to take over responsibility from the marines that had been reduced in numbers under new guidelines issued by the MND. On 1 February 2000, the CGA was formally established and took over responsibility for the security of the two islands from the MND.[19] The number of coast guard personnel deployed to Itu Aba was the same as the marines, and were armed with the same weapons. However, a token number of personnel from the army remained for logistical purposes. It was envisaged that during a crisis coast guard personnel would be placed under the command of the armed forces.

In transferring responsibility for the security of the islands from the MND to the CGA, some legislators and observers in Taiwan criticized the government's lack of transparency and also questioned whether the policy move meant that the government intended to abandon the ROC's territorial claims in the South China Sea. In response, the MND argued that it was misleading to characterize the change of personnel as a form of demilitarization, and that the ROC was not abandoning its claims to sovereignty over the islands. The MND reiterated that it would defend every square inch of the country's territory, no matter how remote those areas were from the main island. Despite these reassurances, however, some experts still questioned if the CGA was capable of defending ROC territory, and whether or not in light of the volatile situation in the Spratlys, the substitution of the marines with coast guard personnel was a wise decision. If CGA personnel were not able to defend the islands, they argued, the PRC might be tempted to launch a military attack. The presidential candidate from the Democratic Progressive Party (DPP) for the 2000 election, Chen Shui-bian, derided the move as "retreatism", and a concession towards the PRC that would have a negative impact on Taiwan's national sovereignty.[20] Across the Taiwan Straits, Beijing regarded the move as a signal that Taipei might abandon the South China Sea islands in accordance with Lee's "special state-to-state" initiative,[21] even though in reality there was no connection between the two events.

The replacement of marine forces by CGA personnel seemed ill timed. After the issuance of the "special state-to-state relationship" proclamation in July 1999, Taipei detected unusual activities by the People's Liberation Army Navy (PLA-Navy) to the northeast of the Pratas Islands. Taipei responded by dispatching warships to Itu Aba. Taiwan was very concerned that the PRC might use force against the islands in retaliation for Lee's July statement,[22] and that a crisis in the Taiwan Straits might spill over into the South China Sea. Beijing might even invade the Pratas Islands or Itu Aba to embarrass the Lee administration.[23] However, Taipei knew it was difficult to effectively defend Itu Aba, and the change of personnel would expose the PRC to international criticism if it attacked the two islands where only non-military coast guard forces were stationed.

The ROC government had traditionally viewed the Spratly Islands under its control as a predominantly military issue, but in 1999 some experts argued that Taiwan should adopt a more comprehensive approach to consolidate its legal claims over the disputed islands. The Taiwan Research Institute — a KMT affiliated think-tank close to President Lee — as well as the Kaohsiung City Government under the DPP Mayor Frank Hsieh, called for a loosening of military control and economic development of the islands. In response, in June 1999, at the Eighth South China Sea Task Force Meeting, Taipei decided to allow private enterprises to develop tourism on the two islands (see Table 4.1). The MND argued that Taiwan would be able to strengthen its sovereignty claims to the islands by promoting civilian economic activities and infrastructure development.

TABLE 4.1
ROC South China Sea Task Force Meetings, 1992–99

3 December 1992	Adopted South China Sea Policy Guidelines; Task Force to meet every three months.
26 May 1993	Decided to hold a conference on the South China Sea and organize trips to Pratas Island and Itu Aba.
21 March 1994	Discussed field trip reports to the islands and implemented decisions taken at the conference on the South Sea China.
24 November 1994	Explored the possibility of cooperation with the PRC in the South China Sea.
13 June 1995	The Executive Yuan approved the establishment of a South China Sea Emergency Management Task Force.
2 November 1995	The Executive Yuan changed South China Sea Task Force meetings from every three months to an ad hoc basis.
23 December 1997	Explored the possibility to develop Pratas Island and sponsor an international conference on the South China Sea.
4 June 1999	Proposed the establishment of an international investment corporation with Vietnam, the PRC and the Philippines to jointly develop projects in the South China Sea. Also permitted private corporations to apply Build-Operate-Transfer formula to construct harbours on Itu Aba and Pratas Island.

Source: Compiled by the authors.

In Beijing's view, the motive behind Taiwan's policy readjustments was not economic, but political. Beijing feared that Taipei would adopt a separate and different South China Sea policy from that of the PRC, thus portraying Beijing as more militant.[24] Moreover, Beijing argued that Taipei's manoeuver had weakened China's claims in the South China Sea and strengthened those of the Southeast Asian claimants.

After the controversial policy of deploying coast guard personnel to the South China Sea, President Lee instructed Vice President and KMT candidate for the 2000 presidential election Lien Chan to visit the Pratas Islands in January 2000, two months before the election, with a view to quelling any doubts about the government's determination to maintain control of its possessions in the South China Sea.

Whatever the motives behind Taipei's readjustment of its military garrison in the South China Sea, arguably it served as a unilateral confidence-building effort by Taiwan to diffuse tensions in the Spratlys. After Taipei announced the plan, the MND urged the other claimants to replace military personnel with police or civilian units in order to reduce the risk of armed conflict and pre-empt the seizure of unoccupied islands in the South China Sea. However, ASEAN paid scant attention to Taipei's decision, perhaps because it was more preoccupied with discussing a regional code of conduct for the South China Sea with the PRC. Even though Taiwanese participants at the South China Sea Workshop raised the issue of demilitarizing the occupied atolls in December 1999, the final statement did not mention their proposal. For some ASEAN claimants, Taiwan's military presence kept the largest island in the Spratlys from being occupied by the PRC, and thus they did not wish to see any major move by Taiwan that would provide the PRC with an opportunity for military adventurism. Taiwan's policy adjustment in 1999 did not have a positive demonstration effect on the other claimants, as both China and Vietnam increased the number of troops stationed on the islands they occupied.

PRESIDENT CHEN'S SOUTH CHINA SEA POLICY AND DECISION TO CONSTRUCT AN AIRSTRIP ON ITU ABA

Before President Chen Shui-bian, Taiwanese leaders had been more preoccupied with defending the main island against military threats from the PRC. Thus, even though the ROC government was the first to send troops to the Spratly Islands after 1945, Taiwan was careful not to implement any policies that might provoke a hostile response from the Southeast Asian claimants and which would force Taiwan to divert its attention away from its primary security threat. During its years in the opposition throughout the 1990s, some members of the DPP had been critical about the KMT government's ambiguous legal positions on the South China Sea and the lack of an effective policy-making structure. After Chen took office in May 2000, the DPP government gradually adopted a more proactive approach to promoting Taiwan's status as a party to the South China Sea dispute.

President Chen first raised the idea of establishing Taiwan as a "maritime nation" in 2000. The idea was formally incorporated into Taiwan's first Ocean Policy White Paper in 2001. He also visited the Pratas Islands for the first time in December 2000. In November 2002, Taiwan's Ministry of Foreign Affairs issued a statement protesting the signing of the Declaration on the Conduct of Parties in the South China

Sea (DoC) between ASEAN and China. The statement reiterated the ROC's sovereignty over the islands in the South China Sea, and expressed regret that Taiwan had not been invited to sign the DoC and that its rights and interests had been ignored. Notwithstanding renewed attention to the South China Sea, during President Chen's first term between 2000 and 2004, Taiwan's main policy challenge continued to be cross-straits relations. In fact, the relationship between Taipei and Beijing plummeted due to the DPP's rejection of the "1992 consensus" and Chen's reference to cross-straits relations as "one country on each side" (of the Taiwan Straits) in August 2002.[25] It deteriorated further after Chen's decision to hold a referendum in response to China's missile deployment against Taiwan on 20 March 2004, the same day as Taiwan's presidential election. The decision was condemned by the PRC as "a plot to change the cross-straits status quo" and a threat to peace and stability in the Taiwan Straits.[26] It was not until Chen's re-election in May 2004 that the DPP government began to focus on implementing its maritime policies more actively, in order to safeguard Taiwan's national sovereignty and interests in the South China Sea.

The May 2006 National Security Report recommended that the government elevate decision making for maritime issues and "utilize oceanic resources for sustainable development, interact with other democratic maritime countries, and together respond to threats from the sea".[27] The same year, the DPP government moved decision-making on South China Sea issues from the Ministry of Interior Affairs to the National Security Council. In addition, the DPP government adopted further measures to consolidate Taiwan's legal claims over the disputed islands. The most significant decision was to build an airstrip on Itu Aba. In addition, it also decided to build port facilities on Itu Aba and the Pratas Islands. Moreover, the government decided to open Pratas to tourism, and turned the islands into a national park in 2007. President Chen paid two more visits to the Pratas Islands in July 2005 and February 2008,[28] and in early 2008 he became the first ROC leader to visit Itu Aba.

Construction of the airstrip on Itu Aba began in the first half of 2007 and was completed within nine months. The main purpose of the airstrip was not only to reinforce Taiwan's sovereignty over the island, but also to improve maritime safety. Chen's controversial decision to build the airstrip may have been prompted by his annoyance at Taiwan's exclusion from the Joint Marine Seismic Undertaking (JMSU), an agreement signed by the national oil companies of China, the Philippines and Vietnam in March 2005 to explore for energy resources in disputed waters in the South China Sea. Even though designated areas covered by the JMSU appeared to include Itu Aba, Taiwan was not consulted nor invited to participate in the negotiations. Also, the JMSU was signed on the same day Beijing adopted the Anti-Secession Law, which provides a legal basis for the use of force against Taiwan under certain conditions including a declaration of independence.[29] For these reasons, Taiwan clearly regarded the JMSU as a violation of its sovereignty.

On 2 February 2008, President Chen made a historic visit to Itu Aba to officially open the airstrip. During his trip he also announced a "Spratly Initiative" which consisted of four points: first, that Taiwan was willing to accept the spirit and principles of the DoC on the basis of sovereign equality; second, that the claimant countries should utilize the resources of the South China Sea in more ecological and sustainable manner; third, that Taiwan would invite environmental specialists to conduct scientific research on and around the Pratas Islands, Itu Aba and Ban Than Reef; and fourth, that the claimant countries should not allow disputes over sovereignty to impede cooperation, and that they should establish non-governmental research organizations to discuss conflict prevention.[30]

The Spratly Initiative received little attention from the other claimants. This was in sharp contrast to their responses to the construction of the airstrip on Itu Aba and President Chen's visit to the island. In reaction to the latter, PRC Foreign Ministry spokesman Liu Jianchao reiterated that

> China has indisputable sovereignty over the Nansha Islands and adjacent waters. Taiwan is an inseparable part of the Chinese territory. China is willing to solve the South China Sea disputes through friendly consultation with relevant countries and work with them to safeguard peace and stability there.[31]

Beijing believes that any facilities constructed by Taiwan in the South China Sea belong to the PRC. An airstrip on Itu Aba would, therefore, be seen by Beijing as a positive, as it could bolster China's presence in the South China Sea *vis-à-vis* the ASEAN claimants, especially if Taipei agreed to jointly defend Chinese sovereign rights in the area.

Vietnam and the Philippines strongly criticized Taiwan's moves. On 2 February 2008, Vietnamese Foreign Ministry Spokesman Le Dzung denounced Chen's visit to Itu Aba as "an extremely serious act of escalation, violating Vietnam's territorial sovereignty over the Truong Sa [Spratly] archipelago, causing tension and more complication to the region. Taiwan is fully responsible for all consequences caused by their move."[32] Philippine Foreign Secretary Alberto Romulo issued a statement expressing "serious concern over this reported development that works against the joint efforts by claimant countries in the South China Sea to achieve peace and stability in the region in accordance with the Declaration on the Conduct of Parties in the South China Sea (DoC)." He added that "it is unfortunate that Taiwan is resorting to what may be considered as irresponsible political posturing that could be of no possible advantage to the peace-loving Taiwanese people."[33]

Some observers in Taiwan saw Chen's Itu Aba visit as a "practical demonstration of Taiwan's sovereignty over the Spratly Islands",[34] and his Spratly Initiative as a commendable way of protecting the environment and promoting cooperation among the claimants.[35] All in all, during Chen Shui-bian's presidency, Taiwan improved the effectiveness of decision-making on the South China Sea as well as the infrastructure on Pratas and Itu Aba. Chen also succeeded in raising rival claimants' attention to its existence as a party to the South China Sea dispute.

PRESIDENT MA AND CROSS-STRAITS COOPERATION IN THE SOUTH CHINA SEA

Although tensions had been rising in the South China Sea since 2007–8, cross-straits relations began to improve after President Ma Ying-jeou assumed office in May 2008. On the basis of the "1992 consensus", Taipei and Beijing revived institutional dialogue through Taipei's Straits Exchange Foundation and Beijing's Association for Relations Across the Taiwan Straits. Improved relations provided a new impetus for cross-straits cooperation in the South China Sea. In mainland China, analysts and commentators suggested that the dispute could provide the basis for confidence-building activities between the Chinese and Taiwanese armed forces.[36] PRC access to Itu Aba could also ease logistical problems for the PLA in a conflict situation. On 14 May 2014, PRC Taiwan Affairs Office spokesperson Ma Xiaoguan asserted that "Safeguarding the country's sovereignty and territorial integrity as well as the overall interests of the Chinese nation should be a common obligation of compatriots of the two sides", and confirmed that Beijing had called for Taiwan's cooperation through various channels.[37] All these reflect the PRC's view that cross-straits cooperation should progress from economic to military and political issues, and eventually set the stage for reunification.

Within Taiwan, the idea of joint territorial defence with the PRC in the South China Sea is welcomed by those who advocate reunification. It has also been suggested that Taiwan could take advantage of China's territorial and maritime boundary claims to reinforce its own position as a party in the dispute. However, the Ma government has exercised caution. Responding to a proposal that Taiwan and the PRC build a new airport on Itu Aba in 2010, Government Information Office Minister Johnny Chi-chen Chiang said the feasibility of such a project would have to be carefully deliberated before a decision could be made, and that "any decision we make will be in the best interests of the people of Taiwan".[38] At a press conference in May 2012, Vice Chairman of Taiwan's Mainland Affairs Council (MAC), Liu Der Hsun, stated that sovereignty in the South China Sea belonged to the ROC, that it would defend the islands against any attacks and that there was no need to cooperate with the PRC.[39] In May 2014 this message was underscored by MAC spokeswoman Wu Mei-hung when, in response to Beijing's proposal, she said that Taiwan did not think there was any possibility of cross-straits cooperation on territorial disputes in the South China Sea. However, it welcomes all parties concerned to develop and share resources in the region peacefully.[40]

The Ma government's position on the South China Sea was expressed in a statement issued by the Ministry of Foreign Affairs shortly after the showdown between Chinese Foreign Minister Yang Jie-chi and U.S. Secretary of State Hillary Clinton over her comments on the dispute in July 2010 at the ASEAN Regional Forum (ARF) in Hanoi. The statement, in full, reads as follows:

1) No matter from what perspective one uses — history, geography or international law — one can see that the Nansha Islands (Spratly Islands), Shisha Islands (Paracel Islands), Chungsha Islands (Macclesfield Islands), Tungsha Islands (Pratas Islands), as well as their surrounding waters, and respective seabed and subsoil, all consist of the inherent territory of the Republic of China (Taiwan). These archipelagos without a doubt fall under the sovereignty of the government of the Republic of China (Taiwan). Therefore, the government reasserts that it enjoys all rights over the islands and their surrounding waters. Furthermore, it cannot accept any claim to sovereignty over, or occupation of, these areas by other countries or territories.

2) The government of the Republic of China (Taiwan) calls on countries bordering the islands to respect the principles and spirit of the Charter of the United Nations and the United Nations Convention on the Law of the Sea (UNCLOS), and to refrain from adopting unilateral

measures that might upset the peace and stability of the region and the South China Sea.

3) The government of the Republic of China (Taiwan) reiterates that it upholds the basic principles of "safeguarding sovereignty, shelving disputes, peace and reciprocity, and joint exploration" and remains willing to work with other countries in exploring the resources of the South China Sea.

4) The government of the Republic of China (Taiwan) also urges the neighbouring countries bordering the South China Sea to exercise self-constraint so that peaceful resolutions to South China Sea disputes can be reached through consultation and dialogue. Taiwan remains willing to participate in dialogue aiming to form resolutions to disputes and promote regional peace, stability and development.[41]

Ma's government has steadfastly reiterated Taiwan's territorial claims in the South China Sea, and has endeavoured to demonstrate its determination to uphold them through a combination of hard and soft power approaches. Taiwan has issued numerous official statements objecting to the other claimants' attempts to assert sovereignty. On 2 February 2009, for instance, Taiwan protested the passage of legislation in the Philippines that incorporated Scarborough Shoal and parts of the Spratly Islands into Philippine territory.[42] In May 2009, Taiwan's Ministry of Foreign Affairs issued statements opposing the submission by Vietnam, and a joint submission by Vietnam and Malaysia, to the UN Commission on the Limits of the Continental Shelf (CLCS), extending the outer limits of their continental shelves.[43] It further declared that, since the ROC was not a signatory or a party to UNCLOS, its government was not bound by the May 2009 deadline for submitting claims to the CLCS, and "after this date, this country shall remain entitled to make claims on the outer limits of its extended continental shelf beyond 200 nautical miles with respect to the waters of the East China Sea, the Eastern Taiwan, and the South China Sea."[44]

In addition to these diplomatic moves, President Ma visited the Pratas Islands on 10 September 2008. During the trip he stressed that Taiwan should continue to harden its defence capability so that it could negotiate with the PRC from a position of strength.[45] In July 2010, Jiang Yi-huah, Taiwan's Minister of Interior Affairs, visited Pratas to inaugurate the Tungsha Management Station of the Tungsha Atoll National Park. Since 2011, steps have been taken to improve Taiwan's defence capabilities on Taiping Island. For example, in April 2011, the government announced that coast guard personnel stationed on Itu Aba would be trained by the marines and that Taiwan would therefore have combat ready personnel in the disputed region for the first time since 2000.[46] A live-fire training exercise was subsequently held on the island in July at a time of heightened tensions between Vietnam and China. In 2012 coast guard forces received additional weapon systems. In April 2014, the ROC Marine Corps conducted an amphibious landing drill on Itu Aba, its largest in fifteen years.[47] Finally, in early 2014 Taiwan began to repair and expand its dock and runway as well as build a lighthouse on the island, all of which were completed in September 2015.[48] In addition to improving the island's defences, in December 2011 Taiwan announced the inauguration of a new solar power generating system on Itu Aba. The 120 kilowatt-peak solar power system is expected to generate an estimated 175,920 kilowatt hours of electricity per year, which will save $24,260 in fuel costs and help eliminate 119 tons of carbon emissions per year.[49]

During the summer of 2011, the Taiwan government sponsored and facilitated two college-level study tours of the South China Sea. The first tour, conducted during 12–18 July on Itu Aba, was organized by the National Taiwan Ocean University with the support of MND, and attended by twelve graduate students.[50] The second tour, co-organized by the CGA, MND and the Ministry of Education, sent twenty-three college students to the Pratas Islands for four days in early August.[51] Both events aimed to enrich young people's understanding and support for the government's efforts to protect Taiwan's maritime claims and marine environment.

Without prejudice to Taiwan's claim of sovereignty over the islands, President Ma, like his predecessors, has also advocated strengthening cooperation with other stakeholders in resolving disputes peacefully and promoting peace, stability and development in the region. Specifically, Ma has proposed that an international research centre be created on the Pratas Islands for ecological conservation. In addition, Ma has called for cooperation with international conservation organizations to turn Itu Abu and Ban Than Reef into a South China Sea peace park.[52] In 2014 Ma further suggested that his "East China Sea Peace Initiative"[53] could be applied to the South China Sea too.[54] Ma's South China Sea Initiative was formally proposed in May 2015. In terms of cross-straits functional cooperation in the South China Sea, Taipei and Beijing have made some important breakthroughs. For example, the two sides have revived cooperation in the exploration and development of offshore hydrocarbon resources. This cooperation began in 1993 but was suspended in 2004 as a result of rising cross-straits tensions. In December 2008, the China National Offshore Oil Corporation (CNOOC) and Taiwan's

China Petroleum Corporation (CPC Taiwan) signed four agreements to conduct joint exploration in the Taiwan Straits and off the southern coast of Guangdong Province in the northern part of the South China Sea.[55] The business model created by the two companies might be applied in the future to joint hydrocarbon exploratory efforts in the Spratlys under appropriate conditions. In addition, since mid-2008, Taiwan and China have negotiated and signed twenty-three agreements. Some of those agreements — including the Cross-Straits Sea Transportation Agreement, Agreement on Joint Crime Fighting and Judicial Mutual Assistance and Cross-Straits Agreement on Cooperation in Respect of Fishing Crew Affairs — offer possible legal foundations for future cross-straits cooperation in the South China Sea in areas such as humanitarian assistance, anti-piracy, combating illegal trafficking and conservation of fish stocks. In November 2009, the two sides successfully initiated a joint project called "Southeast Asia Network for Education and Training" at the 19th South China Sea Workshop. This was the first cross-straits initiative since the inception of the workshops in 1990.[56] And in July 2011, experts from Taiwan and China published a joint report assessing the situation in the South China Sea during 2010. The report provided a comprehensive analysis of the increasingly complex dispute. It is worth-noting that the final chapter, entitled "Prospects of Cooperation in the South China Sea", called for the creation of a cross-straits mechanism to deal with the disputes in the South China Sea. It also suggested the establishment of a cross-straits military coordination mechanism so that the PRC and Taiwan could defend their territorial claims together, and if necessary, conduct combined naval patrols in the South China Sea. The report received a mixed reception, and Taiwanese officials have dismissed the possibility of cooperation in this regard.[57] Nonetheless, the report represented a serious effort by academics and policy thinkers across the Taiwan Straits to build confidence. A second and third report, published in October 2012 and December 2013 respectively, urged the two sides to strengthen functional cooperation and create a mechanism to coordinate maritime jurisdictional matters. To date, a total of five such reports have been published.

With the recent improvement in cross-straits relations, Beijing has not opposed, and perhaps even welcomed, Taiwan's reiteration of its sovereignty claims in the South China Sea. The PRC's attitude is understandable given that since May 2008 Taipei and Beijing have recommitted themselves to the "1992 consensus". President Ma accepts that there is only one China and that cross-straits relations are not state-to-state relations, but "special" relations, even though he maintains that

"China" is "the Republic of China". Since Taiwan is excluded from multilateral forums where the South China Sea has been raised, such as the ARF, ASEAN Plus Three and East Asia Summit, China remains the one that dictates the interpretation of "One China".

Both the PRC and Taiwan have used the "U-shaped" line map to claim a substantial portion of the South China Sea.[58] In its 1993 policy guidelines, Taiwan claimed that the maritime space within the U-shaped line represented the ROC's "historic waters", wherein it possesses "all rights and interests".[59] However, since 2000, Taiwan has rarely referred to the line in its official statements, and it is debatable whether it still maintains the claim.[60] The PRC has not officially explained what the nine-dash line denotes, although it clearly maintains such a claim. The nine-dash line claim has neither been recognized by the other South China Sea claimants nor internationally. Nonetheless, the PRC has moved to reinforce its jurisdictional claims within the line.[61] In short, Taiwan's territorial claims, as well as its uninterrupted occupation of the Pratas Islands and Itu Aba since 1956, form an indispensable component of the Chinese claim. From Beijing's perspective, as long as Taiwan continues to be an integral part of the state of China, Beijing will have a stronger legal ground to assert and enforce its own claims, and Taiwan's sovereignty claims in the South China Sea may well be tolerated so as to defend the Chinese position against those of the other claimants.

All this suggests a strong linkage between Beijing's insistence on the "One China" principle in cross-straits relations and the South China Sea disputes. Sovereignty over all the insular features in the South China Sea has considerable implications for China's rights and jurisdiction over the living and non-living resources, as well as control over sea lines of communications, and Taiwan is a crucial element in the PRC's expanding national interests as a maritime power. In this context, it can be argued that regardless of whether or not Beijing has officially pronounced the South China Sea as a "core interest", it is at least an element of China's core interests, if not one in its own right. Consequently, Taiwan has much to consider when evaluating its cooperation with the mainland in the South China Sea.

CHALLENGES AND OPPORTUNITIES FOR TAIWAN'S SOUTH CHINA POLICY

Several factors linked to cross-straits relations have been impacting Taiwan's South China Sea policy choices since May 2008. This first factor is Taiwan's domestic politics. Cross-straits relations remain a highly sensitive and divisive issue in Taiwanese domestic politics. The two main political parties, the KMT and the DPP, disagree on how cross-straits relations should be conducted. The DPP has criticized President Ma for undermining Taiwan's political and economic independence by negotiating and undertaking cooperation with Beijing on the basis of the "One China" formula, even though Ma's definition of "China" differs from Beijing's. The DPP also blamed Ma for failing to protest China's May 2014 deployment of the oil rig Hai Yang Shi You-981 (HYSY-981) in waters surrounding the Paracel Islands claimed by China, Taiwan and Vietnam. This helped reinforce the impression of Taiwan as part of China and contributed to subsequent indiscriminating attacks on Taiwanese businesses during the anti-China riots in Vietnam in May 2014.[62]

A government led by the DPP would probably be more active in promoting international as well as multilateral approaches to managing disputes in the South China Sea. As indicated in the National Security Chapter of the DPP's Ten-Year Policy Platform released in August 2011, the party believes that "the disputes and conflicts related to waters surrounding Taiwan, including the South China Sea, should be resolved by those countries whose interests are affected, as well as within a multilateral framework, and in the spirit of 'joint development and setting aside controversies'". The DPP also supports "the establishment of a multilateral consultation in areas such as maritime resource development, pollution prevention, and navigation security, with the goal of jointly maintaining the sustainability of maritime resources as well as peace and security on the seas".[63]

Secondly, Taiwan and the PRC continue to face the challenge of building mutual trust. Beijing's deployment of missiles aimed at Taiwan, and its refusal to renounce the use of force against the island, means that the PRC remains Taiwan's primary security threat.[64] In addition, Taipei and Beijing still have to overcome considerable political differences to enable Taiwan to deepen and widen its international space. In regard to the latter, Taiwan has formally expressed discontent at being excluded from the process leading to the adoption of the guidelines for implementing the DoC and regional efforts to negotiate a formal Code of Conduct (CoC) for the South China Sea. In a press release issued after ASEAN and China had agreed on implementation guidelines for the DoC in July 2011, Taiwan's Ministry of Foreign Affairs reiterated its basic principles on the South China Sea, namely, "safeguarding sovereignty, shelving disputes, promoting peace and reciprocity, and encouraging joint exploration", and its readiness to work with other relevant parties in the region to resolve the dispute. At the same time, it stated that "As the government should be included in the dispute dialogue mechanism, it will not recognize any resolution reached without its participation."[65]

Public opinion also seems to have become more concerned about how the Ma government reacts to developments in the East and South China Seas, including China's unilateral moves that could undermine Taiwan's sovereignty. For example, on 23 November 2013, China announced the establishment of an Air Defence Identification Zone (ADIZ) in the East China Sea. The ADIZ, which covers the disputed Senkaku/Diaoyu Islands also claimed by the ROC, overlaps with Taiwan's ADIZ. The next day, Taiwan's National Security Council (NSC) issued a four-point statement. Although the statement expressed deep concern over this development it did not protest China's action. Instead it asserted, *inter alia*, that the ROC's sovereignty over the islands would not be affected by China's ADIZ and that the government would continue to defend its territorial sovereignty, protect fishing rights and ensure the safety of its airspace.[66] A few days later, political party caucus leaders (including the ruling KMT) of the Legislative Yuan passed a non-binding resolution by consensus, urging the government to lodge a formal protest with Beijing over the ADIZ. In response, the government issued another five-point statement. The statement recalled the NSC statement, but added that China's failure to consult with Taiwan before demarcating its ADIZ had "not contributed to positive cross-strait relations" and that the government would "express our firm and serious concern to the mainland [China] through appropriate channels". In addition, "the military will increase inspections in the area to enhance air and sea defenses to protect national security and public interests". Finally, Taiwan's Civil Aeronautics Administration would handle issues related to the requirement imposed by China concerning commercial flights notification in accordance with relevant International Civil Aviation Organisation rules.[67]

Thirdly, if Taipei decides to pursue military cooperation with Beijing in the South China Sea, it risks further alienating itself from the Southeast Asian claimants as well as from the United States. There has been increasing suspicion about whether or not Taipei is collaborating with Beijing in the South China Sea, since not only do the two hold similar territorial claims, but also because while Taiwan has consistently objected to the Southeast Asian claimants' unilateral actions in recent years, it has not criticized the PRC's growing assertiveness. As the United States has become more actively involved in the disputes since 2010, and has been at loggerheads with China over the definition of freedom of navigation, the appropriate legal bases for territorial and maritime boundary claims and the best way to manage and eventually resolve the disputes, Taiwan's policy dilemma has grown. Although the United States claims that it does not support one party's claims over another,[68] the administration of President Barack Obama clearly disagrees with China's legal claims, particularly the nine-dash line.[69] Washington has supported the Philippines' arbitral case against China under Chapter VII of UNCLOS and proposed an immediate freeze on activities likely to escalate tensions, as well as a binding CoC between ASEAN and China.[70] Moreover, the United States has been tightening security ties with Vietnam, the Philippines and other countries in Asia. All of these are perceived as U.S. strategies to balance the PRC's growing power in the region. Conflict between the United States and the PRC in the South China Sea would place Taiwan in a very difficult position.[71] If Taiwan allies itself with the PRC, this could force America to reconsider its commitment to defend Taiwan should it come under attack from China.[72] However, if Taiwan openly supports an increased U.S. presence in the South China Sea, this could rekindle Beijing's suspicion of Taiwan's intentions, and lead to a setback in cross-straits relations.

Nevertheless, these challenges have also created opportunities for the Ma government to reassert ROC or Taiwan's role as a party and a constructive player in the South China Sea. For example, with the arbitration case between the Philippines and China underway, the call for Taiwan to clarify the meaning of the U-shaped line has also intensified. Some have even urged Taiwan to abandon its claims based on the line altogether.[73] Officials at the ROC Foreign Ministry rejected the latter suggestion, restating the four groups of land features in the South China and their surrounding waters are "inherent parts of Taiwan's territory". On 1 September 2014, Taiwan's Ministry of Interior and Academia Historica opened the first ever Exhibition of Historical Archives on the Southern Territories of the Republic of China. The exhibition makes public a substantial amount of documentary evidence, including the 1947 U-shaped map, in support of the ROC's territorial claims. The government also finished remapping some 220 islands and other maritime features in the East and South China Seas by December 2015. On 12 December 2015, Taiwan's Minister of Interior Chen Wai-zen led a delegation to Itu Aba to preside over a ceremony marking the opening of a wharf and lighthouse. He used the opportunity to recall President Ma's South China Sea Peace Initiative and reiterate that Itu Aba is an "island" and not a "rock" under Article 121 of UNCLOS.

Chen's visit was followed by more official visits. The most notable one was led by President Ma on 28 January 2016.

Taiwan has also demonstrated its commitment and ability to resolve disputes peacefully and in accordance with international law. A case in point was how Taiwan dealt with the Philippines over the 2013 "Guang Da Xing No. 28 Incident". On 9 May 2013, a Taiwanese fishing boat, the Guang Da Xing No. 28, while operating in overlapping areas of Taiwan and the Philippines' EEZs, came under attack by a vessel belonging to the Philippine Coast Guard (PCG). The incident resulted in the death of sixty-five-year-old Taiwanese fisherman Hung Shi-cheng. On 10 May the PCG chief Rear Admiral Rodolfo Isorena admitted that a shooting incident had occurred, but claimed that it had taken place in Philippine waters and that the trawler had been fishing illegally. Taiwan protested the Philippines' claims, and demanded that within seventy-two hours Manila officially apologize, conduct an investigation, punish the perpetrators, offer compensation to the victims and open talks on a bilateral fishery agreement to prevent similar incidents from happening again. The Philippine government rejected Taiwan's demands and refused to issue a formal apology while investigations were on-going.[74] It also stated that a resolution to the issue would have to adhere to the "One China" principle since Manila only recognized Beijing and did not have diplomatic relations with Taiwan.[75] Consequently, on 15 May 2013 Taiwan imposed eleven sanctions against the Philippines.[76] On 16 May, Taiwan's navy and coastguard conducted a joint air and sea drill in the area in which the incident had taken place. This was the first time a Taiwanese naval ship had assisted the coast guard in protecting Taiwanese fishermen.[77]

To avert a further escalation of the crisis, Taiwan and Philippines agreed to conduct a parallel investigation into the shooting incident. On 14 June the two sides also held the first preparatory meeting on fisheries cooperation in Manila, where they reached agreement on four points: first, to refrain from the use of force or violence in law enforcement actions; second, to share maritime law enforcement procedures in order to establish a maritime law enforcement security mechanism; third, to inform the other when hot pursuit, boarding, inspection, arrest, detention or related administrative or judicial procedures are carried out against fishing boats from the other side; and fourth, to set up a mechanism for the prompt release of detained fishing vessels and their crews should arrests take place.[78] These points subsequently culminated in the bilateral Agreement Concerning the Facilitation of Cooperation on Law Enforcement in Fisheries Matters signed on 5 November 2015.

On 7 August 2013, the Philippine government released its investigation report. It concluded that PCG personnel had caused the death of the fisherman and recommended that eight crew members be prosecuted for homicide, and four for obstruction of justice.[79] On 8 August, Amadeo R. Perez Jr., Chairman of the Manila Economic and Cultural Office (MECO), delivered a formal apology on behalf of Philippine President Benigno S. Aquino III and the Philippine people to the family of the Taiwanese victim. An agreement on compensation was also reached between the family and MECO. As a result, Taiwan lifted its sanctions against the Philippines.[80]

In addition to a satisfactory conclusion to the above incident, in stark contrast to recent tensions in the South and East China Seas, the Ma government managed to sign agreements with the Philippines and Japan as provisional measures to protect Taiwan's fishing interests, avoid escalation of disputes and promote the rule of law in overlapping waters.[81] Both agreements were concluded after Ma proposed the "East China Sea Peace Initiative". The agreements embody the main spirit and principles contained in the initiative and the government's declared South China Sea policy. Taiwan's cooperative approaches in managing the crisis in the South and East China Seas received wider appreciation from the international community.[82] These agreements did not create any serious problems in cross-straits relations, either. This may be because both Beijing and Taipei were anxious to maintain the positive momentum in their relationship, and because the agreements directly concerned the immediate interests of Taiwanese fishermen, and were bilateral and without prejudice to the issue of sovereignty.

CONCLUSION

Since the early 1990s, Taiwan has taken concrete steps to respond to the growing rivalries in the South China Sea. In addition, developments in cross-straits relations have invariably played a role in Taiwan's South China Sea policy deliberations. This has caused Taiwan to adopt certain measures that may seem at odds with the prevailing situation in the South China Sea at a particular time, as illustrated by President Lee's attempt to de-escalate tensions in the South China Sea between 1999 and early 2000, President Chen's construction of an airstrip on Itu Aba in 2007 and his visit to the island in 2008, and President Ma's pursuit of cross-straits functional cooperation after May 2008. Overall though, Taiwan's approaches towards the South China Sea dispute have been more restrained than the other claimants, particularly the PRC, Vietnam and the Philippines. Moreover, since the early 1990s Taiwan's South China Sea policy has consistently been guided by the principle that although Taiwan will defend its sovereignty claims in the South China Sea, it remains committed to the concept of joint development of living and non-living resources under international law. In addition, Taiwan has expressed its support for the principle of freedom of navigation in the South China Sea.[83] Most importantly, Taiwan has consistently called for all the claimants to put aside their sovereignty disputes and conduct joint research into the development and sustainable management of maritime resources, activities that would not prejudice their respective claims or hinder the eventual resolution of the dispute. The various proposals put forward by Taiwanese leaders demonstrate the island's support for an open and inclusive approach to regional cooperation. Unfortunately, Taiwan's initiatives have been all but ignored by the other claimants, either because they question Taipei's motives or because of Beijing's stance that South China Sea dispute is primarily bilateral i.e. between the PRC and each of the claimants.

Since President Ma came to power in 2008, Taiwan has continued to maintain a cautious approach to cooperating with the PRC in terms of territorial and maritime boundary defence and joint development. During Ma's first term between 2008 and 2012, improved cross-straits relations provided a window of opportunity for Taipei and Beijing to cooperate in the South China Sea. In his second term, from 2012 to May 2016, bilateral cooperation has been continuing mainly at the academic and track-II levels. On the other hand, differences between Taiwan's South China Sea policy approaches and those of Beijing's have become more visible. Ma has stated that in the future when negotiations or talks are held regarding the South China Sea, the ROC must be present, as the nation has an important role to play in such discussions.[84] Moreover, the government has been more actively promoting its preference towards "soft power" and bilateral as well as multilateral cooperative approaches in managing the South China Sea dispute. Finally, the Ma government has declined Beijing's official call for co-defending sovereignty in the South and East China Seas. How such a development might impact cross-strait cooperation and Taiwan's posture in the South China Sea remains to be seen.

The Ma government hopes better cross-straits relations will not only create a win-win situation in terms of energy security, but also that Beijing will adopt a more flexible approach towards Taiwan's status as a party to the South China Sea dispute. A more flexible approach would be for Beijing to allow Taipei to participate in multilateral forums where cooperation among the claimants can be pursued, as well as for Taiwan to be included in talks between ASEAN and China to implement the DoC and negotiate a CoC. Beijing, however, seems to be more interested in strengthening cooperation between the two sides so as to bolster China's legal claims and position relative to the other claimants. Meanwhile, Beijing will continue to ensure that Taipei's unilateral moves to reiterate the ROC's sovereignty over the islands and waters in the South China Sea, or its vocal support for joint cooperation with the other parties, do not amount to Taiwan's *de jure* independence, "Two Chinas" or the "internationalization" of the dispute. Taiwan's South China Sea policy-makers face the increasingly complicated dual challenge of protecting the ROC's sovereignty and interests as a claimant without undermining progress already achieved in cross-straits relations or hampering its relations with Southeast Asian claimants and the United States.

Notes

1. J.K.T. Chao, "South China Sea: Boundary Problems Relating to the Nansha and Hsisha Islands", in *Fishing In Troubled Waters: Proceedings of an Academic Conference on Territorial Claims in the South China Sea*, edited by R.D. Hill, Norman G. Owen, and E.V. Roberts (Hong Kong: Centre for Asian Studies, University of Hong Kong, 1991), p. 88.
2. For a detailed review of the origin and background of the line, see Zou Keyuan, "The Chinese Traditional Maritime Boundary Line in the South China Sea", *International Marine and Coastal Law* 14 (1999): 27–55.
3. Statement by Malaysian scholar B.A. Hamzah in 1995, cited in Cheng-yi Lin, "Taiwan's South China Sea Policy", *Asian Survey* 37, no. 4 (April 1997): 328.
4. Kristen Nordhaug, "Explaining Taiwan's Policies in the South China Sea, 1988–99", *The Pacific Review* 14, no. 4 (2011): 488–89.
5. Yann-Hui Song, "The South China Sea Workshop Process and Taiwan's Participation", *Ocean Development and International Law* 41 (2010): 262.
6. "Landmark Activities of Marine Affairs Developments in Taiwan since 1949", compiled by Alfred Nien-Tsu Hu, March 2012, available at <http://marinepolicy.nsysu.edu.tw/news/Landmark-activities-of-marine-affairs-in-Taiwan.pdf>.
7. Tammy C. Peng, "ROC Will Protect Its Air and Sea Zones", *Free China Journal* (16 October 1992): 1.
8. Nordhaug, "Explaining Taiwan's Policies", op. cit., p. 498.
9. The full English text of the guidelines is appended in Kuan-Ming Sun, "Policy of the Republic of China towards the South China Sea: Recent Developments", *Marine Policy* 19, issue 5 (1995): 408.
10. "S$14b Firm Proposed", *Straits Times*, 23 August 1995.
11. Lin, "Taiwan's South China Sea Policy", op. cit., p. 330.

12. For a review of the relevant legislative background, see Yann-Huei Song and Zou Keyuan, "Maritime Legislation of Mainland China and Taiwan: Developments, Comparison, Implications and Potential Challenges for the United States", *Ocean Development & International Law* 30 (2001): 303–45.

13. Similarly, the PRC did not include Pratas Island or Itu Abu in the Declaration of the Government of the People's Republic of China on the Baselines of the Territorial Sea of the People's Republic of China of 15 May 1996, available at <http://www.un.org/depts/los/LEGISLATIONANDTREATIES/ PDFFILES/DEPOSIT/chn_mzn7_1996.pdf>.

14. Beijing maintains that "China" is the "People's Republic of China", while the KMT government insists that "China" is the "Republic of China" which was established in 1912 and which continued to exist on Taiwan after 1949. The term "1992 consensus" was not formally adopted during the cross-straits consultations between 1992 and 1993. It was created in 2000 by former chairperson of the ROC's Mainland Affairs Council Dr Su Chi for the convenience of describing historical events during that period in which the two sides decided to move ahead with the Singapore talks despite their different interpretations of "One China". China has never formally accepted Taiwan's interpretation that the "1992 consensus" means "both sides adhere to one China, but each side with its own definition of that China". Rather, it regards the "1992 consensus" as the minimum required common denominator between the two sides on "One China". The Democratic Progressive Party, which ruled Taiwan between 2000 and 2008, denies the existence of the "1992 consensus".

15. "Interview with Taiwan President Lee Teng-hui with *Deutsche Welle* Radio", Taipei, 9 July 1999, available at <http://www.taiwandc.org/nws-9926.htm>.

16. Richard C. Bush, *Untying the Knot: Making Peace in the Taiwan Strait* (Washington, D.C.: Brookings Institution Press, 2005), p. 115.

17. "Defense Minister Tang Fei Explained the Replacement of Marine with Coast Guard Personnel", *Chingnian Ribao* [Youth Daily News], 10 December 1999.

18. Perris Lee Choon Siong, "Taiwan Can't Defend Spratlys, Says Tang", *Taiwan News*, 19 November 1999; see also "Tang Fei: We Have No Capability to Defend Pratas and Itu Aba", *Lianhebao* [United Daily News], 25 November 1999.

19. "Pratas and Itu Aba Garrison Transferred to Coast Guard Administration from February 1", *Lianhebao* [United Daily News], 28 January 2000.

20. "Chen Shui-bian: Marines Replaced by Coast Guard a Kind of Retreat", *Lianhebao* [United Daily News], 20 November 1999.

21. *An Analysis of Taiwan's Withdrawal of Its Military from the Spratlys* (China Institute of Marine Affairs, October 2000), p. 2.

22. Tzou Ching-wen, *Lee Teng-hui Zhizheng Gaobai Shilu* [The Record of Lee Teng-hui Presidency] (Taipei: INK, 2001), pp. 234–35.

23. U.S. Department of Defense, *Military and Security Developments Involving the People's Republic of China 2012* (May 2012), p. 19.
24. *An Analysis of Taiwan's Withdrawal of Its Military from the Spratlys*, op. cit., p. 3.
25. "President Chen: 'One Country on Each Side' Our Own Taiwanese Road", *Taiwan Communiqué*, no. 102 (International Committee for Human Rights in Taiwan, September 2002), available at <http://www.taiwandc.org/twcom/tc102-int.pdf>.
26. "China Condemns Taiwan Referendum", 25 February 2004, available at <http://wcm.fmprc.gov.cn/pub/ce/ceus/eng/zt/twwt/t67961.htm>.
27. *2006 National Security Report* (Taipei: National Security Council, 2006), p. 93.
28. Chiu Yu-tzu, "Chen Travels to the Disputed Pratas Island", *Taipei Times*, 29 July 2005.
29. Article 8 of the Anti-Secession Law, available at <http://english.peopledaily.com.cn/200503/14/eng20050314_176746.html>.
30. See Song Yian-huei, "The Political Implication of 'Spratly Initiative' for President Chen Shui-Bian's Visit to Taiping Island", *Coast Guard Administration Bimonthly* 32 (April 2008): 15–20, available at <http://www.cga.gov.tw/GipOpen/wSite/public/Attachment/f1258860349508.pdf>.
31. "Foreign Ministry Spokesperson Liu Jianchao's Regular Press Conference on 5 February 2008", available at <http://www.fmprc.gov.cn/eng/xwfw/s2510/2511/t406590.htm>.
32. "Taiwan is Fully Responsible for All Consequences Caused by Their Move", available at <http://biengioilanhtho.gov.vn/eng/taiwanisfullyresponsibleforall-nd-3cf1a549.aspx>.
33. "Taiwan Leader Lands on Disputed Spratlys", *Philippine Daily Inquirer*, 2 February 2008, available at <http://globalnation.inquirer.net/news/breakingnews/view/20080202-116412/UPDATE-Taiwan-leader-lands-on-disputed-Spratlys>.
34. Song, "Political Implication", op. cit. p. 17.
35. Ibid.
36. "Liang an he zuo shi feng qi shi" [It's Time for Cross-Strait Cooperation in the South China Sea], *China Review News*, 10 April 2010, available at <http://www.chinareviewnews.com/doc/1012/8/1/5/101281568.html?coluid=137&kindid=4701&docid=101281568&mdate=0410001310>.
37. "Mainland Proposes Cross-Strait Cooperation on South China Sea Issue", *Taiwan Affairs Office of the State Council PRC*, 14 May 2014, available at <http://www.gwytb.gov.cn/en/SpokespersonRemarks/201405/t20140515_6164340.htm>.
38. Frühere Ausgaben, "GIO Minister Reaffirms ROC Sovereignty over Spratlys", *Taiwan Review*, 2 September 2010, available at <http://taiwanreview.nat.gov.tw/site/tr/ct.asp?xitem=116228&ctnode=293&mp=1>.
39. "Lu wei huei: nan hai jhu cyuan bu xu liang an he zuo" [Mainland Affairs Council: No Need of Cross-Straits Cooperation on Sovereignty Issues Relating

to South China Sea], 3 May 2012, available at <http://taiwan.dwnews.com/big5/news/2012-05-03/58724060.html>.

40. "MAC Sees No Room for Cross-Strait Cooperation on Territorial Issues", *Focus Taiwan News Channel*, 15 May 2014, available at <http://focustaiwan.tw/news/acs/201405150040.aspx>.

41. "Ministry of Foreign Affairs of the Republic of China (Taiwan) Reiterates Its Position on the South China Sea", Press Release no. 143, 29 July 2010, available at <http://www.mofa.gov.tw/official/Home/Detail/8ead9c15-967f-4ebc-a9b8-ba05f3a8268d?arfid=8f8092a6-b477-4f92-bf94-031da11665cd&opno=0ab69338-b476-449c-8554-2c7d26534828>.

42. "Solemn Declaration of the Ministry of Foreign Affairs of the Republic of China Concerning the Philippine Senate Bill 2699 and House Bill 3216", Ministry of Foreign Affairs, Republic of China (Taiwan), Statement, 6 February 2009, available at <http://www.mofa.gov.tw/webapp/ct.asp?xItem=36914& ctNode=1902&mp=6>.

43. Statement no. 002, 11 May 2009, available at <http://www.mofa.gov.tw/webapp/ct.asp?xItem=38046&ctNode=1548&mp=1>.

44. Declaration of the Republic of China on the Outer Limits of Its Continental Shelf, Press Statement no. 003, 12 May 2009, available at <http://www.mofa.gov.tw/webapp/content.asp?cuItem=38077&ctNode=1036&mp=6>.

45. Office of the President, Republic of China (Taiwan), News Release, 10 September 2008, available at <http://www.president.gov.tw/Default.aspx?tabid=131& itemid=14180&rmid=514&word1=%e6%9d%b1%e6%b2%99%e5%b3%b6>.

46. Cindy Sui, "Taiwan to Boost Forces in Disputed Spratly Islands", *BBC*, 12 April 2011, available at <http://www.bbc.co.uk/news/world-asia-pacific-13130208>.

47. Gavin Phipps and James Hardy, "Taiwan Holds Biggest Spratly Islands Drill in 15 Years", *IHS Jane's Defence 360*, 29 April 2014, available at <http://www.janes.com/article/37245/taiwan-holds-biggest-spratly-islands-drill-in-15-years>.

48. The new pier is expected to accommodate 3,000-ton naval frigates and coastguard cutters. Angela Tsai and Y.F. Low, "Spratly Islands Pier May be Completed Ahead of Schedule", *Focus Taiwan News Channel*, 12 July 2014, available at <http://focustaiwan.tw/news/aipl/201407120023.aspx>.

49. "Solar Power Station Opens on Taiping", *Taipei Times*, 14 December 2011, available at <http://www.taipeitimes.com/News/front/archives/2011/12/14/2003520688>.

50. Grace Soong, "Taiping Island Camp Shows Sovereignty: Ma", *China Post*, 19 July 2011, available at <http://www.chinapost.com.tw/taiwan/national/national-news/2011/07/19/310238/Taiping-Island.htm>.

51. "23 Students Visit Dongsha on Sovereignty Trip: CGA", *China Post*, 4 August 2011, available at <http://www.chinapost.com.tw/taiwan/national/national-news/2011/08/04/312200/23-students.htm>.

52. Song, "The South China Sea Workshop", op. cit., p. 262.

53. "Remarks by President Ma at the 2014 East China Sea Peace Forum", *Mainland Affairs Council*, 5 August 2014, available at <http://www.mac.gov.

tw/ct.asp?xItem=109736&ctNode=5909&mp=3>; see also, "MAC Sees No Room for Cross-Strait Cooperation on Territorial Issues", op. cit.

54. The East China Sea Peace Initiative was propounded by Ma in August 2012 amid the crisis over Japan's "nationalization" of the Senkaku/Diaoyu Islands and calls for self-restraint, laying aside dispute, peaceful settlement of dispute, a code of conduct and cooperation including joint development. For the full text, see Ministry of Foreign Affairs, Republic of China (Taiwan), "The Republic of China (Taiwan) Proposes: The East China Sea Peace Initiative", available at <http://www.mofa.gov.tw/en/cp.aspx?n=A3C75D6CF8A0D021>.

55. Yuanming Alvin Yao, "Energy Cooperation beyond the Taiwan Strait", available at <http://www.mac.gov.tw/public/Attachment/04115571725.pdf>.

56. Song, "The South China Sea Workshop", op. cit., pp. 260–63.

57. *An Assessment Report of the South China Sea Regional Situation in 2010* (Taipei: Institute of International Relations and National Institute for South China Sea Studies, 2011), pp. 101–2; Shih Hsu-chuan, "Academics Suggest Cross-Strait Effort on Sea Dispute", *Taipei Times*, 6 August 2011, available at <http://www.taipeitimes.com/News/front/print/2011/08/06/2003510050>.

58. For a comprehensive review of the ROC's (Taiwan's) claims in the South China Sea, including the "U-shaped" line, see Kuan-Hsiung Wang, "The ROC's Maritime Claims and Practices with Special Reference to the South China Sea", *Ocean Development & International Law* 41, no. 3 (2010): 237–52. C.f. Zou Keyuan, "China's U-Shaped Line in the South China Sea Revisited", *Ocean Development & International Law* 43, issue 2 (2012): 18–34.

59. Suu, "Policy of the Republic of China towards the South China Sea", op. cit.

60. According to one Taiwanese international law of the sea expert, although Taiwan has not formally renounced the nine-dash line claim, in practice, the DPP government quietly terminated the 1993 guidelines by an internal note in 2005, while the Ma government has refrained from raising the "historic waters" argument. Michael Sheng-Ti Gau, "The U-Shaped Line and a Categorization of the Ocean Disputes in the South China Sea", *Ocean Development and International Law* 43, issue 1 (2012): 57–69. However, in the first batch of the Republic of China territorial sea baseline surrounding the Taiwan island and nearby sea area announced by the Executive Yuan in 1999, it was noted "the Spratly archipelagos within the traditional U-shaped line belong to our country". The same reference was kept intact after minor revisions to the 1999 announcement in 2009.

61. Zou, "China's U-Shaped Line", op. cit., pp. 20–23.

62. Chris Wang, "MOFA Condemns Protests against China in Vietnam", *Taipei Times*, 15 May 2014, available at <http://www.taipeitimes.com/News/front/archives/2014/05/15/2003590373>.

63. "DPP Releases 10 Year Policy Platform: National Security Strategy Chapter", 23 August 2011, available at <http://dpptaiwan.blogspot.com/2011/08/dpp-releases-10-year-policy-outlook.html>.

64. In the ROC 2013 National Defense Report, PRC's military threat is considered to remain the primary threat of Taiwan's security environment, Chapter 2, Sec. 3 of the report, available at <http://report.mnd.gov.tw/en/m/part5.html>.

65. MOFA Press Release No. 232, 20 July 2011, English translation available at <http://www.boca.gov.tw/content.asp?cuItem=4736&mp=1>.

66. "ROC Statement on Beijing's Announcement of the East China Sea Air Defence Identification Zone", *National Security Council of ROC*, 25 November 2013, English text available at <http://www.nsb.gov.tw/documents/The%20ROC%E2%80%99s%20National%20Security%20Policy%20and%20Position%EF%BC%88Added%20December%2017%EF%BC%89.pdf>.

67. Chris Wang and Shih Hsiu-chuan, "Resolution Urges Air Zone Protest", *Taipei Times*, 30 November 2013, available at <http://www.taipeitimes.com/News/front/archives/2013/11/30/2003577976/1>.

68. See Yann-huei Song, *United States and Territorial Disputes in the South China Sea: A Study of Ocean Law and Politics* (Baltimore, Maryland: School of Law, University of Maryland, 2002).

69. See Ronald O'Rourke, "Maritime Territorial and Exclusive Economic Zone (EEZ) Disputes Involving China: Issues for Congress", *Congressional Research Service*, 5 August 2014, available at <http://fas.org/sgp/crs/row/R42784.pdf>.

70. This was part of the Philippines' "Triple Action Plan" presented at the 47th ASEAN's Foreign Ministers' Meeting (AFMM) on 8 August 2014 in Nay Pyi Taw, Myanmar, available at <http://www.dfa.gov.ph/index.php/2013-06-27-21-50-36/dfa-releases/3789-philippines-presents-triple-action-plan-at-47th-asean-foreign-ministers-meeting-in-nay-pyi-taw>. U.S. Secretary of State John Kerry's opening remarks at the ASEAN Regional Forum echoed this and called on claimants to "voluntary and jointly freeze the sorts of activities that would complicate or escalate tension", 10 August 2014, available at <http://www.state.gov/secretary/remarks/2014/08/230518.htm>.

71. See, for example, Robert Kaplan, "The South China Sea is the Future of Conflict: The 21st Century's Defining Battleground is Going to be on Water", *Foreign Policy*, issue 188 (September/October 2011): 76–83.

72. For a summary of the various arguments on why the United States should abandon its defence commitment to Taiwan, see Shelly Rigger, "Why Giving Up Taiwan Will Not Help US with China", American Enterprise Institute, 29 November 2011, available at <http://www.aei.org/article/foreign-and-defense-policy/regional/asia/why-giving-up-taiwan-will-not-help-us-with-china/>.

73. William Stanton, a former director of the American Institute in Taiwan (AIT), offered such a suggestion during a speech in Taipei in September 2014. The AIT clarified later that that his comments did not represent the official view of the U.S. government. Tang Pei-chun and Evelyn Kao, "Stanton's

Advice to Taiwan on South China Sea Not Official", *Focus Taiwan News Channel*, 15 September 2014, available at <http://focustaiwan.tw/news/aipl/201409150039.aspx>.

74. "Taiwan Gives Philippines Ultimatum After Shooting of Fisherman", Reuters, 13 May 2013, available at <http://www.reuters.com/article/2013/05/13/us-taiwan-philippines-idUSBRE94C02H20130513>.

75. "Philippines Agrees to 3 out of 4 Demands: Reports", *Taiwan News*, 14 May 2013, available at <http://www.taiwannews.com.tw/etn/news_content.php?id=2220439>.

76. Remarks at an international conference, David Y.L. Lin, Minister of Foreign Affairs, Republic of China (Taiwan), 17 May 2013, available at <http://www.mofa.gov.tw/EnOfficial/Topics/TopicsArticleDetail/9e22ffe1-5d7b-4bc0-8104-1d7dd48ddf61>.

77. "Taiwan Holds Joint Navy, Coast Guard Drill in Overlapping Waters with Philippines", *China Post*, 17 May 2013, available at <http://www.chinapost.com.tw/taiwan/foreign-affairs/2013/05/17/378760/Taiwan-holds.htm>.

78. ROC Ministry of Foreign Affairs, Press Conference Background Information No. 071, 15 June 2013, available at <http://www.mofa.gov.tw/EnOfficial/Topics/TopicsDetail/e9c4dba2-6bd6-48f0-91d0-94adc92b6e2f?TopicsUnitLinkId=3f6abead-825c-4419-86c9-0d44218a395e>.

79. "The Republic of China Government Express Affirmation of the Philippine Government's Recommendation for Homicide Charges in Its Investigative Report on the ROC Fishing Boat Guang Da Xing No. 28 Shooting Incident", ROC Ministry of Foreign Affairs, Press Release No. 200, 7 August 2013, available at <http://www.mofa.gov.tw/EnOfficial/Topics/TopicsDetail/449b4590-8792-4e38-9488-b8c16f86683d?TopicsUnitLinkId=3f6abead-825c-4419-86c9-0d44218a395e>.

80. "Taiwan Lifts Sanctions on the Philippines", ROC Ministry of Foreign Affairs, Press Release, available at <http://www.mofa.gov.tw/EnOfficial/Topics/TopicsDetail/b004c344-8efc-4fa9-9f82-04154f01ac1a?TopicsUnitLinkId=3f6abead-825c-4419-86c9-0d44218a395e>.

81. Shih Hsiu-chuan, "Taiwan, Japan Ink Fisheries Agreement", *Taipei Times*, 11 April 2013, available at <http://www.taipeitimes.com/News/front/archives/2013/04/11/2003559323>. For a comprehensive account of the background and content of the agreement, see "The Taiwan-Japan Fisheries Agreement: Embodying the Ideals and Spirit in the East China Sea Peace Initiative", ROC Ministry of Foreign Affairs, available at <http://www.mofa.gov.tw/Upload/WebArchive/979/The%20Taiwan-Japan%20Fisheries%20Agreement%20(illustrated%20pamphlet).PDF>.

82. For example, the United States and Australia, see Joseph Yeh, "Kerry Applause Taiwan–Japan Fishery Pact", *China Post*, 15 August 2014, available at <http://www.chinapost.com.tw/taiwan/intl-community/2014/08/15/414925/Kerry-applauds.htm>; "President Ma Received Eisenhower Medallion for

Peace Initiative", *Taipei Economic and Cultural Office in Australia Press Release*, 24 September 2014, available at <http://www.roc-taiwan.org/AU/ct.asp?xItem=548275&ctNode=1596&mp=212>. President Ma also received the Eisenhower Medallion award on 19 September 2014 from the People to People International for the East China Sea Peace Initiative.

83. Press Release No. 186, Ministry of Foreign Affairs, 6 July 2011, available at <http://www.mofa.gov.tw/webapp/ct.asp?xItem=52800&ctNode=1547&mp=1>.

84. "President Ma Attends Opening Ceremonies of Exhibition of Historical Archives on the Southern Territories of the Republic of China", Press Release, Office of the President of the ROC, 1 September 2014, available at <http://english.president.gov.tw/Default.aspx?tabid=491&itemid=33215&rmid=2355>.

5

THE SOUTH CHINA SEA: PRIMARY CONTRADICTIONS IN CHINA–SOUTHEAST ASIA RELATIONS

Alice D. Ba

The emergence and re-emergence of disputes in the South China Sea as a high-profile security challenge offers bookends on an important chapter in China–Southeast Asia relations. That chapter began in the early 1990s, when the South China Sea last posed major challenges to relations between China and several Southeast Asian countries; it concludes in 2008 with the eruption of fresh tensions after more than a decade of relative calm and significantly improved relations. The significance of the South China Sea dispute is that it brings together outstanding concerns that have come to define contemporary relations between China and Southeast Asian states. These include power asymmetries, the questions and expectations generated by China's historical centrality in East Asia, and the uncertainties and dynamics associated with the United State's strategic role in the region. Each of these concerns has, moreover, been exacerbated by China's growth in military capabilities and self-confidence on the international stage during the intervening years.

Yet, if the past offers any insights, tensions in the South China Sea will also press states to find new ways to stabilize and improve their relations. The 1990s, for example, witnessed the expansion and improvement of Sino–Southeast Asian relations that few expected at the time; it also saw the South China Sea mostly, though not completely, relegated to the background as an issue. While the resurgence of tensions clearly destabilizes these trends, they also do not completely negate them.

This chapter situates the South China Sea dispute within a "big picture" view of China–Southeast Asia relations. It begins with an overview of states' core concerns, with reference to both the previous and current periods of tensions in the South China Sea. It then identifies the conditions and processes that have facilitated both the downgrading of the South China Sea disputes and the improvement of China–Southeast Asia relations over the last decade as a way to gain insight into the dispute's resurgence at this particular time. The chapter concludes that while the diplomatic processes and economic dynamics created over the last twenty years offer incentives and opportunities to moderate disputes, recent tensions have nevertheless prompted all parties to reassess existing strategies, priorities and relations. U.S.–China dynamics are also likely to challenge relations more than they did during the previous period. Ultimately, how each side chooses to address both their own and the other's reassessments, as well as their respective relations with the United States, will largely determine how dramatically new the next chapter of China–Southeast Asia relations will be compared to the last.

SOUTH CHINA SEA BOOKENDS: PARALLEL AND PERSISTENT CONCERNS

The latest chapter of China–Southeast Asia relations ended, in many ways, much as it had begun: namely, with the emergence of tensions in the South China Sea and questions about how a more capable China would relate to less capable powers on its periphery. Bookending periods exhibit notable parallels. Both are associated with a still evolving maritime regime — the United Nations Convention on the Law of the Sea (UNCLOS) — and the "grab what you can" incentives it created;[1] heightened administrative actions and attention, especially, but not exclusively, from China; global-systemic change (the end of the Cold War in the first period and a Euro-America centred economic crisis in the latter period); and Chinese leadership transitions — indeed, the two most sensitive leadership transitions of China's reform era (first, Deng Xiaoping to Jiang Zemin and most recently from Hu Jintao to Xi Jinping[2]).

Such parallels serve to illustrate that drivers and relational dynamics that have characterized the most recent period of tensions since 2008 are not new, but rather illustrate sources of insecurity and uncertainty that were also present in the early- and mid-1990s. The eruption of tensions is indicative of mutually held insecurities that persist despite the stabilization of relations in the intervening period. A brief overview of China's and ASEAN's defining uncertainties and concerns during the 1990s when the South China Sea last posed a major threat to relations serves to contextualize post-2008 developments in China–ASEAN relations and the challenges posed by the dispute.

For the smaller ASEAN states, the strategic challenges of the South China Sea in the 1990s — much as today — are associated with geopolitical questions about China's growing capabilities and strategic reach, especially against growing questions about U.S. strategic and economic commitments. The potential link between China's military modernization and the South China Sea appeared as early as 1988 when China took physical possession of its first islands in the Spratlys in a naval clash with Vietnam — though most ASEAN states at the time tended to treat the clash as something particular to Sino–Vietnamese relations, as Vietnam at the time was not an ASEAN member and relations between those two countries remained tense over a host of historical issues, including Vietnam's occupation of Cambodia.[3]

ASEAN states' concerns, however, grew in the early 1990s with new post-Cold War U.S. retrenchments and Chinese maritime actions partly in response to the incentives created by the UNCLOS regime. For example, as UNCLOS gained the requisite ratifications that brought it into effect in 1994, interested states began clarifying maritime positions and acting on their understood maritime rights. For the ASEAN states, two Chinese actions drew particular attention. The first was an administrative action, namely the passage in February 1992 by China's National People's Congress of the "Law of the PRC on its Territorial Waters and Contiguous Areas", which specified island claims and maritime rights, including the rights of control as well as innocent passage. The second was China's construction in late 1994 of structures on Mischief Reef, which is located within the Philippines' 200 nautical miles (nm) exclusive economic zone (EEZ) and also claimed by Vietnam in addition to China and Taiwan. The most southerly projection of a Chinese presence up until that point, China's structures on Mischief Reef were also additionally significant for being the first time China had directly challenged a claim made by an ASEAN member. While the construction may have been undertaken without Beijing's authorization,[4] it seemed consistent with other developments, including China's building of facilities in the southern part of the country and an airstrip on the Paracel Islands.

With Mischief Reef, the South China Sea emerged as a "litmus test"[5] of China's great power ambitions *vis-à-vis* ASEAN states. Singapore's then Prime Minister Goh Chok Tong, in his comments to Chinese officials in May 1995, gave voice to the regional insecurities raised by the Mischief Reef incident: "It is important to bring into the open this underlying sense of discomfort, even insecurity, about the political and military ambitions of China."[6] In 1996, the Chairman of the Jakarta-based Centre for Strategic and International Studies, Jusuf Wanandi, characterized the two issues considered most critical by Southeast Asia as being "China's claims in the South China Sea and the lack of transparency in its military affairs".[7] In 1999, Philippine President Joseph Estrada characterized China's actions in the South China Sea as a threat to "Southeast Asia's bottom line security".[8] As elaborated below, for most ASEAN states, post-2008 events have tended to reinforce, not lessen, the significance of the South China Sea as a measure of China's commitment to its Southeast Asian relations and to regional security in general.

China's key concerns were different. But while different from ASEAN states, these concerns prove to be quite enduring. While assessments often begin with the assumption of China as the stronger, advantaged party, China, as a late occupier of Spratly features, has generally viewed itself as the disadvantaged, even victimized, party in the dispute; that is, from China's vantage point at the time, other states had taken advantage of China's domestic crises and relative military weakness during the 1970s and 1980s.[9] Even with its seizure of several more features following its 1988 clash with Vietnam, China's total features count was only eight (including Mischief Reef) — still short of the thirty plus features occupied by the Philippines, Malaysia, and especially Vietnam, which occupies over twenty.[10] According to this view, China has been reactive to both a larger historical pattern and specific instances of Southeast Asian provocations and occupations through the early 1990s.[11] Even the Mischief Reef incident was viewed by the People's Liberation Army (PLA) as having been provoked by prior Philippine actions.[12]

Meanwhile, the fact that the PLA-Navy may have built those structures without Beijing's authorization speaks to the challenges of China's "fragmented authoritarian" system,[13] bureaucratic politics, and policy coordination that will also reappear in the post-2008 period of tensions. In particular, China's heightened maritime interest and activity took place in a context of uncertain party-military relations, especially after Beijing's

Tiananmen Square crackdown in 1989 when the military's support for Party leaders came into question. The most serious challenge to regime legitimacy of China's reform era, the Tiananmen crisis also marked China's transition to a post-revolutionary leadership under Jiang Zemin, who owed his own ascendance to political crisis.[14] As others have detailed, such domestic concerns have loomed large in the priority accorded to military modernizations (and professionalization) in the early 1990s.

A second source of Chinese insecurity stemmed from the possibility that the United States might mobilize its allies and other strategic partners against China. Concerns about possible anti-China coalitions, for example, informed China's decision to participate in the ASEAN Regional Forum (ARF), an arrangement created in 1994 largely to manage the regional security situation created by China's activities in the South China Sea and military modernization[15] — though there remained concerns that ASEAN members and the United States might use new forums to "gang up" on China. A second concern specifically regarded the South China Sea: that is, the same countries might use such forums to internationalize the dispute, e.g., via the introduction of third parties.[16] A larger interest in moderating China–ASEAN relations and in developing the ARF as a potential mechanism of "multipolarization" ultimately outweighed those other concerns; however, as events of the most recent period illustrate, it did not erase them completely.[17]

At the same time, heightened tensions also created new incentives for ASEAN and China to work towards moderating the dispute. What followed was smart, effective diplomacy on both sides: ASEAN states practised inclusive diplomacy with a view towards moderating China's concerns and insecurities; China, especially after 1997, became more proactive in responding to Southeast Asian insecurities.[18] The result of their mutual efforts was a growing network of diplomatic, economic and institutional linkages that correlated with a steady improvement in relations. Indeed, it is generally agreed that China's overtures were relatively successful in mitigating some of the ASEAN states' more acute concerns in the economic and security spheres.[19] New cooperation and improved relations defined a new chapter of relations such that the South China Sea became a much diminished issue.[20]

As the renewal of tensions in 2008 shows, however, the improvement of relations did not erase China's and the ASEAN states' respective concerns over the South China Sea. In fact, developments since 2008 suggest that key concerns remain more or less the same as they had been in the early 1990s: ASEAN states remain worried about how China would utilize its growing military capabilities; China remains concerned about the possibility of third party involvement, U.S.-led "small group military cooperation", and the emergence of a "Pacific network" or "coalition to counter-balance China's growing power",[21] and how they might undermine China's economic growth and domestic legitimacy and deny China recognition of great power status.[22] Moreover, ASEAN states' and China's respective concerns were and remain clearly linked and interdependent: ASEAN states' interest in third party assistance is strongly correlated with heightened questions about Chinese power and intent provoked by its maritime activities and uncompromising rhetoric; China's maritime and rhetorical assertiveness have been sharpened by what it sees to be third party meddling. That linkage also highlights the interactive dynamics of their actions and insecurities. On both sides, insecurities have intensified: ASEAN states because of the increased frequency and assertiveness of China's maritime patrols in the South China Sea, Chinese administrative and operational developments, and the sharpening of Beijing's rhetoric on both the dispute and towards individual ASEAN states; China because of expanded strategic cooperation between the United States and Southeast Asian states, a concern made recently more salient by the U.S. "pivot" or "rebalance" of military forces towards and within Asia under President Barack Obama.[23]

Thus, for much of the intervening period between 1997 and 2008, the South China Sea was best understood as a "latent" challenge to relations — latent because it remained unresolved and, more importantly, because it remained a persistent and periodic irritation, even if mostly overshadowed by the general improvement in relations in other areas. Sino–Philippine relations, in particular, experienced more than one serious challenge during the late 1990s — but until 2008, the South China Sea did not challenge the broader structure or cooperative trajectory of China–Southeast Asia relations.

SOUTH CHINA SEA REDUX

Why, after a decade of relative calm, has the dispute once again become such a challenge to relations? In part, the timing can be explained by developments in maritime law, including a May 2009 UNCLOS deadline on outer continental shelf claims, at which time Malaysia and Vietnam made a joint submission to the United Nations Commission on the Limits of the Continental Shelf (CLCS) for an outer continental shelf beyond the 200 nm from their territorial baselines. That, in turn, prompted formal responses from both China and the Philippines. China responded with a *note verbale* to the CLCS to which it attached the controversial nine-dash line map that seemed to suggest Beijing's claim to 80 per cent of the South China Sea. While China had long referenced the map, it was the first time it had been formally included in a UN submission.[24]

Insight into the resurfacing of tensions can also be gained by examining the conditions that had helped suppress the conflict between 1997 and 2008. This was a question examined by Ralf Emmers in 2007 shortly before the upsurge in tensions in 2008. Emmers outlined six trending conditions that had contributed to the diminished prominence of the South China Sea as an issue in China–ASEAN relations: first, limited proven oil reserves; second, Vietnam's membership in ASEAN; third, limited Chinese power projection capabilities; fourth, a lessening of China threat perceptions; fifth, the downplaying of nationalist rhetoric; and sixth, America's relatively hands off approach to the dispute.[25] Developments in 2008–14 point to instabilities in all of those trending conditions with the possible exception of the first two. On the first, for example, the existence of significant oil reserves in the area remains largely speculative, though rising energy prices due to political crises in the Middle East, along with global economic crises, have meant that oil prospects, even if only potential, remains an important driver of the dispute. As for Vietnam, its membership in ASEAN has, as Emmers argues, helped buffer Sino–Vietnamese relations, but developments also show that ASEAN itself may not be buffered from the challenges of that bilateral relationship. The coincidence of Vietnam's ASEAN and ARF chairmanships in 2010 gave Hanoi the opportunity, for example, to make the South China Sea an agenda item, internationalizing the dispute in ways that ASEAN as an institution had previously avoided and which China had opposed. An important difference between this period and the last is also the fact that ASEAN as an institution confronts much higher expectations and risks higher diplomatic and strategic stakes this time for inaction or mismanagement.

As for the other trends highlighted by Emmers, developments suggest that each of those trends has been disrupted. Chinese naval modernization and the strengthening of the PLA's power projection capabilities not only continue apace but have also become more visible due to the increasing frequency of Chinese patrols, the development of the Sanya naval base on the southern tip of Hainan Island and most recently, China's well-publicized reclamations in the South China Sea. And while the existence of the Sanya naval base had been known as early as 2002, widely published satellite imagery in 2008 offered greater detail as to its capacities and functions.[26] Other developments have served to impress upon Southeast Asian states of China's increased maritime reach, including the "long distance training exercises" of its North Sea Fleet.[27]

Emmers' fourth and fifth conditions also display instabilities. While not all Southeast Asian states are equally concerned, the notion of a "China threat" has regained some currency as a result of recent tensions and exchanges (both diplomatic and physical). China threat images also reflect mutually reinforcing nationalist sentiments concerning ownership of the atolls in the South China Sea in Vietnam, the Philippines,[28] as well as China, whose "words and actions" on the issue became increasingly "strident", especially during the second half of 2009 and through 2011.[29] While China's "official" and "authoritative" responses to specific maritime incidents have moderated somewhat since, public commentary has grown more sharply nationalist and critical of both Southeast Asian claimants and the United States as regards the disputes.[30] As the International Crisis Group concluded, "The Chinese public … overwhelmingly believes that China's territory encompasses the whole area" contained within the nine-dash line.[31] The politics of leadership transition at a particular time of regime insecurity also created few incentives for political leaders, commentators, or other elites to take more moderate stances — in fact, just the opposite. Nationalist emotions have similarly run high in Vietnam and the Philippines, which of the ASEAN states, have experienced the most volatile exchanges with Beijing on the issue. In particular, Vietnamese nationalism has been especially galvanized by the South China Sea disputes. In 2011, eleven to twelve consecutive weeks of anti-China street protests took place in Vietnam, a country where such protests are not usually tolerated and certainly not for so long.[32] In May 2014, China's placement of an oil rig in waters near the Paracels and in Vietnam's EEZ triggered new popular protests in cities across Vietnam, as well as attacks on Chinese factories operating in southern Vietnam.[33]

Lastly, the resurfacing of tensions corresponds with unprecedented U.S. interest in the dispute. Brantly Womack, for example, explains the timing of tensions with reference to two developments that bring into focus shifting global balances of power and influence that make the United States a more interested and concerned third party to the South China Sea dispute than previously. The first was a U.S. and European-centred global financial crisis, which began in 2008. That crisis widened the material gap between the United States and China, intensifying U.S. anxieties about China's challenge to its future place and position and, in turn, building

Chinese confidence in its own "revival". Some Southeast Asian officials have also expressed the view that China has been emboldened by perceptions of U.S. decline.[34] The second was the 2008 election of President Ma Ying-jeou in Taiwan and the subsequent stabilization of cross-straits relations. As Womack puts it, the significance of Ma's election is that it freed China — and also the United States — to "think about somewhere else other than Taiwan".[35]

Two other developments also contributed to the timing of U.S. interest. One was the November 2008 election of Barack Obama, whose administration entered office determined to reclaim some of the diplomatic and strategic ground reputedly lost to China during the administration of President George W. Bush — i.e., "the pivot/rebalance" to Asia.[36] The second were the March 2009 incidents concerning the *USNS Victorious* and *USNS Impeccable*, both of which had been undertaking surveillance activities in China's EEZ and which were subjected to "aggressive" policing efforts by Chinese-flagged vessels.[37] These incidents have been characterized as catalysing U.S. strategic thinking on the South China Sea.[38] While all ASEAN states generally welcome a continued U.S. security role, Washington's more active involvement in the dispute, as Emmers suggests and as further detailed below, also introduces complicating dynamics and challenges to the China–Southeast Asia relationship.

In short, a number of developments coincided to destabilize the trending conditions that had moderated the dispute in the previous period and to make the period since 2008 an opportune time for tensions to resurface. But while opportune, the deeper issue is that despite the last decade's improvement of relations, the China–Southeast Asia relationship is still in many ways defined by the same insecurities of the early 1990s. The difficulties faced by states in moving the relationship to another level are, at a minimum, a reminder of the fact that the improvements seen in China–Southeast Asia relations over the last fifteen years are relatively recent. Consequently, diplomatic credibility remains to be fully achieved on both sides. In such relationships of uncertainty, each side continues to face a high burden of proof in terms of convincing the other of its good intentions. The challenge is even greater at times of growing power asymmetries. Similarly, in such relationships, any contradiction in behaviour, or reversion to past behaviour, will be accorded greater significance. While each side during the 1990s made significant headway in convincing the other of their regard for the other's needs and interests, recent developments in the South China Sea challenge relations precisely because they offer contradictions to the diplomatic message each has supposedly been trying to convey to the other. Kavi Chongkittavorn has characterized the South China Sea as the "Achilles heel" of China–Southeast Asia relations,[39] but perhaps more accurately the South China Sea has become for both sides illustrative of the primary contradictions in their contemporary relations. The discussion below outlines these primary contradictions and questions raised by recent events for both sides.

PRIMARY CONTRADICTIONS

China's Contradictions

For most Southeast Asian states, both claimants and non-claimants, China's rhetoric and actions on the South China Sea have seemed more reminiscent of a revisionist, pre-reform China than the enlightened power that Beijing's "peaceful rise" rhetoric has portrayed. Explanations for China's contradictions range from the alarmist to the benign. Some see China's contradictions as reflective of what former Philippine Defense Secretary Orlando Mercado characterized as a "talk and take" strategy,[40] where diplomacy serves to obfuscate and/or buy China time to build its power-projection capacities.[41] Others see China's contradictions as products of a leadership transition made especially sensitive by the fact that Hu Jintao's successor would be the first leader not to enjoy Deng Xiaoping's personal sanction. Characterized as more proactive than his predecessors, Xi Jinping and his efforts to consolidate his power base may also be factoring into recent tensions. At a minimum, China's succession politics, which have been punctuated by political scandal and other exposes of top leaders, have given wider berth to more nationalist and hawkish positions than they otherwise might have enjoyed.

Still others trace China's contradictions — indeed, policy incoherence — to the increasing pluralism and complexity of China's policy processes: inter-bureaucratic politics that go beyond the PLA-Navy versus Ministry of Foreign Affairs (MFA) debates of the early 1990s. Today, China's South China Sea policies and actions are also reflective of a multitude of bureaucratic interests that include the Ministry of Land and Mineral Resources, the Bureau of Fisheries Administration (Agriculture Ministry), and the China Marine Surveillance (State Oceanic Administration), the China Coast Guard, the China Customs Anti-Smuggling Bureau, the Maritime Safety Administration, the National Tourism Administration and the environment ministry, as well as local and provincial authorities motivated by economic reasons, specific issues, personal ambition or just over enthusiasm, as opposed to top-down grand strategy.[42] Also affecting the policy process today more so than the 1990s are China's energy companies, including the China National Offshore Oil Corporation (CNOOC), a powerful state-owned company responsible for the placement of the oil rig that triggered the crisis in Vietnam–China relations in May 2014 and whose chairman is quoted as characterizing such oil rigs as a "mobile national territory and strategic weapon for promoting the development of [China's] offshore oil industry".[43] Notably, in this pluralist mix of actors, the MFA — the one agency "experienced in handling diplomatic affairs and authorized to negotiate with neighbouring countries over the South China Sea disputes" — is often bypassed or overshadowed by other, more powerful actors.[44] The MFA's weaker status is one similarity to the early 1990s that works against more durable diplomatic outcomes.

Beijing's efforts to "harmonize" and reconcile policy contradictions (via, for example, the creation of a higher-level coordinating or advisory unit on maritime affairs) may lend some credence to the pluralist explanation of China's contradictions and speak to concerns about their diplomatic and strategic consequences,[45] though China's continued assertiveness on maritime disputes since the official leadership transition to Xi Jinping also suggests that it is the harder line, not the diplomatic line, that may prevail at least on maritime questions. Meanwhile, China's continued active engagement of ASEAN states on the economic front — in trade, investment, and developmental assistance — also underscore the contradictions and tensions between the security and economic tracks of China–ASEAN relations.[46] Regardless of the cause, however, the South China Sea has become emblematic of a "perceived mismatch between China's words and actions", which is hardly reassuring to Southeast Asian states.[47] Once again, China's approach to the South China Sea has become "a critical test" of China's intentions towards Southeast Asia.[48]

China's decision in May 2014 to deploy an oil rig in Vietnam's EEZ offers a particular illustration of the contradictions in Chinese policy. Much attention has been given to where exactly the rig was placed; however, the timing of the decision is just as notable. Specifically, the decision took place at a time when diplomatic processes seemed to be moving forward. For example, China–ASEAN negotiations on a Code of Conduct (CoC) had resumed, and Sino–Vietnamese relations seemed to have improved since 2011 when tensions between them were especially high. Regardless of the legal merits of the case, China's decision undermines ASEAN states' trust in China's sincerity and commitment to ongoing diplomatic processes.

China's nine-dash line map, which, as noted earlier was officially submitted to the CLCS in 2009, has become especially emblematic of Southeast Asian insecurities and of what is perceived as disturbing contradictions in Chinese policy, behaviour and rhetoric. Concerning the map, there are at least two related issues for Southeast Asian states: first, the expansiveness of China's claim, and second, the historical evidence used to justify it. While China has increasingly referenced UNCLOS in its legal filings, the map's invocation of "historic rights" contradicts that trend.[49] Notably also, it is the historical claim, not UNCLOS, that justifies the expansiveness of China's claim. For example, based on UNCLOS alone, China would have difficulty justifying the entirety of the area suggested by its map, especially given questions as to whether the Spratlys are in fact "islands" and thus able to generate EEZs.

As noted, it is not entirely clear what exactly is claimed by the map, but it does, at a minimum, allow China to make a broader claim by implication.[50] As noted, many observers interpret the map as China's claim to nearly 80 per cent the South China Sea. While the MFA has said that China is not claiming sovereignty over all of the South China Sea and official diplomatic wording in UN submissions has also been more limited (referring to the South China Sea islands and "their adjacent waters"),[51] the contradictions remain. First, "the attitudes of other government agencies and the general public are often at odds with the MFA's statements".[52] Second, those who understand legal and sovereign distinctions the best are typically not the ones most influential in the policy process. Even with MFA comments, there nevertheless still remain ambiguities in China's position. For example, while it is generally agreed that "adjacent waters" refers to a 12 nm territorial sea, China's official notes state that the Spratly Islands are entitled to an EEZ and continental shelf.[53] "Unwilling or unable" to clarify fully what the map references,[54] Beijing has thus created an opening for other Chinese-domestic actors to interpret the map for themselves and act based on those interpretations, actions and interpretations that may or may not be consistent with China's official position or, at least, preferred policy/approach of its top leadership.[55] All this contributes to Southeast Asian views of China's duplicity.

Most of all, as regards the map, it is simply very difficult for Southeast Asian states to understand why China would want to claim such an extensive area beyond its own shores. China may view itself as the disadvantaged party when it comes to occupations and activities in the South China Sea, but it has been disadvantaged for exactly the same reason that Southeast Asian states find China's claim suspect — namely, the physical distance that separates China and the Spratlys archipelago. Similarly, China's argument that its claims are no different from that of France, the United Kingdom, or the United States, each of which claim islands far afield, only serve to underscore concerns about Chinese expansionism since those other claims are products of imperialist practices and an era of imperialism.

Both the historical basis and expansiveness of China's claim also suggest a sense of regional entitlement.[56] Widespread media reports in March 2010 that Chinese officials had described the South China Sea to be a "core interest" — and thus comparable to Taiwan — reinforced those suspicions, intensifying Southeast Asian insecurities. While there is controversy over what in fact Chinese officials said,[57] the key issue for Southeast Asian states is that Chinese officials have also not explicitly denied it. The "core interest" concept was also used in subsequent Chinese press reports,[58] as well as by "military and mid-ranking civilian officials".[59]

In short, China's map represents both a physical and symbolic claim. China may justifiably see double standards in play given that Vietnam's claim is nearly as expansive, the fact that others similarly base their own claims on controversial maps and histories, and that others, too, have relied on assertive patrols and administrative actions; however, China's claims and actions are complicated by questions of size and history in ways that the others are not. Indeed, China's efforts to counter "China threat" perceptions with "peaceful rise" and portrayals of China as a "moral power" can make any Chinese action to the contrary an even more blatant and obvious contradiction.[60]

ASEAN's Contradictions

The ASEAN states are not the only ones to perceive contradictions. China sees the increase in fishing and oil exploration activities by Vietnam and the Philippines at odds with the provision in the 2002 Declaration on the Conduct of Parties in the South China Sea (DoC) that parties should exercise "self-restraint". It also sees double standards at work. In China's view, for example, Manila has been equally assertive in patrolling its claims.[61] For China, the ASEAN states' turn to the United States for assistance on the South China Sea also sit in tension with their stated commitment to non-confrontational and regional solutions. Just as Beijing's actions in the South China Sea play to Southeast Asian insecurities as lesser powers about their giant neighbour to the north, the latter's interest in, and even active solicitation of, U.S. involvement plays to Chinese concerns about U.S.–ASEAN anti-China collusion. Viewed in this way, China's actions, as in the 1990s, might be seen as "reactive and conservative rather than assertive and innovative".[62]

The contradictions in ASEAN's approach to China also have more than one source. Similar to China's domestic policy tensions, ASEAN states are not always of one mind. States vary in their concern about the South China Sea and certainly in how hard a line to take *vis-à-vis* China. ASEAN's approach can also vary significantly depending on who occupies the rotating chair. As noted, it was under Vietnam's chairmanship in 2010 that the South China Sea became more internationalized within ASEAN's formal frameworks. Notably also, it was under Vietnam's chairmanship of ASEAN that the United States confronted China at the ARF. Indonesia — though more wary of embracing America too closely — continued to support discussion of the South China Sea at the ARF when it assumed the chairmanship in 2011. In contrast, Cambodia as ASEAN chair in 2012, was much more deferential to China and worked against putting the South China Sea on the ASEAN agenda.[63] At that meeting, differences, especially between Cambodia and the Philippines, were such that states were unable to arrive at even a minimalist ASEAN consensus, the result being the organization's unprecedented failure to produce a joint communiqué at its annual ASEAN Ministerial Meeting (AMM) — indeed, the first time in the organization's then forty-five years of history.

Other intra-ASEAN differences and sources of ASEAN contradiction regard the question of a U.S. role in the dispute. While all ASEAN states support, to varying degrees, U.S. strategic engagement, they have also traditionally differed on how closely to embrace the United States and the kind of strategic role it should play.[64] In the case of the Philippines, where electoral turnovers take place, changes in government can also add to the perceived inconsistencies in policy. For example, President Gloria Macapagal Arroyo's policies were generally more favourable towards China, generally less adverse to bilateral approaches to the dispute, and more keen to work out deals with China. In contrast, President Benigno Aquino III has been more forceful in engaging the United States and in pushing for multilateral, regional responses to the dispute.[65]

Recent contradictions in ASEAN also reflect growing intra-ASEAN differences and dissatisfaction from states such as the Philippines regarding the organization's generally non-confrontational approach towards China

on the question of the South China Sea. As it had done in the 1990s,
the Philippines since 2010 challenged ASEAN to play a more "decisive
role" in response to geopolitical changes, one that would "not evade"
the question of a U.S. role.[66] As Aileen Baveira details, "Manila appears
convinced that it is time to move beyond mere confidence building
to a resolution of the conflict, but the response from other ASEAN
countries has been tepid."[67] Vietnam shares the Philippines' interest in
internationalizing the South China Sea dispute. Intra-ASEAN differences
contribute to Philippine and Vietnamese concerns that "other [ASEAN]
states will not support them in negotiating with China".[68] Manila, in
particular, sees itself as an "orphan" when dealing with China.[69] Such
dissatisfactions tend to sustain Manila's interest in non-ASEAN options.
Such options include closer strategic cooperation with the United States
(and also Japan). Also, in January 2013, after Cambodia's contentious year
as ASEAN chair, Manila also decided — without consultation with other
ASEAN states — to submit the dispute to the International Tribunal on
the Law of the Sea (ITLOS).

Intra-ASEAN differences about the kind of role the United States
might play speak to another potential source of tension in ASEAN's overall
approach to regional security: namely, what some have characterized as a
dual strategy[70] or "hedging strategy" pursued by ASEAN states.[71] ASEAN's
strategy is in essence a mix of approaches — a combination of constructive
bilateral and institutional engagement (via, for example, ASEAN processes)
and "soft balancing" in which states seek to offset their China-related
vulnerabilities with a variety of third party relationships and multilateral
mechanisms/processes. That mix reflects states' expanding economic
interests with China coupled with the uncertainties of their strategic
environment. Here it is worth underscoring that "uncertainty" means
exactly that: neither the security situation nor China–Southeast Asia
relations are understood as pre-determined. ASEAN's dual strategy plays to
the hope that relations can be transformed or redefined through positive
engagement and institutional "enmeshment",[72] while at the same time
appreciating the stabilizing effects of U.S. strategic engagement.

While ASEAN states do not see contradictions in their approach,
there is potential for the strategy to send mixed messages, especially if
"soft balancing" becomes of the "harder" kind. While China has generally
viewed the intensification of U.S.–Southeast Asia strategic relations as
U.S.-initiated and manipulated,[73] Southeast Asian states have been willing
partners. Of special note have been new and renewed strategic ties between
the United States and Vietnam and the United States and Indonesia. These

relationships exist alongside expanding arrangements with America's more established partnerships with the Philippines, Singapore, and to a lesser extent, Thailand. In June 2011, U.S. Defense Secretary Robert Gates announced plans to forward deploy up to four U.S. Navy Littoral Combat Ships in Singapore.[74] That announcement was followed by President Obama's trip to Australia where he and Prime Minister Julia Gillard officially announced the establishment of a U.S. Marines presence in Darwin, Australia beginning in 2012. Reaffirmed in August 2014, the twenty-five-year agreement commits the countries to first 250, then 1,200, and ultimately 2,500 U.S. Marines who would be rotated through Darwin on six-month tours.[75] These strategic moves — along with Washington's heightened diplomatic attention to Southeast Asia and ASEAN — are also associated with Washington's "Pacific Pivot" or "Re-balance to Asia", which was officially introduced in 2011 and further developed in 2012.[76] Such activities play to Chinese fears of a "containment" policy in the making.[77]

For China, the moment perhaps most symbolic of its concerns about ASEAN came in 2010, at the ARF, where U.S. Secretary of State Hillary Clinton — supported by a number of ASEAN states — expressed concern about developments in the South China Sea and their implications for freedom of navigation. Clinton also offered to work with China and the ASEAN members to develop a mechanism to help manage the dispute. From the U.S. and most ASEAN members' viewpoints, Clinton's diplomatic intervention called attention to the contradictions of Chinese policy and its efforts to consolidate its claims without harm to its relations with Southeast Asia. By pushing the issue onto the ARF agenda, Washington both broke and set precedent, opening the possibility for discussion at the ARF and other multilateral forums.

While Washington eventually moderated its stance and retracted its offer to mediate in response to ASEAN concerns about the fallout, the 2010 ARF meeting was, for China, still symbolic of unresolved questions and insecurities about ASEAN highlighted earlier. From China's perspective, actions taken at the ARF were seen as confirmation of its original fears and insecurities, namely, that others would use multilateral forums to "gang up" on China. As China's Foreign Minister Yang Jiechi put it, for example, Clinton's "seemingly fair remarks [at the ARF] were actually aimed to attack China by creating an illusion that the situation of the South China Sea is alarming".[78] Some of China's more belligerent commentary on the South China Sea, including some comments from those who have historically been more moderate, took place following Clinton's remarks at the ARF meeting.[79]

The question is the extent to which such developments encourage minority views in China that Sino–ASEAN relations need to be reassessed. While China's economic engagement of ASEAN has thus far remained quite strong, and in fact has become more proactive despite heightened maritime tensions, developments could still change that. For example, China's questions about ASEAN could shift the balance of what Michael Swaine characterizes as China's own "hedging strategy" in which a dominant diplomatic and economic strategy has co-existed with a secondary, "realpolitik" approach to its territorial and maritime interests.[80] The contradictions associated especially with ASEAN states' strategic engagement of the United States could flip the order of the two strategies. This, of course, will only sharpen the contradictions that ASEAN states already see in China's approaches to the South China Sea. China's harsh (over) reaction to Clinton's remarks, including not so subtle warnings to ASEAN states, tended to reinforce, rather than negate, Southeast Asian concerns about China.[81] What this underscores is that China's and ASEAN's key concerns about the other are clearly linked and that there are action-reaction dynamics that can create a momentum of their own and ever larger obstacles to more cooperative outcomes.

CONCLUSION: RECONCILING AND RISING ABOVE THE CONTRADICTIONS

It is difficult to imagine who exactly would gain if the South China Sea were to become any more politicized than it has been already, and each side has already lost something important *vis-à-vis* the other. For one, each side has already lost some credibility. ASEAN has lost a little bit of its prior neutrality, which has been considered one of its greatest attributes and sources of "soft power". China has lost some important, hard-won diplomatic ground and goodwill. The costs of further politicization are extremely high. For China, such politicization would require "diplomatic and military efforts of the utmost magnitude" if the damage to relations were to be overcome.[82] Those efforts also come with opportunity costs, as it diverts both attention and resources from other domestic, regional and global priorities.[83] This is to say nothing of the effects it has on China's longstanding interest in social status, international legitimacy and recognition as a "Great Power".[84]

For Southeast Asia, further politicization and thus deterioration of relations with China also risks critical economic interests that have bearing on both domestic politics and regime stability, as well as global competitiveness. It also heightens Sino–U.S. tensions in ways that will make it more difficult for ASEAN states to reconcile these two very critical relationships. As Aileen Baviera notes, there is already the "palpable fear that Southeast Asia may become a theatre in which a possible US–China conflict might occur in the foreseeable future".[85]

On China's side, its greatest challenge is how to reconcile what appears to be a growing domestic consensus as to the need for greater vigilance in defending its maritime interests *and* also the need to maintain good and improved relations with its neighbours, thus preserving a stable, more certain regional neighbourhood, which has been an important objective for the past two decades.[86] If China is still concerned about the latter, the problem is that the South China Sea has become, as Womack puts it, the material symbol of Southeast Asian uncertainties and insecurities about China.[87] China's position has been that geographic proximity has no weight on legal sovereignty questions,[88] but developments show that it does have quite a lot of weight on political and strategic perceptions of China. It is worth underscoring that the sheer expansiveness of China's claim is what regional and global actors most take issue with. At a minimum it feeds into other actors' worst suspicions about China wanting to seek regional domination. Again, the expansiveness of China's claim, the historic, extra-UNCLOS justifications associated with its nine-dash line map, and also its assertive South China Sea patrols and other actions constitute a tremendous contradiction in its diplomacy of peaceful rise *vis-à-vis* Southeast Asia.

Thus, one important challenge for China is whether it can adjust the extensiveness of its South China Sea claim and/or reassess the map in ways that are both more constraining and more consistent with UNCLOS. For example, it could claim the Spratlys as a line of islands or make the map simply a reference to specific Spratly features. The latter option would also give clarity to the map, which has been a critical source of ambiguity, concern and insecurity. Potential loss of face may also be mitigated by the very fact that China has not fully clarified the map (and is thus not necessarily retracting already stated claims).

Still, it is worth noting that the map's ambiguity has already worked against a key Chinese concern, namely, that the dispute not be internationalized. At least twice, questions about the map have drawn in non-claimants as interested third parties — Indonesia in the 1990s (because the map appears to overlap with the EEZ projected by the Natuna Islands) and the United States following China's submission of its map to the CLCS.[89] Clearly, any adjustments to the map would not solve the problem of overlapping claims, but they could, as Patrick Cronin puts it, have "the benefit of limiting suspicions that China's core interests are expanding"[90] and that China approaches the region with a sense of historical entitlement, thus moderating China's primary contradictions *vis-à-vis* the ASEAN states. Clarification of the map could also ease functionalist efforts like joint development which are difficult to pursue without a clear delineation of where the overlapping claims are located.[91]

Most of all, China faces challenges associated with the regional insecurities generated by its growing capabilities. China increasingly has a "Goliath" problem that is not helped by the extensiveness of its claim. The underlying fear in Southeast Asia is that China might use its newfound military capabilities to deny them resources, security and autonomy. Most important, for China, there are limits and costs to such coercive strategies. Coercion may be an effective short-term strategy, but it can be very expensive (materially, normatively and socially) in the long run given the resistance strategies of lesser powers, as well as the strategic interests of other major powers. China's diplomacy of the last decade — with notable exceptions, including the South China Sea — has been mostly guided by that cautionary logic. Stable relationships, especially those defined by growing disparities of power, depend on actors understanding both the limits and consequences of coercion.[92] The challenge for China, especially as it grows in capacity, is to remember those limits and consequences, as well as the insecurities generated by its growing capacities.

Indeed, the critical question for most in Southeast Asia is ultimately less the *fact* of Chinese power in and of itself. The Philippines' Jose Almonte characterized ASEAN's position thus:

> ASEAN can accommodate the idea of China as the East Asian superpower. All it asks is that China remember that demographic magnitude, economic weight, and military power by themselves do not command respect. Respect must be earned — and it can only be earned if a superpower's attributes include moral authority.[93]

At the same time, if the relationship is to be stable, respect for the other's interests and concerns cannot be all one-sided. If ASEAN states expect China to exercise self-restraint, for example, they must also do the same. Otherwise, their criticisms of China lack credibility. In particular, all states need to be less aggressive in their patrol efforts. Governments also have to try leading public opinion, rather than capitalizing on nationalist sentiment. Ultimately, if China's challenge is to remember the limits of power and coercion, the challenge for ASEAN's smaller states is to remember the limits of China's forbearance, especially in the face of domestic constraints and increased voices calling for a more muscular foreign policy at a time when regime insecurity also remains high.[94]

One of the toughest challenges for ASEAN may very well be to forge unified positions on specific issues such as the applicability of UNCLOS, which areas might be eligible for joint development, as well as their position on the internationalization of the dispute via ASEAN and beyond. This would have the benefit of reconciling some of ASEAN's contradictions, offering a firmer stand as to ASEAN's expectations as to proper conduct (for all concerned) and facilitating the creation of conflict management processes. This was a point that Indonesia's Foreign Minister Marty Natalegawa tried to press home in July and August 2012 following ASEAN's very public and reputation-damaging failure to produce a communiqué in Phnom Penh. As he put it, the absence of a "collective and common approach" on the South China Sea increased the "risk of further tensions" in the South China Sea for all.[95] Of course, China could object, as it did with ASEAN's effort to insert a clause in the DoC referencing intra-ASEAN consultations before its meetings with China. However, a more coherent ASEAN stance could reduce some of the activities in the South China Sea. For example, a united, common ASEAN stance could have a deterrent effect, as it would express the seriousness with which ASEAN treats the South China Sea. Also, ASEAN claimants might feel more supported, which, in turn, might increase their confidence in a common solution and thus encourage self-restraint. In both cases, it would help moderate some of the uncertainties of ASEAN's position that have contributed to some of the action-reaction dynamics described. As John Hemmings has argued, China "might soften its stance if ASEAN's position on this was clear and consistent".[96]

A particular challenge for ASEAN states is also how to engage both the United States and China in ways that do not increase a sense of zero-sum competition between them and reassure both that they have a place in East Asia. Again, ASEAN states were relatively successful in meeting this challenge in the 1990s, especially via the ARF. The challenge this time is arguably harder because the material gap between the United States and China has narrowed. That narrowing also has psychological effects: China is more confident; the United States more anxious about its pride of place. This time around, Beijing is less compelled by material or political circumstances (e.g., Tiananmen 1989), to accept arrangements with which it takes issue; Washington is less confident that concessions to China will not ultimately harm America's status and position.

Ultimately, U.S. attention to East Asia, and especially its heightened interest in the South China Sea, is double-edged for the ASEAN states. On the one hand, it serves to bolster the seriousness of Southeast Asian objections to China's extensive claims. On the other, it introduces the very sensitive dynamics of U.S.–China relations to China–Southeast Asian relations that can complicate the search for a *modus vivendi* on the issue. For China, its relations with the United States, for example, are far more sensitive and charged compared to its relations with Southeast Asian countries. Strategically, China's sense of vulnerability is also sharper in that the United States could cut off vital lifelines, as well as undermine growth and regime legitimacy. Both considerations complicate a more moderate Chinese stance. For Southeast Asian states, such U.S.–China dynamics may complicate efforts at a diplomatic or cooperative outcome, for example, by raising the stakes for China or by introducing issues that are separate from their relations with China and beyond Southeast Asian states' ability to influence.

Here, it is worth underscoring that Southeast Asian and U.S. concerns about the South China Sea are not necessarily the same. Both may share a general concern for safety/security of the seas and the peaceful resolution of disputes, but the United States and ASEAN states have different priorities and issues *vis-à-vis* China. For example, the specific "bone of contention" between the United States and China regards "competing definitions and interpretations of military use of EEZs".[97] In addition, U.S.–China dynamics in Asia — despite their protestations to the contrary — are also made distinct by an intensified sense of geopolitical and strategic rivalry. Such issues are different from those between China and the ASEAN states, namely, questions concerning the appropriate bases for determining territorial claims, how resources should be shared, and more generally, the autonomy of Southeast Asian states. Recent exchanges suggest that China is especially sensitive to U.S. efforts to intervene in the dispute and more likely to overreact in such cases.

Heightened U.S. attention thus presents different challenges for ASEAN and China. For China, it will remain a challenge to remember that America's strategic commitment to Southeast Asia offers Southeast Asian states "strategic peace of mind" and the confidence to engage China with the view of achieving "win-win" outcomes. For the ASEAN states, it is how to maintain the U.S. strategic relationship without stoking China's own legitimate insecurities and concerns.[98] As Singapore Prime Minister Lee Hsien Loong put it, "The biggest challenge is to rebalance strategically in a way that gives the Chinese more space without unsettling things and destabilizing longstanding, gradually built-up relationships."[99]

To conclude, on both sides, recent South China Sea developments draw attention to contradictions and inconsistencies that each perceives in the other. These contradictions are not new, but recent developments have brought them back to the fore. In the early 1990s, ASEAN's internal contradictions were eventually reconciled, resulting in new regional processes that balanced U.S. and Chinese engagement, a more confident and internationally recognized ASEAN, a more sensitive and politically assured China — indeed, an impressive (and even envied) period of Chinese diplomacy in Southeast Asia — and new commitments by states to stabilize the regional security situation. Clearly, there are important differences this time around. China is a more powerful country, while the insecurities of both Southeast Asian states as lesser powers and the United States as the established status quo power have grown greater. But an additional, significant difference is that China–Southeast Asia relations are also much more extensive than before. Consequently, there are now considerable interests, linkages and venues that give states additional incentives and resources to moderate and diffuse tensions. Developments show that such interests and resources can be brought to bear on how each side manages the dispute. China's and ASEAN's states ongoing efforts to fashion a CoC is a good start.

Ultimately, as Womack has argued, a "mature", stable relationship between greater and lesser powers depends on there being a reciprocating sense of the other's needs and insecurities, as well as one's own limitations.[100] China–Southeast Asia relations have progressed and expanded in large part because for much of the last decade, both sides understood that. The question, again, is whether each side will be able to transcend the contradictions that have defined this most recent post-2008 period of tensions and return to the successful strategies that bestowed each of them important security and international recognition as responsible actors.

Notes

1. Lui Ning quoted in Michael Leifer, "Chinese Economic Reform and Security Policy: The South China Sea Connection", *Survival* 37, no. 2 (Summer 1995): 49.
2. The Deng–Jiang transition was made most sensitive by the crisis politics and threat to the regime associated with Beijing's 1989 Tiananmen crackdown. The Hu–Xi transition is made most sensitive by the fact of its being the first succession not directed by Deng Xiaoping.
3. See, for example, "Defense Analysts on Spratlys War Scenario", *Manila Business World*, 21 April 1995 in FBIS-EAS 95-079. Also, Mark J. Valencia, *China*

and the South China Sea Disputes, Adelphi Paper no. 298 (New York: Oxford University Press for the International Institute for Strategic Studies, 1995), pp. 6–7.

4. See Ian Storey, "Creeping Assertiveness: China, the Philippines and the South China Sea Dispute", *Contemporary Southeast Asia* 21, no. 1 (April 1999): 95–118.

5. ASEAN diplomat quoted by Michael Richardson, "China's Neighbors Aim for a 'Litmus Test' on Spratlys", *New York Times*, 13 May 1995. See also Barry Wain, "South China Sea Provides a Litmus Test for China", *Wall Street Journal,* 25 July 1994.

6 Nicholas Cummings-Bruce, "China Makes More Mischief in the South China Sea", *The Guardian*, 22 May 1995.

7. See Jusuf Wanandi, *Asia-Pacific After the Cold War* (Jakarta: Centre for Strategic and International Studies, 1996).

8. Philippine Presidents Fidel Ramos and Joseph Estrada quoted in Ian Storey, "China and the Philippines: Moving Beyond the South China Sea Dispute", *China Brief* 6, issue 17 (9 May 2007). The Philippines has especially characterized the South China Sea as a litmus test of China's intentions. See also, documents cited in "Philippines Seeks Chinese Withdrawal from Spratlys", *Kyodo News*, 27 July 1997.

9. Chi-kin Lo, *China's Policy Towards Territorial Disputes: The Case of the South China Sea Islands* (New York: Routledge, 1989), p. 179.

10. Numbers tend to vary; it is also not always clear whether the features referenced are in fact "islands" or "rocks".

11. For example, Malaysian commandos occupied Swallow Reef (Terumbu Layang-Layang) in August 1983, the Dallas (Ubi) and Mariveles (Matanani) Reefs in November 1986. See Joseph Chin Yong Liow, "Malaysia–China Relations in the 1990s: The Maturing of a Partnership", *Asian* Survey 40, no. 4 (2000): 672–91. See also Elina Noor's chapter in this volume in which she notes Malaysia's occupation of five features. According to Chinese reports, Vietnam occupied five more islands between 1989 and 1991. See Chen Jie, "China's Spratly Policy: With Special Reference to the Philippines and Malaysia", *Asian Survey* 34, no. 10 (October 1994): 893–903.

12. You Ji, *The Armed Forces of China* (New York: I.B. Tauris, 1999), p. 223.

13. Kenneth Lieberthal and Michel Oksenberg, *Policy Making in China: Leaders, Structures, and Processes* (Princeton: Princeton University Press, 1988).

14. You Ji, "The South China Sea: A Test Case for China's Defense and Foreign Policies", *Contemporary Southeast Asia* 16, no. 4 (1995): 394–95.

15. Ralf Emmers, "The Influence of the Balance of Power Factor in the ASEAN Regional Forum", *Asian Survey* 23, no. 2 (2001): 275–91.

16. Chen, "China's Spratly Policy", op. cit.

17. Kuik Cheng-Chwee, "Multilateralism in China's ASEAN Policy: Its Evolution, Characteristics and Aspiration", *Contemporary Southeast Asia* 27, no. 1 (April

2005): 102–22; Emmers, "The Influence of the Balance of Power Factor", op. cit.

18. See, for example, Alice Ba, "The Politics and Economics of 'East Asia' in China–ASEAN Relations", in *China and Southeast Asia: Global Changes and Regional Challenges*, edited by Ho Khai-Leong and Samuel C.Y. Ku (Singapore: Institute of Southeast Asian Studies, 2005), pp. 170–94.

19. See, for example, Aileen Baviera, "The China Factor in US Alliances in East Asia and the Asia Pacific", *Australian Journal of International Affairs* 57, no. 2 (2003): 339–52; Wanandi, *Asia-Pacific After the Cold War*, op. cit; Joshua Kurlantzick, *Charm Offensive: How China's Soft Power is Transforming the World* (New York: Yale University Press, 2007).

20. This was, for example, the general sentiment expressed by researchers interviewed by the author in Singapore and Kuala Lumpur in August 2002.

21. See discussion in Michael Swaine, "Chinese Leadership and Elite Responses to the US Pacific Pivot", *China Leadership Monitor*, no. 38 (Summer 2012): 6, including footnote 32.

22. See Michael Swaine, "China's Strategy and Security in the Post-Cold War Era", in *China's Rise in Historical Perspective*, edited by Brantly Womack (Lanham: Rowman and Littlefield, 2010), pp. 89–106.

23. Ibid.

24. Robert Beckman, "South China Sea: How China Could Clarify Its Claims", *RSIS Commentary* 116/2010 (16 September 2010), available at <http://cil. nus.edu.sg/wp/wp-content/uploads/2009/08/RSIScommentaries-ProfBeckman-16Sep2010.pdf>.

25. Rolf Emmers, "The De-escalation of the Spratly Dispute in Sino-Southeast Asian Relations", RSIS Working Paper 129 (6 June 2007). See also, You Ji, "A Test Case", op. cit.

26. See, for example, "China Building Underground Nuclear Sub Base", *Straits Times*, 3 May 2008; Thomas Harding, "Chinese Nuclear Submarine Base", *The Telegraph*, 1 May 2008; Jackie Northam, "China's Underground Submarine Base Scrutinized", *National Public Radio*, 9 May 2008, available at <http://www.npr.org/templates/story/story.php?storyId=90309537>.

27. Evan A. Laksmana, "Is China Failing SE Asia's Litmus Test?", *Jakarta Post*, 10 June 2010.

28. Anti-China protests have occurred in both Vietnam and the Philippines in response to Chinese actions in the South China Sea. In the Philippines, policies towards China and how to approach the South China Sea have precipitated various charges of treason and nationalist betrayal. See Aileen Baviera, "The Influence of Domestic Politics on Philippine Foreign Policy: The Case of Philippines–China Relations Since 2004", RSIS Working Paper 241 (5 June 2012), available at <http://www.rsis.edu.sg/wp-content/uploads/rsis-pubs/WP241.pdf>; Tarra Quismundo, "Ailing Philippine Ambassador to

China, Brady, Flown Home", *Philippine Daily Inquirer*, 23 September 2012; Cathy C. Yamsuan and Norman Bordadora, "Enrile Accuses Trillanes of Working for China", *Philippine Daily Inquirer*, 20 September 2012; Noemi Gonzales, "Secret Talks with China Cause Infighting", *Business World*, 20 September 2012.

29. Michael Swaine, "Perceptions of an Assertive China", *China Leadership Monitor* 32 (Spring 2010), available at <http://carnegieendowment.org/files/CLM32MS1.pdf>.

30. Swaine, "Chinese Leadership", op. cit.

31. International Crisis Group, "Stirring Up the South China Sea (I)", *Asia Report* no. 223 (23 April 2012), p. 17, available at <http://www.crisisgroup.org/~/media/files/asia/north-east-asia/223-stirring-up-the-south-china-sea-i.pdf>.

32. See Alice D. Ba and Ian Storey, "Developments in the South China Sea in 2012: Continuity Over Change", paper presented at The South China Sea: Cooperation for Regional Security and Development, Diplomatic Academy of Vietnam and Vietnam Lawyers' Association, Ho Chi Minh City, Vietnam, 19–21 November 2012.

33. Chinese factories were not the only ones attacked. There were also reports of mobs torching Taiwanese factories, as well as Singaporean, South Korean and Japanese factories. See Euan McKirdy, "Protestors Torch Factories in Southern Vietnam as China Protests Escalate", *CNN* (14 May 2014), available at <http://edition.cnn.com/2014/05/14/world/asia/south-china-sea-drilling-duplicate-2/>.

34. See Jane Perlez, "Singaporean Tells China U.S. Is Not in Decline", *New York Times,* 6 September 2012.

35. Brantly Womack, "The Spratlys: From Dangerous Ground to Apple of Discord", *Contemporary Southeast Asia* 33, no. 3 (December 2011): 370–87. On the effects of the 2008 global financial crisis on China, see also Thomas Christensen, "The Advantages of an Assertive China: Responding to Beijing's Abrasive Diplomacy", *Foreign Affairs* 90, no. 2 (March/April 2011), available at <http://www.brookings.edu/research/articles/2011/03/china-christensen>.

36. See, for example, Alice Ba, "Systemic Neglect: A Reconsideration of US Southeast Asia Policy", *Contemporary Southeast Asia* 31, no. 3 (December 2009): 369–98; Swaine, "Chinese Leadership", op. cit.

37. See Alice Ba, "Staking Claims and Making Waves in the South China Sea", *Contemporary Southeast Asia* 33, no. 3 (December 2011): 269–91.

38. See, for example, Bronson Percival, "Dangerous Waters: Exercise Caution", Conference on Maritime Security in the South China Sea, Center for Strategic and International Studies (CSIS), Washington D.C., 21 June 2011. See also comments by Admiral Timothy Keating quoted in "China: US Naval Vessel Violated Laws", *Agence France-Presse*, 6 May 2009.

39. Kavi Chongkittavorn, "Southeast Asia Now Running a New Powerful Playground", *China Post*, 16 August 2010.

40. Joel D. Adriano, "Sinophobia on the Rise in the Philippines", *Asia Times*, 13 July 2011; Mark Valencia, "Did the US Push China Over the Edge?", *The Diplomat*, 24 June 2011.

41. Taylor Fravel, "China's Strategy in the South China Sea", *Contemporary Southeast Asia* 33, no. 3 (December 2011): 292–319.

42. Li Mingjiang and Kwa Chong Guan, *China–ASEAN Sub-Regional Cooperation: Progress, Problems and Prospect* (Singapore: World Scientific, 2011); Li Mingjiang, "Non-Confrontational Assertiveness: China's New Security Posture", *RSIS Commentary* 80 (16 May 2011); Da Wei, "Has China Become Tough?", *China Security* 6, no. 3 (2010): 35–42.

43. Dirk van der Kley, "The China–Vietnam Standoff: Three Key Factors", *Lowy Interpreter* (8 May 2014), available at <http://www.lowyinterpreter. org/post/2014/05/08/China-Vietnam-standoff-Three-key-factors. aspx?COLLCC=1124359996&COLLCC=2717631039&>.

44. For a discussion of recent intra-bureaucratic dynamics, see International Crisis Group, "Stirring Up the South China Sea (I)", op. cit. For a discussion of the PLA-Navy v. MFA debates of the early 1990s, see John Garver, "China's Push through the South China Sea: The Interaction of Bureaucratic and National Interests", *China Quarterly* 132 (December 1992): 999–1028.

45. See, for example, Da Wei, "Has China Become Tough?", op. cit.; Li and Kwa, *China–ASEAN Sub-Regional Cooperation*, op. cit.; Christensen, "The Advantages of an Assertive China", op. cit.

46. For a discussion of recent trends in China's economic engagement of ASEAN and Southeast Asia, see Alice Ba, "Is China Leading? China, Southeast Asia, and East Asian Integration", *Political Science* 66, no. 2 (2014): 143–65.

47. Adriano, "Sinophobia on the Rise", op. cit.

48. Evelyn Goh, "Limits of Chinese Power", *YaleGlobalOnline*, 26 April 2011; Evan Laksamana, "Is China Failing SE Asia's Litmus Test?", *The Diplomat*, 10 June 2010.

49. This is not to say that historical use does not have a bearing on claims but UNCLOS has "deliberately avoid[ed] the issue of historic rights or historic waters" outside territorial seas and internal waters. See, for example, Zou Keyuan, "Historic Rights in International Law and in China's Practice", *Ocean Development and International Law* 32, no. 2 (2001): 150–52.

50. Douglas H. Paal, "Beware the South China Sea", *The Diplomat*, 15 July 2011, available at <http://the-diplomat.com/2011/07/15/beware-the-south-china-sea/>; Clive Schofield, Ian Townsend-Gault, Hasjim Djalal, Ian Storey, Meredith Miller and Tim Cook, "From Disputed Waters to Seas of Opportunity", *NBR Special Report No. 30* (July 2011); Robert Beckman, "South China Sea: Worsening Dispute or Growing Clarity in Claims", *RSIS Commentary* 90/2010 (16 August 2010), available at <http://www.rsis.edu.sg/wp-content/uploads/2014/07/RSIS09020103.pdf>.

51. See Robert Beckman, "The China–Philippines Dispute in the South China Sea: Does Beijing Have a Legitimate Claim?", *RSIS Commentary* 36/2012 (7 March 2012), available at <http://cil.nus.edu.sg/wp/wp-content/uploads/2010/12/ProfBeckman-RSIS-China-PhilippinesDisputeinSCS-7Mar2012.pdf>. See also the 29 February 2012 comments of Chinese Foreign Ministry Spokesperson Hong Lei cited in Li Mingjiang, "China's Rising Maritime Aspirations: Impact on Beijing's Good-Neighbor Policy", *RSIS Commentary* 53/2012 (28 March 2012), available at <http://www.rsis.edu.sg/wp-content/uploads/2014/07/CO12053.pdf>.

52. International Crisis Group, "Stirring Up the South China Sea (I)", op. cit., p. 17.

53. Beckman, "The China–Philippines Dispute", op. cit.

54. See Fravel, "China's Strategy in the South China Sea", op. cit.

55. Li and Kwa, *China–ASEAN Sub-Regional Cooperation*, op. cit.; Li Mingjiang, "Non-Confrontational Assertiveness: China's New Security Posture", *RSIS Commentary* 80/2011 (16 May 2011).

56. Peter Kien-hong Yu, "The Chinese (Broken) U-shaped Line in the South China Sea: Points, Lines, and Zones", *Contemporary Southeast Asia* 25, no. 3 (December 2003): 405–30.

57. Michael Swaine's close reading of official Chinese sources, for example, "failed to unearth a single example of a PRC official or an official PRC document or media source that publicly and explicitly identifies the South China Sea as a PRC 'core interest'". See Michael Swaine, "China's Assertive Behavior: On Core Interests (Part I)", *China Leadership Monitor* 34 (22 February 2011). According to Jeffrey Bader who served in the Obama administration as senior director for East Asian affairs on the National Security Council from January 2009 to April 2011, Dai Binguo had referred to China's rights in the South China Sea as a national priority (a more mild term) and not, as was reported, a "core interest". See Jeffrey Bader, *Obama and China's Rise: An Insider's Account of America's Asia Strategy* (Washington, D.C.: Brookings Press, 2012), pp. 75–76.

58. Shen Dingli, "2011: Cooling Temperatures in the South China Sea", AsiaSociety.org, 26 December 2011, available at <http://asiasociety.org/blog/asia/2011-cooling-temperatures-south-china-sea>.

59. Bader, *Obama and China's Rise*, op. cit., p. 105.

60. For a discussion of the complex politics of China's "soft power" strategy, see Michael Barr, *Who's Afraid of China?* (London and New York: Zed Books, 2012).

61. Michael Swaine and M. Taylor Fravel, "China's Assertive Behavior (Part Two)", *China Leadership Monitor* 35 (Summer 2011), available at <http://carnegieendowment.org/2011/06/24/china-s-assertive-behavior-part-two-maritime-periphery/1c6>.

62. Christensen, "The Advantages of an Assertive China", op. cit.
63. "China has ASEAN arguing over East Sea status", *Thanh Nien News*, 6 April 2012.
64. See Alice Ba, *(Re)Negotiating East and Southeast Asia* (Stanford: Stanford University Press 2009), Chapters 2 and 6.
65. See, for example, discussion in Ba and Storey, "Developments in the South China Sea", op. cit.
66. See comments by former Philippine Foreign Minister Raul Manglapus quoted in Ba, *(Re)Negotiating East and Southeast Asia*, op. cit., Chapter 6, and recent remarks made by current Philippine Foreign Minister Alberto del Rosario quoted in Baviera, "The South China Sea Disputes", op. cit.
67. Baviera, "The South China Sea Disputes", op. cit.
68. "Indonesia Frets About U.S., Japanese interference in S. China Sea", *Mainichi Daily News*, 22 January 2011.
69. Former Philippine Foreign Minister Lauro Baja quoted in Shaun Narine, *Explaining ASEAN: Regionalism in Southeast Asia* (Boulder: Lynn Reinner, 2001), pp. 87–88; Carlyle Thayer, "Is the Philippines an Orphan?", *The Diplomat*, 2 May 2012, available at <http://thediplomat.com/2012/05/is-the-philippines-an-orphan/>.
70. Alice Ba, "A New History? The Structure and Process of Southeast Asia's Relations with a Rising China", in *Contemporary Southeast Asia*, 2nd ed., edited by Mark Beeson (London: Palgrave Macmillan 2008), pp. 192–207.
71. Evelyn Goh, "Meeting the China Challenge: The US in Southeast Asian Regional Security Strategies", *Policy Studies* 16 (Washington, D.C.: East-West Center, 2005); Kuik, "Multilateralism in China's ASEAN Strategy", op. cit.; Ian Storey, *Southeast Asia and the Rise of China* (Abingdon, Oxon.: Routledge, 2011), pp. 47–51.
72. Goh, "Meeting the China Challenge", op. cit.
73. See, for example, comments of Zhou Yongsheng at China's Foreign Affairs University in Rick Wallace and Michael Sainsbury, "Between a Rock and a Reef", *The Australian*, 24 September 2012. See also Swaine, "Chinese Leadership", op. cit., p. 10.
74. See News Transcript of Secretary of Defense Robert M. Gates, "Remarks by Secretary Gates at the Shangri-La Dialogue, International Institute for Strategic Studies, Singapore", 10th Annual IISS Shangri-La Security Dialogue, 3 June 2011, available at <http://www.defense.gov/Transcripts/Transcript.aspx?TranscriptID=4831>. See also, "Singapore, U.S. Formally Announce Deployment of U.S. Littoral Combat Ships", *Kyodo News Service*, 3 June 2012.
75. Jackie Calmes, "U.S. and Australia Seal Expanded Military Ties", *New York Times*, 16 November 2011.
76. Swaine details five stages of the "Pacific Pivot": (1) Washington's stepped up diplomatic and institutional engagement beginning 2009; (2) an explicit

U.S. concern with East and South China Sea territorial disputes between China and other Asian states (2010–11); (3) several coordinated actions and statements — "policy moves" — including such strategic actions as the stationing of marines in Darwin and forward deployment of littoral combat ships to Singapore (June 2011); (4) new defence guidelines that identified Asia (and the Middle East) as a key defence priority and China (along with Iran) as a potential anti-access threat (January 2012); and (5) the announcement of the Joint Operational Access Concept (JOAC). See Swaine, "Chinese Leadership", op. cit.

77. Goldstein cites, for example, Navy Senior Captain Li Jie's (Naval Research Centre in Beijing, the PLAN's premier think-tank) concerns that a new Cold War scenario emerging, justifying more concerted preparations by China. Lyle Goldstein, "Chinese Naval Strategy in the South China Sea", *Contemporary Southeast Asia* 33, no. 3 (December 2011): 320–47.

78. "China Rejects U.S. Suggestion for Asean Mediation on Territory", *Wall Street Journal,* 26 July 2010.

79. See Goldstein, "Chinese Naval Strategy", op. cit.; Christensen, "The Advantages of an Assertive China", op. cit.

80. Michael Swaine, *America's Challenge* (Washington, D.C.: Carnegie Endowment for International Peace, 2011), pp. 34–35, 42–45. As early as 1995, You Ji identified a latent "discord" between China's economic priorities, diplomatic objectives and military interests. See You Ji, "A Test Case", op. cit.

81. Abdul Khalik, "ASEAN Unity 'Key to Handling' US–China Rivalry in the Region", *Jakarta Post*, 16 August 2010.

82. Toshi Yoshihara and James R. Holmes, "Can China Defend a 'Core Interest' in the South China Sea?", *Washington Quarterly* 34, no. 2 (Spring 2011): 45–59.

83. Womack, "The Spratlys", op. cit.

84. Yong Deng, *China's Struggle for Status: The Realignment of International Relations* (Cambridge: Cambridge University Press, 2008). See also Yan Xuetong's chapters — "Comparative Study of Pre-Qin Interstate Philosophy" and "Xunzi's Interstate Philosophy and Its Message for Today", in *Ancient Chinese Thought, Modern Chinese Power*, edited by Daniel Bell and Sun Zhe (Princeton: Princeton University Press, 2011), pp. 21–69, 70–106.

85. Baviera, "The South China Sea Disputes", op. cit.; Rizal Sukma, "ASEAN, Regional Security, and the Role of the United States: A View from Southeast Asia", 2004, available at <http://www.iips.org/04sec/04asiasec_sukma.pdf>.

86. Li, "China's Rising Maritime Aspirations", op. cit.

87. Womack, "The Spratlys", op. cit.

88. See, for example, Yi Ping (School of Law, Peking University), "The Philippines Lacks Legal Ground to go to Tribunal", Embassy of the PRC in

the Republic of the Philippines, 15 May 2012, available at <http://ph.china-embassy.org/eng/sgdt/t931868.htm>.

89. Ba, "Staking Claims", op. cit.
90. Patrick Cronin, "How China, US See Each Other at Sea", *The Diplomat*, 29 May 2011, available at <http://thediplomat.com/2011/05/how-china-us-see-each-other-at-sea/>; Robert Beckman and Leonardo Bernard, "Disputed Areas in the South China Sea: Prospects for Arbitration or Advisory Opinion", at the Third International Workshop on the South China Sea, Hanoi, 3–5 November 2011.
91. Beckman and Bernard, "Disputed Areas in the South China Sea", op. cit.
92. See especially Chapters 10 and 11 in Brantly Womack, *China and Vietnam: The Politics of Asymmetry* (New York: Cambridge University Press, 2006), pp. 212–37, 238–56.
93. Jose T. Almonte, "Ensuring Security the 'ASEAN Way'", *Survival* 39, no. 4 (Winter 1997–98): 80–92.
94. Christensen, "The Advantages of an Assertive China", op. cit.
95. Li Xiaokun and Zhou Wa, "China Seeks to Boost Southeast Asian Ties", *China Daily*, 10 August 2012.
96. John Hemmings, "The South China Sea Dispute: A Legal Solution Needed", *East Asia Forum* (7 December 2011).
97. Zha Daojiong, "South China Sea Diplomacy: More Needs to be Done", *RSIS Commentary* 102/2011 (13 July 2011); Valencia, "Did the US Push China Over the Edge?", op. cit.
98. Brantly Womack, "China and Vietnam: Managing an Asymmetric Relationship in an Era of Economic Uncertainty", *Asian Politics and Policy* 2, no. 4 (2010): 597.
99. Perlez, "Singaporean Tells China U.S. Is Not in Decline", op. cit.
100. Womack, *China and Vietnam: The Politics of Asymmetry*, op. cit.

6

RISING TENSIONS IN THE SOUTH CHINA SEA: SOUTHEAST ASIAN RESPONSES

Ian Storey

At the height of the May–July 2014 crisis between Beijing and Hanoi over the deployment of the large Chinese oil rig Hai Yang Shi You-981 (HYSY-981) into Vietnam's claimed exclusive economic zone (EEZ), Singapore Prime Minister Lee Hsien Loong pointed out that the South China Sea dispute was only one facet of relations between the Association of Southeast Asian Nations (ASEAN) and the People's Republic of China (PRC) and that it should not be allowed to overshadow the many positive aspects of the relationship.[1]

Prime Minister Lee's point was well taken. Since the end of the Cold War in the early 1990s, relations between ASEAN and China, and between the PRC and each of the ten members which comprise Southeast Asia's premier regional organization, have been transformed, and largely for the better. Two-way trade, the bedrock of the relationship, has expanded from a mere US$7.5 billion in 1990 to $366.5 billion by 2014, making China ASEAN's largest external trade partner.[2] The economic nexus between ASEAN and China is set to strengthen with an upgraded free trade agreement and as improved air, sea and road linkages increase "connectivity" between China and Southeast Asia. At the political level, with the exception of Vietnam and the Philippines, Beijing's diplomatic relations with Southeast Asian countries are relatively cordial and cooperative, and the

PRC has become a central player in all of the various ASEAN-led forums such as the ASEAN Regional Forum (ARF), ASEAN Plus Three (APT) and East Asia Summit (EAS). Due to Beijing's active defence diplomacy, military and security ties between China and the countries of Southeast Asia have also expanded in ways that would have been unthinkable during the Cold War — or even in the 1990s.[3]

Notwithstanding the enormous strides in relations between Southeast Asia and China over the past quarter of a century, since 2007–8 the South China Sea dispute has become a growing source of diplomatic tension between China and the Southeast Asian claimants — particularly Vietnam and the Philippines — and this has had an impact on ASEAN–China relations as a whole. If allowed to fester, or deteriorate, the dispute could undermine the economic, political and security gains that ASEAN and China have achieved over the past few decades. Perhaps more seriously, a worsening of tensions in the South China Sea could push ASEAN unity to breaking point, put pay to the notion of ASEAN "centrality" and allow Great Powers such as the United States and China to determine the future strategic environment of Southeast Asia.

This chapter examines how ASEAN as an organization has approached the South China Sea dispute since the early 1990s, the degree to which a consensus has been forged, and the problem of unity when crises have arisen. Particular attention is given to efforts by ASEAN to manage the problem with China through initiatives such as the 2002 Declaration on the Conduct of Parties in the South China Sea (DoC) and the proposed Code of Conduct for the South China Sea (CoC). The chapter goes on to explore how Southeast Asian countries as individual entities view the dispute, and the policies they have put in place to protect their sovereignty claims, national interests and foreign relations.

THE ASEAN RESPONSE

Although perceptions of and approaches to the South China Sea problem varies among Southeast Asian countries, its potential to generate regional instability, military conflict and Great Power rivalry has meant that ASEAN has accorded the dispute a high priority since the early 1990s. However, even though four of its members are claimants, from the outset ASEAN has tried to maintain a neutral stance: it does not take a position on the merits of the competing territorial claims, nor has it arrogated itself a central role in resolving the dispute as this can only be achieved among the claimants themselves or through international legal arbitration. Instead, ASEAN has focused on a process of conflict management by engaging China in a dialogue with the aim of reducing tensions, building trust and confidence among the parties and establishing an environment conducive to a peaceful resolution of the problem.

After more than two decades, however, the ASEAN–China conflict management process has yielded mixed results, to say the least. Part of the problem lies with China's reluctance to negotiate concrete crisis prevention mechanisms with ASEAN, preferring instead non-binding, largely symbolic agreements that do not restrict its freedom of action in the South China Sea. Yet ASEAN itself must also bear some of the responsibility for the lack of progress. Over the years, the organization has struggled to forge a strong consensus on how to deal with China over the issue, reduce the risk of conflict and identify pathways to a resolution. This lack of a strong consensus is partly the result of overlapping claims among four of the ASEAN members but mainly due to differing geopolitical perspectives and interests, and the emphasis member states' place on their bilateral relations with China. Thus while some members have pushed for a more robust response to China's actions in disputed waters, others have advocated for a more conciliatory approach so as not to offend Beijing. As tensions have surged since 2007–8, and the dispute has become an issue of contention between Washington and Beijing, ASEAN solidarity has come under increasing strain, culminating in a very public and highly embarrassing display of disunity under Cambodia's chairmanship in 2012. Unity was subsequently restored, but it remains fragile, and a very serious incident in the South China Sea, such as a military clash, could shatter it.

For much of the 1980s ASEAN was preoccupied with ending Vietnam's occupation of Cambodia. The easing of superpower tensions in the late 1980s eventually led to a resolution of the Cambodian problem, but even before the Cold War had fully thawed the situation in the South China Sea had become highly charged. In 1988, Chinese and Vietnamese naval forces clashed at Johnson Reef in the Spratlys, resulting in nearly seventy Vietnamese fatalities, and in 1992 China moved to formalize its territorial claims in the South China Sea through the passage of domestic legislation. These developments took place against the backdrop of a sustained effort by China to modernize the People's Liberation Army (PLA) and a reduction in America's military presence in Southeast Asia following the closure of U.S. bases in the Philippines in 1992.

Conscious of the need to check growing tensions and maintain stability in the South China Sea, ASEAN issued its first statement on the dispute in July 1992: the ASEAN Declaration on the South China Sea (also known as the Manila Declaration):[4] in it, the ASEAN members explicitly acknowledged that "adverse developments" in the South China Sea "directly affect peace and stability in the region" and called for a peaceful resolution of the problem without the use of force; urged the parties to exercise "self-restraint" and pursue cooperative confidence-building measures (CBMs); and negotiate a "code of international conduct".[5]

It would be another decade before ASEAN and China made tangible progress towards better conflict management. This despite the fact that during the intervening period, tensions continued to rise, principally between Vietnam and China, and the Philippines and China. The dispute reached a turning point in 1995 when China occupied Mischief Reef, 130 miles west of Palawan Island and within the Philippines' EEZ — the first time China had seized a feature claimed by an ASEAN member.[6] The occupation triggered a crisis in Sino–Philippine relations, and in response ASEAN closed ranks behind Manila: it issued a statement expressing "serious concern" at the deteriorating situation in the South China Sea, and, for the first time, ASEAN foreign ministers collectively raised the issue with their Chinese counterpart at a summit meeting later that same year.[7] Thereafter, however, ASEAN unity dissipated: the 1997–98 Asian Financial Crisis provoked bickering among the member states, while the accession of new members — Vietnam in 1995, Laos and Myanmar in 1997 and Cambodia in 1999 — made the process of consensus-building more difficult, especially on a contentious issue such as the South China Sea in which some members had a clear stake and others did not. As a result, ASEAN failed to take a united stand in response to several events in the late 1990s: in 1997 when Sino–Vietnamese tensions erupted in the Gulf of Tonkin; in 1998 when China upgraded its structures on Mischief Reef; and in 1999 when Malaysia occupied two atolls in the Spratlys.[8]

Although the 1992 Declaration had called on the parties to work towards a code of conduct, China resisted, insisting instead on a bilateral approach (e.g. in 1995 it signed a code of conduct with the Philippines, though that agreement proved ineffectual). By the late 1990s, however, China had become more accustomed to participating in regional forums, such as the ARF, and increasingly recognized the utility of multilateralism to promote its national interests. In 1999, therefore, China agreed to begin talks with ASEAN on a Code of Conduct.

The outcome of those talks was not a code but the Declaration on the Conduct of Parties in the South China Sea (DoC), signed on 4 November 1992.[9] The DoC was not quite the outcome envisioned in the Manila Declaration. While some ASEAN members — principally Vietnam and the Philippines — had pushed for a legally binding code, China, supported by Malaysia, favoured a less legalistic approach.[10] The result was a non-binding political statement that lacks enforcement mechanisms or sanctions. Hanoi wanted the DoC to cover the Paracel Islands, but as China does not recognize that a dispute exists with Vietnam over sovereignty of the archipelago, the precise geographical scope of the agreement was left unstated. The central goals of the DoC are to better manage the conflict by freezing the status quo in terms of the number of atolls occupied and create an environment conducive to a peaceful settlement by promoting dialogue and building trust through cooperative activities. While the DoC builds on the Manila Declaration, it also contained new provisions, such as a commitment to freedom of navigation, a prohibition on "inhabiting" unoccupied features and a pledge to exercise "self-restraint in the conduct of activities that would complicate or escalate the dispute".[11] As a concession to those members who had advocated a binding code, in the final paragraph of the DoC the parties agreed to work towards the adoption of a Code of Conduct (CoC) to "further promote peace and stability in the region".[12]

When the DoC was inked, it was touted as an important step towards efforts to better manage the dispute. It was subsequently credited for an easing of South China Sea tensions in the first half of the 2000s, and a seemingly new-found spirit of cooperation, exemplified by the 2005 Joint Marine Seismic Undertaking (JMSU), an agreement among China, the Philippines and Vietnam to explore for energy resources in the South China Sea. In hindsight, however, it is clear that the DoC was unworthy of such credit because once it was signed the parties put very little effort into putting its provisions into effect. In 2005 ASEAN and China convened a Senior Officials Meeting (SOM) on the Implementation of the DoC, and agreement was reached to establish a Joint Working Group (JWG) to draw up implementation guidelines and establish cooperative projects. However, the JWG met only three times between 2005 and 2008. Moreover, by 2009 its work had become paralyzed over a minor procedural point. In accordance with the 2008 ASEAN Charter, member states are required to "coordinate and endeavour to develop common positions" in the conduct of external affairs.[13] As such, ASEAN officials wanted to include a clause in the implementation guidelines which stated that they would consult among themselves prior to meeting with their Chinese counterparts. China, however, demurred on the grounds that not all ASEAN members are claimants. In an effort to accommodate China's reservation, ASEAN rephrased the clause more than twenty times; but China rejected it each time.[14]

Serious friction in Sino–Philippine and Sino–Vietnamese relations over the South China Sea dispute during 2010–11 increased frustration in some Southeast Asian capitals at China's intransigence and ASEAN's failure to break the impasse over DoC implementation. As ASEAN Chair in 2011, Indonesia articulated regional concerns and frustrations. Foreign Minister Marty Natalegawa warned that unless a breakthrough was achieved the dispute could "spiral out of control" and undermine regional stability, while President Susilo Bambang Yudhoyono declared ASEAN must "send a strong signal to the world that the future of the South China Sea is a predictable, manageable and optimistic one".[15] Fundamentally, ASEAN's inability to make progress towards operationalizing the DoC had called into question its credibility as the custodian of Southeast Asian security — a credibility problem exacerbated by military clashes between Thai and Cambodian security forces at Preah Vihear Temple earlier that year.

With its credibility on the line, ASEAN finally conceded China's objection and in July 2011 a set of implementation guidelines was issued. The offending clause was watered down to read "The Parties to the DoC will continue to promote dialogue and consultation in accordance with the spirit of the DoC".[16] Overall, the guidelines were very disappointing, as they merely reiterated the parties' commitment to promote peace and stability in the South China Sea, pursue a peaceful resolution of the dispute and implement the DoC in a "step-by-step" manner. The Philippines, which had advocated for a more detailed and comprehensive set of guidelines, was the most vocal critic. Foreign Secretary Albert del Rosario complained that "the necessary elements to make the guidelines a success are still incomplete" and therefore the DoC "lacked teeth".[17] China, which had made no concessions, but which had emerged looking like a constructive player in the process, was clearly satisfied with the outcome. Foreign Minister Yang Jiechi called the conclusion of the guidelines of "great significance".[18]

Implementing the DoC, Establishing a CoC

Agreement on the implantation guidelines opened the possibility of progress on two fronts in the ASEAN–China conflict management process: first, cooperative projects; and second, a formal and binding CoC.

The DoC calls for cooperative activities in five areas: maritime environmental protection; marine scientific research; safety of navigation and communication at sea; search and rescue (SAR) operations; and tackling transnational crime.[19] In November 2011, Beijing announced that it was willing to fund joint projects in these areas from a $476 fund set up to improve "connectivity" between ASEAN and China.[20] The JWG began discussing the issue of cooperative projects in these areas in early 2012, and at a meeting in Suzhou, China in September 2013, agreement was reached in principle to establish an SAR hotline.[21] After almost eleven years it was a sign of progress, but it was hardly cause for major celebration.

Even as talks on implementing the DoC continued, the real focus of attention was on the CoC. Among the ASEAN members there was consensus on the need to push forward with a CoC.[22] By mid-2012, ASEAN had agreed on a set of "proposed elements", including avenues to resolve disputes arising from violations or interpretations of the code. Indonesia subsequently used the proposed elements to draw up a "zero paper" that contained several new ideas.[23] However, China's lack of enthusiasm for a code was apparent from the outset. Although in late 2011 Chinese officials had signalled that they were ready to begin discussions on the CoC, by mid-2012 China slammed on the brakes when Vice Foreign Minister Fu Ying declared that the time was "not ripe" for talks to begin.[24] According to China, there was little reason to discuss the code when, in its view, Vietnam and the Philippines were repeatedly violating the DoC (an allegation both countries rejected and also levelled at China itself).[25] Moreover, China also indicated that ASEAN's proposed elements and Indonesia's zero paper could not be the basis for discussions as it wanted to start talks with a clean slate.[26]

China's decision to defer talks with ASEAN on the CoC coincided with two important and interrelated developments. In April–May 2012, a tense standoff between Chinese and Philippine patrol boats occurred at Scarborough Shoal, a tiny reef located near Luzon which is technically not part of the Spratlys but claimed by both the Philippines and China. The incident began when a Philippine warship was prevented by Chinese vessels from detaining Chinese fishermen deemed to be operating illegally in waters surrounding the shoal. Under a U.S. brokered deal, both sides agreed to withdraw: China, however, did not keep to its end of the bargain and kept its vessels on station.[27] Although technically China could argue that it had not "inhabited" the shoal, by exerting de facto control over it Beijing had violated the DoC.

At a meeting of ASEAN foreign ministers in Phnom Penh in July, the Philippines and Vietnam wanted the final communiqué to reflect their concerns over a series of incidents in the South China Sea — including Scarborough Shoal and several cable cutting incidents involving Vietnamese-chartered ships — but Cambodia, which held the ASEAN Chair and which has established close economic and political ties to China under Prime Minister Hun Sen since 1997,[28] refused arguing that the incidents constituted bilateral disputes. Attempts by the foreign ministers to reach a compromise failed, and for the first time since its establishment in 1967 ASEAN was unable to issue a final communiqué.[29] Cambodia was widely criticized for its truculence and even accused of having acted at the behest of China so as to secure continued economic assistance.[30] Singapore's Foreign Minister K. Shanmugam lamented that the fiasco had caused a "severe dent" in ASEAN's credibility, while Natalegawa said it had called into question ASEAN's "centrality".[31] The lack of ASEAN solidarity over the South China Sea had been publicly and embarrassingly exposed. In an effort to restore a semblance of unity, Natalegawa subsequently travelled to five ASEAN capitals. His shuttle diplomacy resulted in a six-point statement that reaffirmed ASEAN's bottom-line consensus but broke no new ground.[32]

New leadership led to some progress in 2013. As Chair, Brunei pledged that the CoC would be an ASEAN priority. Over the next twelve months, Brunei adroitly used its diplomatic skills to maintain consensus among the ten members, thereby preventing a repeat of the July 2012 debacle. But the impasse over talks on the CoC could only be broken by China. In March, Wang Yi was appointed foreign minister and immediately demonstrated greater flexibility on the South China Sea than his predecessor. In April and May, Wang indicated to his ASEAN counterparts that China was ready to begin exploratory talks on the CoC "under the framework of the implementation of the DoC" and in a "step-by-step" manner.[33] China's tactical change was probably designed to relieve pressure from some ASEAN members and other countries over the CoC, and also to enable Beijing to focus attention on the deteriorating situation with Japan over the disputed Senkaku/Diaoyu Islands in the East China Sea.

Progress towards establishing the CoC, however, proved painfully slow. In May, a meeting of the JWG in Bangkok made little headway. In September, in Suzhou, at Beijing's insistence, the ASEAN–China SOM on the implementation of the DoC agreed to delegate formal consultations on the CoC to the lower-level JWG. China also pushed for the creation of a technical experts group at the Track 1.5 or Track 2 level — known as the Eminent Persons Expert Group — though its composition and how it would complement the JWG remained unclear. Moreover, while ASEAN had called for an "early conclusion" to the CoC, Wang Yi dismissed these calls as "unrealistic" and declared China was in "no rush".[34] Accordingly, China had determined the pace of negotiations: dead slow ahead. A meeting of the JWG in Singapore in March 2014, and the SOM in Pattaya in April failed to make headway.[35]

Myanmar assumed the rotating Chairmanship in 2014 and, as with Brunei, promised to make the CoC a priority. Having developed close ties with China during the 1990s and 2000s, but moving to reduce its dependence on its giant northern neighbour from 2011 by initiating political and economic reforms thus paving the way for better relations with the West, observers wondered whether Beijing would be able to influence Naypyidaw as it had with Cambodia in 2012. A week prior to the 24th ASEAN Summit on 10–11 May, China had moved its most advanced oil rig, HYSY-981, to an area south of the Paracels but within Vietnam's claimed EEZ. It was the first time China had deployed an oil rig to disputed waters in the South China Sea, and its presence led to a surge in tensions between Vietnam and China and also provided another test of ASEAN unity. Under Myanmar's chairmanship, ASEAN was able to pass that test when it agreed to Hanoi's request that a stand-alone statement on the crisis be released.[36] On the one hand the statement repeated ASEAN's existing position — that the parties should exercise self-restraint, resolve their disputes peacefully, implement the DoC and work "expeditiously" towards an early conclusion of the CoC. On the other hand, it was important in three respects. First, for the first time since 1995 the ASEAN foreign ministers had expressed "serious concerns" at developments. Second, in the past, ASEAN had avoided commenting on issues associated with the Paracels dispute, which was at the centre of the HYSY-981 crisis. In doing so, ASEAN implicitly recognized that the Paracels dispute affected the peace and stability of the entire region. Third, ASEAN had maintained unity over the issue. However, the Sino–Vietnam standoff — together with the announcement by the Philippines that China was undertaking large-scale reclamation work on seven atolls in the Spratlys[37] — seriously called into question the DoC/CoC process. Since it was signed in 2002, all of the parties have, to varying degrees, violated the spirit, if not the letter, of the

DoC. Yet China's behaviour has been particularly troubling: the cable-cutting incidents off the Vietnamese coast in 2012, harassment of survey ships at Reed Bank in 2011, attempts to block supplies reaching the Philippine Marines on Second Thomas Shoal, the dispatch of HYSY-981 and the reclamation works in the Spratlys can all be interpreted as contravening the "self-restrain" clause in Article V. And while China can technically argue that it has not "inhabited" any "uninhabited" reefs, events at Scarborough Shoal in May 2012 amount to a de facto occupation. If the CoC is designed to prevent such incidents from occurring, then it is clearly at odds with China's strategy to enforce its territorial and jurisdictional claims within the nine-dash line. Little wonder that Chinese Foreign Minister Wang Yi declared his government was in "no rush" to conclude the CoC.[38]

SOUTHEAST ASIAN COUNTRY RESPONSES TO THE SOUTH CHINA SEA

Beyond the ASEAN consensus on the South China Sea, each of the ten members naturally have developed their own positions and policies depending on whether they are a claimant or not, their geopolitical interests and also their bilateral relationships with China and the United States. When analysing individual Southeast Asian responses to the dispute it is customary to divide the ten countries into two groups: the four claimants i.e. Brunei, Malaysia, the Philippines and Vietnam and the six non-claimants i.e. Cambodia, Indonesia, Laos, Myanmar, Singapore and Thailand. However, a more useful dichotomy is to divide the ten members into those countries that make claims and/or have significant economic and strategic interests in the South China Sea (the four claimants plus Indonesia and Singapore), and those ASEAN members which do not perceive a direct stake in the dispute and have developed close political, economic and security ties with China (Cambodia, Laos, Myanmar and Thailand).

The first group of six can be further subdivided into three pairs: Vietnam and the Philippines, who view the dispute as an acute national security issue; Malaysia and Brunei, which have adopted a low-key approach; and Indonesia and Singapore, which are not claimants but which have significant interests in the South China Sea and who have both called on China to clarify its claims and for a speedy conclusion of the CoC. The second group can be subdivided into two groups: Laos, Myanmar and Thailand, which have refrained from expressing strong views on the problem, and Cambodia which, as described earlier, may have been heavily influenced by its close relationship with China. The following sections examine in brief the perceptions and policies of the ten Southeast Asian countries towards the South China Sea dispute.

Vietnam

Vietnam is the key Southeast Asian actor in the South China Sea dispute: it is the only Southeast Asian country to claim sovereignty over the Paracels and all of the Spratly Islands; it is the only Southeast Asian claimant to have clashed militarily with China in the South China Sea (in 1974 in the Paracels and 1988 in the Spratlys); and it occupies more than twenty features in the Spratlys, more than any other claimant. Since the clash at Johnson Reef, the dispute has been a constant source of friction in Sino–Vietnamese relations, though tensions have ebbed and flowed. However, since 2007, and especially during 2010–11 and again in 2014, the dispute has placed a major strain on bilateral relations. As China's neighbour, ideological comrade and major trade partner, Hanoi strives to maintain stable and productive ties with China, but stands ready to parry Chinese thrusts in the South China Sea in both word and, should push come to shove, probably deed.

Sino–Vietnamese interaction in the South China Sea has been characterized by an action-reaction dynamic in which each side protests the other's move as a violation of its sovereignty, followed by a countermove. Two prominent examples illustrate this dynamic. In May 2009, China protested submissions made by Vietnam, and Vietnam and Malaysia, to the United Nations (UN) body that assesses extended continental shelf claims, the Commission on the Limits of the Continental Shelf (CLCS).[39] China's protests provoked counter-protests from Vietnam.[40] In 2012, Vietnam's national assembly passed a "marine law" which reiterated the government's territorial claims in the Paracels and Spratlys.[41] China promptly declared the Vietnamese legislation to be "illegal and invalid" and proceeded to raise the administrative status of Sansha — the administrative body established by China in 2007 to "govern" its territorial claims in the South China Sea — from country to prefectural level.[42]

Quite apart from the ultrasensitive issue of territorial sovereignty, Hanoi views China's moves in the South China Sea as a flagrant attempt to undermine its maritime economic interests. Vietnam's EEZ contains sizeable reserves of oil and gas, while fisheries provide the country with a lucrative export trade. In 2007, China exerted pressure on several oil majors — including BP and ExxonMobil — to withdraw from energy development projects off the Vietnamese coast.[43] Following complaints from the United States, Beijing has been less inclined to use this tactic. However, between 2010 and 2012 China applied a more aggressive means to dissuade energy companies from conducting exploratory work in Vietnam's EEZ by using patrol boats and trawlers to sever equipment towed by survey vessels. The two most serious, and well publicized incidents occurred in May and June 2012, and were condemned by Hanoi as "premeditated attacks" and a "grave violation" of the country's sovereignty.[44] The cable-cutting incidents sparked anti-China protests in Hanoi and Ho Chi Minh City over eleven consecutive weekends.[45] Hanoi was further angered when the state-owned China National Offshore Oil Corporation (CNOOC) invited foreign energy companies to bid for exploration rights in nine blocks at the outer-edge of the nine-dash line, but within Vietnam's EEZ.[46] Disputes over fishing grounds has also been a serious source of tensions in bilateral relations. Hanoi has repeatedly protested China's annual unilateral fishing ban (typically imposed from mid-May to August) in northern areas of the South China Sea as a violation of the country's sovereign rights. During the ban, and also at other times of the year, Chinese authorities have detained and fined Vietnamese fishermen, confiscated their equipment and even fired warning shots at Vietnamese trawlers.

Although Sino–Vietnamese tensions in the South China Sea subsided in 2013, this did not mean that Vietnamese anxieties dissipated. In his keynote address at the Shangri-La Dialogue in 2013, Prime Minister Nguyen Tan Dung alluded to the disconnect between China's attempts to reassure its Southeast Asian neighbours, and its assertive activities in the South China Sea when, without actually mentioning China, he remarked that "Somewhere in the region, there have emerged preferences for unilateral might, groundless claims, and actions that run counter to international law and stem from imposition and power politics."[47] Nguyen's concerns proved prescient. Less than a year after his speech, China had parked HYSY-981 off the coast of Danang and well within Vietnam's claimed EEZ. The deployment of HYSY-981 triggered the gravest crisis in Sino–Vietnamese ties since the normalization of relations in 1991, and arguably since their armed forces clashed along the border in 1979 and in the Spratlys in 1988. Hanoi immediately condemned the presence of HYSY-981 as a violation of its sovereignty and Vietnamese attempts to challenge the flotilla surrounding it resulted in hundreds of ramming incidents.[48] Peaceful anti-China protests in Hanoi and Ho Chi Minh City were followed by attacks on foreign-owned factories which led to the deaths of several Chinese citizens. Although no lives were lost at sea during the ten-week standoff, the large number of skirmishes between vessels of both sides could have resulted in an exchange of gunfire and an unintended escalation of the crisis.

In managing its dispute with China, Vietnam has been pursuing five strategies simultaneously: first, holding regular dialogue with China via government, party and military exchanges; second, as a member of ASEAN, Vietnam has pushed China to implement the DoC and negotiate a CoC; third, Vietnam has sought to "internationalize" the problem by raising it at regional and international forums and by hosting a regular series of academic conferences; fourth, Vietnam has accelerated its defence modernization programme with an emphasis on improving the military's air and naval capabilities to deter China and defend its territorial claims; and fifth, by diversifying the country's foreign policy and signing "strategic/ comprehensive partnerships" with a broad range of countries such as the United States, China, Japan, India and Russia.

HYSY-981 has called into question the efficacy of those strategies. According to Vietnam, when the crisis broke, China refused to discuss the matter through diplomatic, party or military channels. When the first high-level meeting did take place — between Chinese State Councillor Yang Jiechi and Vietnamese Foreign Minister Pham Binh Minh in June — China berated Vietnam for "hyping" the issue and called on it to stop harassing Chinese vessels.[49] A hotline between the two countries established in 2013 for precisely this kind of crisis situation was apparently not utilized. Vietnam persuaded its fellow ASEAN members to issue a statement of serious concern on 10 May, but this did little to ameliorate tensions. Vietnam's recently acquired military hardware — including sophisticated jet fighters, submarines and frigates from Russia — failed to deter Beijing from dispatching the rig, and once it began drilling, Vietnam was keen to avoid a clash with China's superior air force and navy. Instead, Hanoi relied on its coast guard which, outnumbered and outgunned by its Chinese counterpart, looked on helplessly as the rig continued to operate. And while Vietnam's policy of forging relationships with a wide range of countries has no doubt paid economic dividends, during the crisis it was painfully apparent that Vietnam was on its own.

The HYSY-981 incident also exposed fissures within the Communist Party of Vietnam (CPV) on the best way to deal with China. Although decision-making within the CPV is notoriously opaque, several analysts have noted the heated debates within the Party between those who have used the crisis to advocate for a harder line against China and a closer relationship with America, and those who remain distrustful of Washington's intentions and favour closer relations with China for historical and ideological reasons as well as geopolitical realities.[50] No doubt these heated debates will continue until and even beyond the all-important Party Congress in 2016. Yet Vietnam seems to have little choice but to continue with the same strategies. Perhaps the only additional strategy it can pursue is to follow the Philippines' lead and mount a legal challenge to China's claims at the International Tribunal of the Law of the Sea (ITLOS), the dispute resolution body established under UNCLOS. During the crisis Vietnamese leaders had suggested that they were actively considering taking China to international legal arbitration, but once the rig was removed such talk dissipated. Nevertheless, it remains an option, and one that Hanoi will almost certainly reconsider should China send another oil rig into its EEZ.

In late August, Vietnamese Politburo member Le Hong Anh visited Beijing in an effort to mend fences. Although both sides promised to repair relations and avoid actions that would "complicate" the dispute, neither side made any concessions, and within a matter of days Hanoi had accused China of violating its sovereignty by conducting tourist cruises in the Paracels and harassing Vietnamese fishermen.[51] Meanwhile China's state-run press was warning Vietnam not to "play tricks" and urged it to recognize Beijing's expansive claims in the South China Sea.[52] Although by late 2014 Sino–Vietnamese relations had stabilized, many observers felt that another crisis was just a question of time.

The Philippines

Alongside Vietnam, the Philippines is Southeast Asia's other "frontline state" in the South China Sea dispute. Manila's claims to approximately fifty features in the Spratlys — which the government refers to as the "Kalayaan Island Group" in the "West Philippine Sea" — and to Scarborough Shoal has come to overshadow Sino–Philippine relations over the past two decades. Unlike Vietnam, the Philippines has never been involved in a military clash with China, though the two countries armed forces and civilian maritime agencies have been involved in numerous risky and alarming standoffs over contested atolls and maritime resources, and given the acceleration of negative trends over the past few years, a serious military confrontation between China and the Philippines may only be a question of time.

The ebb and flow of tensions in the South China Sea since the end of the Cold War has determined the tenor of Sino–Philippine relations. Ownership of the Spratlys Islands emerged as a source of bilateral discord in the late 1980s, but it was not until China's occupation of Mischief Reef in 1995 that the Philippines came to view the dispute as a major national security problem — and China as a source of threat. In the second half of the 1990s, a militarily-weak Philippines looked on helplessly as China reinforced its position at Mischief Reef, leaving Manila little option but to pursue bilateral and multilateral diplomacy to manage the problem. Relations improved markedly in the first half of the 2000s as President Gloria Macapagal Arroyo (2001–10) took advantage of China's regional "charm offensive" to stimulate trade and investment ties between the two countries in the hope that the Spratlys problem would be relegated to the backburner or, better yet, become a source of cooperation.[53] The 2002 DoC, the 2005 JMSU, and a surge of Chinese investment into the Philippines seemed to indicate that Arroyo's China policy was on the right track. However, by 2007–8 China had reverted to a more assertive posture in the South China Sea, and this coincided with the collapse of high-profile Chinese-funded infrastructure projects under the weight of corruption allegations.[54] Even the JMSU, which the Arroyo administration had championed, was quietly allowed to expire in 2008 when its constitutionality was called into question.[55]

President Benigno Aquino's (2010–present) China policy represents a 180-degree turn from that of his predecessor. Frustrated with the slow progress of the DoC/CoC process, the Aquino government has put forward proposals which it hopes will promote a resolution to the dispute. At the same time, in response to increasing Chinese assertiveness, Manila has strengthened military ties with its treaty ally, the United States, and begun to seriously address the capability deficiencies of the Armed Forces of the Philippines (AFP). Aquino's policies have angered Beijing. But unlike his predecessor, Aquino seems determined to press the Philippines' sovereignty claims in the South China Sea at the expense of economic ties with China.

Aquino's boldest move was made in January 2013 when his government unilaterally submitted Sino–Philippine overlapping jurisdictional claims for legal arbitration at the UN.[56] The Philippine's submission does not seek a resolution of the sovereignty dispute — only the International Court of Justice could adjudicate ownership of the atolls and the consent of all parties would be required for the case to be heard — but challenges

China's claim to sovereign rights within the maritime space encompassed by the nine-dash line. The Philippines requests the UN to issue an award that, *inter alia,* declares China's maritime claims based on its nine-dash line to be contrary to UNCLOS and therefore invalid; requires China to bring its domestic legislation into conformity with UNCLOS; declares China's occupation of certain reefs to be illegal and a violation of Philippine sovereign rights; declares that China has unlawfully claimed maritime entitlements beyond 12 nautical miles (nm) from certain features (including Scarborough Shoal); and requires China to desist from unlawful activities in the Philippines' EEZ, including the exploitation of living and non-living resources.

Manila's audacious move was motivated by the failure of the two countries to resolve their disputes, disappointment with the ASEAN–China conflict management process and a series of Chinese moves which undermined Philippine claims.

Under international law, disputing parties are encouraged to discuss their overlapping claims bilaterally with a view to reaching a mutually-acceptable resolution. According to Manila, despite numerous exchanges and consultations since China's occupation of Mischief Reef, the two sides have failed to resolve their disputes over ownership of insular features, delimitation of maritime zones as well as rights to fishery, energy and mineral resources in the South China Sea.[57]

Other Philippine attempts to resolve the dispute in partnership with the other claimants also failed. In 2011, the Aquino government put forward a proposal to transform the sea into a Zone of Peace, Friendship, Freedom and Cooperation (ZoPFF/C). The ZoPFF/C called on the parties to clarify their maritime claims, designate the Spratly Islands as a disputed zone, demilitarize the atolls and establish a joint development agency to manage undersea resources.[58] Beijing, however, rejected the proposal out of hand, and none of the Philippines' ASEAN partners, except Vietnam, chose to support it, effectively killing the imaginative concept.

A series of moves by China between 2011 and 2012 catalysed Manila's decision to pursue arbitration. In March 2011, two Chinese patrol boats harassed a survey ship near Reed Bank, an area off Palawan Island that is rich in natural gas and within the Philippines' EEZ. The survey ship had been chartered by Forum Energy which had been awarded a contract by the Philippine government to explore for gas.[59] As described earlier, a more serious incident occurred in April–May 2012 when the Philippines was forced to concede Scarborough Shoal in the face of superior Chinese maritime power. These events simply exacerbated Manila's frustration over the inability of ASEAN and China to effectively implement the DoC and negotiate a CoC.

In accordance with its long-standing policy not to submit its territorial, border or maritime boundary disputes to international legal arbitration, China refused to participate in the proceedings citing its "indisputable sovereignty" over all the atolls in the South China Sea and its preference for a bilateral solution.[60] China's foreign ministry declared the Philippine submission was "factually flawed", "contained false accusations" and violated the DoC.[61] Notwithstanding China's objections and refusal to participate in the case, legal proceedings continued. ITLOS appointed an Arbitral Tribunal composed of five judges and on 30 March 2014 the Philippines submitted a memorial in support of its arguments. In the run-up to the deadline for the memorial, China stepped-up pressure on the Philippines to withdraw the case by harassing Filipino fishermen near Scarborough Shoal and, more seriously, trying to prevent the AFP from resupplying a group of marines on a navy ship grounded on Second Thomas Shoal in the Spratlys.[62] Should the Tribunal accept jurisdiction over the case and rule that China's claims are not compatible with UNCLOS, the decision will not be enforceable but will represent a legal and moral victory for the Philippines. It will also put the onus on China to provide legal justification for its expansive claims. China, however, in all likelihood will simply ignore the ruling though that would incur reputational costs. A decision is expected in 2016.

Another strategy adopted by the Aquino government is to modernize the country's armed forces and strengthen its alliance with the United States. *Vis-à-vis* its territorial dispute with China, Manila has always been disadvantaged by the weakness of the AFP. In the wake of the Mischief Reef incident, a defence modernization programme was promulgated in 1995 but never implemented due to lack of funds. Post-9/11, the United States provided financial support to the AFP, but the focus was on helping improve the army's ability to counter internal security threats. In response to Chinese actions at Reed Bank in 2011, however, the Aquino administration raised defence spending, thus enabling the armed forces to place orders for trainer jets from South Korea and radars from Israel.[63] The United States has also been an important source of capacity-building support for the Philippines. In 2011–12, America transferred two refurbished coast guard cutters to the Philippine navy, and the U.S. military has stepped up training exercises with the AFP. Most significantly, during President Barack Obama's trip to the Philippines in April 2014, the two country's signed a ten-year Enhanced Defense Cooperation Agreement (EDCA) that will increase the U.S. military presence in the Philippines on a rotational basis. Under the agreement the U.S. armed forces will be given greater access to Philippine military bases and also allowed to preposition supplies and equipment.[64] Obama's visit to the Philippines was designed to reassure the Philippines of America's "ironclad commitment" to its security, the administration was also at pains to stress that EDCA was not aimed at China.[65] However, America's refusal to clarify the circumstances in which it would support the Philippines if the AFP came under attack in the South China Sea left many Filipinos unconvinced of U.S. commitment.[66] Meanwhile, Chinese media commentaries castigated EDCA as part of a U.S.-led strategy to contain China, and predicted that it would embolden the Philippines to become more assertive in the South China Sea.[67]

Malaysia and Brunei

Malaysia and Brunei have adopted a very different approach to the dispute than Vietnam and the Philippines. Both countries have tended to downplay tensions in the South China Sea and in contrast to Hanoi and Manila, the dispute has thus far not generated major diplomatic or military tensions in their relationships with Beijing. Malaysia and Brunei have been strong proponents of the consensus-based ASEAN-approach to the problem, including the implementation of the DoC and the need for a CoC. However, neither country has been supportive of their fellow claimants in their various maritime run-ins with China, nor Philippine initiatives such as the ZoPFF/C or its legal challenge to Beijing's claims at the UN. Malaysia and Brunei's relatively relaxed positions over the South China Sea is partly due to cordial political ties and partly because of the luxury of distance from China compared to Vietnam and the Philippines. Nevertheless, continued Chinese assertiveness in an effort to enforce its territorial and jurisdictional claims to the outer limits of the nine-dash line could well strain bilateral relations and impel Malaysia and Brunei to recalibrate their policies towards China. Insofar as Malaysia is concerned, this recalibration may already be underway due to PLA-Navy exercises near the contested James Shoal in 2013–14.

Malaysia claims twelve atolls in the Spratlys archipelago and occupies five. Since the late 1980s the imperative to defend those territorial claims has been a major factor in the country's defence modernization programme, including the acquisition in 2009 of two French-built submarines home ported in Sabah close to the Malaysian-occupied atolls. Malaysia has also forged a strong defence and security relationship with the United States over the past four decades in recognition of America's indispensable role as regional balancer. In contrast, Malaysia's military-to-military ties with China are extremely thin.[68] Yet even as Malaysia equips its arms forces for conflict scenarios in the South China Sea, and nurtures close defence ties with Washington, its official line since the early 1990s has been that a rising China presents economic opportunities rather than strategic threats. As a consequence, Malaysia's China policy has been focused on growing trade and investment links with Asia's largest economy.

While the development of Sino–Malaysian relations has not been impeded by the dispute, nor has it been completely immune from it. Rising tensions in the late 2000s prompted Malaysia's leaders to call for the faster implementation of the DoC and a peaceful resolution of the dispute in accordance with international law.[69] Absent a resolution, Malaysia has promoted joint development as a way to lower tensions, and has suggested the Thailand–Malaysia joint development zone in the Gulf of Thailand as a possible model.[70] However, Malaysia's confidence that the South China Sea dispute would not upset the positive tenor of bilateral relations received a jolt in March 2013 when four Chinese warships conducted a high-profile amphibious landing exercise near James Shoal, a mere 80 km from the Malaysian coast. The PLA-Navy's presence near the disputed atoll — which lies within Malaysia's EEZ — unnerved the country's security establishment and led one observer to opine that the incident had undermined Sino–Malaysian relations and may have even "sowed the seeds for Malaysia to rethink its China strategy".[71] Within a year, the PLA-Navy had conducted another exercise near James Shoal.[72] Though the Malaysian authorities chose to downplay the first incident, and denied that the second had ever taken place, increased Chinese assertiveness in the southern area of the South China Sea is likely to have been a factor in the government's decision to construct a small naval base near to James Shoal and establish a marine corps with U.S. assistance.[73] Should the situation deteriorate, Malaysia may well increase cooperation and coordination with the other claimants, strengthen its military presence in the South China Sea and step up security ties with America — none of which would sit well with Beijing.

Although Brunei is always listed as a claimant in the South China Sea dispute, unlike the other claimants it has never formally made a sovereignty claim to, nor occupied, any of the features in the Spratlys, including the two low-tide elevations — Louisa Reef and Rifleman Bank — inside its EEZ. Nevertheless, because of China's sovereignty claim to the disputed atolls, and the fact that the nine-dash line significantly cuts into Brunei's EEZ, Beijing and Bandar Seri Begawan are rival claimants (in 2009 Malaysia dropped its claim to Louisa Reef when it recognized Brunei's EEZ[74]). Brunei and China have not discussed the dispute substantively, though at summit meetings between leaders of the two countries China has often pushed the idea of joint development.[75] In 2013, the two countries agreed to strengthen cooperation between their state-owned energy companies and explore joint exploration and exploitation of oil and gas resources.[76] As noted earlier, as ASEAN Chair in 2013 Brunei did an excellent job of ensuring ASEAN consensus was maintained and that the dispute did not disrupt any of its meetings.

Indonesia and Singapore

Neither Indonesia nor Singapore take a position on the territorial claims of the various parties in the South China Sea. However, as both countries have significant economic and strategic interests in the South China Sea, and were key players in the negotiations which led to UNCLOS, Indonesia and Singapore have been extremely unsettled by China's expansive claims represented by the nine-dash line.

Indonesia has been more demonstrative in articulating its concerns than Singapore, mainly because if two of the segments of the line are joined together it cuts into the 200 nm EEZ generated by the Natuna Islands in Riau Province. The waters surrounding the Natunas contain significant reserves of natural gas. In 1993, Indonesia asked China to clarify its claims in the area; two years later China responded that while it recognized Indonesia's sovereignty over the Natunas, the maritime boundary between the two countries should be delimited. However, because Indonesia considers the U-shaped line to be incompatible with UNCLOS, it rejected China's assertion and in the mid-1990s increased its military presence on the Natunas as a signal to Beijing of its determination to uphold its sovereign rights.[77]

As an issue in bilateral relations, the Natuna issue did not resurface again until the late 2000s. In May 2009, China attached a copy of the nine-dash line map to a protest note to the CLCS following a joint submission by Malaysia and Vietnam. Indonesia responded in July 2010 by submitting a letter to the UN Secretary General which asserted that the map had no basis under international law and contravened UNCLOS.[78] Indonesian concerns that China intended to enforce its claims within the nine-dash line were reinforced by a series of incidents in 2010 and 2013 in which Indonesian patrol boats were prevented from detaining Chinese fishermen operating illegally in the Natuna's EEZ by armed Chinese vessels.[79] Yet the Indonesian government continued to maintain that it was a neutral party in the dispute because, in its view, the nine-dash line is not compatible with international law, a position reiterated by Foreign Minister Natalegawa in March 2014.[80] Indonesia is thus a self-proclaimed non-claimant in the dispute, though how China sees it is another matter. As noted earlier, Indonesia has been a strong advocate of the DoC/CoC process.

Singapore shares Indonesia's concerns over the legal status of the nine-dash line map. However, it was not until 2011 — following a visit to the city-state by a Chinese patrol vessel which the Chinese media characterized as a sovereignty-reinforcing mission — that Singapore formally called on China to clarify its claims and abide by UNCLOS.[81] Subsequently several of Singapore's foremost legal experts challenged the validity of the nine-dash line.[82] Aside from the legality of China's claims, Singapore has another major concern regarding the dispute: the threat of instability or even conflict in the South China Sea which could disrupt or curtail the free flow of maritime trade on which the country's prosperity depends. In order to protect Singapore's vitally important sea lanes, its armed forces have been equipped with an impressive array of naval and air capabilities, including state-of-the-art frigates, submarines and jet fighters. And since the end of the Cold War, Singapore has actively facilitated America's military presence in Asia by regularly hosting visits by U.S. ships and aircraft. As with Indonesia, Singapore is also a strong advocate of the CoC.

Cambodia, Laos, Myanmar and Thailand

With the notable exception of Vietnam, the states of mainland Southeast Asia do not consider the dispute to be a priority issue in the conduct of their foreign policies. Laos is a landlocked country; Thailand has been preoccupied with its domestic political problems since 2006; Myanmar's maritime interests are located in the Bay of Bengal and Andaman Sea; while Cambodia's coast fronts the Gulf of Thailand. Moreover, since the end of the Cold War (and in Thailand's case since the late 1970s), each of these four countries have forged close economic, political and security ties with China, and none of them wish to disrupt those ties by taking positions on the dispute which run counter to Beijing's interests and preferences. Thus, since tensions began to rise in 2007–8, Laos, Thailand and Myanmar have been *sotto voce* on the problem, while Cambodia has been more sympathetic to China's position than any other ASEAN member. As noted earlier, as chair of ASEAN in 2012 Cambodia acted at China's behest to keep the dispute off the organization's agenda, though in subsequent years it has been more supportive of its ASEAN partners and did not oppose the organization's statement of concern issued in May 2014.

CONCLUSION

Clearly ASEAN cannot "resolve" the South China Sea dispute — that can only be accomplished when the claimants finally muster the political will to pursue a legal or negotiated settlement. Absent a resolution — and based on current trends the prospects are receding — ASEAN will maintain its "neutral" position and attempt to reduce tensions, preserve the status quo and foster cooperation among the parties concerned. To date, however, the ASEAN–China conflict management process has been disappointing. More than a decade after it was signed, the DoC has yet to be even partially implemented and most of the claimants have violated the spirit of the agreement through unilateral and provocative actions. China's behaviour — at Scarborough Shoal, Second Thomas Shoal, Johnson Reef South and through the deployment of HYSY-981 — have been especially troubling. Moreover, Beijing is clearly opposed to a substantive and credible CoC that would constrain its freedom of action in an area in which increasingly has the capabilities to press its sovereignty and "historic rights" claims. As such, it will likely seek to draw out the negotiations for as long as possible until the final result is a largely symbolic agreement that is long on symbolism, short on details and is unlikely to reverse negative trends. The individual responses of ASEAN member states to the problem — which include diplomacy, force modernization, international legal arbitration and silence — have also yielded mixed results and failed to influence China's behaviour. As a consequence, the dispute is likely to smolder for the foreseeable future.

Notes

1. "Asean–China Ties 'Multifaceted', Not Just About Sea Spat", *Straits Times*, 21 May 2014.
2. "ASEAN Trade by Partner Country/Region 2014", ASEAN Secretariat statistics, available at <http://www.asean.org/images/2015/July/external_trade_statistic/table24_asof17June15.pdf>.
3. See Ian Storey, "China's Defence Diplomacy in Southeast Asia", *Asian Security* 8, no. 3 (October 2012): 287–310.
4. ASEAN Declaration on the South China Sea, Manila, 22 July 1992, available at <http://www.asean.org/3634.htm>.
5. Ibid.
6. Ian Storey, "Creeping Assertiveness: China, the Philippines and the South China Sea Dispute", *Contemporary Southeast Asia* 21, no. 1 (April 1999): 95–118.
7. "Philippines says ASEAN has One Voice on Spratlys", Reuters, 5 April 1995.
8. Ibid.
9. Declaration on the Conduct of Parties in the South China Sea, 4 November 2002, available at <http://www.asean.org/asean/external-relations/china/item/declaration-on-the-conduct-of-parties-in-the-south-china-sea>.
10. Christopher Chung, "Southeast Asia and the South China Sea Dispute", in *Security and International Politics in the South China Sea: Towards a Cooperative Management Regime*, edited by Sam Bateman and Ralf Emmers (Abingdon, Oxford: Routledge, 2009), p. 104.
11. Declaration on the Conduct of Parties, op. cit.
12. Ibid.
13. *The ASEAN Charter* (Jakarta: ASEAN Secretariat, 2007), p. 31.
14. Comment made by Termsak Chalermpalanupap, Director of the Political and Security Directorate of the ASEAN Secretariat at "Maritime Security in the South China Sea", Center for Strategic and International Studies, Washington D.C., 20 June 2011.
15. "Speed Up Talks on South China Sea Code", AFP, 19 July 2011.
16. Guidelines for the Implementation of the DoC proposed by ASEAN, July 2011.
17. Ibid.
18. Remarks with Chinese Foreign Minister Yang Jiechie before their meeting, U.S. Department of State, 22 July 2011.
19. See Paragraph 6 of the Declaration on the Conduct of Parties in the South China Sea, op. cit.
20. Taylor M. Fravel, "All Quiet in the South China Sea", *Foreign Affairs*, 22 March 2012, available at <http://www.foreignaffairs.com/articles/137346/m-taylor-fravel/all-quiet-in-the-south-china-sea>.

21. "China to Promote Maritime Cooperation with ASEAN Countries", Xinhua News Agency, 15 September 2013.

22. "ASEAN Community in a Global Community of Nations", Joint Communiqué of the 44th ASEAN Foreign Ministers' Meeting, Bali, Indonesia, 19 July 2011.

23. Mark J. Valencia, "Navigating Differences", *Global Asia* 8, no. 1 (Spring 2013).

24. "Sea Code Threatens to Fuel Tensions", *South China Morning Post*, 12 July 2012.

25. "Better to be Safe than Sorry", *China Daily*, 30 July 2012.

26. Author discussions with ASEAN officials, Jakarta, August 2012.

27. "Why there was No ASEAN Joint Communique", Department of Foreign Affairs, Manila, 19 July 2012.

28. See Ian Storey, "Cambodia and China: A Tightening Relationship", in *Southeast Asia and the Rise of China: The Search for Security* (Abingdon, Oxon: Routledge, 2011), pp. 181–88.

29. "S. China Sea Row Forces ASEAN to Forego Communiqué for 1st Time in 45 Years", *Straits Times*, 12 July 2012.

30. Donald K. Emmerson, "ASEAN Stumbles in Phnom Penh", *Asia Times*, 17 July 2012; Ernest Z. Bower, "China Reveals Its Hand on ASEAN in Phnom Penh", Center for Strategic and International Studies, 20 July 2012, available at <http://csis.org/publication/china-reveals-its-hand-asean-phnom-penh>.

31. "Asean Meeting Fails to Reach Agreement on Joint Statement", *Straits Times*, 14 July 2012.

32. "Statement of ASEAN Foreign Ministers on ASEAN's Six-Point Principles on the South China Sea", Cambodian Ministry of Foreign Affairs, 20 July 2012, available at <http://www.mfaic.gov.kh/mofa/default.aspx?id=3206>.

33. "Territorial Spats 'Must Not Harm Asean–China Trust'", *Straits Times*, 19 April 2013; "China and Brunei Darussalam Issue Joint Press Release", Ministry of Foreign Affairs, China, 5 May 2013.

34. "China Warns Against Rush to set Code of Conduct in the South China Sea", Xinhua News Agency, 5 August 2013.

35. "China, Asean to Meet in S'pore for Talks on Code of Conduct", *Straits Times*, 8 March 2014; "ASEAN and China to Continue Building Mutual Trust and Cooperation", ASEAN Secretariat News, 23 April 2014.

36. ASEAN Foreign Ministers' Statement on the Current Developments in the South China Sea, Nay Pyi Taw, 10 May 2014, available at <http://www.asean.org/news/asean-statement-communiques/item/asean-foreign-ministers-statement-on-the-current-developments-in-the-south-china-sea>.

37. "China 'Violated Declaration on Conduct in S. China Sea'", *Straits Times*, 20 May 2014.

38. "China Warns Against Rush to set Code of Conduct in the South China Sea", op. cit.
39 For Vietnam's submission and Chinese protest, see <http://www.un.org/Depts/los/clcs_new/submissions_files/submission_mysvnm_33_2009.htm> and <http://www.un.org/Depts/los/clcs_new/submissions_files/submission_vnm_37_2009.htm>.
40. Ibid.
41. "Vietnam Marine Law Should Not Harm Relations with China: Phuc", Bloomberg, 21 June 2012.
42. "China Summons Vietnam Ambassador to Dispute Maritime Claims", Bloomberg, 21 June 2012; "Spat Over Disputed Islands Intensifies", *Straits Times*, 23 June 2012.
43. "Tussle for Oil in the South China Sea", *South China Morning Post*, 20 July 2008.
44. "Sea-spat Raises China–Vietnam Tensions", *Straits Times*, 10 June 2011.
45. "Hundreds of Vietnamese Protest Against China in Sea Dispute", DPA, 5 June 2011.
46. "Notification of Part of Open Blocks in Waters under Jurisdiction of the People's Republic of China Available for Foreign Cooperation in the Year of 2012", 23 June 2012, available at <http://en.cnooc.com.cn/data/html/news/2012-06-22/english/322127.html>.
47. "Building Strategic Trust for Peace, Cooperation and Prosperity in the Asia-Pacific Region: Nguyen Tan Dung", Keynote Address, Shangri-La Dialogue, 1 June 2013.
48. "China Accuses Vietnam of Ramming Its Ships in Disputed Waters", *Straits Times*, 8 June 2014.
49. "China Scolds Vietnam for 'Hyping' South China Sea Oil Rig Row", Reuters, 18 June 2014.
50. Alexander Vuving, "Did China Blink in the South China Sea?", *The National Interest*, 27 July 2014; Zachary Abuza, "Vietnam Buckles Under Chinese Pressure", *Asia Times Online*, 29 July 2014.
51. "China Wants to Mend Ties with Vietnam: Xinhua", *Thanh Nien*, 28 August 2014.
52. Ke Xiaozhai, "Hanoi Should Give Up on Opportunism", *Global Times*, 4 September 2014.
53. See Storey, *Southeast Asia and the Rise of China*, op. cit., pp. 259–64.
54. Ian Storey, "Trouble and Strife in the South China Sea Part II: The Philippines and China", *China Brief*, vol. 8, issue 9 (28 April 2008).
55. Barry Wain, "Manila's Bungle in the South China Sea", *Far Eastern Economic Review* (January–February 2008).
56. Notification and Statement of Claim, Department of Foreign Affairs, Manila, 22 January 2013, available at <http://www.dfa.gov.ph/>.

57. Ibid.
58. Ian Storey, "ASEAN and the South China Sea: Movement in Lieu of Progress", *China Brief,* vol. XII, issue 9 (27 April 2012).
59. Ian Storey, "China and the Philippine: Implications of the Reed Bank Incident", *China Brief,* vol. 11, issue 8 (6 May 2011).
60. "Chinese Ambassador: China Has Indisputable Sovereignty over South China Sea Islands", Xinhua News Agency, 23 January 2013.
61. "China Rejects Philippines' Arbitral Request: FM", Xinhua News Agency, 19 February 2013.
62. "China Summons Manila Envoy over South China Sea Legal Case", Reuters, 31 March 2014.
63. "Philippines to Buy 12 South Korean Fighters for $422 Million", Reuters, 21 February 2014; "Philippines to Seal P2.68-B Radar Deal with Israel", *Philippine Star*, 6 May 2014.
64. For the full text of the Enhanced Defense Cooperation Agreement, see <http://www.scribd.com/doc/220920869/Enhanced-Defense-Cooperation-Agreement>.
65. "US–Manila Defence Pact 'Not to Curb China'", *Straits Times*, 29 April 2014; "US Pledges 'Ironclad' Military Support", *Straits Times*, 30 April 2014.
66. See, for instance, Ricardo Saludo, "After Aquino: What His Successor Must Fix", *Manila Times*, 27 April 2014; "Can the US be Counted On?", *Manila Times*, 4 May 2014.
67. "Philippines to Push for Sea Conduct Code", *Global Times*, 9 May 2014.
68. Ian Storey, "China's Defence Diplomacy in Southeast Asia", *Asian Security* 8, no. 3 (October 2012): 287–310.
69. See, for instance, comments made by Prime Minister Najib Razak and Defence Minister Ahmad Zahid Hamidi at the June 2011 Shangri-La Dialogue in Singapore.
70. Keynote Address, Prime Minister Najib Razak, 27th Asia-Pacific Roundtable, Kuala Lumpur, 3 June 2013.
71. Tang Siew Mun, "The Beting Serupai Incident", *New Straits Times*, 16 April 2013.
72. "Chinese Ships Patrol Southernmost Territory", Xinhua News Agency, 27 January 2014.
73. "China Not Encroaching on Our Waters", *New Straits Times*, 29 January 2014; Dzirhan Mahadzir, "Malaysia to Establish Marine Corps, Naval Base close to James Shoal", *IHS Jane's Defence Weekly*, 15 October 2013.
74. Ian Storey, "Brunei's Contested Sea Border with China", in *China and Its Borders: Twenty Neighbors in Asia*, edited by Bruce Elleman, Stephen Kotkin and Clive Schofield (New York: M.E. Sharpe, 2012), pp. 37–46.
75. In 2006, for instance, Premier Wen Jiabao suggested joint development to Sultan Hassanal Bolkiah. "Brunei, China Eye Trade Boost", *The Borneo Bulletin*, 1 November 2006.

76. "China, Brunei Agree to Seek Closer Maritime Energy Cooperation", Xinhua News Agency, 11 October 2013.
77. Storey, *Southeast Asia and the Rise of China*, op. cit., p. 199.
78. See <http://www.un.org/Depts/los/clcs_new/submissions_files/mysvnm33_09/idn_2010re_mys_vnm_e.pdf>.
79. Ann Marie Murphy, "The End of Strategic Ambiguity: Indonesia Formally Announces Its Dispute with China in the South China Sea", PacNet #26 (1 April 2014).
80. Evan Laksmana, "Why There is No 'New Maritime Dispute' Between Indonesia and China", Strat.Buzz, 2 April 2014, available at <http://thecardinal.wordpress.com/2014/04/02/why-there-is-no-new-maritime-dispute-between-indonesia-and-china/>.
81. "MFA Spokesman's Comments in Responses to Media Queries on the Visit of Chinese Maritime Surveillance Vessel Haixun 31 to Singapore", Ministry of Foreign Affairs, Singapore, 20 June 2011.
82. See Keynote Address by Professor S. Jayakumar, CIL Conference on Joint Development and the South China Sea, Singapore, 16 June 2011; Tommy Koh, "Mapping Out Rival Claims in the South China Sea", *Straits Times*, 13 September 2011.

7

THE PHILIPPINES AND THE SOUTH CHINA SEA DISPUTE: SECURITY INTERESTS AND PERSPECTIVES

Aileen S.P. Baviera

The geographic configuration of the Philippines — a mid-ocean archipelago consisting of over 7,100 islands and its strategic location at the crossroads of major waterways including the Pacific Ocean, Celebes Sea and South China Sea, make it the quintessential coastal state.[1] Only a few towns or cities in the country are more than 100 km from the coast; 78 per cent of its provinces and 54 per cent of municipalities, almost all major cities and 62 per cent of the population are considered coastal. International navigation straits crisscross the country, including the Babuyan and Balintang Channels, and the Luzon, San Bernardino, Mindoro, Surigao and Balabac Straits. Shipping provides the major means of linking the islands and facilitating movement of domestic goods and people. Moreover, the country's long maritime tradition is reflected in the fact that one out of every four registered workers on the world's oceangoing vessels is a Filipino and that today, the Philippines hosts the world's fourth biggest shipbuilding industry (after China, South Korea and Japan).[2]

The critical importance of the maritime environment on the Philippines' national identity and sense of vulnerability was evident throughout the decades-long negotiations for the United Nations Convention on the Law of the Sea (UNCLOS), when the near exclusive goal of the Philippines was to obtain recognition by other countries of its unique need to exercise sovereignty over the waters connecting the islands in much the same way as it would over its terrestrial domains.[3] Today this "archipelagic doctrine" is enshrined in Part IV of UNCLOS. The Philippines was among the first countries to sign and ratify UNCLOS, though it was not until 2009 that its provisions could be actively implemented following the passage of an amended archipelagic baselines law.

As one of the South China Sea littoral states, the Philippines has long-standing interests in this maritime space, and the islands, waters and resources of the sea that are closest to the country's main archipelago. The South China Sea is vitally important in providing the Philippines with security against external threats, in light of its long irregular coastlines (altogether longer than that of the United States) and the resultant vulnerability to intrusions or attacks. The sea lines of communication (SLOCs) which pass through the South China Sea sustain the Philippines' transport and economic linkages with the rest of the world. Ocean resources, such as fisheries and other marine life and minerals, are a major source of livelihood, nutrition and materials. The Philippines draws 25 per cent of its annual fisheries production from the waters west of Palawan Island.[4]

In its western seaboard facing the South China Sea, which directly borders eleven provinces, past conflicts or tensions have occurred with other states. These states include Japan, which prior to the Second World War had occupied Spratly Island and used it as a base during military operations in Southeast Asia; the Republic of China (ROC) or Taiwan with whom there were disagreements over fisheries and navigation rights following Taipei's occupation of Itu Aba (the largest of the features in the Spratlys) in 1955; Malaysia with whom in the southern reaches there were disputes over fisheries and the unresolved historical issues over Sabah in North Borneo; Vietnam which is a rival claimant over islands and waters in the Spratlys; and China, which has become the biggest security concern for the Philippines in the South China Sea, particularly after its 1994 occupation of Philippine-claimed Mischief Reef in the Spratlys and a standoff between Manila and Beijing over unoccupied Scarborough Shoal in 2012. In addition to interstate conflicts, the Philippines is concerned with a number of other threats that may emanate from the sea including piracy, activities of armed insurgents, smuggling, trafficking in illegal drugs, weapons and persons, oil spills and other environmental hazards that may threaten marine ecosystems and the frequent occurrence of natural disasters at sea.

Following a brief background on Philippine claims in the South China Sea, this chapter will examine recent developments pertaining to the disputes, the conditions that explain the worsening security environment for the Philippines and how they impact the country's political and security interests.

PHILIPPINE TERRITORIAL CLAIMS IN THE SOUTH CHINA SEA

The Philippine claim in the South China Sea centres on a group of features in the Spratly Islands which the government refers to as the Kalayaan Island Group (KIG). These features became the subject of Philippine interest even before the country attained independence in 1946, but Filipino adventurer Tomas Cloma claimed discovery of the islands in 1947 on the grounds that they were unoccupied and belonged to no one.[5] Following the ROC's occupation of Itu Aba in 1955, and until the late 1960s, periodic tensions erupted between Taiwanese troops and Filipino nationals, including local officials and residents of Palawan province who, when visiting the area, would be challenged by ROC military personnel. In response, the Philippines established military outposts on some of the KIG atolls.[6]

In the early 1970s, oil and gas reserves were discovered on the Philippines' continental shelf, leading to explorations in 1976 in the Reed Bank area located 80 km from Palawan province. This was a time of rising tensions in the South China Sea. In 1974–75, after China had seized Vietnamese-occupied islands in the Paracels, Hanoi began occupying features in the Spratlys. The martial law government of then President Ferdinand Marcos issued a decree in 1978 claiming sovereignty over the KIG, citing history, indispensable need and effective occupation and control as justification. Another decree establishing a 200 nautical miles (nm) exclusive economic zone (EEZ) around the main Philippine archipelago was also issued, which included a substantial part of the KIG.[7] Thereafter the Marcos government established a presence on eight of the islands: Thitu Island, Northeast Cay, Loaita Island, Lankiam Cay, West York Island, Flat Island, Nanshan Island and Commodore Reef. Second Thomas Shoal has also hosted a small unit of Philippine Marines since 1999.

Aside from the KIG claim, Philippine Treaty Limits (defined by the 1898 U.S.–Spain agreement known as the Treaty of Paris) continued to shape the outer limits of what the Philippines considers its territorial waters.[8] Some legal scholars questioned the legality of both the KIG boundaries and the Treaty limits, as they appeared to be lines drawn on water rather than maritime zones emanating from sovereignty over land features.[9] From the Philippine point of view, at issue was also the fact that there were territories it owned or claimed that lay outside the KIG and Treaty of Paris limits, such as Scarborough Shoal (known locally as Panatag or Bajo de Masinloc) and North Borneo (a historical claim by heirs of a former Philippine sultan which has been largely dormant but which Manila has yet to officially drop).[10] On the other hand, a certain island that had been granted in 1928 through international arbitration to the Netherlands, and which now belongs to Indonesia (Isla de Las Palmas or Miangas),[11] is situated inside the Treaty limits.

Despite its early ratification of UNCLOS in 1982 (being the eleventh state to do so), without a clear and consistent definition of the metes and bounds of Philippine territory, there was little basis for Manila to pursue either the settlement of territorial disputes or maritime boundary delimitation with its neighbours. This situation only changed in 2009 when the Philippines passed Republic Act 9522, adjusting its archipelagic baselines to comply with UNCLOS. The law also reiterated Philippine sovereignty over the KIG and asserted that baselines over the features, as well as over Scarborough Shoal, shall be determined consistent with the "regime of islands" under UNCLOS.[12] While the new law did not entirely resolve the ambiguity of Philippine claims over the waters of the KIG and within Treaty limits, thereafter the Philippines indicated its serious intent to resolve territorial disputes by recourse to international courts.

In 1988 the Philippines watched with concern as China and Vietnam clashed militarily at Johnson Reef in the Spratlys. This incident, and China's passage of a law on its Territorial Sea and Contiguous Zone in February 1992, led Manila to rally the Association of Southeast Asian Nations (ASEAN) to issue a statement in July — the 1992 Manila Declaration on the South China Sea — calling on the parties to exercise self-restraint and commit to peaceful resolution of the dispute.[13]

Serious military tensions between the Philippines and China began in January 1995 with the discovery that the People's Liberation Army-Navy (PLA-Navy) had occupied Mischief Reef (Panganiban Reef) which is part of the KIG and within the Philippines' EEZ. The PLA-Navy's occupation of Mischief Reef was a wake-up call for Manila. It triggered the Philippine legislature to pass an Armed Forces Modernization Law in February 1995, and subsequently sign a Visiting Forces Agreement (VFA) with the United States in February 1998 that paved the way for the resumption of U.S.–Philippine defence cooperation following a hiatus after the Philippine Senate had voted to terminate the lease on U.S. military bases in 1991.

At the time of the Mischief Reef occupation, the United States made it abundantly clear that it would not take sides in the dispute, and that its main interests were with a peaceful resolution of the dispute and the preservation of freedom of navigation.[14] Fortunately for the Philippines, it was able to secure collective support from ASEAN to discuss the dispute with China, and the ASEAN–China Senior Officials Meeting in Hangzhou in April 1995 marked the first of many multilateral consultations between ASEAN and China concerning the problem.[15]

Since the Mischief Reef incident, Manila's relations with Beijing have experienced ups and downs, with tensions arising particularly following intrusions by Chinese fishing boats and reported attempts by China to set up markers and buoys that Manila feared were precursors to new construction and occupation. A brief naval face-off occurred in 1996,[16] and by the end of the decade the Philippine Navy, coastguard and fisheries authorities, singly or in joint operations, were actively apprehending Chinese fishermen accused of illegally entering Philippine waters.[17] The fishermen were subsequently tried in Philippine courts, leading to wrangling between interest groups including even local stakeholders such as environmentalist non-governmental organizations (opposed to Chinese illegal fishing practices) and an ethic Chinese-dominated Chamber of Commerce in Palawan province,[18] as well as the affected fishing communities on Hainan Island. Manila actively pursued diplomatic initiatives, both bilaterally with Beijing (including agreement on guiding principles for a code of conduct in 1995 and high-level military confidence-building exchanges) as well as multilaterally. The latter took the form of ASEAN–China code of conduct discussions and a tripartite pre-exploration oil survey agreement involving Manila, Beijing and Hanoi known as the Joint Marine Seismic Undertaking (JMSU). Before the ink on the agreements was dry, however, actions undertaken by one side or the other that were perceived as violations of the spirit of the agreements, led to a resumption of the war of words between the Philippines and China.

Efforts at pursuing joint resource development also came to naught. In the case of the short-lived JMSU, the project became entangled in domestic political opposition to then President Gloria Macapagal Arroyo, but ultimately failed because of the Filipino public's suspicion that the government had traded away sovereignty too easily.[19] The JMSU deserves emphasis as the nearest that the Philippines, China and Vietnam have come thus far towards pragmatic "minilateral" functional cooperation. Its failure left unanswered the question of whether joint development of resources might lead to mitigation or even resolution of the disputes. However, it was also a testament to the basic resiliency of Sino–Philippines ties that other aspects of relations, notably trade and people-to-people linkages, continued and even flourished through the highs and lows of the conflict.

While some related disputes and disagreements with Vietnam and Malaysia also emerged during this period, for the Philippines the South China Sea dispute was seen primarily as a test of its relations with China, its largest, closest and most powerful neighbour to the north.

THE DETERIORATING SECURITY SEASCAPE[20]

Many South China Sea experts point to an apparent change in the behaviour and security dynamics among the major claimants and other stakeholders in the disputed areas beginning in 2007–8, resulting in a sharp deterioration in the security environment. The years since then have been especially tense among the various claimants, with the greatest concern arising over more assertive behaviour by the most powerful claimant, China. Actions which fuelled these tensions included the following: construction activities by the Taiwanese authorities on Itu Aba in January 2008;[21] warnings by China to international energy companies (including British Petroleum and Exxon Mobil) in 2007 and 2008 to desist from working with Vietnam in offshore areas;[22] the approval in 2007 by China's State Council to create Sansha City to administer the country's territorial claims;[23] renewed tensions in the Gulf of Tonkin in January 2008 when China accused Vietnam of attacking its fishermen;[24] construction of a submarine base on Hainan Island in 2008;[25] China's unilateral imposition of annual fishing bans and its May 2009 formal submission of its nine-dash line claim in response to the passage of a new archipelagic baselines law in the Philippines and a joint Vietnam–Malaysia submission regarding continental shelf claims to the UN;[26] tensions between the Indonesian Navy and Chinese fisheries administration vessels in mid-2009 near the Natuna Islands following the arrest of seventy-five Chinese fishermen;[27] the planting of the Chinese flag on the South China Sea seabed in 2010;[28] the standoff between the Philippines and China on Scarborough Shoal in 2012; Philippine filing of a case challenging China's nine-dash line before the International Tribunal on the Law of the Sea (ITLOS) in January 2013, which China has rejected;[29] the conduct of PLA activities close to Malaysia's James Shoal;[30] Xinhua's publication of a new "vertical" map including the entire sea in June 2014; China's stationing of an oil rig in the Paracels leading to violent anti-Chinese riots in Vietnam and its reclamation and construction on several reefs beginning in May 2014.[31]

For the Philippines, which continued to experience episodic problems with China since the 1995 Mischief Reef incident, tensions began to mount anew in the first six months of 2011 when Chinese civilian maritime law enforcement vessels harassed the Philippine-chartered energy survey ship *MV Veritas Voyager*[32] near Reed Bank in March and in two separate incidents in May and June severed the cables of Vietnamese survey vessels within Vietnam's EEZ.[33] They further escalated in April 2012 when an attempt by the Philippine Navy to arrest Chinese fishermen who had collected sharks, corals and endangered giant clams in the vicinity of Scarborough Shoal was blocked by Chinese government vessels, leading to a ten-week standoff between the two countries that were publicly played out in their respective media.[34] Efforts by the two sides to negotiate a simultaneous pull-out from the shoal in early June — reportedly facilitated by U.S. Assistant Secretary of State for East Asia and Pacific Kurt Campbell in talks with Chinese Vice Foreign Minister (and former envoy to the Philippines) Fu Ying — failed, as only the Philippine vessels withdrew, leaving the shoal under de facto Chinese control. Philippine Foreign Secretary Albert del Rosario then bitterly accused China of reneging on a commitment to simultaneous withdrawal, while the Chinese Foreign Ministry denied that such an agreement was ever reached.[35] During the height of the standoff, it was reported that the number of Chinese vessels and fishing boats in the vicinity of the shoal reached almost a hundred.

The 2012 Scarborough Shoal standoff was a watershed for Philippine policy, and possibly to some degree for the United States and China itself. Much like the Chinese occupation of Mischief Reef, the resulting Chinese takeover had "changed the facts on the ground" anew. Filipinos were denied fishing rights in what were traditional fishing grounds and part of their country's EEZ. However, compared with the Philippines' KIG claim, this tiny rock had historically, administratively and economically been assumed to be part of the country, as the ancient names "Panacot" indicated in a 1774 Spanish map (predating the use of "Scarborough Shoal" or "Huangyan Dao") and "Bajo de Masinloc" indicate. Founded in 1607, Masinloc is the name of the oldest town in Zambales province.

The loss of Scarborough Shoal provided the impetus for the government in Manila to file suit against China at ITLOS seeking, among others, invalidation of China's nine-dash line as without legal basis in international law. It was also a driver in the Philippine decision to further strengthen security cooperation with the United States, exemplified by the two countries' signing of an Enhanced Defense Cooperation Agreement (EDCA) during a visit by President Barack Obama to Manila in April 2014.

Chinese security analysts considered Chinese actions in Scarborough Shoal so significant that some began to speak of a "Scarborough Shoal model",[36] which involved strategies of "extended coercion" (a play on the United States' "extended deterrence") through which China could pressure U.S. allies even while keeping America itself at a safe distance. More importantly for the Chinese, by relying on "salami-slicing" tactics,[37] and a so-called "cabbage strategy"[38] rather than placing the PLA at the forefront, the United States could not play the deterrent role expected of it. Indeed, it became increasingly apparent that the territorial dispute between the Philippines and China had become an element of the broader U.S.–China strategic competition.

Years before the Scarborough standoff, Chinese opposition to U.S. military activities in its EEZ had also raised tensions in the South China Sea. The most well-known incident occurred in March 2009 when five Chinese-flagged vessels conducted aggressive maneuvers in close proximity to the *USNS Impeccable* which was conducting survey activities close to Hainan Island and within China's EEZ.[39]

An unfortunate convergence of interactive conditions thus appeared to undermine regional stability, among them renewed interest in exploiting energy resources in the South China Sea given the political instability in the Middle East, advances in China's military capabilities, increasing nationalism (particularly in China, Vietnam and the Philippines), efforts by coastal states to consolidate their legal claims, especially continental shelf claims, ahead of the 13 May 2009 deadline set by the United Nations Commission on Limits of the Continental Shelf (CLCS), the failure of cooperative initiatives such as the JMSU and the earlier code of conduct discussions with China, regional arms build-ups, and last but not the least, renewed U.S. determination to maintain its primacy in the Western Pacific through the so-called "pivot" or "rebalance".

Perhaps the most important reason for the uptick in tensions after 2007–8 was changes in China's behaviour. Gradually departing from paramount leader Deng Xiaoping's exhortations to "hide our capacities and bide our time", in 2003 Chinese leaders began to speak of China's "peaceful rise"; then upon realizing the potential blowback against its own predictions of a "rise", they shifted their rhetoric to that of "peaceful development".[40] In military terms the "rise" translated into a rapid improvement in both the quality and lethality of the PLA, dubbed by one observer as a "Revolution in Military Affairs with Chinese characteristics".[41] Increasingly these improvements have allowed the PLA-Navy to conduct operations far from China's shores such as counter-piracy patrols in the Gulf of Aden beginning in 2008. As the PLA continued to modernize, U.S. assessments of Chinese military capabilities began to change, especially with regard to its relative strength in a Taiwan Straits conflict scenario. Moreover, although the direction of Chinese maritime strategy was still being debated within China, other regional states were becoming concerned about the PLA-Navy's growing power projection capabilities.

Meanwhile, following three years of ASEAN–China negotiations on a Code of Conduct (CoC) for the South China Sea, the two sides were able to agree only on a political "declaration" in 2002 that mostly stated principles, rather than the expected legally-binding or more formal "code" that would have instituted clearer rules of behaviour. This agreement was known as the Declaration on the Conduct of Parties in the South China Sea (DoC). It took another nine years before implementation guidelines for the DoC were finalized in July 2011. While discussions were on the backburner, Manila's decision not to extend the JMSU that would have allowed companies from Vietnam and China to participate in oil development in maritime zones close to the Philippines meant the loss of an anchor around which energy cooperation could be built. As mentioned earlier, in 2007–8 China was reported to have begun applying pressure on oil giants BP and Exxon Mobil to abandon offshore projects with Vietnam.[42] And as also noted earlier, in 2011 the Philippines and Vietnam were alarmed when Chinese vessels tried to disrupt oil exploration and survey activities in the South China Sea.[43] To date, there has been no major progress in the CoC negotiations between China and ASEAN nor in joint development initiatives among the claimants.

In 2010, China's Fisheries Administration announced that they had initiated regular patrols in the South China Sea, operating from Sanya on the southern coast of Hainan Island, to "reinforce" Chinese fishing rights.[44] China also continued to upgrade its submarine base on Hainan, and in 2010 for the first time launched large-scale military exercises involving the PLA-Navy's South, East and North Sea Fleets.[45] The latter was an apparent response to U.S.–South Korea military exercises (in the wake of the sinking of the *Cheonan* and Pyongyang's shelling of the South Korean coastal village of Yeonpyeong on 26 March and 23 November 2010 respectively) that China said encroached on its EEZ in the Yellow Sea.[46] China also appeared to be reacting to growing military ties between Vietnam and the United States, as seen in their cooperation in search-and-rescue training and visits by Vietnamese officials to U.S. warships.[47]

More than merely responding to perceived "provocations" from other claimants, China's growing assertiveness, in rhetoric as well as its military posture, was clearly triggered by what it perceived as attempts by the United States to constrain its rising power. Long before the Obama administration had announced that the U.S. military would "pivot" to Asia, the renewed U.S. emphasis on the maritime domain in its National Security Strategy was no doubt a major factor contributing to Chinese nationalism and assertiveness. As early as 2007, U.S. Navy strategy stressed the need for new maritime partnerships, and zeroed in on the importance of military cooperation with Indonesia, Vietnam and India, in addition to its traditional alliances with Japan, South Korea, Australia, the Philippines and Thailand, raising Chinese suspicions of U.S. encirclement.[48] The U.S. Defense Department's *2010 Quadrennial Defense Review Report (QDR 2010)*, on the other hand, emphasized the need to preserve the "global commons", which it defined as

> domains or areas that no one state controls but on which all rely. They constitute the connective tissue of the international system. Global security and prosperity are contingent on the free flow of goods shipped by air or sea, as well as information transmitted under the ocean or through space.[49]

QDR 2010 anticipated that America would be "increasingly challenged in securing and maintaining access to the global commons". China may have felt singled out when the report claimed that *QDR 2010* "gives solid direction on developing capabilities that counter the proliferation of anti-access and area-denial threats, which present an increased challenge to our maritime, air, space, and cyber forces."[50] Other observers were more explicit in saying that the new maritime strategy was directed against a possible "peer competitor", with China as the only possible candidate.[51]

This new security environment raises a number of questions with respect to the management of the South China Sea disputes. The resurgence of Great Power competition of the sort not seen since the end of the Cold War will likely delay any progress towards resolving territorial and maritime boundary claims, especially as far as China is concerned. Indeed these disputes may themselves become areas of contention in Sino–U.S. relations, especially if China were confronted by an array of countries with competing maritime claims but which were also aligned with the United States, e.g. the Philippines, Vietnam, Japan, and to some extent, Indonesia and India.

Then U.S. Secretary of State Hilary Clinton articulated America's position in 2010, as follows:

> The United States supports a collaborative, diplomatic process by all claimants for resolving the various territorial disputes without coercion. We encourage the parties to reach agreement on a full code of conduct. The United States, like every nation, has a national interest in freedom of navigation, open access to Asia's maritime commons and respect for international law in the South China Sea.[52]

Since that time, Washington has found itself hard put to maintain a position of neutrality or the stance of an "honest broker" with respect to the various sovereignty claims. It began to acknowledge that larger strategic interests are at stake, particularly if inaction in the face of Chinese provocations would severely undermine U.S. alliances and the new partnerships that it is trying to strengthen or build, especially with Vietnam, Japan and the Philippines.

THE IMPACT ON PHILIPPINE SECURITY: THREE LEVELS OF ANALYSIS

Against this backdrop of growing complexity and shifting power balances, Philippine policy on the South China Sea over the last decade — spanning the administrations of President Arroyo (January 2001–June 2010) and Benigno S. Aquino III (July 2010–present) — has been pulled in different directions. National policies have been shaped by various sets of factors operating at different levels: the first arising from changes occurring in the international system (i.e. China's rise, America's relative decline, Sino–U.S. competition particularly in the maritime domain); the second pertaining to evolving threat perceptions and conceptions of national interest, with implications for how the security alliance between the Philippines and the United States and the role of regional mechanisms are perceived; and the third by the vicissitudes of domestic politics.

The Impact of Sino–U.S. Competition

From its preoccupation with the post-9/11 "war on terror" and the subsequent military interventions in Iraq and Afghanistan, the United States briefly refocused its attention on the Asia Pacific under the Obama administration, but only to be distracted once more by Middle East issues including the challenge from the new movement Islamic State (IS) in 2014. Moreover, there are perceptions in the region that America is in relative decline *vis-à-vis* China. The strengthening of China's armed forces, especially in the realm of so-called anti-access/area denial (A2/AD) capabilities, is viewed as having the potential to erode the U.S. military's capacity to intervene in crises (e.g. across the Taiwan Straits) in the East Asian littoral. In response, the United States has undertaken major initiatives to strengthen defence ties with traditional allies (including the Philippines) and cultivate new security partners (such as Vietnam).

This has important implications for the Philippines, a formal treaty ally of the United States since 1951, but one where the bilateral security relationship has been laden with controversy since a cooling of ties following the closure of U.S. military bases in 1992. U.S.–Philippine military-to-military ties were normalized after the terrorist attacks of 9/11, when the presence of extremist groups in the southern Philippines with links to al-Qaeda provided Washington with an opportunity to renew military cooperation, particularly in terms of holding training and combined exercises. However, unlike the Cold War *raison d'etre* of the alliance, which was directed at external threats, the U.S. military post-9/11 became involved in supporting the Armed Forces of the Philippines (AFP) in its struggle against domestic terrorist threats.

Even during the Cold War, successive Philippine governments had tried in vain to elicit from Washington a clearer commitment to provide assistance in relation to Manila's own external security needs, particularly with respect to its territorial claims in the South China Sea. Post-Cold War, following the Mischief Reef incident which was a watershed event in Philippine external threat perceptions of China, the United States continued to maintain that it did not take a position on the merits of Manila's claims (or those of any of the parties), and that America's primary interests lay in ensuring freedom of navigation and a peaceful settlement of the disputes. In Philippine eyes, the seeming neutrality and ambiguity of U.S. commitment to assist it in a scenario of armed confrontation in disputed areas undermined the usefulness of the alliance as an instrument for its own hedging policy, possibly leading it to rely more on regional diplomacy, including closer engagement with China. In the meantime, as the Philippines remained preoccupied with internal security challenges, it did not invest in developing external defence capabilities and was thus forced to rely on diplomacy to forestall an escalation of tensions.

Since early 2011, however, particularly following the first Philippines–U.S. Bilateral Strategic Dialogue, the United States has agreed to step up cooperation with the Philippines to upgrade the capabilities of the AFP. This time, unlike the post-9/11 period, the focus has been on improving the AFP's ability to provide for maritime security and territorial defence rather than internal security. In 2011, the United States transferred a refurbished ex-U.S. Coast Guard cutter to the Philippine Navy, followed by another in 2013. The two sides continue to discuss further transfers of military equipment to improve maritime domain awareness, including radars for the country's Coast Watch system, aircraft, helicopters and patrol ships.[53] In the aftermath of the Scarborough Shoal standoff and having filed the arbitration suit against China at ITLOS, in August 2013 the Philippines announced that it was ready to allow "increased rotational presence (IRP)" by U.S. soldiers in various parts of the country. Philippine Foreign Secretary Albert del Rosario stated that, "For Philippine diplomacy, this raises our already deep and historic strategic relations with a key partner to even greater heights. By highlighting our treaty commitments under our Mutual Defense Treaty and the Visiting Forces Agreement, we serve to keep our region stable and secure."[54] Although not quite leading to the establishment of permanent U.S. bases such as those that had existed before 1992, the IRP demonstrated the Aquino government's disposition to engage in some form of balancing behaviour against China.

President Obama's visit to Manila in April 2014, however, gave mixed signals to the Philippines. It resulted in the signing of the EDCA, which emphasized the value of the U.S.–Philippine alliance — EDCA would grant U.S. troops, ships and planes rotational access to facilities of the AFP, but not permanent bases which are prohibited under the Philippine Constitution — with the result of reducing response time should an external threat from a common adversary crystallize. In a statement rarely heard in the recent history of bilateral ties, Obama acknowledged the strategic location of the Philippines and said America has an "ironclad commitment" to the defence of the Philippines in the event of an external attack.

However, he was careful to emphasize that the agreement was not directed against China nor made in the context of territorial disputes. Instead, he expressed support for the Philippine approach of seeking arbitration under UNCLOS and merely reiterated the longstanding U.S. position that

> international law must be upheld, the freedom of navigation must be preserved and commerce must not be impeded … Our goal is not to counter China, our goal is not to contain China. Our goal is to make sure that international rules and norms are respected, and that includes the area of maritime disputes.[55]

Given the perceived decline in U.S. influence and the Philippines' growing economic interdependence with China, one of the key questions confronting Manila is which direction it wishes to take its defence cooperation with the United States. Are rival claimants to the South China Sea, in particular China, perceived to be a significant enough threat that the Philippines might shift to outright balancing behaviour, as opposed to soft balancing or hedging policies? Will Manila then emphasize its bilateral alliance with the United States, and possibly increased coordination with other U.S. allies, at the expense of multilateral diplomacy pursued within the ASEAN framework, and to the exclusion of substantive bilateral engagement with China? More strategically, how will the country's elite and foreign policy establishment assess the impact of relative U.S. decline on the alliance relationship? Will the Philippines envisage for itself a role, possibly along with other regional states, in facilitating what is bound to be a difficult power transition to a post-American world?

Defining Philippine National Interests

Aside from upholding its territorial claims and sovereign rights and jurisdictions in the South China Sea, one of the Philippines' primary interests is to generate revenue from and utilize oil and gas reserves, particularly in the area of Reed Bank. The Aquino government's focus on this area is in part an attempt to correct what it perceives as President Arroyo's blunder of including Reed Bank — which the Philippines considers undisputed — in the area surveyed under the rubric of the JMSU.[56] More frequent sightings of Chinese naval and law enforcement vessels in this area (including the skirmish between a Philippine-chartered survey ship and a Chinese fishery protection vessel in March 2011) and reports of China putting pressure on Western oil companies to desist from operating off the Vietnamese coast, have made clear China's strong opposition to other countries unilaterally drilling for oil, but at the same time underscored the need for the Philippines to do more to defend its rights to those resources. To this end, the Aquino administration pledged to increase defence spending to modernize the country's decrepit navy and air force with the explicit goal of protecting the country's offshore resources. This comes after a decade of single-minded attention by the country's security leaders to the requirements of internal security in relation to counter-insurgency and counter-terrorism.

It is in this context that the country has sought to define its policy on energy resources. The Philippines proposed to ASEAN in 2011 to turn the South China Sea into a Zone of Peace, Freedom, Friendship and Cooperation (ZoPFF/C) which, despite the failure of the JMSU, suggested a continuing interest in the possibility of joint development of ocean resources with the other claimants. A prerequisite to cooperation, according to its proponents in the Department of Foreign Affairs, was that the concerned states need to clarify the status of maritime zones and clearly identify disputed from undisputed areas based on UNCLOS principles. For Manila, the 2009 passage of the Archipelagic Baselines Law, its submission of partial continental shelf claims to the CLCS, its protest against China's own submission of the nine-dash line map to the CLCS (with China filing a counter-protest), and pending bills in Congress on maritime zones as well as archipelagic sea lanes have been steps in this direction.

Another major step — and one which some commentators consider a potential game changer — was the decision in January 2013 to file the case against the nine dash-line and Chinese acts in the Philippines' EEZ at ITLOS. Manila's complaint triggered the formation of an Arbitration Tribunal that has proceeded to discuss the matter even without China's consent or participation in the proceedings. Specifically, the Philippines is requesting the Arbitral Tribunal to issue an award that, among others:

> Declares that China's rights in regard to maritime areas in the South China Sea, like the rights of the Philippines, are those that are established by UNCLOS, and consist of its rights to a Territorial Sea and Contiguous Zone under Part II of UNCLOS, to an EEZ under Part V, and to a Continental Shelf under Part VI;

> Declares that China's maritime claims in the SCS based on its so-called nine-dash line are contrary to UNCLOS and invalid;

> Requires China to bring its domestic legislation into conformity with its obligations under UNCLOS; and

> Requires that China desist from activities that violate the rights of the Philippines in its maritime domain in the West Philippine Sea.

Decisions that are favourable to the Philippines, assuming there would be no obstacles to enforcement, may pave the way for the Philippines to claim its sovereign rights to explore and exploit its EEZ resources, notwithstanding the territorial disputes. However, arriving at any decision may take as long as three to four years, according to experts.[57] Meanwhile, China has stated on numerous occasions that they have no intention of participating in the proceedings nor abiding with the Tribunal's decisions.

As indicated earlier, external defence and the protection of energy resources are also not the only important interests of the Philippines in the South China Sea. Ocean governance and cooperative management by littoral states with respect to maritime security (especially against piracy and terrorism), addressing transnational crime (e.g. illegal trafficking in people, narcotics and arms), marine environmental protection, disaster response, and search and rescue are critically important to the Philippines as the quintessential coastal state. In contrast, how China's expansive claims in the South China Sea inform its approach to ocean management has yet to be spelled out.

Another vital interest of the Philippines is regional security and stability, whereby it seeks cooperation with neighbouring states based on common principles, shared norms and the rule of law. This underpins the Philippines' strong support for a binding CoC, its high expectations and hopes for ASEAN to move together and in the same direction on the matter of the territorial disputes, and its general openness to confidence-building and deepening engagement with China, regardless of the tough rhetoric that has characterized recent dealings. One might even detect risk-taking behaviour on the part of the Philippines when it challenged China to bring the maritime disputes before ITLOS, as some would argue that its claim is no stronger than China's or any of the other claimants.

The emphasis on peaceful, diplomatic, norms- and rules-based solutions to the disputes also underpinned previous Philippine initiatives, both bilateral and multilateral. These include the 1992 ASEAN Declaration on the South China Sea (signed in Manila), and the 1995 Philippines–China bilateral agreement on "principles for a code of conduct" which established working groups for confidence-building measures, fisheries and marine environmental protection. Manila also played an active role in persuading ASEAN and China to negotiate a CoC, resulting in the DoC, and its insistence on moving the agreement forward into a legally binding agreement.

Yet there have also been periods of inconsistency in Philippine diplomacy, such as shifting from emphasis on multilateralism to bilateralism and then back again and blowing hot and cold with Beijing on the South China Sea. To some extent, this inconsistency has been a function of leadership change and regime interests, but they have also reflected

Manila's frustration with bilateral talks with China and disappointment with the ASEAN–China processes. Ultimately, however, the Philippines has thus far prioritized peaceful diplomacy and regional cooperation rather than a major military build-up or outright balancing or containment strategies involving extra-regional partners.[58] In any case, the Philippines does not have the financial means to embark on a major modernization of its armed forces, nor did it think it could fully rely on the United States for support. However, Manila did have other alternatives, such as inaction or free-riding, which is essentially what some of the other ASEAN claimants have been doing. Yet that would have allowed the problems to fester — though ultimately fester they have — due to ASEAN's failure to take collective action and the lack of political will to confront the hard issues. The debacle at the ASEAN Ministerial Meeting in Phnom Penh in July 2012, when for the first time in forty-five years ASEAN ministers did not issue a joint communiqué because of their failure to agree on the text that included mention of tensions at Scarborough Shoal, is evidence of this. Aside from fence-sitting, another option would have been for the Philippines to make even bolder unilateral assertions of sovereignty, such as drawing baselines from the main archipelago to include the KIG and Scarborough Shoal, instead of merely enclosing them in a regime of islands as provided by UNCLOS.[59]

In other words, the Philippines' actions have been directed towards building an atmosphere conducive to establishing cooperative regional regimes, more than they were mere assertions of sovereignty or moves to strengthen its claims.

Domestic Drivers

In analysing the political and security implications of the dispute, it is important to look at the role of domestic politics and especially domestic actors as drivers of the Philippines' South China Sea policy.

The Philippine approach to the disputes and towards China underwent a sea change when power was transferred from President Arroyo to President Aquino. In contrast to Arroyo's readiness to pursue cooperation with China, officials of the Aquino government have not been afraid to take a stronger line with Beijing. The strong nationalist rhetoric and populist appeal of President Aquino (his statement delivered in Filipino included the phrase "What is ours is ours"),[60] echoed by senior diplomatic and defence officials, have struck a chord among ordinary Filipinos who are increasingly wary of Chinese assertiveness. If cyberspace is any indication, the Filipino public has grown resentful at what they see as the arrogance and hubris of the Chinese official and quasi-official media in its war of words with the Philippine government.[61]

In addition, the Aquino administration was all along suspicious of the previous administration's close ties to China. After Arroyo left office, corruption charges were brought against her, some of which implicated Chinese investment projects as well as the JMSU. Arroyo's JMSU initiative had represented a break from the previous position of the Philippine government (under Presidents Fidel Ramos and Joseph Estrada) that it would pursue multilateral solutions to the dispute within the ASEAN framework and international law; she instead accommodated China's preference for a bilateral approach. Arroyo's approach to the South China Sea issue had been criticized as having undermined ASEAN solidarity and damaged Manila's credibility.[62] Since Arroyo's departure, the Aquino government has been hard pressed to try to restore a more multilateralist framework for managing the dispute, as seen in the run up to ASEAN's Phnom Penh meetings in July 2012.

There may be alternative explanations for the Philippines' change of tack from ASEAN-centred multilateralism to China-centred bilateralism, but in tracing the decision-making that led to the JMSU, what stands out is that the policymakers involved in the tripartite agreement were not foreign policy or security experts from the Department of Foreign Affairs, National Security Council or the Department of National Defense, agencies that had long been handling policy on the Spratlys disputes. Instead, certain key individuals, who enjoyed the confidence of President Arroyo as well as the Chinese side, stood out as its main champions.[63]

The military establishment has also become a more influential player in the Philippine's South China Sea policy. In particular, the Aquino administration's focus on upholding the country's territorial sovereignty and sovereign rights in the South China Sea has meant that the navy and air force, which had long been neglected in favour of the army as it tackled internal security threats, are both receiving a larger slice of the budgetary pie. This is arguably long overdue: for too long the Philippines has been exclusively focused inward and not out to the sea where many challenges exist.

Other domestic stakeholders in the dispute include the Philippine Senate, which ratifies treaties and which in recent years has been assertive in helping shape foreign policy (relevant issues being the 1991 vote to close down U.S. bases, and subsequently to approve the VFA). Some senators have spoken of the need to review or even abrogate the 1951 Mutual Defense Treaty with the United States but the debate over this issue has diminished in light of China's more confrontational behaviour. These debates will be informed by both the actions of China and the United States in the coming years.

The business community, which would be the first to be affected if the dispute deteriorated into armed conflict, has yet to make its views publicly known on recent developments in the South China Sea. Moreover, considering that the ethnic Chinese are among the most affluent members of the Philippine business community, some with close links to China, this could develop into a very sensitive issue.

CONCLUSION

As a strategically located maritime nation, the Philippines considers itself a major stakeholder in the South China Sea, with a broad range of interests including territorial claims, economic rights and environmental concerns. Successive governments have therefore taken an active lead in diplomatically engaging the other stakeholders in order to protect and promote those interests. Because of the weakness of its armed forces, and due to its legal traditions and pragmatic outlook, Manila's approach to the dispute has emphasized international legal norms, agreement among the various claimants on codes of conduct and cooperative initiatives.

On another level, however, the Philippines is also engaged in hedging against the possibility of an aggressive China, and thus relies on whatever deterrent effect its alliance with the United States may have on Beijing's assertive behaviour. As with many other countries in the region that have developed close economic ties with China but remain wary of its growing military strength and increasingly assertive posture in the maritime domain, the Philippines must tread a fine line between its desire to have a cooperative relationship with China and its fear of Chinese domination.

The South China Sea, which the Aquino government has now labelled the West Philippine Sea, has become the most critical issue in both Philippine foreign and defence policies. In this maritime domain are intersecting questions for the country involving first and foremost the definition of its territory and therefore its nation-state identity, preservation of its archipelagic integrity and sovereignty, equitable and sustainable access to the ocean's resources for future generations, the character of its relationships with China and ASEAN, the *raison d'être* for the continuing alliance with the United States and its commitment to regional peace and stability.

Notes

1. The phrase "quintessential coastal state" was first used to refer to the Philippines by the UN Partnership in Environmental Management for the Seas of East Asia and has often been used since.

2. The International Maritime Organization estimates that there are 330,000 Filipinos out of 1.5 million seafarers worldwide, making the Philippines the world's largest supplier of sailors. Nilo Palaya, "IMO Secretary General Sekimizu Visits PH", Department of Foreign Affairs, 10 February 2012, available at <http://dfa.gov.ph/main/index.php/newsroom/dfa-releases/4737-imo-secretary-general-sekimizu-visits-ph>; Michael Cohen, "SUBIC Freeport: Hanjin Shipyard Expanding to Hire 10,000 Workers", *Ground Report*, 15 May 2012, available at <http://www.groundreport.com/Business/SUBIC-Freeport-Hanjin-shipyard-expanding-to-hire-1/2946153>; "Philippines Now the Fourth Largest Shipbuilding Country in the World", *Manila Bulletin*, 7 February 2013, available at <http://ph.news.yahoo.com/philippines-now-fourth-largest-shipbuilding-country-world-091605468.html>.

3. Henry Bensurto, "Filipino Archipelagic Agenda for the 21st Century and the South China Sea: Unlocking the Gridlock", paper presented at the Conference on Entering Uncharted Waters? ASEAN and the South China Sea Dispute, Institute of Southeast Asian Studies, Singapore, 18 February 2011. The author was then Secretary General of the Philippine Maritime and Ocean Affairs Commission Secretariat, Department of Foreign Affairs.

4. Bureau of Agricultural Statistics, *Fisheries Statistics of the Philippines 1997–2001* (Quezon City: Department of Agriculture, 2002), available at <http://www.bas.gov.ph/?ids=publications_view&id=87>.

5. Aileen S.P. Baviera, "The Kalayaan Islands (Spratlys) in Philippine Foreign Policy", *Panorama*, vol. 2 (Manila: Konrad Adenauer Stiftung, 1999), p. 64, citing Jose Abueva, Arnold Alamon and Ma. Oliva Domingo, *Admiral Tomas Cloma: Father of Maritime Education and Discoverer of Freedomland/Kalayaan Islands* (Quezon City: UP Center for Leadership, Citizenship and Democracy, 1999). See also Aileen S.P. Baviera and Jay Batongbacal, "The West Philippine Sea: The Territorial and Maritime Jurisdiction Disputes from a Filipino Perspective", 15 July 2013, available at <http://philippinesintheworld.org/sites/default/files/FINAL_West Phil Sea Primer_UP (15 July 2013).pdf>.

6. Baviera, "The Kalayaan Islands (Spratlys) in Philippine Foreign Policy", op. cit., pp. 64–65.
7. "Presidential Decree No. 1599 of 11 June 1978 Establishing an Exclusive Economic Zone and for other Purposes", available at <www.un.org/Depts/los/LEGISLATIONANDTREATIES/PDFFILES/PHL_1978_Decree.pdf>.
8. Lowell Bautista, "The Philippine Treaty Limits and Territorial Waters Claim under International Law", *Social Science Diliman* 5, issues 1–2 (January 2008–December 2009): 107–27.
9. Ibid., citing Joseph W. Dellapenna, "The Philippines Territorial Waters Claim in International Law", *Journal of Law and Economic Development* 45 (1970–71).
10. For background, see website of Philippine Senate President Juan Ponce Enrile, available at <http://www.jpenrile.com/advocacies/article.asp?advocacy=reforms&folder=speech&article=007>.
11. "The Island of Palmas (or Miangas)", in *The Hague Justice Portal,* available at <http://www.haguejusticeportal.net/index.php?id=6142>.
12. Section 2 of Republic Act 9522, 10 March 2009, "An Act to Amend Certain Provisions of Republic Act no. 3046, as Amended by Republic Act no. 5446, to Define the Archipelagic Baseline of the Philippines and for Other Purposes", available at <http://www.lawphil.net/statutes/repacts/ra2009/ra_9522_2009.html>.
13. Declaration on the Conduct of Parties in the South China Sea, 4 November 2002, available at <www.aseansec.org/1196.htm>.
14. Congressional Research Service, CRS Report for Congress, "China's Maritime Territorial Claims: Implications for U.S. Interests", 12 November 2001, p. 15. It was only in 1999 that the United States took a somewhat stronger position, issuing a State Department press guidance dated 11 February that "the United States closely monitors activities in the South China Sea and follows developments regarding China's military modernization."
15. For a more detailed account of the Philippines–China engagement on the South China Sea in the wake of the Mischief Reef Incident, see Aileen S.P. Baviera, "Waltzing with Goliath: Philippines' Engagement with China in Uncharted Waters", in *Living with China: Regional States and China through Crises and Turning Points*, edited by Amitav Acharya, Li Mingjiang and Tang Shiping (New York: Palgrave Macmillan, 2009), pp. 173–92.
16 Ross Marlay Ross and Sam Stanton, "An Unequal Contest: China versus the Philippines in the South China Sea", in *Weaving a New Tapestry, Asia in the Post-Cold War World: Case Studies and General Trends*, edited by William Head and Edwin Clausen (Westport: Praeger, 1999), pp. 143–59.
17. Because of the lack of assets and the huge demands of securing the archipelago, the Philippine navy would be deputized to undertake civilian law enforcement operations or participate in joint operations.

18. Author's interviews, Puerto Princesa City, 1997–99.
19. Manuel L. Quezon III, "Today the Spratlys, Tomorrow Palawan", *Philippine Daily Inquirer*, 27 February 2008.
20. I am grateful to Alexander Vuving who brought to my attention the term "seascape" when we worked together on a special issue of the journal *Asian Politics and Policy*, titled "How China's Rise is Changing Asia's Landscape and Seascape", *Asian Politics and Policy* 4, issue 3 (July 2012): 289–464.
21. "Itu Aba Island [Taiping Island], Spratly Islands", available at <http://www.globalsecurity.org/military/world/taiwan/taiping.htm>.
22. Wikileaks, "(C) BP Prefers to Manage Chinese Pressure over South China Sea in Commercial Channels", *The Telegraph*, 4 February 2011, available at <http://www.telegraph.co.uk/news/wikileaks-files/london-wikileaks/8305028/C-BP-PREFERS-TO-MANAGE-CHINESE-PRESSURE-OVER-SOUTH-CHINA-SEA-IN-COMMERCIAL-CHANNELS.html>; Yee Kai Pin, "China Pressures Exxon, Vietnam on South China Sea Project", *Dow Jones Newswires*, 24 July 2008, available at <http://www.rigzone.com/news/article.asp?a_id=64661>.
23. Lan Shinzhen, "Sansha by the Sea", *Beijing Review*, 5 July 2012, available at <http://www.bjreview.com.cn/nation/txt/2012-07/02/content_464645.htm>.
24. Ian Storey, "Maritime Security in Southeast Asia: Two Cheers for Regional Cooperation", in *Southeast Asian Affairs 2009*, edited by Daljit Singh (Singapore: Institute of Southeast Asian Studies, 2009), p. 50.
25. Thomas Harding, "Chinese Nuclear Submarine Base", *The Telegraph*, 1 May 2008, available at <http://www.telegraph.co.uk/news/worldnews/asia/china/1917167/Chinese-nuclear-submarine-base.html>.
26. Paolo Romero and Pia Lee-Brago, "GMA Signs Baselines Bill into Law, Triggers China Protest", *PhilStar.com.*, 12 March 2009, available at <http://www.philstar.com/Article.aspx?articleId=447737&publicationSubCategoryId=63>.
27. Keith Loveard, "Caution over Natuna", *Jakarta Globe*, 2 July 2009, available at <http://www.thejakartaglobe.com/columns/the-thinker-caution-over-natuna/315800>.
28. "Robot plants Chinese Flag on Seabed", *Associated Press*, 26 August 2010, available at <http://www.ndtv.com/article/world/robot-plants-chinese-flag-on-seabed-47371>.
29. "Philippines to Push Through with UN Arbitration Despite China's Rejection", *GMA News Online*, 20 February 2013, available at <http://www.gmanetwork.com/news/story/295805/news/nation/phl-to-push-through-with-un-arbitration-despite-china-s-rejection>.
30. B.A. Hamzah, "China's James Shoal Claim: Malaysia the Undisputed Owner", *RSIS Commentary* 122/2014, 1 July 2014, available at <www.rsis.edu.sg/wp-content/uploads/2014/07/CO14122.pdf>.
31. For a detailed report, see Rupert Wingfield-Hayes, "China's Island Factory", BBC, available at <http://www.bbc.co.uk/news/special/2014/newsspec_8701/index.html>.

32. "Philippine Military Accuses China in Sea Spat", *Agence France-Presse*, 3 March 2011, available at <http://www.google.com/hostednews/afp/article/ALeqM 5iwEI0PzHfznq6BOGJaFfc94aKKAw?docId=CNG.5eda08e8eb1b42b79c 577796fd7c8cba.261>.

33. "Vietnam Accuses China in Seas Dispute", *BBC News Asia Pacific*, 30 May 2011, available at <http://www.bbc.co.uk/news/world-asia-pacific-13592508>.

34. See "Scarborough Shoal Standoff: A Timeline", *Philippine Daily Inquirer*, 9 May 2012, available at <http://globalnation.inquirer.net/36003/scarborough-shoal-standoff-a-historicaltimeline>.

35. Ellen Tordesillas, "Back Channels of Diplomacy: Trillanes, MVP, US talk to China for PHL", *GMA News*, 21 September 2012, available at <http://www.gmanetwork.com/news/story/274903/news/nation/back-channels-of-diplomacy-trillanes-mvp-us-talk-to-china-for-phl>.

36. Ely Ratner, "Learning the Lessons of Scarborough Reef", *The National Interest*, Center for a New American Security, 21 November 2013, available at <http://www.cnas.org/content/learning-lessons-scarborough-reef#.VCfrw-dDvWE>.

37. The slow accumulation of small changes, none of which in isolation amounts to a *casus belli*, but which add up over time to a substantial change in the strategic picture. See Robert Haddick, "America Has No Answer to China's Salami-slicing", 6 February 2014, available at <http://warontherocks.com/2014/02/america-has-no-answer-to-chinas-salami-slicing/>.

38. According to General Zhang Zhaozhong of the PLA, the "cabbage strategy" consists of surrounding a contested island with concentric layers of Chinese fishing boats, fishing administration ships, maritime enforcements ships, and warships such that "the island is thus wrapped layer by layer like a cabbage". Ibid.

39. "Pentagon says Chinese Vessels Harassed U.S. Ship", *CNN*, 9 March 2009, available at <http://articles.cnn.com/2009-03-09/politics/us.navy.china_1_chinese-ships-chinese-vessels-chinese-media?_s=PM:POLITICS>.

40. Guo Sujian, "Introduction: Challenges and Opportunities for China's Peaceful Rise", in *China's Peaceful Rise in the 21st Century: Domestic and International Conditions*, edited by Guo Sujian (Farnham, UK: Ashgate Publishing Co., 2006), p. 2.

41. *China's National Defense in 2004* (Beijing: Information Office of the State Council of the People's Republic of China, December 2004), available at <http://www.china.org.cn/e-white/20041227/index.htm>. For details, see Jacqueline NewMyer, "The Revolution in Military Affairs with Chinese Characteristics", *The Journal of Strategic Studies* 33, no. 4, (August 2010): 383–404.

42. Greg Torode, "Beijing Pressure Intense in South China Sea Row", *South China Morning Post*, 11 September 2011.

43. Ian Storey, "China and the Philippines: Implications of the Reed Bank Incident", *China Brief* 8, issue 11 (6 May 2011), available at <http://www.jamestown.org/single/?no_cache=1&tx_ttnews%5Btt_news%5D=37902/>.

44. Xinhua News Agency, 26 April 2010.
45. *China Security Report 2011* (Tokyo: Japan National Institute of Defense Studies, 2011), p. 16.
46. "South Korea–US Military Exercises Stoke Tensions", *BBC News Asia Pacific*, 28 November 2010, available at <http://www.bbc.co.uk/news/world-asia-pacific-11855162>.
47. Donald Kirk, "US–Vietnam Ties Strengthen with Military Exercises, to China's Chagrin", *The Christian Science Monitor*, 12 August 2010, available at <http://www.csmonitor.com/World/Asia-Pacific/2010/0812/US-Vietnam-ties-strengthen-with-military-exercises-to-China-s-chagrin>.
48. James Conway, Gary Roughead and Thad W. Allen, "A Cooperative Strategy for 21st Century Seapower", Department of the Navy, Washington D.C., October 2007, available at <http://www.navy.mil/maritime/Maritimestrategy.pdf>.
49. U.S. Department of Defense, *Quadrennial Defense Review Report 2010* (Washington D.C: U.S. Department of Defense, February 2010), p. 8, available at <http://www.defense.gov/qdr/qdr%20as%20of%2029jan10%201600.PDF>.
50. Ibid., p. 103.
51. James Kurth, "The New Maritime Strategy: Confronting Peer Competitors, Rogue States, and Transnational Insurgents", *Orbis* (Fall 2007): 589–90; Christopher Layne, "China's Role in American Grand Strategy: Partner, Regional Power, or Great Power Rival?", *The Asia Pacific: A Region in Transition*, edited by Jim Rolfe (Honolulu: Asia Pacific Center for Security Studies, 2004), pp. 54–80.
52. Hillary Rodham Clinton, Secretary of State, Remarks at Press Availability, National Convention Center, Hanoi, Vietnam, 23 July 2010, available at <http://www.state.gov/secretary/rm/2010/07/145095.htm>.
53. Gilbert Bayoran, "AFP to get Warships, Helicopters", *The Visayan Daily Star*, 7 May 2012, available at <http://www.visayandailystar.com/2012/May/07/topstory8.htm>; "US Military to Help Philippines Monitor Coastal Waters", *The Telegraph*, 13 June 2012, available at <http://www.telegraph.co.uk/news/worldnews/asia/philippines/9328427/US-military-to-help-Philippines-monitor-coastal-waters.html>.
54. "Statement of the Hon. Albert F. Del Rosario at the Media Briefing to Announce the Start of Negotiations on the PH (DND) — US (DoD) Framework Agreement on Increased Rotational Presence", 12 August 2013, available at <https://www.dfa.gov.ph/index.php/2013-06-27-21-50-36/dfa-releases/510-statement-of-the-hon-albert-f-del-rosarlo-at-the-media-briefing-to-announce-the-start-of-negotiations-on-the-ph-dnd-us-dod-framework-agreement-on-increased-rotational-presence>.
55. Aileen S.P. Baviera, "Implications of the US–Philippines Enhanced Defense Cooperation Agreement", *Asia Pacific Bulletin*, no. 262, East-West Center,

9 May 2014, available at <http://www.eastwestcenter.org/publications/implications-the-us-philippines-enhanced-defense-cooperation-agreement>.

56. Barry Wain, "Manila's Bungle in the South China Sea", *Far Eastern Economic Review* (January/February 2008).

57. For details of the Philippine complaint, see the website of the Department of Foreign Affairs at <https://www.dfa.gov.ph/index.php/2013-06-27-21-50-36/unclos>.

58. Aileen S.P. Baviera, "Philippine Interests and Positions on the South China Sea Disputes", Remarks at a Forum on the South China Sea organized by the Carlos P. Romulo Foundation and Institute of Southeast Asian Studies, Manila, 17 October 2011, available at <http://bavierablogonintlrelations.blogspot.com/2011/11/philippine-interests-and-positions-on.html#more>.

59. Ibid.

60. President Benigno S. Aquino III, Second State of the Nation Address before the Joint Session of Congress, 25 July 2011, available at <http://www.interaksyon.com/article/9275/full-text-of-president-benigno-aquino-iiis-2011-sona-in-english>.

61. Mong Palatino, "Why Filipinos are Angry at China", *The Diplomat*, 11 June 2012, available at <http://thediplomat.com/asean-beat/2012/06/11/why-filipinos-are-angry-at-china/>.

62. Interviews with various Philippine officials, July–September 2011.

63. For details, see Aileen S.P. Baviera, "The Influence of Domestic Politics on Philippine Foreign Policy: The Case of Philippines–China Relations since 2004", RSIS Working Paper 241, available at <http://www.rsis.edu.sg/publications/WorkingPapers/WP241.pdf>.

8

A VIETNAMESE PERSPECTIVE ON THE SOUTH CHINA SEA DISPUTE

Hoang Anh Tuan

The South China Sea has tremendous geostrategic and geoeconomic importance, and the dispute over conflicting territorial and boundary claims resonates across the Asia-Pacific region and beyond. At the root of current tensions is China's expansive maritime claims as indicated by its nine-dash line map, which covers over 80 per cent of the 3.5 million square kilometres of the South China Sea, and which overlaps with the 200 nautical miles (nm) exclusive economic zones (EEZ) of the four Southeast Asian claimants: Brunei, Malaysia, the Philippines and Vietnam.[1] China's growing assertiveness in the South China Sea has contributed to rising tensions since 2007–8. As some of the claimants have been rapidly modernizing their military forces, and nationalist sentiment is rising, the risk of armed conflict is growing. In the event that conflict does break out, it could be wider in scope and longer in duration than previous clashes. The repercussions, moreover, would be global.

Developments over the past several years have given rise to a number of important questions. Has China deviated from Deng Xiaoping's principle of "hiding capabilities and biding time" (*Tao guang, yang hui*) in order to pursue a more assertive foreign policy which challenges the existing regional and international order?[2] What has motivated China's recent assertiveness? Is there a linkage between China's more strong-willed posture and America's "pivot" or "rebalancing" in the Asia Pacific, or between the Philippine and Vietnamese "assertiveness" as claimed by

China? How should the international community respond to the situation in the South China Sea? Most importantly, how can the risk of conflict in the area be reduced? This chapter attempts to answer these questions from the Vietnamese perspective.

CHINA'S GROWING ASSERTIVENESS IN THE SOUTH CHINA SEA

Since the establishment of the People's Republic of China (PRC) in 1949, Beijing has consistently pursued the goal of asserting its sovereignty claims in the South China Sea in an effort to dominate the entire maritime region. However, during the period from 1949 to 1979, China was restricted from enforcing its extensive claims due to the limited capabilities of the People's Liberation Army Navy (PLA-Navy). This did not, however, prevent China from seizing opportunities to expand its presence in the South China Sea when they arose, such as the seizure of the western Paracels from the Republic of Vietnam (South Vietnam) in 1974, which took place as U.S. forces were about to withdraw from that country. China's actions in the Paracels took place at a time when South Vietnam was focusing its attention and resources on countering the military offensive from the Democratic Republic of Vietnam (DRV, or North Vietnam). China deployed overwhelming power, and the PLA-Navy quickly took control of the islands from South Vietnam's demoralized troops. The DRV's measured response does not mean, however, that it approved of China's action.[3] At the time, the DRV's priority was the liberation of South Vietnam and the unification of the country, and its overall relationship with the PRC was good, though it had deteriorated since the mid-1960s.[4] Nevertheless, the generally positive nature of Sino–North Vietnam ties suggested that Beijing had merely "liberated" and "kept" the Western Paracels on behalf of Hanoi with the aim of preventing the United States from using the islands as a launching pad to attack the DRV. The DRV's confidence was based on the fact that China had returned Dragon Tail Island (*Beilong Wei*) in the Gulf of Tonkin in 1956, two years after Hanoi had asked Beijing to take over the island from the defeated French under the Geneva Agreement.[5] However, the situation in the 1970s differed dramatically from that of the 1950s in that China's action was motivated more by territorial ambitions than revolutionary solidarity with Vietnam.

After a brief naval battle with Vietnam in 1988, China took control of Johnson Reef (*Đá Gạc Ma*) in the Spratlys. The seizure represented a turning point in China's strategy because for the first time since 1974

Beijing had demonstrated its readiness to occupy atolls under the control of other claimants by using force instead of seizing unoccupied islands or reefs. Thereafter, the PRC moved to increase its presence in the South China Sea and ramped up its rhetoric regarding ownership of the disputed atolls.

China has adjusted its policies concerning the handling of disputes in the South China Sea at least three times since 2008, each time without diverging from the goal of dominating the entire area within the nine-dash line. At the ASEAN Regional Forum (ARF) meeting in Hanoi in July 2010, 12 of the 27 participating countries expressed concern at developments in the South China Sea, including China's increasing assertiveness.[6] In response, from July 2010 until March 2012, China softened its position somewhat and refrained from taking provocative actions against the other claimants. The third period, starting from March 2012 until the present, has been characterized by a new round of Chinese assertiveness, with the Philippines and Vietnam bearing the brunt.

In spite of a statement to the National People's Congress in March 2012 by Premier Wen Jiabao that China would prioritize good relations with regional states, Beijing's renewed burst of assertiveness, and its efforts to bolster its sovereignty and jurisdictional claims in the South China Sea, has elicited concern from some of its neighbours, especially Vietnam and the Philippines.[7] During the summer of 2011 and 2012, protesters in Hanoi and Ho Chi Minh City called on the government to defend the country's sovereignty and territorial integrity and resist PRC "aggression".[8] In the Philippines, President Benigno Aquino's popularity surged after he took a strong stand against China's assertiveness in the South China Sea.[9]

After China completed its leadership transition from President Hu Jintao and Premier Wen Jiabao to President Xi Jinping and Premier Li Keqiang in 2012–13, Southeast Asian countries had high hopes of China's "second charm offensive". Within a year, both Xi and Li had visited all ten ASEAN members and promised to elevate Sino–ASEAN relations to a new height. However, these hopes were soon dashed, as China undertook a series of assertive actions in the maritime domain, including seizing Scarborough Shoal in 2012, declaring an Air Defence Identification Zone over the disputed Senkaku/Diaoyu Islands in November 2013 and deploying the Hai Yang Shi You-981 oil rig into Vietnam's EEZ between May and July 2014. These and other developments have called into question whether Beijing is serious about negotiating a Code of Conduct for the South China Sea (CoC) with ASEAN and managing the dispute peacefully with the other claimants.

The international community has been increasingly concerned about the South China Sea dispute and its potential impact on maritime security, and freedom of navigation in particular. At the July 2010 ARF meeting, U.S. Secretary of State Hillary Clinton expressed concern over recent developments in the South China Sea. Specifically, Clinton made it clear that America has a national interest in the maintenance of freedom of navigation in the South China Sea.[10] Since then, the United States has continuously raised its concerns over tensions in the area at various regional forums such as the Shangri-La Dialogue, the ASEAN Defence Ministers' Meeting Plus (ADMM-Plus) and the East Asia Summit (EAS).[11]

China has offered a number of justifications in support of its nine-dash line map. First, Beijing has repeatedly stated that it is the legal heir to the claims of the Chiang Kai-shek regime, including the U-shaped line map that the Kuomintang issued in 1947.[12] Second, China has argued that the majority of Chinese people consider the line as China's southern territorial border, and thus no Chinese leader would dare give up the claims and risk a nationalist backlash. Third, China has claimed that the U-shaped line is consistent with international law since China first announced it in 1947, long before the United Nations Convention on the Law of the Sea (UNCLOS) came into effect and, thus, the international community must recognize this historic reality. Fourth, China has pointed to the fact that until recently none of its neighbours objected to the nine-dash line map.[13]

In pursuit of its sovereignty and jurisdictional claims within the nine-dash line, China's policy consists of six strategies. The first is to strengthen administrative control over the Paracel and Spratlys Islands and their surrounding waters. China's recent moves include the upgrading of Sansha city's administrative status on the Paracels from county to prefectural level in 2012.[14] The second is attempts to strengthen its jurisdictional claims by, for instance, submitting the nine-dash line map to the United Nations Commission on the Limits of the Continental Shelf (CLCS) in May 2009. The third strategy is to undertake diplomatic campaigns intended to defend its claims and demonstrate its preparedness to respond to international criticism. For example, on the one hand, China has repeatedly warned the United States to stay out of the South China Sea dispute and stated that the disputes should be settled on a bilateral and not a multilateral basis. On the other, China has begun resorting to UNCLOS to explain its claims in the South China Sea.[15] The fourth strategy is to increase the presence of the PLA-Navy in disputed areas, a move made possible because of China's growing military capabilities and rising defence expenditure. In 2013, China's military budget grew to $116 billion, an increase of 10.7 per cent as compared to the previous year.[16] Between 1999 and 2008, China increased its defence spending by an average of 16.2 per cent a year.[17] The Chinese leadership has prioritized the modernization of the PLA-Navy. At the 18th Congress of the Chinese Communist Party in 2012, China openly stated the goal of becoming a global maritime power.[18] The fifth strategy is to put pressure on energy companies not to explore or drill for oil in the EEZs of the Philippines and Vietnam.[19] Finally, China incites nationalist sentiment at home to elicit broad popular support for its policies in the South China Sea and uses this as leverage in talks with the other claimants.

Thus, China remains intent on finding ways to buttress its sovereignty and sovereign rights claims in the South China Sea. However, by doing so it has increased tensions with the other claimants, and complicated relations with its Southeast Asian neighbours.

CHINA'S STRATEGIC MISCALCULATION OR STRATEGIC DILEMMA?

China's behaviour in the South China Sea has prompted its neighbours, as well as other members of the international community, to question why the Chinese leadership has adopted a much harder line, even aggressive policy, in pursuit of its territorial and sovereignty claims. Regional states, including the major powers, wonder whether the assertion of China's sovereignty and sovereign rights within the nine-dash line is an attempt by Beijing to establish a new regional order dominated by the PRC. Some observers have suggested that China's increasingly militant behaviour in the South China Sea is a response to the "rebalancing" of U.S. military forces towards Asia. Others have argued that China's increased focus on the South China Sea stems from a desire to divert domestic attention outward, away from China's internal problems such as growing social unrest and the political fallout from the Bo Xilai affair, the latter being particularly important in the run up to the 2012 18th National Congress of the Communist Party of China which saw the transfer of power from the fourth to the fifth generation of leaders.[20] In addition to the long list of domestic issues, the political turmoil in Hong Kong in 2014 over how the territory's leader should be chosen might be another reason for China's possible assertiveness in managing territorial disputes with its neighbours.

Whatever the explanation behind Beijing's strategic choices, it appears that the government's calculations have placed the country on a collision course with the other claimants. In the final analysis, China's policy in the South China Sea will be counterproductive for the country's long-term strategic interests for four reasons. First, sovereignty disputes with ASEAN have severely weakened China's position in the region and the world. China's recent assertiveness in the South China Sea has undermined its "peaceful development" thesis and provoked concern within Asia over its future intentions. As such, some have described China as "a lonely power".[21] Contrary to the sense that China's national strength is on the rise, its influence abroad is actually declining.

The second reason is that Washington has made clear that Beijing's policy in the South China Sea undermines U.S. national interests. Accordingly, America has adopted new policies to protect its interests. One is the rebalancing of military forces towards and within Asia. Another is the Trans-Pacific Partnership (TPP), a proposed free trade agreement among eleven countries in the Asia-Pacific region, excluding China. The TPP would blunt China's efforts over the last several years to sign free trade agreements with its Asian neighbours that have excluded America. Both policies are designed to offset China's economic and political influence in Asia, and counter its growing military power. China has perceived these new policies as part of U.S. efforts to encircle or even contain the country.[22] In reality, however, China's assertive behaviour has both prompted and facilitated the tightening of alliance relationships between the United States and Japan, South Korea, Australia, the Philippines and even New Zealand. As part of its policy of rebalancing military forces, the United States will rotate 2,500 marines through Darwin, Australia, and forward deploy up to four littoral combat ships to Singapore. During his visit to Tokyo in April 2014, President Barack Obama reiterated that the U.S.–Japan security treaty covered the defence of the Senkaku/Diaoyu Islands. Continued Chinese assertiveness is likely to galvanize increased strategic cooperation between the United States and its allies and partners, especially if China ignores the interests or concerns of countries with a stake in the South China Sea.

Thirdly, China's behaviour negatively affects its standing with its neighbours in Asia as well as countries in other parts of the world. If a country is to become a global power it must maintain good relations with its neighbours. One reason why the United States was able to expand its influence across the globe is because of its largely trouble-free relations with Canada and Mexico. However, so long as China is unable to enjoy the same level of trust and friendship with its neighbours, global power status will remain out of reach. Moreover, if China cannot maintain close ties with its immediate neighbours, countries further away will be disinclined to pursue policies favourable to PRC interests.[23] China is aware of this problem, and is trying to correct it by prioritizing regional relations.[24]

Fourth, China's moves to enforce its sovereignty claims in the South China Sea has undermined the stable environment it needs to achieve economic development and hence achieve its Great Power aspirations. All of the claimants have strengthened their military capabilities and shown a determination to defend their sovereignty claims. This raises the risk of a conflict that would disrupt maritime traffic in the South China Sea as well as freedom of navigation. As nearly 80 per cent of China's energy supplies pass through the sea, as well as a significant proportion of its exports, the country would be hit hard by instability in the South China Sea.[25]

In addressing the South China Sea problem, Vietnam rejects China's argument that the disputes are exclusively bilateral in nature. In Vietnam's view, the disputes are simultaneously bilateral, multilateral and international. The Paracels is a bilateral dispute between China and Vietnam, while the Spratlys is a multilateral problem involving China, Taiwan, Vietnam, Malaysia, the Philippines and Brunei. Issues such as maritime security, safety of navigation and freedom of navigation are international. Even if the other claimants accepted China's argument that the South China Sea disputes are purely bilateral, this does not mean that Beijing would accept negotiated settlements between the Southeast Asian claimants; in its view the disputes can only be resolved by China and each of the claimants on a one-on-one basis.

Regional developments and global dynamics thus increasingly shape the South China Sea dispute and complicate the PRC's efforts to enforce its claims. Put simply, the more assertive China becomes the more countries in the region unite to resist it, facilitating a greater U.S. military presence in the region. Ultimately, this undermines China's strategic interests in the Asia Pacific and beyond.

China argues that it has indisputable historical evidence to support its claims. Several crucial points are worth noting. First, Imperial Japan was the first country to claim the entirety of the South China Sea during the Second World War.[26] The KMT government made claims to the South China Sea, but those claims never had any traction in the region. China only officially claimed the nine-dash line in May 2009 in a response to Malaysia and Vietnam's joint submission of outer continental shelf claims to the CLCS. At that point, the world began to pay attention to China's claims and the territorial dispute in the South China Sea. Although China claims it has long held sovereign rights within the nine-dash line, in fact, it has neither effectively administered nor controlled the islands, islets or shoals within the nine-dash line. China did not control all the Paracels until it invaded the western part of the archipelago in 1974. In contrast, five countries (China, Brunei, Malaysia, Vietnam and the Philippines) and Taiwan each control some maritime space, which provides a stronger basis for their sovereignty claims.

Second, newly available sources suggest that until 1904, Qing Dynasty maps did not even show the Paracels or Spratlys.[27] They only showed Hainan Island as China's southernmost island. In contrast, various maps in Vietnam's possession indicate that as early as the seventeenth century, the Nguyen Dynasty of Vietnam administered both the Paracels and the Spratlys and exploited their sources.

Third, in legal terms even if China's domestic laws or maps show the nine-dash line, UNCLOS — which the PRC ratified in 1996 — prevails over domestic law. According to UNCLOS, coastal countries are eligible to claim up to 200 nm of EEZ from coastal baselines. Additionally, the territorial waters for uninhabited islands such as the Paracels and Spratlys extend 12 nm from the baseline. Thus, there is a legal foundation for the nine-dash line that overlaps with the EEZs of the Southeast Asian claimants, but that legal construct does not support the vast claims to the entire South China Sea that Beijing makes. A question that emerges from UNCLOS is this: if the nine-dash line has a solid legal foundation as China claims, what has prevented Beijing from challenging the other claimants in an international court?

Fourth, the nine-dash line was drawn randomly with no specific coordinates, thus allowing for various inconsistent interpretations by China. In addition to claiming that the nine-dash line represents the limits of China's "historic rights", some in China now interpret the line as the outer maritime boundary of the Paracels and Spratlys, which are treated as inhabited islands and therefore eligible for a 200 nm EEZ according to UNCLOS. Countries such as the United States, Indonesia and Singapore have repeatedly asked China to clarify the legal basis of the line.[28] China, however, has never responded in a satisfactory manner.

In view of all this, China is now faced with a strategic dilemma: backing away from its claims regarding ownership of the atolls within the nine-dash line would represent a concession from a position of weakness; but continuing to assert China's sovereign rights within the line will further irritate China's neighbours, and exacerbate tensions with countries that are increasingly inclined to stick together and insist on the application of international laws and legal norms to resolve the dispute. As Kishore Mahbubani has noted, "The 'nine-dotted line' that China has drawn over the South China Sea may prove to be nothing but a big geopolitical millstone around China's neck."[29]

CHINA'S ASSERTIVENESS AND REGIONAL AND INTERNATIONAL SECURITY

It is difficult to determine precisely what strategic calculations China's leaders have in mind concerning the South China Sea. Intriguingly, the authors of a recent eight-volume book entitled, *The Rise of Great Powers* (*Daguo Jueqi*), examined the emergence of maritime powers in the eighteenth and nineteenth centuries, including Portugal, Spain, the Netherlands, France, Japan and the United Kingdom. The authors concluded that China should first attain maritime power status before seeking to become a global power because history shows that maritime power does not always assure a country will be able to sustain its global power status especially since power is directly related to the extent to which a country possesses advanced economic institutions.[30] That both former President Hu Jintao and current President Xi Jinping emphasized the need for China to become a maritime power is an indication of how influential this publication has been on the Chinese leadership.[31] Indeed, it appears that China is pursuing a course of action in the South China Sea that follows in the footsteps of past maritime powers, at least as interpreted by *The Rise of Great Powers*. From this perspective, it would seem that dominating the South China Sea is merely the beginning of this grand strategy. Interestingly, it appears that China has had greater success in establishing and maintaining stable relations with large land powers, such as India and Russia. China's relations with Russia are considered to be on a positive keel, while the possibility of border conflict with India has been minimized, although the risk of conflict still exists.

Thus, what is motivating Beijing to press forward with its aggressive strategy, and what are the consequences of this course of action for China?

From Beijing's perspective, the sea lanes that pass through the South China Sea are vitally important for trade and commerce. Preserving a dominant position in the South China Sea allows the PRC to maintain economic growth and fulfill its Great Power ambitions. However, overdependence on these sea routes has also exposed China's Achilles heel; if and when the security situation in the South China Sea deteriorates, China can no longer be confident in its formula for sustained growth, unchallenged regional dominance and increasing global stature.

Many Chinese analysts are of the view that the Obama administration's strategic focus on Asia is aimed at containing China's rise and curbing its influence. China sees the U.S. "pivot" to Asia as overwhelming unfavourable, especially since the PRC still has many unresolved territorial disputes with its neighbours. Classical Realists tend to think that in the chaotic international system, conflict between a rising power, i.e. China, and an established power, i.e. the United States, is inevitable. Many historical lessons have also pointed out that the narrower the power gap between the established and rising power, the higher the possibility of conflict between them. Various forecasts have predicted that China might overtake the United States in terms of GDP by 2020 or 2030 at the latest. However, it remains to be seen whether this advantage in economic power will enable China to wield greater military power than the United States. In the case of America, even though it had surpassed Great Britain in terms of industrial output by 1870, it took another seventy-five years, and two world wars, for it to become the world's most powerful country. It is not clear that China can make the transition from an economic powerhouse to a global strategic force, especially when regional countries combine to thwart its ambitions in the South China Sea.

Taylor Fravel — who has studied patterns of China's behaviour in territorial conflicts with its neighbours since 1949 — has observed that it only resorted to the use of force or took pre-emptive action when it was either in a weak position or envisioned the possibility of a power shift in its opponents' favour.[32] Based on Fravel's argument it would appear that the shift of 60 per cent of U.S. naval assets to the Asia Pacific and the possible impact of American efforts to consolidate strategic partnerships with countries in East Asia is a sufficient explanation for the PRC's recent assertiveness. From China's perspective, if the United States is successful in undertaking the strategic adjustments necessary to position itself as a core power and central influence in Asian affairs, this would diminish the possibility of China's realizing the dream of dominating the South China Sea. This could explain the logic behind China's thinking that there is a firm strategic basis for asserting sovereignty within the nine-dash line sooner rather than later.

However, if China intended to cope with America's Asian rebalance by aggressively staking out its expansive claims in the South China Sea, then it must be chagrined at the way in which some Southeast Asian countries have robustly opposed its efforts, and drawn closer to America, entering into partnerships with Washington that are likely to have long term strategic consequences for China's vision of its role in and relations with the region.

It is important to restate the oft-observed assertion that the rich natural resources in the South China Sea are sufficient motivators for China's assertiveness. Unlike the United States, but similar with Japan and South Korea, China is heavily dependent on the import of energy resources for its economic development. China's dependency on imported fossil fuels will only deepen if its economy continues to grow at the current rate of 8 per cent a year. Meanwhile, the South China Sea is estimated to hold reserves ranging from 28 billion to as high as 213 billion barrels of oil, as well as huge volumes of natural gas.[33] However, although countries such as Vietnam, Malaysia and Brunei have been conducting oil and gas exploitations in their EEZs for decades without any complaints, China is now stating that these countries are "stealing" China's natural resources in its "territorial waters", and that China has never exploited a drop of oil from the South China Sea. China has recently constructed deep-water drilling rigs and announced its intention to operate them in the disputed waters of the South China Sea.[34] The recent announcement by the state-owned China National Offshore Oil Company that had discovered large reserves of natural gas in the South China Sea only emboldens Beijing's claims.[35] Yet it is not clear whether these steps will yield economic dividends in terms of exploitable oil and gas resources. Moreover, it is also unclear that the political costs for China of alienating the other claimants at a time when these countries are primed to cooperate more closely to resist Chinese actions in the South China Sea are worth it.

In China, the South China Sea conflict has fostered the growth of nationalistic sentiments. According to Li Mingjiang, "Chinese netizens have constantly expressed their extremely harsh views on other claimant states, particularly Vietnam, and the Philippines as well as the United States."[36] Fortified by this nationalism, China has taken a provocative path that has alarmed regional claimants, and telegraphed the message that Beijing is prepared to deploy resources, and use them forcefully, to uphold its territorial ambitions. However, China's actions have sacrificed decades of hard work to build mutual trust between it and the countries of Southeast Asia. China's policy towards the region, once lauded as a "charm offensive", seems increasingly to lack any charm at all. Yet Beijing professes a continued commitment to developing sustainable, positive and mutually beneficial relations with its neighbours in the region. Even if both sides are sincere in their efforts to build trust and resolve conflicts, it may take a generation or more to heal the wounds and reset the situation — without any assurances that it would lead to the restoration of the status quo and "normal" ties between the PRC and Southeast Asian nations.

China's assertiveness in the South China Sea has caused serious rifts among ASEAN members. In July 2012, ASEAN failed to reach a consensus on China's activities in disputed waters and was unable to issue a joint statement for the first time in its forty-five-year history. However, the failure to produce a joint statement did not weaken ASEAN or cause the South China Sea dispute to fade away. Instead, it became apparent that China had used its political and economic influence over Cambodia, the ASEAN Chair, to ensure that the dispute was not mentioned in the final communiqué. In the end, thanks to Indonesian Foreign Minister Marty Natalegawa's shuttle diplomacy, ASEAN issued a separate six-principle Statement on the South China Sea for the first time since 1995[37] — an achievement few thought possible. Furthermore, ASEAN members also agreed on the key elements of a Code of Conduct for the South China Sea (CoC), which could serve as a basis for negotiations with China. In the final analysis, the entire episode demonstrated that a divided ASEAN is not in the interests of any country, including China. Thus, to a significant extent, China's campaign to divide and conquer ASEAN instead produced an unprecedented effort to maintain corporate unity when it came to matters of regional security.

It seems that China's assertiveness has only prodded ASEAN members and its dialogue partners to pay closer attention to the dispute. The manner in which Beijing has gone about "managing" the conflict has in effect done more to multilateralize the South China Sea issue in ways that run counter to China's interests. In the period from 2000 to 2007–8, the South China Sea was not a prominent security issue in Asia. However, since then, due to China's growing assertiveness, the dispute has been one of the most debated topics at regional security forums, such as the Shangri-La Dialogue and the ARF. At the ARF meeting in Cambodia in 2012, for instance, 20 out of 27 participants raised the South China Sea dispute, whereas two years previously only 12 countries had done so.

Tensions in the South China Sea have compelled a number of countries in Southeast Asia to increase their defence budgets in an effort to modernize their militaries, particularly their naval forces. The Philippines has sought not only to strengthen its navy, but also to upgrade and tighten its alliance with the United States.[38] The Philippines has also strengthened maritime cooperation with Japan, South Korea and Australia. For its part, Indonesia has also raised its military spending and acquired new fighter jets from Russia.[39] Malaysia may buy four additional *Scorpene*-class submarines from France bringing the number of submarines in its inventory to six.[40] Since 2010, Vietnam has rapidly modernized its air and naval forces with Indian-made multi-purpose BrahMos missiles, 6 *Kilos*-class submarines, 3 frigates and 20 SU-30 MK fighters from Russia.[41] The trend of naval modernization in the region is likely to continue for the foreseeable future.

China's assertiveness has had consequences for Beijing's strategic interests beyond Southeast Asia. Fearful that China will make similar moves over the disputed Senkaku/Diaoyu Islands, Japan has become more strident in defending its territorial claims. In 2012, despite its friendly relations with China, Russia detained as many as 36 Chinese fishermen and seized 2 ships fishing in Russian waters.[42] In addition, as mentioned, China's assertiveness has given a certain momentum to America's Asian rebalance. Finally, developments in the region have compelled countries to seek new forms of alignment. For example, since 2011 the annual Japan–U.S. bilateral security dialogue has been expanded to incorporate India to become a trilateral dialogue. Other newly formed trilateral security dialogues or security triangles include the U.S.–Japan–Australia and United States–Australia–India dialogues. It is no coincidence that the United States' largest multilateral naval exercise in 2012, Rim of the Pacific, included the participation of 22 countries, up from 14 in 2010.[43]

CONCLUSION

As tensions have risen in the South China Sea, the once peaceful sea has been transformed into a potential powder keg and an international security issue. Much of the blame for this situation can be ascribed to China's more assertive, even aggressive behaviour. Yet the more assertive China becomes, the more counterproductive it is for China's regional image and international stature. In order to restore its standing in the region, China needs to regain the respect of its Southeast Asian neighbours. This could be achieved in part if China were to pursue a Charm Offensive 2.0 in a more serious manner, in which Beijing emphasizes the supremacy of international law, and particularly UNCLOS as a basis for resolving the dispute. China should then enter into negotiations with ASEAN for a binding CoC that will establish norms of behaviour, defuse tensions and build trust. Even as it talks to ASEAN about a code, it should also clarify what it is claiming in the South China Sea and abandon the nine-dash line once and for all, despite the monumental change in mindset that this will require. Only the PRC can reverse the negative trends in the South China Sea and win back the trust and goodwill of its Southeast Asian neighbours.

Notes

1. Though Taiwan is a party to the conflict, its position on maritime and territorial issues is similar to that of China. That is, both Taiwan and China's claims are based on identical historical events. See International Crisis Group, "Stirring up the South China Sea (II): Regional Responses", Asia Report N°229 (24 July 2012), p. 2, available at <http://www.crisisgroup. org/-/media/Files/asia/north-east-asia/229-stirring-up-the-south-china-sea-ii-regional-responses>.

2. Some scholars have observed that Deng Xiaoping's principle of "hiding capabilities and biding time" no longer works for two reasons. First, it is now extremely difficult for China to play an active diplomatic role as it is already the second biggest economy in the world and second, because China needs to take a proactive diplomatic approach to address threats to its security. See, for example, Ely Ratner, "The Emergent Security Threats Reshaping China's Rise", *The Washington Quarterly* 34, no. 1 (Winter 2011): 29–44; Aaron Friedberg, *A Contest for Supremacy: China, America, and the Struggle for Mastery in Asia* (New York and London: W.W. Norton & Company, 2011); Randall Schweller and Xiaoyu Pu, "After Unipolarity: China's Visions of International Order in an Era of U.S. Decline", *International Security* 36, no. 1 (Summer 2011): 41–72; and Michael Swaine, "China's Assertive Behavior — Part One: On 'Core Interests'", *China Leadership Monitor*, no. 3 (Winter 2011), available at <http://www.carnegieendowment.org/files/CLM34MS_FINAL.pdf>.

3. Stein Tonneson argues that "The Paracel islands played a significant role in the deterioration of the relationship between China and North Vietnam towards the end of the Vietnam War." See Stein Tonneson, "Sino–Vietnamese Rapprochement and the South China Sea Irritant", *Security Dialogue* 34, no. 1 (March 2003): 60.

4. John L. Gaddis traces the causes of the Sino–Vietnamese War of 1979 to the fragmentation of the Sino–Vietnamese alliance during the late 1960s and early 1970s. See John L. Gaddis, Foreword in *China and the Vietnam Wars, 1950–75*, by Qiang Zhai (Chapel Hill: University of North Carolina Press, 2000), p. x. Nicholas Khoo argues that the causes can be traced to the 1964–68 period. See Nicholas Khoo, "The Breaking the Ring of Encirclement: The Sino-Soviet Rift and Chinese Policy toward Vietnam, 1964–1968", *Journal of Cold War Studies* 12, no. 1 (Winter 2010): 3–42.

5. Fravel Taylor cites Chinese sources indicating Mao Zedong himself ordered the transfer of White Dragon Tail Island (*Bailongwei Dao*) in the Gulf of Tonkin to North Vietnam in an effort to aid Hanoi in its conflict with the United States. See Fravel Taylor, "Regime Insecurity and International Cooperation: Explaining China's Compromises in Territorial Disputes", *International Security* 30, no. 2 (Fall 2005): 63. Hanoi at that time mistakenly interpreted this as China's goodwill and an indication that socialist China had no territorial ambitions towards Vietnam.

6. Greg Torode, "ASEAN Shows Sudden Resolve Against Beijing", *South China Morning Post*, 6 August 2010.

7. "Report on the Work of the Government", delivered at the Fifth Session of the Eleventh National People's Congress on 5 March 2012 by Wen Jiabao, Premier of China's State Council, p. 28, available at <http:online.wsj.com/public/resources/documents/2012NPC_GovtWorkReport_English.pdf>.

8. "Vietnam Breaks Up Anti-China Protests", *The Guardian*, 9 December 2012.

9. President Aquino received an approval rating of 78 per cent in September 2012, a huge surge from a low of 67 per cent in May. See Kim Arveen Patria, "Almost Halfway His Term, Aquino Still Getting High Ratings", *Yahoo! Southeast Asia Newsroom*, 13 December 2012, available at <http://ph.news.yahoo.com/almost-halfway-his-term--aquino-still-getting-high-ratings-085813139.htm>.

10. At the ARF Meeting in Hanoi in July 2010, U.S. Secretary of State Hillary Clinton stated that the U.S. has "a national interest in freedom of navigation, open access to Asia's maritime commons, and respect for international law in the South China Sea". See Lye Liang Fook, "ASEAN and the South China Sea Disputes", *EAI Bulletin* 12, no. 2 (October 2010), available at <http://www.eai.nus.edu.sg/EAI%20Bulletin%20 (Oct2010).pdf>.

11. Leszek Buszynski, "Rising Tensions in the South China Sea and Implications for Regional Security", in *The South China Sea: Towards a Region of Peace, Security and Cooperation*, edited by Tran Truong Thuy (Hanoi: The Gioi Publishers, 2011), pp. 89–100; Ian Storey, "China's Missteps in Southeast Asia: Less Charm, More Offensive", *China Brief*, vol. X, issue 25 (17 December 2010); Jason Szep and James Pomfret, "Tensions Flare over South China Sea at Asian Summit", Reuters, 19 November 2012.

12. "The Bully of the South China Sea", *Wall Street Journal*, 14 August 2012.
13. Author's interviews with Chinese experts in various research institutions such as the China Institute of Contemporary International Relations (CICIR), the China Institute of International Studies (CIIS) and the Shanghai Institute for International Studies (SIIS) during November 2010 to July 2012.
14. "China Establishes Sansha City", Xinhua News Agency, 24 July 2012, available at <http://news.xinhuanet.com/english/china/2012-07/24/c_131734893.htm>.
15. Tania Branigan, "China Lambasts US over South China Sea Row", *The Guardian*, 6 August 2012; Ronald O'Rourke, "Maritime Territorial and Exclusive Economic Zone (EEZ) Disputes Involving China: Issues for Congress", *Congressional Research Service*, 9 April 2013, available at <http://www.fas.org/sgp/crs/row/R42784.pdf>.
16. Kathrin Hille, "China Boosts Defence Spending by 10.7%", *Financial Times*, 5 March 2013.
17. "China Raising 2012 Defense Spending to Cope With Unfriendly 'Neighborhood'", *Bloomberg News*, 5 March 2012, available at <http://www.bloomberg.com/news/2012-03-04/china-says-defense-spending-will-increase-11-2-to-106-4-billion-in-2012.html>.
18. "China Should Become 'Maritime Power', Hu Jintao Says", *South China Morning Post*, 8 November 2012.
19. Jonathan Adams, "South China Sea: The Coming War?", *Global Post*, 27 June 2010; Patrick Barta and Cris Larano, "Drilling Plans Raise Stakes in Disputed Seas", *Wall Street Journal*, 3 August 2011; "Gazprom Falls Victim to China–Vietnam Territorial Dispute", RT.com, 29 June 2012, available at <http://rt.com/business/gasprom-oil-gas-057/>.
20. "Philippines on Alert over Anti-China Protest", Reuters, 10 May 2012, available at <http://www.reuters.com/article/2012/05/11/us-philippines-china-idUSBRE84A05S20120511>.
21. John Lee, "Lonely Power, Staying Power: The Rise of China and the Resilience of US Pre-eminence", *Strategic Snapshot* 10 (Sydney: Lowy Institute for International Policy, September 2011); Zhu Feng, "China's Rise will be Peaceful: How Unipolarity Matters", in *China's Ascent: Power, Security, and the Future of International Politics*, by Robert S. Ross and Zhu Feng (Ithaca and London: Cornell University Press, 2008), pp. 34–54.
22. "Pivotal Concerns", *The Economist*, 11 May 2013; Ely Ratner, "Rebalancing to Asia with an Insecure China", *The Washington Quarterly* (Spring 2013): 21–38; Bonnie Glaser, "US Pivot to Asia Leaves China Off Balance", *Comparative Connections: A Triannual E-Journal on East Asian Bilateral Relations, CSIS/Pacific Forum CSIS*, January 2012; Wang Yong, "The Politics of the TPP are Plain: Target China", *Global Asia*, March, 2013, available at <http://www.globalasia.org/V8N1_Spring_2013/The_Politics_of_the_TPP_Are_Plain_Target_China.html>.

23. As China increases its investment, trade and political relations with Africa, anti-China sentiment on the continent is growing and some countries have become concerned about the possibility of being "colonized" by China. See Benoit Faucon and Sherry Su, "Hostility Toward Workers Cools Angola–China Relationship", *The Wall Street Journal*, 10 August 2010; Loro Horta, "Africa's Poor Don't See China as a Great Power", *Asia Sentinel*, 20 November 2009, available at <http://www.asiasentinel.com/index.php?option"com_content&task"view&id"2154&Itemid"422>; Gavin du Venage, "Is China's Africa Safari Faltering?", *The Diplomat*, 14 November 2011, available at <http://thediplomat.com/2011/11/14/is-china%E2%80%99s-africa-safari-faltering/>.

24. In his address to the National People's Congress in March 2012, Chinese Prime Minister Wen Jiabao mentioned relations with neighbours first, followed by relations with developing countries and big countries. See Tan Yingzi, "Focus Turns to Good Neighborly Relations", *China Daily*, 8 March 2012, available at <http://www.chinadaily.com.cn/cndy/2012-03/08/content_14783969.htm>.

25. Will Rogers, "Rocking the Boat in the Energy Rich South China Sea", *Consumer Energy Report*, 12 July 2012, available at <http://www.consumerenergyreport.com/2012/07/02/rocking-the-boat-in-the-energy-rich-south-china-sea/>.

26. "10 December 1941: Japan Becomes Master of the Pacific and South China Sea", *History Today*, available at <http://www.history.com/this-day-in-history/japan-becomes-master-of-the-pacific-and-south-china-sea>.

27. "Qing Dynasty Map Shows No China Claim in Spratlys", Reuters, 26 July 2012, available at <http://www.abs-cbnnews.com/global-filipino/world/07/26/12/qing-dynasty-map-shows-no-china-claim-spratlys>.

28. "U.S. Calls for More Clarity on South China Sea Claims", Reuters, 23 July 2011; Jennifer Chen, "Understanding the Claims and Claimants in the South China Sea", *East Asia Forum*, 28 June, 2011, available at <http://www.eastasiaforum.org/2011/06/28/understanding-the-claims-and-claimants-in-the-south-china-sea/>; "Singapore Urges China to Clarify South China Seas Claim", BBC World News, 20 June 2011, available at <http://www.bbc.co.uk/news/world-asia-pacific-13838462>.

29. Kishore Mahbubani, "Is China Losing the Diplomatic Plot?", *Project Syndicate*, 26 July 2012, available at <http://www.project-syndicate.org/commentary/is-china-losing-the-diplomatic-plot>.

30. Andrew S. Erikson and Lyle J. Goldstein, "China Studies the Rise of Great Powers", in *China goes to Sea: Maritime Transformation in Comparative Historical Perspective*, edited by Andrew S. Erikson, Lyle J. Goldstein and Carnes Lord (Annapolis, Maryland: Naval Institute Press, 2009), pp. 401–26.

31. "China Should Become 'Maritime Power', Hu Jintao Says", *South China Morning Post*, 8 November 2012; Jeremy Page, "For Xi, a 'China Dream' of Military Power", *Wall Street Journal*, 13 March 2013.

32. Taylor Fravel, "Power Shifts and Escalation Explaining China's Use of Force in Territorial Disputes", *International Security* 32, no. 3 (Winter 2007/8): 44–83.

33. Randy Fabi and Manuel Mogato, "Insight: Conflict Looms in South China Sea Oil Rush", Reuters, 28 February 2012, available at <http://www.reuters.com/article/2012/02/28/us-china-spratlys-philippines-idUSTRE81R03420120228>.

34. Paul Eckert, "China: CNOOC–Nexen Deal Seen Helping China's South China Sea Thrust", Reuters, 3 August 2012, available at <http://uk.reuters.com/article/2012/08/03/china-southchinasea-cnooc-idUKL2E8IVI0M20120803>.

35. Joseph Keefe, "CNOOC: South China Sea Gas Discovery", *World Energy News*, 15 September 2014, available at <http://www.worldenergynews.com/news/cnooc-south-china-sea-gas-discovery-612596>.

36. Li Mingjiang, "Chinese Debates of South China Sea Policy: Implications for Future Developments", RSIS Working Paper 239, p. 5, available at <http://www.rsis.edu.sg/publications/WorkingPapers/WP239.pdf>.

37. ASEAN's six-point position on the South China Sea was issued on 20 July 2012: (i) the full observation of the Declaration on the Conduct of Parties in the East Sea (DoC); (ii) the guidelines for the implementation of DoC; (iii) early conclusion of the Code of Conduct (CoC); (iv) absolute respect for universally recognized principles of international law, including the 1982 UN Convention on the Law of the Sea (UNCLOS); (v) pursuit of self-restraint and renunciation of the threat or the use of force among relevant parties; (vi) peaceful settlement of disputes in accordance with international law, including the UNCLOS. See "ASEAN Announces Six-point Principle on East Sea", Vietnam's Government Website, 20 July 2012, available at <http://news.gov.vn/Home/ASEAN-announces-sixpoint-principle-on-East-Sea/20127/15134.vgp>.

38. Jean Magdaraog Cordero, "U.S., Philippines Reinforce Defense Ties", *Asia-Pacific Defense Forum*, 12 April 2013; "Philippines, U.S. Reinforce Their Alliance", *IIP Digital*, 21 April 2013, available at <http://iipdigital.usembassy.gov/st/english/inbrief/2013/04/20130402145121.html#axzz2Wezzv05P>.

39. "Indonesia to buy 6 Su-30 Jets from Russia", Xinhua News Agency, 30 December 2011, available at <http://www.chinadaily.com.cn/world/2011-12/30/content_14360315.htm>.

40. "Navy Plan to Buy More Submarines", *New Straits Times*, 26 April 2012, available at <http://www.nst.com.my/latest/navy-plan-to-buy-more-submarines-1.77968>.

41. "India to Sell BrahMos Missile to Vietnam", 20 September 2012, available at <http://www.indiandefence.com/forums/indian-strategic-forces/11247-india-sell-brahmos-missile-vietnam.html>; "Vietnam Builds Naval Muscle",

Asia Times, 29 March 2012, available at <http://www.atimes.com/atimes/Southeast_Asia/NC29Ae01.html>; "Vietnam to Buy Second Batch of Gepard 3.9 Class Stealth Frigates from Zelenodolsk Shipyard", *Interfax*, 9 December 2011, available at <http://www.navyrecognition.com/index.php?option=com_content&task=view&id=237>.

42. "Russia Arrests Chinese Fishermen", *Australia News Network*, 18 July 2012.

43. "RIMPAC World's Largest International Maritime Exercise", 19 December 2012, available at <http://www.marinelink.com>.

9

THE SOUTH CHINA SEA DISPUTE: OPTIONS FOR MALAYSIA

Elina Noor

The South China Sea contains approximately 200 insular features, including islets, rocks and reefs. Most of these are only visible at low tide and many are permanently submerged and uninhabitable, rendering current regional tensions seemingly trivial and baffling at first glance. What gives the Spratly Islands dispute its geopolitical salience are the sea lanes which pass through the South China Sea and connect the Indian and Pacific Oceans, and Northeast Asia with Southeast Asia. On an annual basis, more than half the world's shipping passes through the South China Sea carrying manufactured goods and commodities such as crude oil, liquefied natural gas, coal and ore, making the sea a vital life line of energy supply for countries in the Asia-Pacific region and beyond.[1] Below the surface, the South China Sea purportedly holds vast reserves of oil and gas.

This chapter examines Malaysia's interests and claims in the South China Sea, and offers a number of options in moving forward towards a resolution of the dispute. First, it outlines the promise of energy resources as the primary driver behind Malaysia's stake in the South China Sea. Second, it contextualizes Malaysia's claim through the lens of geography and national security. Third, it discusses developments to date with specific regard to Malaysia's claim. Fourth, it explores the possible political, legal and diplomatic options that Malaysia might pursue to resolve the dispute.

THE SOUTH CHINA SEA:
WHAT IS AT STAKE FOR MALAYSIA?

With demand for hydrocarbon resources from Asia's vibrant economies projected to rise, the reserves that are reputed to lie beneath the waters of the South China Sea has become of key interest for regional states and international energy companies. Accurate assessments of those oil and natural gas reserves have been near impossible to obtain due to conflicting territorial claims which have ruled out comprehensive exploratory drilling in the area. It bears caution to note therefore that estimates of energy reserves vary wildly: between 28 to 213 billion barrels (bbl) for crude oil, and between 900 trillion cubic feet (tcf) and 2 quadrillion cubic feet for natural gas.[2] However, as an indication of its potential, there are at least 4 to 6 tcf of proven natural gas reserves near the Spratly Islands, as uncovered by Husky Energy and the Chinese National Offshore Oil Corporation (CNOOC) in April 2006.[3]

Although Malaysia's gross natural gas production has been rising steadily at a rate of 50 billion cubic metres per year,[4] reaching 2.7 tcf in 2010, domestic consumption of natural gas has also increased, reaching 1.1 tcf in 2010 and representing 42 per cent of production.[5] Malaysia does hold fairly substantial reserves: at 83 tcf of proven natural gas reserves as of January 2011, it is the fourth largest source of natural gas reserves in the Asia Pacific, after Australia, China and Indonesia.[6] The current figure, however, represents a drop from 88 tcf in 2008, which is the equivalent of 14.67 bbl of oil or approximately three times the size of 5.46 bbl of crude oil reserves. Given Malaysia's production rate in 2008, the country's gas reserves are expected to last another 36 years,[7] a decrease from 51.2 years at the 2002 rate of production.[8] If estimates by the U.S. Geological Survey and others that 60–70 per cent of the South China Sea's hydrocarbon resources comprise natural gas are correct, the declining trend in Malaysia's gas reserves could be substantially slowed over the medium term.[9]

Some projections forecast that Malaysia could become a net energy importer by the middle of this decade. Either way, the country's oil production has been declining since its peak of 862,000 barrels per day in 2004. The trend is almost certain to continue in an environment of increasing energy demand, maturing offshore reservoirs and expiring petroleum agreements with Malaysia's neighbours.[10]

With the oil and gas sector accounting for about 40 per cent of Malaysia's revenue and its identification as a National Key Economic Area under the government's Economic Transformation Programme, a validation of Kuala Lumpur's claim in the South China Sea would give Malaysia access to hydrocarbon reserves which in turn could help raise total gross national income contribution to US$75 billion by 2020 — Malaysia's target date for achieving fully developed nation status — from $34 billion in 2009.[11]

UNDERSTANDING MALAYSIA'S TERRITORIAL CLAIMS

As with the other claimant countries, Malaysia's interests are partly driven by resource access and economic security. There is, however, a more fundamental aspect to Malaysia's claim rooted in the normative conception of the post-Westphalian nation-state and its attendant principles of sovereignty and territorial integrity, as well as the stark realities of geography. As a country cleaved in two by the vast body of water that is the South China Sea, the imperative of upholding territorial integrity and sovereignty strongly resonates in Malaysia.

At its narrowest point, the distance between Peninsular Malaysia ("west Malaysia") and the states of Sabah and Sarawak (collectively referred to as "east Malaysia") on the island of Borneo is approximately 600 km. At its widest point, that distance increases to about 1,600 km. What this means militarily for a small country with a modest defence budget of about 6 per cent ($4.3 billion) is that the Royal Malaysian Armed Forces (RMAF) has to divide its air, land and sea deployments between separate parts of the country.

In contrast to the ease of transportation afforded by the land borders between Malaysia and Singapore and Malaysia and Thailand, there is no alternative mode of shuttling Malaysians between east and west Malaysia other than by sea and air. Unsurprisingly, the physical distance between Peninsular Malaysia and Borneo has only compounded the perceptual distance between the respective communities in west and east Malaysia. It has also, rightly or wrongly, perpetuated feelings of alienation among east Malaysians from their fellow countrymen to the west. For multi-ethnic Malaysia, where national unity is a paramount concern, managing this distance — real and perceived — is a national security priority.

The challenges of administrating geographically and socio-culturally separated territories feed into official policy and, by extension, Malaysia's claim in the South China Sea. The national defence policy of Malaysia explicitly states that

> the physical separation between peninsula Malaysia, and Sabah and Sarawak by the South China Sea necessitates central attention towards the sea routes and air space between those territories. Any threat or disruption to the sea routes or air space there could detrimentally affect the integrity of both those territories and Malaysia as a whole.[12]

It is this priority, among others, that informs decisions at the highest levels in Malaysia to ensure the country's capability to protect and defend its sovereignty on land and at sea, including its exclusive economic zone (EEZ), continental shelves, strategic maritime routes and air space.[13]

In so doing, Malaysia bases its claims in the South China Sea on international law, including provisions in the 1958 Convention on the Continental Shelf and the 1982 United Nations Convention on the Law of the Sea (UNCLOS). What this translates to in practical terms is a claim based upon continental shelf and EEZ delimitation. This was affirmed in the country's 1979 "Map Showing the Territorial Waters and Continental Shelf Boundaries of Malaysia" (the so-called *Peta Baru* or "New Map").[14] Subsequent public assertions of the territory and features within those boundaries have also been made on the basis of the continental shelf principle: "Malaysia is of the view that islands and reefs in the continental shelf area of Malaysia are owned by Malaysia and it will continue to maintain sovereignty over the islands it considers to be Malaysian territory." [15]

Malaysia's continental shelf claim has been criticized as weak and problematic because neither UNCLOS nor the country's own 1966 Continental Shelf Act refers to the continental shelf as pertaining to the features above sea level, only to the seabed and subsoil.[16] International law dictates that claims to maritime territory arise from sovereignty over land territory rather than the other way around.[17] Despite this, Malaysia's *Peta Baru* claims remain unmoved. Responding to a parliamentary question in 2010, Deputy Foreign Minister Kohilan Pillay explained that unlike China's extensive claim over the whole of the South China Sea, Malaysia's boundary is calculated 200 nautical miles (nm) from the country's base lines.[18]

As further justification of its claim over parts of the Spratly Islands, Malaysia has also maintained effective occupation of a cluster of features in that area within its continental shelf boundaries. A large part of maintaining sovereignty and exercising sovereign rights, as Malaysia learnt from experience twice before the International Court of Justice (ICJ), is effecting acts evidencing an actual, continued exercise of authority (*effectivités*) over the disputed territories showing the intention and will to act as sovereign (*à titre de souverain*).[19] To that end, Malaysia currently maintains a physical presence on five features in the Spratlys in the form of naval and marine research stations on Terumbu Mantanani (Mariveles Reef), Terumbu Ubi (Ardasier Reef), Terumbu Siput (Erica Reef), Terumbu Peninjau (Investigator Reef) and Pulau Layang-Layang (Swallow Island).[20] Pulau Layang-Layang was initially known as Terumbu Layang-Layang (Swallow Reef). At just 7.5 km long and 2 km wide, it housed a Malaysian naval station constructed and supported by members from all branches of the RMAF. Following land reclamation works, the creation of a 50-acre island on one part of the reef, and the development of a dive resort, the island is now more famously known for its diving and tourism facilities. Terumbu Layang-Layang is also home to a marine research station operated by Malaysia's Fisheries Department.[21]

Malaysia's occupation of these features has not been met without resistance by the other claimants. Perhaps the most notable series of confrontations were with Vietnam in the 1980s over Amboyna Cay, on which Malaysia had placed markers in 1978. Malaysia's claim to sovereignty over the reef was justified by the then deputy minister in charge of legal affairs as a "simple matter of geography".[22] In 1979 Vietnam destroyed those markers and occupied Amboyna Cay. To avoid escalating tensions in the South China Sea, Malaysia has refrained from establishing new installations on any of its occupied features since the construction of a naval station on Terumbu Siput in 1999. In the spirit of promoting a "peaceful, friendly and harmonious environment in the South China Sea" and in accordance with paragraph 5 of the 2002 Association of Southeast Asian Nations (ASEAN)–China Declaration on the Conduct of Parties in the South China Sea (DoC), it is unlikely that Malaysia will risk exacerbating the situation by unilaterally constructing structures on other islets in the area.[23]

It is worth pointing out that as imperative as Malaysia's claim in the South China Sea is in the context of territorial integrity, sovereignty and national security, successive governments have so far refrained from beating the nationalist drum to muster domestic support for its claim. Discussions on the South China Sea dispute in Malaysia usually take place behind closed doors, partly to encourage candour but mainly to insulate the issue from unhelpful publicity. Media reports are occasional and short, and commentaries are typically measured. This approach avoids fanning nationalist emotions and ceding control of the discourse to the media and the masses, which could complicate ongoing diplomatic efforts by hardening positions. This stands in marked contrast to the nationalist fervour surrounding the dispute in Vietnam, the Philippines and China.

At the regional level, Malaysia has also resisted suggestions to open up discussion of the South China Sea to interlocutors beyond the immediate parties to the dispute. Uncomfortable with inviting major power rivalry in its neighbourhood, and cautious about "internationalizing" the issue, Malaysia's position is that discussion of the overlapping claims in the South China Sea should be limited to the claimants. The government maintains that discussions can and should be held within the framework provided by ASEAN and has, in the past, rejected suggestions that the issue be brought up at ASEAN-led multilateral forums such as the ASEAN Regional Forum (ARF) and the East Asia Summit (EAS).[24]

PROGRESS TO DATE

Although Malaysia's expressed preference has been and remains a multilateral, ASEAN approach to calming the waters in the South China Sea, it has not been averse to bilateral agreements where they have proven simple and convenient. On 16 March 2009, Malaysia resolved its overlapping claim with Brunei through an Exchange of Letters (EoL), ending two decades of territorial dispute between them and reducing the number of parties Malaysia has claims with in the South China Sea by one.[25]

The EoL was not without controversy. Prior to the agreement, Malaysia's claim extended to what was eventually conceded to be Brunei's territorial waters. That area included energy Blocks L and M (or J and K, as recognized by Brunei). In a move to assert its claim over Blocks L and M, Malaysia awarded production sharing contracts covering those blocks to Petronas Carigali Sdn. Bhd. and Murphy Oil in 2003 while Brunei awarded concessions to six international companies in the same blocks to assert its own claim. The EoL delimitated the maritime boundaries between Malaysia and Brunei, terminated the Petronas Carigali–Murphy Oil concession and recognized Brunei's sovereign rights over Blocks L and M (or J and K). In the spirit of friendship and neighbourliness, a Commercial Arrangement Area (CAA) for oil and gas was established allowing for Malaysia's participation in the joint development of that area for forty years.[26]

With the exception of the level of disquiet the EoL provoked in Brunei and Malaysia, the agreement received muted response from the other claimants in the Spratlys probably because it appeared to be primarily bilaterally-driven. Apart from the maritime boundary dispute, the agreement also dealt with a land border dispute between the two countries and was not widely picked up by the regional media. Malaysia also has joint development agreements (JDAs) on hydrocarbon exploration and development with Vietnam and Thailand (to the extent that Thailand's involvement in the South China Sea stems from its EEZ and continental shelf). What sets apart the cooperative arrangement between Malaysia and Brunei from the JDAs with Vietnam and Thailand is that while sovereignty over overlapping areas has not yet been resolved with the latter two, the issue has been settled with Brunei through the EoL.

The EoL with Brunei, notwithstanding, Malaysia continues to work with, and through, ASEAN to manage tensions in the South China Sea. The DoC was, by ASEAN standards, a watershed document that initiated a framework for claimant states to begin building trust and cooperation. When cynicism over its inertia set in, and silence in the intervening years was punctuated by occasional flare-ups at sea, the adoption by ASEAN and China in July 2011 of the Guidelines for the Implementation of the DoC restored a measure of optimism.

Since then, however, progress on an actual CoC has been exasperatingly halting, especially in light of escalating tensions. Countervailing perceptions — by ASEAN claimant states of grudging Chinese willingness to actually move discussions forward given its preference for bilateral negotiations, and by China of ASEAN ganging up on it — have resulted in a lack of political will to fast-track any meaningful advancement of the CoC.

There is cautious optimism that vessel collisions, deaths, and particularly, China's expression of interest for an early conclusion to the CoC will reinvigorate momentum for the process.[27] In a joint statement released in Naypyidaw in August 2014, ASEAN foreign ministers "remained seriously concerned" over the South China Sea and agreed to "intensify consultations with China for a legally-binding CoC".[28]

Despite some tentative, positive developments, the South China Sea dispute is likely to remain intractable for the foreseeable future. China seems to be claiming "historic rights" in almost all of the South China Sea and, as with Vietnam, asserts claim over the Spratlys. To add another dimension of complexity, Taiwan's claim over the South China Sea mirrors China's, although Taipei's registration of its "unwavering assertion of sovereignty" is done separately from Beijing's.[29] Overlapping claims between

Malaysia and the Philippines remain outstanding as do those with Vietnam despite Malaysia's and Vietnam's joint submission to the United Nations Commission on the Limits of the Continental Shelf (CLCS) and their joint development agreement.

On 6 May 2009, exactly a week before the expiration of a deadline agreed to by all parties to UNCLOS, Malaysia and Vietnam made a joint submission to the CLCS with respect to the extended continental shelf beyond each country's 200 nm EEZ in the southern part of the South China Sea.[30] Upon public notice of this joint submission — served in accordance with the CLCS' rules of procedure — a series of fervent protests, assertions and counters followed from China, the Philippines, Vietnam and Malaysia. Even Indonesia, a non-claimant state to the South China Sea dispute, found it necessary to weigh in with a *note verbale*.[31] Within a day, China challenged that the joint submission "seriously infringed China's sovereignty, sovereign rights and jurisdiction in the South China Sea". In addition, China stressed "indisputable sovereignty over the islands in the South China Sea and the adjacent waters, and enjoys sovereign rights and jurisdiction over the relevant waters as well as the seabed and subsoil thereof". Vietnam countered the next day, asserting "indisputable sovereignty" over the Paracels and Spratlys. It claimed China's *note verbale* to be "null and void" given its claim to be lacking in "legal, historical or factual basis". Malaysia's response on 20 May was considerably more measured, restrained and diplomatic. It noted that it had informed China of its position prior to its joint submission and that the submission was made without prejudice to the delimitation of the continental shelf or position of states with regard to the land or maritime dispute. Even though the Philippines had been invited to jointly submit with Vietnam and Malaysia, it chose not to do so. Instead, like China, it urged the CLCS to refrain from even considering the joint submission given overlapping claims and "the controversy arising from the territorial claims on some of the islands in the area including North Borneo".[32] Needless to say, Malaysia dismissed the latter as having "no basis under international law" with reference to a Separate Opinion delivered by Judge Frank in the Ligitan–Sipadan dispute brought before the ICJ.[33]

On 26 March 2013, a flotilla of four Chinese navy vessels, led by the amphibious landing ship *Jinggangshan*, sailed near Beting Serupai or James Shoal, some 1,800 km from China's mainland coastline but only 80 km off Malaysia's coast and within the country's EEZ in the South China Sea. The presence of the warships reportedly came at the tail end of China's naval exercises in the South China Sea and culminated in an on-board oath-taking ceremony in which Chinese officers pledged to "defend the South China Sea, maintain national sovereignty and strive towards the dream of a strong China".[34]

On 26 January 2014, Chinese warships again arrived at James Shoal and as reported by Chinese state media, conducted another oath-taking ceremony. The chief of the Malaysian navy, Admiral Tan Sri Abdul Aziz, downplayed the incident and denied the Chinese presence in the area, stating instead that China had notified Malaysia through diplomatic channels of its exercises 1,000 nautical miles away from Malaysia's EEZ.[35] Malaysia's Chief of Defence Forces acknowledged the vessels had "strayed into our waters" but that it was "okay" as long as it was "innocent passage".[36]

China's growing presence in Malaysian waters in recent years has, however, not gone unnoticed. Responding to a question in Parliament on 20 March 2014, Minister in the Prime Minister's Department, Dato' Seri Shahidan Kassim, stated that incursions by Chinese warships into Malaysian waters in the South China Sea had been occurring at least once a year since 2011.[37] In 2013, there had been an increase in the number of incursions by the Chinese navy particularly in the areas of Beting Patinggi Ali (South Luconia Shoals), Beting Patinggi Raja (North Luconia Shoals) and Beting Serupai (James Shoal), all of which lie within Malaysia's EEZ. Since 2013, seven incursions were detected, involving sixteen Chinese warships and civilian maritime law enforcement vessels.

Interactions between the Malaysian navy, in particular, and its Chinese counterpart at the operational level have, however, been professional with a level of predictability that borders on ritualistic so that the motions of notifications of movements at sea have more or less become standard procedure.[38] Barring miscalculations stemming from unforeseen events, this is likely to continue especially with a comprehensive strategic partnership between Malaysia and China now in place. The partnership, announced during President Xi Jinping's visit to Malaysia in October 2013 to commemorate forty years of diplomatic relations between the two countries envisions closer defence and security ties between both countries, amid a raft of primarily socio-economic aspirations.[39]

Reports that Malaysia's plans to establish a marine corps and a naval base near Bintulu, 60 nautical miles away from James Shoal, have provoked speculation that these have been in response to Chinese patrols in the area.[40] It is difficult to determine how much of this planning is attributable to China alone. The Lahad Datu incursion in March 2013 by an armed group of Sulu fighters, after all, also spurred prioritization of an upgrade in defence and security capabilities in that area. However, it would be fair to say that renewed concerns related to credible defence of the country's territorial integrity, sovereignty and natural resources against any incursion — whether by a state or non-state actor — have no doubt contributed to a review of the MAF's capabilities in and off the coast of east Malaysia.

With recent incidents at sea, political posturing, the increasing involvement of external powers and the on-going arms build-up in the region, concerns about an upsurge in tensions in the South China Sea seem well-founded. Speaking at a colloquium convened on the South China Sea in Kuala Lumpur in September 2011, Mohamed Thajudeen Abdul Wahab, the Secretary of the National Security Council in the Prime Minister's Department, warned that,

> Malaysia can no longer adopt a 'silent, wait-and-see attitude' because the stakes are indeed very high. We need to tap all the national expertise that we have — which include our diplomats, defence, legal and mapping experts as well as the academia — to come out with a comprehensive policy on the South China Sea which takes into account not only the strategic but also the legal aspects of the problem pertaining to the South China Sea.[41]

OPTIONS FOR MALAYSIA: A POLITICAL, LEGAL OR DIPLOMATIC SOLUTION?

What then are Malaysia's options in moving forward with its claim? There are three possible routes to a resolution.

Hedging or Bandwagoning?

With tectonic plates shifting as China's power continues to grow and the United States "pivots" or "rebalances" its military forces from the Middle East and Europe to Asia, the region is in a state of some flux. Despite America's repeated assurances that it does not seek to contain, undermine or impede the rise of China, competition seems inevitable as the two giants jostle to redefine their power and influence in a changing space. With a number of countries in the region already openly hedging, the question arises as to whether Malaysia should, at the very least, reassess its position to consider the same.

Of course, the suggestion — and some would argue the fact — is that Malaysia, like many other Southeast Asian countries, has already long been hedging.[42] Although Malaysia–China relations fluctuated in the early years of the country's independence when a communist insurgency supported by China posed a threat to its nascent nationhood, bilateral ties stabilized somewhat during the leadership of Prime Minister Tun Abdul Razak (father of current Prime Minister Najib) who envisioned greater regional security through the neutralization of Malaysia and all other Southeast Asian states. The pragmatism of the past may not have been intended to reap China's goodwill so far into the future, but Chinese leaders to this day fondly remember Prime Minister Razak's visit to China in 1974 when Malaysia became the first ASEAN member to establish formal diplomatic relations with China. Addressing China's rise during his keynote speech at the Tenth Asia Security Summit (the "Shangri-La Dialogue") in 2011, Prime Minister Najib recounted Premier Wen Jiabao's unique and touching request to pay a courtesy call to the former's mother, widow of Prime Minister Razak, when the Chinese premier visited Malaysia in 2011.[43]

The intervening years saw a maturing of economic and political ties between the two countries, particularly during the tenure of Prime Minister Mahathir Mohamad.[44] It is important to recall that even as all this was happening and Mahathir's "Look East" policy appeared to shun the West at least rhetorically, the reality was far from East over West. Malaysia was at the same time developing parallel and equally important relationships with other powers in the region and beyond, including in the West. Malaysia's long-standing defence cooperation with the United Kingdom, Australia, and New Zealand was preserved with the establishment in 1971 of the Five Power Defence Arrangements (which also includes Singapore), even after Britain withdrew its military forces in Asia from 1967. Additionally, U.S. and Malaysian forces began training and exercising together during the Vietnam War, laying the groundwork for ever increasing security and military cooperation in the years to come. U.S.–Malaysia military-to-military relations were institutionalized in 1984 with the Bilateral Training and Consultations agreement which provided for, *inter alia*, combined training exercises, logistical support and intelligence sharing.[45] Malaysia also participates in America's International Military Education and Training (IMET) programme under which fifty Malaysian military personnel are sent for training to the United States every year.[46] In April 2014, during President Barack Obama's visit to Kuala Lumpur, U.S.–Malaysia relations were formalized by way of a comprehensive partnership, promising an upgrade in cooperation in the political, diplomatic, defence, security, economics, trade and socio-cultural ties.[47]

By comparison, Malaysia's defence and security relations with China remain in their infancy. A 2005 Memorandum of Understanding on

Defence Cooperation provides for combined training, personnel exchanges and dialogue between the two countries' armed forces but cooperation thus far has not been very substantive, certainly compared with Malaysia's extant military-to-military relations with other countries.[48]

As China's industrial engine continues to power forward, particularly in relation to the troubled economies of Europe and the United States, it seems likely that Malaysia's engagement with China will remain dominated by trade. The growing economic linkages with this neighbourhood giant, a blossoming sense of Asian solidarity borne of regional mechanisms like ASEAN Plus Three, and temperate, respectful relations with each other all provide a cautious buffer against any sudden unravelling of cordial bilateral ties. At the same time, Malaysia's long and familiar history of security and defence cooperation with the United States, in particular, coupled with generally increasing U.S. engagement in the Pacific part of Asia will ensure a continuation of the present delicate, if dynamic balance, of regional relations. From Malaysia's perspective, neither one of its relationship with China or the United States is developed deliberately with the other in mind, but as the power interplay between the two countries intensifies, so too must Malaysia's ties with both countries.

There are several principled and overwhelmingly pragmatic reasons why bandwagoning or alignment with either the United States or China has not been, and never will be, an option for Malaysia. First, Malaysia has always maintained a non-aligned foreign policy stance, which accords with ASEAN's Zone of Peace, Freedom and Neutrality (ZOPFAN), championed by Malaysian Prime Minister Razak in the 1970s.

Second, the proposition of having to choose between the United States and China assumes that relations between the two countries are inherently competitive and that engagement, especially with regard to the South China Sea, is a zero-sum game. For a claimant country in the South China Sea, viewing this matter merely through this lens can be tempting, but the whole of the U.S.–China relationship is greater than the sum of its parts. Flare-ups may occur, and spats may even escalate. But a tempestuous relationship between two Great Powers in the South China Sea should not be the overriding consideration for Malaysia to tilt one way or the other, not least when the other aspects of Malaysia's (economic) security are integrally bound up with both the United States and China.

Third and related, unlike several of its neighbours, Malaysia enjoys long-standing friendly relations with both countries. Malaysia's decades-old relations with the United States, as discussed above, have been bolstered through increased trade and investment links, expansive defence and security cooperation, and in recent years increasing people-to-people initiatives. Even during the relationship's political nadir in the late 1990s, working level ties remained strong. The relationship has enjoyed a considerable boost since Prime Minister Najib Razak and President Barack Obama took office in 2009. In addition to bilateral meetings between the two leaders, there has been a succession of cabinet-level visits, negotiations over membership of the Trans-Pacific Partnership (TPP), combined military exercises and various educational and socio-cultural programmes to transform the already solid relationship into a comprehensive and enduring partnership for the future.

Malaysia's relationship with China, on the other hand, pre-dates that with the United States by several centuries, as far back as the Ming dynasty and perhaps even farther, when Chinese settlers arrived on the sails of trade and intermarried with the local population. Trade remains a constant in Malaysia–China relations. In 2011, China became Malaysia's largest trading partner and as China's market opens, trade and investment between the two countries seem destined to expand.

There is little reason to change the status quo. Acknowledging China's growth since the Ming Dynasty, and citing China's peaceful record of expansion and engagement, Prime Minister Najib urged an embrace of China's rise:

> ... as the focus of the world's economy has shifted from West to East, from the nations of the Atlantic Ocean to those of the Pacific, China has grown still more assertive, opening up and engaging with its neighbours and competitors. We should see this as cause for optimism, rather than concern ... Today, China is our partner. The United States is also our partner ... It is not about taking sides. We must replace the old bilateralism of the Cold War not with a new bilateralism, but a multilateralism that can rise to the task ahead.[49]

At a time of further U.S. entrenchment in the region and rising Chinese dominance, picking sides would be strategic suicide for Malaysia.

Legal Recourse

UNCLOS, which all of the South China Sea claimant states are party to, provides for a comprehensive dispute settlement system for questions related to the interpretation and application of the Convention.[50] State parties can elect to have their dispute adjudicated at the ICJ or the International

Tribunal for the Law of the Sea (ITLOS), or arbitrated under Article VII or Article VIII of UNCLOS. Until January 2013, when the Philippines instituted arbitral proceedings against China at ITLOS under Annex VII of UNCLOS, none of the claimant states had chosen any of these dispute settlement mechanisms.

Significantly, UNCLOS' compulsory binding dispute settlement system provides for exceptions and limitations, and an "opt-out" clause for disputes concerning sea boundary delimitation, historic bays or titles, military activities or where the UN Security Council is exercising its functions as mandated by the UN Charter. Even if Malaysia and another ASEAN claimant agreed to pursue arbitration, China's position would complicate matters given the breadth of its claim. China's nine-dash line map covering almost the whole of the South China Sea, lack of clarification on the nature of its claim, and invocation of the opt-out clause of UNCLOS' compulsory binding dispute settlement system would impact any other attempt at arbitration by the ASEAN claimant states.

UNCLOS is silent on whether state parties may request an advisory opinion from ITLOS and the Tribunal's own statute is similarly silent.[51] However, Article 138 of the Rules of the Tribunal appears to provide for such jurisdiction provided state parties draw up an agreement to seek an advisory opinion from ITLOS on a legal question. It is unclear how claimant states not party to such an agreement would be affected. The question for Malaysia as a claimant state, however — indeed any South China Sea claimant state — would be whether others would be amenable to such an agreement if Malaysia decided to pursue this option. An advisory opinion does not compel binding finality, but it does carry some weight in providing legal guidance. If Malaysia were to seek further judicial recourse, it would have to consider how an advisory opinion from ITLOS might impact its arguments and ultimately, its strategic interests.

An alternative for Malaysia is to return to The Hague pursuant to Article 36(1) of the ICJ Statute which outlines the Court's jurisdiction to adjudicate based on, among others, special agreement by the parties to the dispute. Malaysia is no stranger to this route having travelled down this path twice before with Indonesia over Sipadan/Ligitan and Singapore in the dispute concerning Pedra Branca/Pulau Batu Puteh.[52] However, it seems from official statements that Malaysian leaders are themselves reluctant to settle the dispute legally before all other avenues have been exhausted. Replying to a question in the Senate on overlapping claims, Ahmad Shabery Cheek, Parliamentary Secretary in the Ministry of Foreign Affairs, explained that, "When overlapping claims become difficult to resolve through negotiations, then reference to a third party becomes an option for resolution." Malaysia, he elaborated, turned to the ICJ on the issue of Pedra Branca/Pulau Batu Puteh because prior negotiations with Singapore had failed.[53] This position was confirmed by Deputy Foreign Minister Kohilan Pillay in Parliament in 2010: "Malaysia's stand is that overlapping claims should be resolved through bilateral negotiations and that reference to third parties such as the ICJ or an arbitration tribunal should be the last option in reaching a settlement."[54]

ICJ judgments are binding and without appeal. The finality of a decision on delimitation and sovereignty in the South China Sea may be a daunting prospect given the stakes involved. There are, however, more practical explanations for Malaysia's reluctance. Taking the South China Sea problem to the ICJ would require the explicit consent of the other parties to the dispute. Even if Malaysia were willing to bring its case before the ICJ, it seems unlikely it would be able to convince the other(s) to do so. And even if it were successful in doing so, it is uncertain how the Court's judgement would impact the claims of other states not party to the adjudication. This final point is an important consideration given the messy, overlapping claims in the South China Sea by multiple parties.

Interestingly, while Malaysia has by and large chosen to reserve comment on the actions of its neighbours in advancing their claims to parts of the South China Sea, Prime Minister Najib specifically acknowledged "international arbitration, as warranted, and in accordance with universally recognized principles of international law, including the United Nations Convention on the Law of the Sea" as legal recourse to the dispute,[55] a tacit — if not explicit — indication that Malaysia is keeping watch on the Philippines' initiated arbitration case at ITLOS.

Diplomatic Negotiations: Bilateral or Multilateral?

China's preference to resolve the dispute is to conduct bilateral discussions with each of the ASEAN claimant states. While Malaysia has repeatedly indicated its willingness to negotiate a resolution to the dispute, it has not specified its preference for a bilateral or multilateral mechanism, often citing both as options.[56]

The case for bilateral negotiations is premised on three suppositions. First, Malaysia's friendly relations with each of the claimant states present a good starting point to negotiate bilaterally. Second, discussions between two parties are invariably less complicated than with multiple parties. This arguably facilitates a more thorough consideration of each party's long-term agenda and interests and affords greater scope for compromise than if negotiations involved a larger number of parties. The applicability of bilateral negotiations is perhaps best seen in cooperative agreements, such as Malaysia's JDAs with Vietnam and Thailand.

Yet, four considerations undercut the bilateral argument. First, as cordial as Putrajaya's relations are with Beijing, Malaysia stands at a natural disadvantage *vis-à-vis* China's sheer size, power and influence in bilateral negotiations. Second, joint development agreements are not the same as agreements delineating territory and determining sovereignty. Third, because of the intricate web of claims in the South China Sea, any and all separate bilateral discussions would somehow need to be coordinated so that each agreement reached would accord with the others. It would be crucial to ensure that no new disputes were created and that existing ones would be minimized in the interim. Thus, even if Malaysia reaches an accord with one or two of the other claimant parties, it would need to harmonize separate agreements with the others. Malaysia would also need to guarantee the preservation of its interests in negotiations conducted by other claimant states. Fourth, bilateral negotiations in a complex, multi-party dispute leave plenty of room for suspicion and distrust over the possibility of secret deals. If Malaysia opts to conduct only bilateral discussions concerning the South China Sea, it risks damaging the image it has carefully cultivated as a champion of multilateralism, as well as its credibility in negotiating other issues in multilateral arenas.

If, on the other hand, multilateral discussions are deemed to be the best way forward, what sort of format might they take? Would claimant states, for example, continue to discuss the problem within the ASEAN framework involving even the non-claimant members? Or would a sub-forum within ASEAN comprising only the claimant states be formed? The procedural norm within ASEAN has been for the affected ASEAN member states to first discuss among themselves prior to bringing the matter to the whole group, then finally to the affected non-ASEAN claimant state, i.e. China. This process effectively isolates China from initial discussions and could, rightly or wrongly, give the impression of the ASEAN claimant states "ganging up" on China for collective bargaining leverage.

If Malaysia's rhetoric of prioritizing discussions among claimant states is to be adhered to, then the usual process might be suspended in this particular case to allow for ASEAN claimant states to negotiate with China before informing or discussing with ASEAN's non-claimant states. It is unclear if the other ASEAN claimant states would acquiesce to this. The

Philippines, for example, appears eager to hasten the pace of resolving the dispute by moving beyond confidence-building measures contained in the DoC. Manila's 2011 proposal for a Zone of Peace, Freedom, Friendship and Cooperation (ZoPFF/C) in the South China Sea aimed to segregate disputed and non-disputed maritime areas. The latter would provide a starting point for negotiating a joint development zone. However, Malaysia expressed "fundamental concerns"[57] regarding the ZoPFF/C which assumes that the disputed and non-disputed areas are in and of themselves indisputable. Foreign Minister Anifah Aman gave as an example the Philippines' claim over Sabah, "whose integrity and sovereignty is recognized by the international community as being part of Malaysia". ASEAN's attention, he underscored, should instead be trained on the effective implementation of the DoC and eventual realization of a CoC.[58]

CONCLUSION

Malaysia's relatively low-key approach to handling the South China Sea dispute so far has elicited speculation that it belies one of two things: a crafty, deliberate long-term strategy or lack of a fully developed and comprehensive policy towards the issue.

On the surface, official statements seem to favour a multilateral approach within the ASEAN framework. However, there are also suggestions that if transparent, bilateral discussions can facilitate intermediate solutions without prejudice to Malaysia's claim (such as JDAs), then Malaysia could consider a dual-track multilateral and bilateral diplomatic approach. While Prime Minister Najib has pledged full commitment "to the common ASEAN position in terms of our engagement with China on the South China Sea", he also expressed equal determination to ensure Malaysia's bilateral relationship with China "remains unaffected and, in fact continues to go from strength to strength".[59]

As government discussions to conclude a CoC plod along, and Malaysia's and Vietnam's joint submission to the CLCS likely only to be considered in 2035 due to the latter's heavy workload,[60] Malaysia must urgently decide on an approach that would best advance its claims and interests in the disputed area. It must also do so without aggravating tensions. Hardening political positions, regional naval modernization programmes and competing resource demands all add to this challenge.

As Malaysia evolves and consolidates its South China Sea policy in response to shifting regional dynamics, there is occasion to drive the CoC process faster and further as the country prepares to take chairmanship of

ASEAN in 2015. This is despite the government's latest pronouncement that the CoC "should not serve as an instrument to resolve territorial and jurisdictional disputes in the South China Sea between the parties concerned".[61] Even though Malaysia has "always believed" that these should instead be resolved "based on existing mechanisms as provided for under international law, including the 1982 UN Convention on the Law of the Sea",[62] a consolidation of positions on the CoC would temporarily provide for a necessary — if insufficient — framework of actions, behaviours and expectations.

With the ASEAN Community due to be realized in 2015, there exists great impetus to complement the region's economic integration with concrete political and security cohesion. Completion of a progressive and substantive CoC by 2015 would be a fitting piece to the ASEAN Political and Security Community puzzle. More importantly, it would offer clarity of action to and by South China Sea claimant states while defusing tensions in the region. As an ASEAN founding member that will chair the organization in 2015, and South China Sea claimant, this is an opportunity Malaysia should not shy away from even as it continues to mull the most appropriate long-term solution to the dispute that would best serve its — and the region's — interests.

Notes

1. GlobalSecurity.org, "South China Sea Oil Shipping Lanes", available at <http://www.globalsecurity.org/military/world/war/spratly-ship.htm>.
2. U.S. Energy Information Administration, "Country Analysis Brief: South China Sea", March 2008, available at <http://205.254.135.7/countries/regions-topics.cfm?fips=SCS>.
3. Ibid.
4. Petronas Gas Berhad, *Msia's Oil & Gas Reserves*, available at <http://www.petronasgas.com/Pages/MsiasOilGasReserves.aspx>.
5. U.S. Energy Information Administration, "Country Analysis Brief: Malaysia", available at <http://205.254.135.7/countries/cab.cfm?fips=MY>.
6. Ibid.
7. Gas Malaysia, *Malaysian National Gas Reserves*, available at <http://www.gasmalaysia.com/about_gas/malaysian_ng_reserves.htm>.
8. *Msia's Oil & Gas Reserves*, op. cit.
9. "Country Analysis Brief: South China Sea", op. cit.
10. Petronas, the national oil and gas corporation, reported that total production for its financial year ended 31 March 2011 had fallen to 2.14 million barrels of oil equivalent (boe) per day, from 2.27 million boe per day in

the preceding financial year. Cecilia Kok, "Petronas Accelerating Efforts to Enhance Production of Oil and Gas for M'sia", *The Star Online*, 16 November 2011, available at <http://biz.thestar.com.my/news/story.asp?file=/2011/11/16/business/9911738&sec=business>.

11. Ibid.

12. The original Bahasa Malaysia language reads, *"[P]emisahan secara fizikal Semenanjung Malaysia dengan Sabah dan Sarawak oleh Laut China Selatan memerlukan negara memberi perhatian utama terhadap laluan laut dan ruang udara di antara kedua-dua wilayah tersebut. Sebarang ancaman atau gangguan di laluan laut dan ruang udara berkenaan boleh menjejaskan keuturhan kedua-dua wilayah tersebut dan Malaysia secara keseluruhannya"*, National Defence Policy, p. 12, available at <http://www.mod.gov.my/images/files/dpn-terbuka.pdf>.

13. Ibid., p. 13.

14. *Peta Baru Menunjukkan Sempadan Perairan dan Pelantar Benua Malaysia* (Kuala Lumpur: Directorate of National Mapping Malaysia, 1979).

15. Transcript of Deputy Foreign Minister Kohilan Pillay's reply to Senator Tunku Abdul Aziz Abdul Rahman's question regarding the Spratlys, 6 May 2010, obtained by Dzirhan Mahadzir, defence journalist; Deputy Foreign Minister Leo Michael Toyad in reply to Senator Tunku Abdul Aziz Abdul Rahman, Hansard, Parliament of Malaysia, DN.29.7.1999, 29 July 1999; Deputy Finance Minister Haji Shafie Mohd. Salleh in reply to Senator Tunku Abdul Aziz Abdul Rahman, Hansard, Parliament of Malaysia, DN.2.5.2000, 2 May 2000.

16. See Mark J. Valencia, Jon M. Van Dyke, and Noel A. Ludwig, *Sharing the Resources of the South China Sea* (Honolulu: University of Hawaii Press, 1999), p. 37.

17. See Chapter 2 in this volume by Clive Schofield, "Untangling a Complex Web: Understanding Competing Maritime Claims in the South China Sea".

18. Deputy Minister of Foreign Affairs Kohilan Pillay in reply to Senator Tunku Abdul Aziz Abdul Rahman, Hansard, Parliament of Malaysia (Senate), DN.28.7.2010, 28 July 2010.

19. "Sovereignty over Pedra Branca/Pulau Batu Puteh, Middle Rocks and South Ledge (Malaysia/Singapore)", Judgement of the International Court of Justice, 23 May 2008; "Sovereignty over Pulau Ligitan and Pulau Sipadan (Malaysia/Indonesia)", Judgement of the International Court of Justice, 23 May 2008.

20. Naval stations "Uniform", "Mike", "Sierra" and "Papa" were constructed on Terumbu Ubi (1986), Terumbu Mantanani (1986), Terumbu Siput (1999) and Terumbu Peninjau (1999), respectively.

21. Marine Research Station Malaysia, available at <http://www.fri.gov.my/marsal/>.

22. Lo Chi-kin, *China's Policy Towards Territorial Dispute: The Case of the South China Sea Islands* (New York: Routledge, 1989), p. 156.

23. "Declaration on the Conduct of Parties in the South China Sea", Secretariat of the Association of Southeast Asian Nations, 4 November 2002, available at <http://www.aseansec.org/13163.htm>.

24. Deputy Foreign Minister Leo Michael Toyad, Hansard, op. cit.; Deputy Finance Minister Haji Shafie Mohd. Salleh, Hansard, op. cit.

25. For a concise explanation of the Malaysia–Brunei Exchange of Letters, see Leong Shen-Li, "A Tale of Two Oil Blocks", *The Star Online*, 9 May 2010, available at <http://thestar.com.my/news/story.asp?sec=nation&file=/2010/5/9/nation/6188182>.

26. "Pak Lah Dismisses Dr M's Claims He Gave Away Oil-rich Areas to Brunei", *The Star Online*, 30 April 2010, available at <http://thestar.com.my/news/story.asp?file=/2010/4/30/nation/20100430183602&sec=nation>; "Petronas: M'sia, Brunei to Jointly Develop 2 Oil-rich Areas", *The Star Online*, 1 May 2010, available at <http://thestar.com.my/news/story.asp?sec=nation&file=/2010/5/1/nation/20100501093852>; "Exchange of Letters Between Malaysia–Brunei Resolved Outstanding Bilateral Issues: Wisma Putra", *Bernama*, 3 May 2010.

27. May Wong, "China Says Keen to Conclude CoC on South China Sea", *Channel News Asia*, 8 August 2014, available at <http://www.channelnewsasia.com/news/asiapacific/china-says-keen-to/1304318.html>.

28. "Joint Communiqué 47th ASEAN Foreign Ministers' Meeting", Nay Pyi Taw, 8 August 2014, available at <http://www.asean.org/images/documents/47thAMMandRelatedMeetings/Joint%20Communique%20of%2047th%20AMM%20as%20of%209-8-14%2010%20pm.pdf>.

29. Shih Hsiu-chuan, "Taipei Reminds Manila of Its South China Sea Claim", *Taipei Times*, 13 March 2012, available at <http://www.taipeitimes.com/News/taiwan/archives/2012/03/14/2003527750>.

30. "Joint Submission to the Commission on the Limits of the Continental Shelf Pursuant to Article 76, Paragraph 8 of the United Nations Convention on the Law of the Sea 1982 in Respect of the Southern Part of the South China Sea", Part I: Executive Summary, by Malaysia and the Socialist Republic of Vietnam, May 2009, available at <http://www.un.org/Depts/los/clcs_new/submissions_files/mysvnm33_09/mys_vnm2009excutivesummary.pdf>; "Receipt of the Joint Submission made by Malaysia and the Socialist Republic of Viet Nam to the Commission on the Limits of the Continental Shelf", CLCS.33.2009.LOS (Continental Shelf Notification), 7 May 2009, available at <http://www.un.org/Depts/los/clcs_new/submissions_files/mysvnm33_09/mysvnm_clcs33_2009e.pdf>.

31. Indonesia suggested that China's own statements led to its "so-called 'nine-dotted-lines-map' ... clearly lack[ing] international legal basis and [is] tantamount to upset (*sic*) the UNCLOS 1982". See submission of *note verbale* by Indonesia to the United Nations Commission on the Limits of the Continental Shelf, No. 480/POL-703/VII/10, 8 July 2010, available

at <http://www.un.org/Depts/los/clcs_new/submissions_files/mysvnm33_09/idn_2010re_mys_vnm_e.pdf>.

32. For a full list of communications, see "Commission on the Limits of the Continental Shelf (CLCS), Outer Limits of the Continental Shelf Beyond 200 Nautical Miles from the Baselines: Submissions to the Commission: Joint Submission by Malaysia and the Socialist Republic of Viet Nam", updated 3 May 2011, available at <http://www.un.org/Depts/los/clcs_new/submissions_files/submission_mysvnm_33_2009.htm>.

33. Case Concerning Sovereignty over Pulau Ligitan and Pulau Sipadan (Permission to intervene by the Philippines), 23 October 2001, available at <http://www.icj-cij.org/docket/files/102/7700.pdf>.

34. Greg Torode, "PLA Navy Amphibious Task Force Reaches Malaysia 'to Defend South China Sea'", *South China Morning Post*, 27 March 2014.

35. Santha Oorjitham, "China Claims Its Vessels Patrolled James Shoal", *The Star*, 31 January 2014, available at <http://www.thestar.com.my/Opinion/Columnists/Temp/2014/01/31/China-claims-its-vessels-patrolled-James-Shoal/>; Stuart Grudgings, "Insight — China's Assertiveness Hardens Malaysian Stance in Sea Dispute", Reuters, 26 February 2014, available at <http://uk.reuters.com/article/2014/02/26/uk-malaysia-china-maritime-insight-idUKBREA1P1Z020140226>.

36. Teoh El Sen, "Chinese Ships Were Just Passing Through — Armed Forces Chief", *Astro Awani*, 20 February 2014, available at <http://english.astroawani.com/news/show/chinese-ships-were-just-passing-through-armed-forces-chief-30493>.

37. Dato' Seri Shahidan Kassim in reply to Dato' Haji Mohd Zaim bin Abu Hasan, Hansard, Parliament of Malaysia (Dewan Rakyat), DN.20.2.2014, 20 March 2014.

38. Author's conversations with serving officials within the Ministry of Defence as well as the Malaysian Armed Forces.

39. "China, Malaysia Agree to Lift Ties to Comprehensive Strategic Partnership", *Xinhuanet*, 4 October 2013, available at <http://news.xinhuanet.com/english/china/2013-10/04/c_132772213.htm>.

40. Dzirhan Mahadzir, "Malaysia to Establish Marine Corps, Naval Base close to James Shoal", *IHS Jane's Defence Weekly*, 15 October 2013, available at <http://www.janes.com/article/28438/malaysia-to-establish-marine-corps-naval-base-close-to-james-shoal>.

41. Mohamed Thajudeen Abdul Wahab, Opening Remarks at the Colloquium on the South China Sea: Issues, Challenges and Strategic Options for Malaysia, National Security Council, Prime Minister's Department, 28 September 2011.

42. For a good summary of the intricate development of Malaysia–China relations from 1949 to 2010, see Ian Storey, "Malaysia and China: Rhetoric

and Reality", in *Southeast Asia and the Rise of China: The Search for Security* (Abingdon, Oxon.: Routledge, 2011), chapter 10.

43. Najib Razak, Keynote Address to the 10th IISS Asia Security Summit (The Shangri-La Dialogue), 3 June 2011, available at <http://www.iiss.org/conferences/the-shangri-la-dialogue/shangri-la-dialogue-2011/speeches/keynote-address/dato-sri-najib-tun-raza/>.

44. Malaysia–China relations underwent a huge expansion after the dissolution of the Communist Party of Malaya in 1989 and with it, the end of the communist threat to Malaysia.

45. Johan Saravanamuttu, *Malaysia's Foreign Policy: The First Fifty Years — Alignment, Neutralism, Islamism* (Singapore: Institute of Southeast Asian Studies, 2010); Richard J. Ellings and Sheldon W. Simon, *Southeast Asian Security in the New Millennium* (New York: National Bureau of Asian Research, 1996).

46. With the exception of a dip in funding allocation in FY 2009, IMET funding for Malaysia increased from $870,000 in FY 2006 to $950,000 in FY 2010. "International Military Education and Training Account Summary", U.S. Department of State, 23 June 2010, available at <http://www.state.gov/t/pm/ppa/sat/c14562.htm>; "Office of Defence Cooperation, Embassy of the United States Kuala Lumpur", available at <http://malaysia.usembassy.gov/odc.html>.

47. "Joint Statement by President Obama and Prime Minister Najib of Malaysia", The White House, 27 April 2014, available at <http://www.whitehouse.gov/the-press-office/2014/04/27/joint-statement-president-obama-and-prime-minister-najib-malaysia-0>.

48. Ian Storey, "Malaysia's Hedging Strategy with China", *China Brief* 7, no. 14 (12 July 2007), available at <http://www.jamestown.org/single/?no_cache=1&tx_ttnews[tt_news]=4298>.

49. Najib Razak, Keynote Address to The Shangri-La Dialogue, op. cit.

50. See Robert C. Beckman and Leonardo Bernard, "Disputed Areas in the South China Sea: Prospects for Arbitration or Advisory Opinion", paper presented at the Third International Workshop on the South China Sea: Cooperation for Regional Security and Development, Hanoi, 3–5 November 2011.

51. Ibid.; You Ki-Jun, "Advisory Opinions of the International Tribunal for the Law of the Sea: Article 138 of the Rules of the Tribunal, Revisited", *Ocean Development and International Law* 39 (2008): 360–71.

52. "Sovereignty over Pedra Branca/Pulau Batu Puteh, Middle Rocks and South Ledge (Malaysia/Singapore)", op. cit., p. 12; "Sovereignty over Pulau Ligitan and Pulau Sipadan (Indonesia/Malaysia)", op. cit., p. 625.

53. Parliamentary Secretary in the Ministry of Foreign Affairs Ahmad Shabery Cheek in reply to Dr Haji Mohd. Puad Zarkashi, Hansard, Parliament of Malaysia (Senate), DN.24.5.2007, 24 May 2007.

54. Deputy Minister of Foreign Affairs Kohilan Pillay, Hansard, op. cit.

55. "Joint Statement by President Obama and Prime Minister Najib of Malaysia", op. cit.
56. See, for example, Deputy Finance Minister Haji Shafie Mohd. Salleh, Hansard, op. cit.
57. Statement made by The Honourable Dato' Sri Anifah Aman, Minister of Foreign Affairs of Malaysia during the ASEAN Ministerial Meeting in Bali, Indonesia, Ministry of Foreign Affairs Malaysia, 15 November 2011.
58. Ibid.
59. Najib Razak, Keynote Address to The Shangri-La Dialogue, op. cit.
60. Nguyen Hong Thao and Ramses Amer, "Coastal States in the South China Sea and Submissions of the Outer Limits of the Continental Shelf", paper presented at an International Conference on Contentious Issues in UNCLOS — Surely Not?, International Hydrographic Organisation/International Association of Geodesy Advisor Board on the Law of the Sea, Monaco, 25–27 October 2010, available at <http://www.gmat.unsw.edu.au/ablos/ABLOS10Folder/S7P1-Pres.pdf>.
61. "COC Not Instrument to Resolve South China Sea Territorial Disputes", Bernama, 10 July 2012, available at <http://www.bernama.com/bernama/v6/newsgeneral.php?id=679543>.
62. Ibid.

10

THE UNITED STATES AND THE SOUTH CHINA SEA: FRONT LINE OF HEGEMONIC TENSION?

Denny Roy

From the standpoint of the United States, the rise of the People's Republic of China (PRC) presents two archetypal possibilities. The first possibility is that China will conform to international norms; will not bully smaller countries; will not seek to dominate the Asia-Pacific region; will not try to overthrow international arrangements that most of the world wants to keep; and will not try to supplant U.S. influence in East Asia. The second possibility is that China will, contrary to its rhetorical promises, strive for regional hegemony; seek to displace the United States from its current position as the strongest strategic player in the region; and use its massive advantages in economic, diplomatic and military weight to pressure or coerce smaller countries to subordinate their own interests to Chinese preferences.

This dichotomy is built into the U.S. policy of hedging which attempts to simultaneously encourage the first outcome while defending against the second outcome. This is somewhat contradictory, since "unfriendly" U.S. policies that imply China is a potential adversary undercut China's confidence that it can achieve its economic and security goals in a region and a world permeated with so many U.S.-sponsored rules and arrangements.

The same dichotomy is also visible in the brief summary of U.S.–China policy that is little changed over the last three presidential administrations, and was recently restated by President Barack Obama as follows:

> We welcome China's rise…. [It's] good for the world, and it's good for
> America. We just want to make sure that that rise occurs in a way that
> reinforces international norms and international rules, and enhances
> security and peace, as opposed to it being a source of conflict either
> in the region or around the world.[1]

In the South China Sea, this dichotomy emerges over the question of
whether the disputes will be settled on the basis of modern international
law, as the United States wishes, or on the basis of the principle that
the dominant regional power sets the guidelines for international affairs.
The latter model prevailed for much of pre-modern history, with China
in the dominant position and many of the other regional states more or
less acquiescing. Some analysts argue that the China-centric model is the
natural state of affairs for East Asia, both past and future.[2] From the U.S.
standpoint, therefore, Beijing's policy towards the South China Sea is an
early and important barometer of the intentions that will guide China's
growth in relative capabilities. On these Chinese intentions, and of course
U.S. reactions to PRC policies, hang the future of Sino–U.S. relations and
America's role in the Asia-Pacific region. This chapter will argue that PRC
policy challenges all the major U.S. interests tied up in the South China
Sea disputes, suggesting this issue will antagonize bilateral relations for the
foreseeable future.

CHINA'S REGIONAL OBJECTIVES

As China becomes a regional Great Power, the expectation should be
that it will strive to make Northeast Asia, Southeast Asia, Central Asia
and possibly parts of South Asia a Chinese sphere of influence if this
objective can be achieved without generating an anti-PRC backlash that
would seriously threaten the country's major strategic interests. A sphere
of influence is a geographic area over which a Great Power enjoys unique
privileges or control.

An example is the Monroe Doctrine proclaimed by the U.S. government
in 1823. President James Monroe declared that from that time forth
Washington would forbid European countries (the Great Powers of that time)
from establishing or re-establishing colonies in the Western Hemisphere.
Thenceforth international affairs in the New World would be dominated
by the United States. Japan's short-lived Greater East Asia Co-Prosperity
Sphere in the 1930s and first half of the 1940s was an attempt to establish
a Japanese sphere of influence in Asia. With its massive territory, population

and resource endowment, China's situation is more analogous to the successful U.S. case than to the unsuccessful Japanese case.

There are several reasons to expect that the PRC will demand a sphere of influence on its periphery, and that these demands will grow stronger commensurate with China's relative capabilities. First, the Chinese have already demonstrated their intentions. Some of the strongest and most belligerent Chinese foreign policy positions involve issues that are geographically located directly south and east of the country. Beijing has staked out proprietary claims of varying degrees over the Yellow Sea, the East China Sea, Taiwan, the South China Sea, and parts of northern Korea (the Koguryo history dispute with South Korea). On these issues, neighbouring states such as Vietnam, the Philippines and Japan perceive China to be illegitimately expansive, while many other regional states are concerned enough about China's intentions that they are increasing their defence cooperation with other governments, particularly the United States. Beijing has taken these strong positions and actions sometimes at substantial cost to other Chinese objectives such as earning international respect and assuring its neighbours that a strong China is nothing to fear. The Chinese government has often bowed to concerted international pressure to fall into line with widely-accepted norms and policies, but this happens less frequently with issues in the PRC's immediate neighbourhood. The Chinese are less responsive to foreign opinion and less deterred by the prospect of anti-China security collaboration when it comes to issues that are close to home, which the Chinese consider especially sensitive or "internal" — chiefly the issues involving disputed territory (including Taiwan), Beijing's treatment of restive ethnic minority communities in western China and the legitimacy of the Chinese Communist Party's (CCP) rule over China.

Second, China is subject to the usual forces of international politics. All states constantly fear harm from other states and strive for as much security as they can get based on their circumstances. For a Great Power, it is feasible to attain additional security by establishing control over the external environment. As a weak country, the PRC had no choice but to tolerate the regional pre-eminence of a Superpower that the Chinese believe is committed to "containing" China. Moreover, neighbouring states have pursued policies that infringe on Chinese interests or preferences. As a strong country, China will follow the typical pattern of strong countries and yield to the compulsion to impose its will upon regional governments and to expunge the strategic influence of external powers such as the United States.

Third, China believes in its historic destiny to become a Great Power once again. The Chinese see their country as the region's pre-eminent political and cultural power for all but a brief period of recorded history. While some Western analysts have defined China based on the sclerotic and feeble performance seen during the early modern period,[3] the Chinese see the so-called "century of humiliation" (1839–1949) as an aberration that is only now being rectified. The Chinese will try to dominate the region because they believe this is China's rightful position. Chinese officials and government-connected commentators argue that history proves China will be a benign power that "will never seek hegemony".[4] This argument is flawed. The circumstances of pre-modernity are different than those of modernity. Pre-modern Chinese elites, for example, had confidence in the superiority and survivability of their cultural and political systems. Even if foreigners managed a military conquest of the seat of government, the Chinese state would swallow them up by Sinicizing them.[5] The present Chinese regime, however, enjoys no such complacency in the world of rival nuclear-armed Great Powers, Western attempts at "peaceful evolution", perceived U.S.-led containment and the threat of Taiwan independence. The reputedly benign behaviour of China as a pre-modern power does not guarantee that modern Great Power China will step on no one's toes in the much different world of our time. The notion that pre-modern China was inoffensive and peace-loving is itself questionable. Ancient China differed little from the European Great Powers: the Chinese fought in thousands of conflicts, made alliances and used force against smaller states.[6] The PRC is an empire built on past Chinese conquests. Vietnam suffered several Chinese invasions and centuries of Chinese occupation. While today's Chinese officials extol the voyages of the fifteenth century admiral Zheng He as goodwill tours, scholars outside China argue that Zheng He was essentially engaged in military campaigns as part of an exercise of what Beijing disparages as "power politics": a stronger country using force to press its self-interests on weaker countries.[7]

U.S. INTERESTS IN THE SOUTH CHINA SEA

The recently increased U.S. attention to the South China Sea corresponds with an apparent rise in the relative importance Washington has accorded to Asia since the election of President Obama in 2008. The United States' South China Sea policy has been a reflection rather than a driver of the overall shift towards greater American interest in the Asia Pacific. This shift includes the Obama administration — to a greater degree than its predecessors did — treating China as an equal partner; the establishment of a new Strategic and Economic Dialogue with China; attempts to strengthen relationships with Japan, South Korea, Australia, the Philippines, Singapore, Malaysia, India, Indonesia and Vietnam; beefing up U.S. forces in Guam and Hawaii; U.S. accession to the Association of Southeast Asian Nation's (ASEAN) Treaty of Amity and Cooperation (TAC); the appointment of a permanent U.S. ambassador to the ASEAN Secretariat in Jakarta; and a stated commitment by the U.S. Secretaries of State and Defense during 2011 to maintain or even increase U.S. military strength in Asia despite budgetary pressures — the so-called "pivot" towards Asia or "rebalancing" of military forces away from the Middle East to the Asia Pacific. China's rise, and the concomitant Chinese demand for greater influence within its own neighbourhood, is thus far meeting not a U.S. withdrawal, but rather a U.S. recommitment to maintaining pre-eminence in the Asia Pacific.

Officially, Washington has no interest in any particular South China Sea claimant country winning or losing its claim. One could speculate about the existence of an unstated agenda. Obviously the United States is more worried about China than the Philippines or Brunei as a potential strategic adversary. In that case, it is logical that far-sighted U.S. strategists would prefer to see additional food and hydrocarbon resources fall into the hands of claimants other than the PRC. Whether U.S. policy is in fact so far-sighted and coherent despite frequent changes in high-level leadership positions is questionable. Four U.S. interests in the South China Sea — none of them inherently anti-China — are clear: stability; freedom of navigation; upholding international law; and maintaining the U.S.-sponsored regional security order.

"Stability" means the absence of conflict or the threat of conflict that might perturb the peace upon which regional economic cooperation is based. This danger ranges from bilateral tensions at the macro level to incidents at sea (or over the sea) at the micro level. Washington has repeatedly expressed an interest in peace in the South China Sea and called for settlement of the disputes through dialogue. The danger of more incidents in the South China Sea between Chinese vessels and the U.S. Navy is a major motivation for the frequent U.S. appeal to the Chinese to strengthen and deepen the bilateral military-to-military relationship.[8] The U.S. government has criticized Chinese attempts to intimidate U.S. and foreign energy corporations involved in exploration on behalf of non-Chinese claimants.[9] The U.S. wish for stability is endangered by the extraordinary scope of the Chinese claim (to the extent the Chinese have explained their claim) and the boldness, even aggressiveness, with which the Chinese have attempted to enforce their claim. Furthermore, the Chinese domestic political environment is a disruptive rather than a pacifying influence on Chinese behaviour. By celebrating its success in leading the country to major power status, the CCP government has stoked the mass public expectation that China will stand up more resolutely for its own interests. Finally, as it attempts to consolidate its authority and influence, the new regime of President Xi Jinping and Premier Li Keqiang can ill afford to alienate the PLA or bring upon itself the wrath of nationalistic public opinion by appearing weak on issues involving Chinese sovereignty.

As long as China eschews relying on international law and institutions to gain its objectives, it will likely feel compelled to attempt to influence developments through extralegal means that bring a high risk of incidents at sea.

Unimpeded use of the South China Sea is something akin to a "core interest" of the United States. This sea connects the Indian and Pacific Oceans. The United States has important commitments as well as military bases in both regions. Rapid movement of U.S. naval forces between these two oceans via the South China Sea is essential to fulfilling the global security role that America has created for itself (and that much of the world endorses, with major exceptions including China). If passage through the South China Sea by U.S. warships was blocked because of China's perceived ownership rights or some other reason, they would be forced to take a longer southerly detour, delaying their arrival and increasing operating costs.

The American side has characterized Chinese policy in the South China Sea as a threat to "freedom of navigation". Top-level U.S. military commanders such as the Commander of the Hawaii-based U.S. Pacific Command have concluded that China "does seek to restrict or exclude foreign, in particular, US, military maritime and air activities in the 'near seas'".[10] The Pentagon's new "air-sea battle" concept features joint operations by the navy and air force to counter China's anti-access/area denial (A2/AD) capabilities that threaten to disable American forces rushing to intervene in a hypothetical Asia-Pacific conflict, especially in the Taiwan Straits.[11] Other American commentators, joined by officials from Australia, India, Japan and some Southeast Asian countries, have supported the argument that China's approach to the South China Sea disputes implies a possible danger to the use of "international waters". According to this argument, the Chinese have generated grounds for suspicion that they might try to impede commerce, humanitarian operations or security cooperation designed to maintain peace in the region. The modernizing People's Liberation Army-Navy (PLA-Navy), and particularly China's large and technologically improving submarine fleet (with a major base at Sanya on Hainan Island at the western edge of the South China Sea), gives the Chinese the capability to cause havoc in the area if they choose to. Chinese officials have responded to these fears by stating they have no intention of restricting freedom of navigation: "The Chinese government has always maintained that the freedom of navigation and overfly in the South China Sea, a right enjoyed by all countries in accordance with the international law, should be fully guaranteed."[12] In the Chinese view, the freedom of navigation argument is a U.S.-invented canard designed to justify American "meddling" in the South China Sea issue in service of the larger U.S. strategy of mobilizing regional states in a strategic encirclement of China.[13]

A "fact check" would be useful here. The PRC generally has not obstructed what is commonly understood under international law as "innocent passage" in the areas of the South China Sea beyond China's immediate shoreline that Beijing claims. In this sense the official PRC position that China poses no threat to freedom of navigation is defensible. China has not impeded commercial traffic, humanitarian operations or transit by foreign warships through the seas beyond its 12 nautical miles (nm) territorial waters limit. Where the Chinese have tried to implement restrictions is in the cases of surveillance (more on this below) and taking resources from the ocean or the seabed. These are not insignificant exceptions; they have led to unilateral annual Chinese fishing bans since 1991, the arrests of non-Chinese fishermen, cable-cutting incidents off the Vietnamese coast during 2010–12 and the harassment of U.S. Navy vessels such as the *USNS Impeccable* in March 2009. Consequently some foreign analysts warn that a Chinese claim to rights over the centre section of the South China Sea potentially threatens the maritime activities of all foreign countries, while the Chinese insist the costs to the region of recognizing the PRC's claims would be limited and manageable.[14]

This is a matter of interpretation rather than fact. A complication for the Chinese position is that even in the semi-official media, the voice of a much tougher nationalistic faction is audible. For example, Chinese legal scholar Pan Guoping wrote in the CCP-affiliated *Global Times* in November 2011 that, "The United States is only a passer-by in the South [China] Sea…. As a country that has no sea coast in the region, does the United States have freedom of navigation and flight in the South [China] Sea? The answer is no! There is no international water in the South [China] Sea."[15] Such outbursts are a reminder that Chinese foreign policymakers are under increasing pressure from groups of elites demanding that the government take a stronger stand in defence of China's interests.

The United Nations Convention on the Law of the Sea (UNCLOS) allows foreign ships the right of passage through coastal waters provided they are not carrying out certain activities specified as forbidden because they are a threat to the coastal state.[16] The law makes a distinction between the waters immediately offshore and more distant waters. Under UNCLOS, spying on a state from its territorial waters is not allowed. UNCLOS does not, however, prohibit military surveillance of a state from its 200 nm exclusive economic zone (EEZ).

The U.S. Navy has been careful to keep its surveillance activities within China's EEZ. The recent high-profile incidents that arose from aggressive Chinese reaction to U.S. surveillance — from the EP-3 collision of 2001 to the 2009 harassment of the *Impeccable* — occurred in or over China's EEZ, not PRC territorial waters. Although the United States has not yet ratified UNCLOS, it has complied with UNCLOS on this point. The political aspect of this issue, however, is a completely different matter. Regardless of what international law says, China objects to foreign military surveillance in its EEZ. In 2007, the PRC passed a domestic law that outlawed spying near China's coast. According to this law, the activities of foreign ships within China's EEZ must "not involve state secrets of China" and must "not damage China's national security".[17] This law reflects the growing sentiment in China that as a Great Power, the PRC should not tolerate unfriendly acts by foreign military forces in the nearby oceans.

It has been difficult for the Chinese to back down from opposition to close-in surveillance. Since China is not accustomed to the superpower game, Chinese tend to see U.S. surveillance within the context of the century of humiliation: hostile treatment by the leading Western power. The Chinese public expects the twenty-first century to be an era in which vestiges of the century of humiliation are swept away, not continued. Alternatively, the United States could alleviate the tensions stemming from this issue by phasing out close-in surveillance missions. Compromise is not easy for the United States, either. There is a debate within the U.S. government over the relative costs and benefits of close-in surveillance of China. Many (but not all) Department of Defense officials argue that the intelligence provided by close-in surveillance is essential for U.S. military planners. This view is reflected in the argument of retired U.S. Navy Admiral Eric McVadon that "this intelligence collection activity is especially important and produces valuable results that would make U.S. actions against the PLA, were it to attack Taiwan, more effective and decisive". In particular, McVadon says,

"The US Navy wants to collect acoustic signatures from the PLA Navy's new submarines, and the PLA navy objects."[18] The close approach of U.S. aircraft and ships to the Chinese coast also allows U.S. forces to monitor the detection capability and response protocols of the PLA units on China's frontiers. Conversely, the prevailing view in the U.S. Department of State is that the intelligence gained through close surveillance is not worth the resulting damage to U.S.–China relations, especially since less provocative ways of intelligence gathering remain available.[19] Leaving aside the question of the value of the intelligence gained from these missions, many in the U.S. government would oppose halting close-in surveillance because it would appear to signal capitulation to China on an important issue.

China's position on the "freedom of navigation" question has three problems. First, as noted earlier, UNCLOS does not support it. Second, the Chinese themselves carry out close-in surveillance when they are able to in such places as Japan's EEZ. Third, a proper way for the Chinese to pursue a complaint about close surveillance by the United States is to file a protest and seek adjudication through international legal institutions rather than trying to change U.S. policies by harassing U.S. ships and aircraft.

The U.S.–China disagreement over the principle of close-in surveillance would fade if China came to accept the rules of superpower interaction that prevailed during the Cold War. In 2013, there were early indications that this might be occurring. The U.S. Department of Defense's annual report on the PLA that year noted "several instances" of PRC "naval activities in the EEZs around Guam and Hawaii". The report said these Chinese activities were hypocritical but lawful. During the Shangri-La Dialogue in Singapore the same year, a PLA officer said Chinese ships and aircraft had entered U.S. EEZs "a few times", although he did not explicitly admit to spying.[20] The Chinese also dispatched a vessel to the waters near Hawaii in July 2014 to observe the multinational Rim of the Pacific (RIMPAC) naval exercise — in which, ironically, PLA Navy ships were participating for the first time — and again in September to monitor U.S.-led exercises off Guam.[21] Resolution of this issue through a tacit reciprocity would of course have the downside of continuing if not increasing the opportunities for an incident at sea between the two rival Great Powers.

Americans are divided into two camps on the question of how to meet the challenge of a rising power. The deterrence model, based on an interpretation of the outbreak of the Second World War in Europe, is still influential. Western European countries unintentionally invited the German invasion of Poland because they chose to appease Hitler rather than stand up to his annexation of part of Czechoslovakia. According to this thinking, appeasement does not satisfy an aggressive state. Rather, it encourages an aggressive government to demand more and more concessions. The appeasing states eventually get the war they hoped to avoid, and only after making the aggressor stronger. This alternative view is captured in the spiral model: a foreign policy that externally looks like aggression is more likely motivated by insecurity than by an endless appetite for expansion. A reasonable and acceptable amount of compromise can satisfy the rising power by meeting its security concerns, thus averting war.[22] This thinking is reflected in U.S. scholar Joseph Nye's famous warning that, "If you treat China as an enemy, China will become an enemy."[23] Those Americans who see Chinese aims as limited, and who believe that a U.S. concession would reduce Chinese fear and distrust of the United States, are inclined to drop antagonizing U.S. policies such as close-in surveillance. Other Americans believe "appeasing" China will set the United States on the path of abandoning Asia to Chinese domination.[24]

Although often accused of partiality and hypocrisy, among the historical Great Powers the United States stands out as a champion of international law. The PRC's South China Sea policy undercuts this effort. Not only has China resisted basing its claims in UNCLOS, but has attempted to gain unfair advantages over the smaller claimants. Ironically, China in effect practices the "power politics" (large countries pursuing their self-interests by bullying smaller countries into submission) that the PRC government has long condemned and criticized other Great Powers over. The United States has attempted to counter by supporting a multilateral resolution process that protects the smaller claimants from being bullied into an unfair settlement by a much larger China.

The most comprehensive and significant statement of U.S. interests in the South China Sea dispute during the first term of the Obama administration came during the ASEAN Regional Forum (ARF) in Hanoi in July 2010. The background of this meeting included the Obama administration's desire to redress the perception that America had lost interest in Southeast Asia; an international consensus that China was increasingly relying on bullying to get Southeast Asia to accept China's claims; and pleas from the Southeast Asian claimants, particularly Vietnam, for stronger diplomatic involvement by Washington.

At the time of the meeting Vietnam and the United States were engaged in a modest upgrade of their bilateral military cooperation. The steps they took were enough to draw from the Chinese media a warning that Vietnam was becoming a "pawn" of the United States.[25]

During the meeting, U.S. Secretary of State Hillary Clinton reasserted the U.S. right to sail in the South China Sea. She said the United States "supports a collaborative diplomatic process by all claimants for resolving the various territorial disputes". Washington supports the 2002 Declaration on the Conduct of Parties in the South China Sea (DoC) and is willing to "facilitate initiatives and confidence building measures" envisioned in the DoC, she said. Finally, Clinton said claims to sovereignty over the sea or the seabed should stem "solely from legitimate claims to land features".[26] Clinton's statement revealed a significant overlap between U.S. interests and international law. The U.S. demand that Chinese claims should be derived from land directly affirmed UNCLOS. Clinton called on China to respect the DoC, a multilateral agreement. Indirect support for international law came from U.S. attempts to prevent a strong country forcing its will on weaker partners, implied in Washington's disapproval of bilateral negotiations that give Beijing an unfair advantage and in the warning that China should not use or threaten to use force in support of its Chinese claims. Clinton's statement was a pointed criticism of PRC policy, and the Chinese reacted strongly to it. A response posted on the PRC Ministry of Foreign Affairs website said Clinton's comments "were in effect an attack on China" and part of "the scheme of some to internationalize the South China Sea issue".[27] As for the Southeast Asian countries that welcomed U.S. intervention, Chinese Foreign Minister Yang Jiechi scolded them for failing to accord a rising China proper deference: "China is a big country and other countries are small countries and that is just a fact", he reportedly said.[28]

In the view of many observers, China's South China Sea policy became even more assertive after 2010 despite the danger to the Chinese that they would undermine their own rhetoric about China's "peaceful rise".[29] This impacted U.S. strategic signalling in two ways. First, the comments of U.S. officials exhibited a harder edge. For example, during a 2013 visit to Singapore, U.S. Vice President Joe Biden mentioned the touchstone of "freedom of navigation", but he also called for the "peaceful resolution of territorial disputes" and said the United States "reject[s] coercion, intimidation, threats and the use of force". These remarks clearly referred to China even though Biden did not name a specific country.[30] U.S. official commentary hardened further when the large Chinese deep-water rig enter Vietnam's EEZ to drill in May 2014. The U.S. Navy's 7th Fleet released a statement saying "provocative or unilateral actions taken by one country could jeopardize the peace and security in the region", while a U.S. Department of State spokeswoman called the Chinese move a "unilateral action [that] appears to be part of a broader pattern of Chinese behavior to advance its claims over disputed territory in a manner that undermines peace and stability in the region."[31]

Second, Washington's criticism of Beijing's South China Sea policy shifted its emphasis from freedom of navigation to the broader question of international norms. In August 2014, for example, U.S. Secretary of State John Kerry said tensions in the South China Sea are "more than claims to islands and reefs and rocks and the economic interests that flow from them. They're about whether might makes right or whether global rules and norms and rule of law and international law will prevail."[32] When the Philippines unilaterally filed a case with the UN's International Tribunal for the Law of the Sea (ITLOS) challenging China's claims in January 2013, Washington publicly endorsed Manila's move, with a State Department spokeswoman saying, "We hope that this case serves to provide greater legal certainty and compliance with the international law of the sea."[33]

International law is often seen as providing protection for weaker states against the actions of stronger states, which often prefer to flout the rules in pursuit of their self-interest. China seems ambivalent about international law even for a major power. For China, UNCLOS is not intrinsically legitimate. Rather, China must grapple with it because the international community considers it legitimate. If confronted with the lack of justification for the nine(or ten)-dash line in UNCLOS, Chinese scholars argue that China had already established sovereignty over the South China Sea over a thousand years before UNCLOS.[34] Moreover, they point out that modern international law was written principally by Western countries and is therefore based on an outlook and historical experience that are alien to Asia. In short, it does not account for the traditional Asian way of conducting international affairs. This line of argument bodes well for China, but not for the other claimants. It suggests that the international rules will be different when Asia (i.e., China) is strong enough to write them. The idea that Asia should reject modern international law in favour of a return to its own form of ordering international affairs is ominous. When combined with the rise of Chinese power, the idea inevitably raises the prospect of a re-establishment of the pre-modern tribute system with China at the apex.

Pax Americana and *Pax Sinica* contend in the South China Sea. The rise of China within a region of longstanding U.S. pre-eminence fits a recurring historical pattern often called "hegemonic transition". The position of hegemon, or dominant power, is valuable not only because a relatively powerful state is safer from attack by its potential adversaries but also because the hegemon has the greatest influence in shaping the rules and norms of international affairs. Invariably the hegemon sponsors an international system that suits its own interests. Since relative power is always in flux, eventually every hegemon faces decline and a challenge by a rising rival for the right to set the rules of the system. The period during which the strength of the rising challenger approaches parity with the strength of the reigning hegemon is conflict-prone. The long-dominant power wants to retain its privileges and is tempted to start a preventive war against the rising challenger. The challenger is anxious to begin enjoying the fruits of its new relative strength. The current relationship between the United States and China is the latest iteration of this historical dynamic.[35] Washington sees itself as the sponsor and protector of regional order that reflects U.S. interests. Americans like to think this order also brings security and prosperity to the other states in the region (except the "rogue" countries that disregard international norms). While China has prospered immensely from global trade and an era of relative peace and stability, the Chinese government and people object to some aspects of the U.S.-managed order. These include: the American quasi-protectorate over Taiwan; U.S. alliances with Japan and South Korea, plus U.S. security cooperation with many other Asia-Pacific countries; the robust U.S. military presence in the region through bases and transiting or visiting military units; and Washington's campaign to encourage political liberalization throughout the region, which countries such as China see as a direct threat to regime security.

Now that China is an emerging Great Power, Chinese public opinion and jingoistic elite interest groups demand that Beijing redress these objectionable aspects of U.S. hegemony. It is conceivable that Washington can be flexible enough, and Beijing patient enough, for both countries to work out a peaceful transition that allows sufficient room for China to peacefully grow into a larger regional leadership role with the assent of the other regional governments. This, however, must be considered an optimistic outlook. On balance, the two Asia-Pacific Great Powers appear to be drifting towards confrontation. China's strategic vision cannot be realized without China driving out America as a regional strategic player and bringing to an end the current collection of regional security cooperation agreements with the United States. U.S. policy works to preserve the U.S.-sponsored order in East Asia by reassuring regional governments that the United States remains a reliable enforcer of peace and stability. Hugh White is among those analysts who argue that a major aspect of Chinese policy is to undermine the confidence of U.S. regional friends in American reliability by demonstrating that the United States will not defend them against Chinese challenges.[36] Failure to maintain U.S. credibility or leadership in Southeast Asia would be costly in itself, but the consequences could magnify if the loss of confidence in America's ability or willingness to play the role of constructive superpower spread to Northeast Asia and other regions. Washington also builds bulwarks against potential Chinese domination by carrying out soft balancing, including increased security cooperation between it and Southeast Asian countries as well as American diplomatic intervention to level the playing field in the South China Sea for the Southeast Asian claimants. If the Chinese strategy is to expose alleged U.S. unreliability and gain submission from its regional neighbours, it is not clear that this strategy is successful. For example, during the China–Philippines standoff over Scarborough Shoal that began in April 2012, although the United States did not directly intervene on behalf of the Philippines, afterward Washington increased annual defence assistance to Manila from $30 million to $50 million and donated a second retired *Hamilton*-class coast guard cutter to the Philippine Navy in 2013. The mutual fear of China also helped grease progress in U.S.–Vietnam relations. In September 2014, the U.S. government was reportedly close to easing an arms embargo against Vietnam to allow Hanoi to purchase P-3 Orion maritime patrol aircraft.[37] This may be a truly zero-sum game between the United States and China.

IS THE SOUTH CHINA SEA THE LEADING U.S.–CHINA FLASHPOINT?

U.S. attention is drawn to the South China Sea because for Washington this strategic waterway is another arena of the sharpening strategic competition with a rising China. The PRC is not only one of the claimants over disputed maritime territory, it has been the most aggressive, even if the Chinese see their own actions as defensive. With its nine-dash line, Beijing's claims go far beyond those of the other claimants. China claims the middle of the South China Sea while others claim the edges. China is alone in claiming that the island-like features generate an EEZ. If other countries used the same logic China uses, half of the North Pacific Ocean between the U.S. west coast and Hawaii would be U.S. territorial waters, and most of the Indian Ocean would be Indian territorial waters. While Southeast Asian claimants have moved ahead unilaterally to strengthen their claims, the PRC has distinguished itself through its fortification of Mischief Reef, its annual declaration of a fishing ban in the northern section of the South

China Sea, bullying of other claimants through acts such as the cable-cutting incidents and the rate at which China is increasing its military and quasi-military presence in the South China Sea not only through ship deployments but also through land reclamation to enlarge seven Chinese-occupied features with the apparent goal of turning them into small military bases.[38]

The Chinese could get most of what they want by appealing to international law. Under UNCLOS guidelines, the Chinese could make a case for rights to a continental shelf and large if partially divided EEZs. Instead, however, Beijing has opted to make what the rest of the world considers an unreasonably large claim, attempting to enforce that claim and hunker down until the other claimants succumb to the conclusion that they cannot prevail against China's overwhelming advantages in relative power. The situation would be completely different if China was not a rising Great Power. Without the expectation that the imbalance in power-projection capability between China and its Southeast Asian neighbours will continue to grow in China's favour, Beijing would have much greater reason to seek a negotiated and mutually-agreeable compromise settlement.

The South China Sea dispute reveals fundamental conflicts of interest in U.S.–China relations on issues of vital interest to both countries. Acquiescence to the apparent Chinese agenda would be tantamount to the United States giving up its role as a Great Power in maritime eastern Asia. Thus, the South China Sea threatens to hasten a U.S.–China conflict that both countries would prefer to avoid. The PRC has specifically warned the United States not to intervene in the South China Sea dispute.[39] The official Chinese rationale is that "internationalizing" the dispute by allowing a non-claimant such as the United States to weigh in will make it harder for the actual claimants to reach a settlement. More importantly, however, U.S. intervention has made it harder for the Chinese to intimidate the smaller claimants into submitting to the PRC's will.

Disappointingly for China, with the "rebalance" policy Washington has reaffirmed a determination to remain a decisive player in the Asia-Pacific region and an agenda setter in maritime Southeast Asia despite the U.S. government's daunting financial problems. Even with the cuts to the U.S. defence budget now planned or contemplated, the United States will remain a formidable regional military power for the foreseeable future. Beijing's South China Sea policy not only clashes with major U.S. objectives in the Asia-Pacific region, it generates pessimism regarding the larger issue of whether or not the rise of China within an international system long under U.S. primacy will result in another classic historical hegemonic conflict between the young challenger and the mature Great Power. Because the Chinese see the South China Sea as part of China's backyard, China's extraordinarily bold policy here may not be indicative of how the PRC will handle other international disputes beyond China's immediate periphery. Even China's periphery, however, encompasses areas important to the United States and its allies and partners. From a U.S. point of view, China's policy sends all the wrong signals: that a strong China intends to push aside international law, insist on a buffer zone free of the influence of major foreign powers and demand deferential behaviour from smaller neighbours. The South China Sea raises fears rather than hopes for the future of U.S.–China relations.

Notes

1. Stephanie Condon, "Obama: We Welcome China's Rise", *CBS News*, 19 January 2011, available at <http://www.cbsnews.com/8301-503544_162-20028958-503544.html>.
2. David C. Kang, *China Rising: Peace, Power and Order in East Asia* (New York: Columbia University Press, 2007).
3. Gerald Segal, "Does China Matter?", *Foreign Affairs* 78, no. 5 (September/October 1999).
4. Xinhua News Service, "China Will Never Seek Hegemony: Vice-Foreign Minister", 14 January 2011, available at <http://news.xinhuanet.com/english2010/china/2011-01/15/c_13691377.htm>.
5. Marshall David Sahlins, Elman Rogers Service and Thomas G. Harding, *Evolution and Culture* (Ann Arbor: University of Michigan Press, 1960), p. 85.
6. See, for example, Alastair Iain Johnston, *Cultural Realism: Strategic Culture and Grand Strategy in Chinese History* (Princeton: Princeton University Press, 1995).
7. Christopher J. Pehrson, *String of Pearls: Meeting the Challenge of China's Rising Power Across the Asian Littoral* (Carlisle: Strategic Studies Institute, US Army War College, July 2006), available at <www.strategicstudiesinstitute.army.mil/pdffiles/PUB721.pdf>; James R. Holmes and Toshi Yoshihara, "Is China a 'Soft' Naval Power?", *China Brief* 9, issue 17 (20 August 2009): 4–7; Geoffrey Wade, *The Zheng He Voyages: A Reassessment*, Asia Research Institute Working Paper no. 31 (Singapore: National University of Singapore, October 2004), pp. 1, 11–16.
8. "Admiral Says Sub Risked a Shootout", *Washington Times*, 15 November 2006, available at <http://www.washingtontimes.com/news/2006/nov/15/20061115-122631-3752r/?page=all>.

9. Remarks by U.S. Secretary of Defense Robert M. Gates during the Shangri-La meeting, Singapore, 5 June 2010, available at <http://www.defense.gov/speeches/speech.aspx?speechid=1483>.

10. Testimony of Admiral Robert F. Willard to House Appropriations Committee, 14 April 2011, available at <http://www.pacom.mil/web/PACOM_Resources/pdf/TestimonyofAdmRobertWillardUSNavy-14April2011.pdf>, p. 10.

11. Air-Sea Battle Office, "The Air-Sea Battle Concept Summary", 10 November 2011, available at <http://www.marines.mil/unit/hqmc/Pages/TheAir-SeaBattleconceptsummary.aspx>.

12. PRC Ministry of Foreign Affairs, "Remarks by Assistant Foreign Minister Liu Zhenmin at the Opening Ceremony of the Workshop on 'Implementing DoC: Maintaining Freedom and Safety of Navigation in the South China Sea'", 19 December 2011, available at <http://ph.china-embassy.org/eng/xwdt/t895100.htm>.

13. Zhong Sheng, "US Should Not Muddy the Waters over South China Sea", *People's Daily*, 20 March 2012, available at <http://www.china.org.cn/opinion/2012-03/20/content_24941973.htm>.

14. Dana Dillon, "How the Bush Administration Should Handle China", Heritage Foundation, 5 September 2001, available at <http://www.heritage.org/research/reports/2001/09/how-the-bush-administration-should-handle-china>; Kanwal Sibal, "China Stance in East Asia At Odds with POK Policy", *India Today*, 11 October 2011, available at <http://indiatoday.intoday.in/story/china-stance-in-east-asia-at-odds-with-pok-policy/1/154470.html>; "Danger At Sea", *Philippine Daily Inquirer*, 22 June 2011, available at <http://opinion.inquirer.net/6771/danger-at-sea>.

15. J. Michael Cole, "South China Sea All PRC's, Op-ed Claims", *Taipei Times*, 29 November 2011.

16. United Nations Convention on the Law of the Sea, Articles 17, 19 and 58, available at <http://www.un.org/depts/los/convention_agreements/texts/unclos/unclos_e.pdf>.

17. "Temporary Management Measures for Survey and Mapping Activities Conducted by Foreign Organizations or Individuals in China", PRC State Bureau of Surveying and Mapping, September 2007, available at <www.sbsm.gov.cn/article//zcfg/bmgz/200709/20070900000644.shtml>.

18. Eric McVadon, "Humanitarian Operations: A Window on US–China Maritime Cooperation", in *China, the United States, and 21st Century Sea Power*, edited by Andrew Erickson, Lyle Goldstein and Nan Li (Annapolis: Naval Institute Press, 2010), pp. 264–65.

19. This assessment is based on the author's confidential discussions with U.S. officials.

20. U.S. Department of Defense, "Annual Report to Congress: Military and Security Developments Involving the People's Republic of China 2013", available at <http://www.defense.gov/pubs/2013_China_Report_FINAL.pdf>;

Rory Medcalf, "Maritime Game-Changer Revealed at Shangri-La Dialogue", *The Diplomat*, 2 June 2013, available at <http://thediplomat.com/flashpoints-blog/2013/06/02/maritime-game-changer-revealed-at-shangri-la-dialogue/>.

21. "Chinese Spy Ship Lurks Around U.S.-led Pacific Naval Drills", *Washington Post*, 21 July 2014; "Chinese Ship Spies on Valiant Shield, and That's OK with US", *Stars and Stripes*, 22 September 2014.

22. Robert Jervis, *Perception and Misperception in International Politics* (Princeton: Princeton University Press, 1976), chapter 3.

23. Jim Mann, "US Starting to View China as Potential Enemy", *Los Angeles Times*, 16 April 1995, available at <http://articles.latimes.com/1995-04-16/news/mn-55355_1_china-today>.

24. For example, U.S. Senator Jim Webb (D-VA) recently said, "We are approaching a Munich moment with China." Transcript from "Meet the Press", NBC-TV, 26 June 2011, available at <http://www.msnbc.msn.com/id/43512460/ns/meet_the_press-transcripts/t/meet-press-transcript-june/>.

25. PRC Foreign Ministry, "Foreign Minister Yang Jiechi Refutes Fallacies on the South China Sea Issue", 26 July 2010, available at <http://www.fmprc.gov.cn/eng/zxxx/t719460.htm>; Geoff Dyer, "Beijing's Elevated Aspirations", *Financial Times*, 10 November 2010, available at <http://www.ft.com/intl/cms/s/0/1cfa57c4-ed03-11df-9912-00144feab49a.html#axzz1hsuZM8I8>.

26. U.S. Department of State, "Remarks at Press Availability", Hanoi, Vietnam, 23 July 2010, available at <http://www.state.gov/secretary/rm/2010/07/145095.htm>.

27. "Foreign Minister Yang Jiechi Refutes Fallacies on the South China Sea Issue", op. cit.

28. Dyer, "Beijing's Elevated Aspirations", op. cit.

29. See, for example, Robert Sutter and Chin-Hao Huang, "China's Shift to Toughness on Maritime Claims — One Year Later", Pacific Forum CSIS, PacNet no. 53, 17 July 2013, available at <http://csis.org/files/publication/Pac1353.pdf>.

30. The White House, Office of the Press Secretary, "Remarks to the Press by Vice President Biden and Prime Minister Lee of Singapore", Singapore, 26 July 2013, available at <http://www.whitehouse.gov/the-press-office/2013/07/26/remarks-press-vice-president-biden-and-prime-minister-lee-singapore>.

31. Erik Slavin, "US Slams 'Provocation' After Chinese Reportedly Ram Vietnamese Ships", *Stars & Stripes*, 8 May 2014, available at <http://www.stripes.com/news/us-slams-provocation-after-chinese-reportedly-ram-vietnamese-ships-1.282098>.

32. Scott Stearns, "Kerry: Law, Not Coercion, Key to Resolving Sea Disputes", *Voice of America News*, 14 August 2014, available at <http://www.voanews.com/content/reu-kerry-says-constructive-relations-with-china-needed-for-regional-stability/2412785.html>.

33. U.S. Department of State Press Statement, "Philippines: South China Sea Arbitration Case Filing", 30 March 2014, available at <http://www.state.gov/r/pa/prs/ps/2014/03/224150.htm>.

34. Sun Xiaoying, "Legitimate Sovereignty: Historical and Legal Evidence Proves China's Indisputable Sovereignty over the South China Sea", *Beijing Review*, no. 32, 12 August 2010, available at <http://www.bjreview.com.cn/world/txt/2010-08/06/content_289282.htm>.

35. Robert Gilpin, *War & Change in International Politics* (Cambridge: Cambridge University Press, 1981); Jack S. Levy, "Power Transition Theory and the Rise of China", in *China's Ascent: Power, Security, and the Future of International Politics*, edited by Robert S. Ross and Zhu Feng (Ithaca: Cornell University Press, 2008).

36. Hugh White, "Explaining China's Behaviour in the East and South China Seas", *The Lowy Interpreter*, 22 May 2014, available at <http://www.lowyinterpreter.org/post/2014/05/22/Explaining-Chinas-behaviour-in-the-East-and-South-China-Seas.aspx?COLLCC=1823521104&>.

37. Lesley Wroughton and Andrea Shalal, "Exclusive: Courting Vietnam, U.S. Prepares to Ease Arms Embargo", Reuters, 23 September 2014, available at <http://www.reuters.com/article/2014/09/23/us-usa-vietnam-relations-exclusive-idUSKCN0HI22I20140923>.

38. "China Says South China Sea Land Reclamation 'Justified'", BBC News, 10 September 2014, available at <http://www.bbc.com/news/world-asia-china-29139125>.

39. Edward Wong, "Beijing Warns US about South China Sea Disputes", *New York Times*, 22 June 2011, available at <http://www.nytimes.com/2011/06/23/world/asia/23china.html?_r=2&ref=world>.

11

THE SOUTH CHINA SEA DISPUTE IN U.S.–ASEAN RELATIONS

Yann-Huei Song

Before 2009, the South China Sea dispute was not a major policy issue in relations between the United States and the Association of Southeast Asian Nations (ASEAN). Since then, however, escalating tensions over sovereignty and maritime boundary claims in the South China Sea has become an increasingly salient issue in bilateral relations. Arguably the South China Sea dispute has been used by the administration of President Barack Obama to support its strategy of increased engagement with Southeast Asia and to push for greater U.S. influence in the Asia-Pacific region more generally. For some ASEAN states, if not for all ten members, the upswing of tensions in the South China Sea has increased the perception that the People's Republic of China (PRC) increasingly poses a strategic threat, making it necessary to move closer to the United States to check Beijing's assertive moves and to counter-balance its growing power in Southeast Asia. One of the indicators of this changing attitude is found in ASEAN's decision to invite the United States to join the East Asia Summit (EAS) and the ASEAN Defence Ministers Meeting-Plus (ADMM-Plus).

On 15 November 2009, a joint statement was issued after the 1st U.S.–ASEAN Leaders' Meeting in Singapore. While Washington and ASEAN agreed to strengthen efforts to combat international terrorism and other transnational crimes such as illicit drug trafficking and piracy, they did not touch upon cooperation on maritime security issues, in particular those related to the South China Sea dispute.[1] Two years later, however, at the 3rd U.S.–ASEAN Leaders' Meeting in Bali on 18 November 2011, the joint statement included the phrase "South China Sea" for the first time, as well as their concern that peace and stability be maintained in the area.[2] U.S. and ASEAN leaders also agreed to make greater efforts to promote "cooperation on maritime issues, including maritime security, search and rescue, and safety of navigation in the region through promotion of capacity building, information sharing and technology cooperation and explore the possibility of utilizing such venues as the ASEAN Maritime Forum".[3] In addition, on 19 November 2011, at the 6th EAS, sixteen of the eighteen countries — including the United States and eight ASEAN members — raised the South China Sea issue. The only two members that did not speak on the issue were Cambodia and Laos. Although the Chairman's Statement of the 6th EAS did not specifically refer to the South China Sea dispute, it included a paragraph in which the EAS members recognized the importance of promoting maritime cooperation and the need to address common challenges on maritime issues in East Asia, including, presumably, the South China Sea dispute.[4]

This chapter examines how the South China Sea dispute impacted the development of U.S.–ASEAN relations between 2009 and 2014. It begins with a discussion of ASEAN's institutional approach towards managing the dispute before moving on to address U.S. concerns and policy responses in the South China Sea. This is followed by a review of recent developments in U.S.–ASEAN relations. The chapter ends by assessing the impact of the South China Sea issue on the development of U.S.–ASEAN relations between 2009 and 2014.

ASEAN AND THE SOUTH CHINA SEA DISPUTE

Due to differing national interests among the ASEAN member states, and the varying degrees of economic, political and security ties they have with China and the United States, ASEAN has always found it difficult to achieve a common stand on the South China Sea dispute, especially since the enlargement of the grouping from six to ten members between 1995 and 1999. In the late 1990s and early 2000s, ASEAN failed to negotiate with China a regional Code of Conduct (CoC) for the South China Sea mainly because consensus could not be reached among the member states. As a result, in 2002 a weaker political document was adopted as a compromise, namely the Declaration on the Conduct of Parties in the South China Sea (DoC), which has been widely criticized for its lack of legally binding enforcement mechanisms.[5]

Another example demonstrating the lack of political solidarity among ASEAN member states over the dispute is related to a paragraph that was included in the proposed draft guidelines to implement the DoC at the 1st ASEAN–China Joint Working Group on the Implementation of the DoC in August 2005; namely that "ASEAN will continue its current practice of consulting among each other before meeting with China."[6] Both the Philippines and Vietnam insisted on the inclusion of this paragraph. China, however, was opposed on the grounds that the disputes in the South China Sea are not between China and ASEAN as a whole and should be settled by the countries directly concerned. It was not until 20 July 2011, at a meeting of ASEAN and China senior officials, that agreement was reached on the adoption of the Guidelines on the Implementation of the Declaration on the Conduct of Parties in the South China Sea.[7] It was only when the original paragraph contained in the 2005 draft guidelines was removed that it became possible for the final adoption of the document after six years of negotiations.[8]

Although the implementation guidelines were criticized as "changing almost nothing",[9] in December 2011 the Chinese proposed establishing a technical workshop on regional oceanographic exchange on the South China Sea, and a track 1.5 international workshop on "Implementing DoC: Maintaining Freedom and Safety of Navigation in the South China Sea" to be held in Qingdao and Haikou attended by participants from China and ASEAN states, as well as international scholars.[10] In addition, at the 14th ASEAN–China Summit, held on 18 November 2011, China proposed a $471 million fund to develop maritime cooperation with ASEAN member states based on the DoC implementation guidelines. At the 4th ASEAN–China Senior Officials Meeting in Beijing on 14 January 2012, it was proposed that China would hold a maritime disaster prevention and mitigation workshop and marine ecological environment and surveillance technology workshop. It was also agreed that Vietnam would hold a maritime search-and-rescue seminar and Singapore a marine ecology and biological diversity seminar. A Joint ASEAN–China Commemorative Workshop for the 10th Anniversary of the DoC was held in November 2012.

Originally ASEAN foreign ministers expressed their common concern over the South China Sea dispute at the 25th ASEAN Ministerial Meeting (AMM) in Manila in July 1992. It was a direct response to the adoption of the Law on the Territorial Sea and Contiguous Zone by China in February 1992, legislation that explicitly asserted Beijing's territorial claims to the Spratly and Paracel Islands. ASEAN foreign ministers emphasized that "any territorial or jurisdictional dispute should be resolved by peaceful means, without resort to force", and urged all parties concerned to exercise self-restraint with a view to creating a positive climate for the resolution of the dispute. They also called on all parties to apply the principles contained in the 1976 Treaty of Amity and Cooperation (TAC) as the basis for establishing a code of international conduct in the South China Sea. The first official policy position of ASEAN on the South China Sea dispute was articulated in a separate declaration issued on 22 July 1992, the "ASEAN Declaration on the South China Sea".[11] Nineteen years later, at the 19th ASEAN Summit in November 2011, ASEAN as a group reiterated its official position on the South China Sea issue, that is: first, reaffirming the importance of the DoC as a milestone document signed between ASEAN and China to ensure peace, stability and security in the South China Sea; second, ensuring the peaceful resolution of the South China Sea dispute in accordance with international law, including the 1982 United Nations Convention on the Law of the Sea (UNCLOS); third, stressing the need to implement the DoC and the adoption of a regional code of conduct in the area; and fourth, welcoming various multilateral mechanisms or forums, at the track one or track two levels for the study and promotion of maritime cooperation in the South China Sea.[12]

Between 2012 and 2014, the position of ASEAN on the South China Sea had been repeatedly stated in its Six-Point Principles on the South China Sea, adopted in July 2012,[13] Joint Communiqués of the 46th and 47th AMM, Chairman's Statement of the 20th, 21st, 22nd, 23rd, and 24th ASEAN Summits, and the ASEAN Foreign Ministers' Statement on the Current Development in the South China Sea, adopted on 10 May 2014.[14]

At present, ASEAN neither supports nor opposes the claims made by its four member states, namely, the Philippines, Vietnam, Malaysia and Brunei. However, as pointed out by Singapore's Ambassador-at-Large, Tommy Koh,[15] and Jusuf Wanandi from the Centre for Strategic and International Studies in Jakarta,[16] collectively ASEAN is a stakeholder in the South China Sea: its main concern is the maintenance of peace, stability and security in the area. In addition, it asks all of the parties concerned to act in accordance with international law, especially UNCLOS. Moreover, ASEAN urges its member states and China to finalize the adoption of a regional CoC. This effort should not, however, be seen as an attempt by ASEAN to counter China or support the claims made by any of its members. Putting these concerns and views together, the official policy line of ASEAN on the South China Sea issue is more or less unchanged since 1992.

U.S. CONCERNS AND POLICY RESPONSES
IN THE SOUTH CHINA SEA

Following a naval clash between Vietnamese and Chinese forces at Johnson Reef in the Spratly Islands in 1988, the administration of President Ronald Reagan responded by stating that while the United States took no position on the merits of competing claims in the South China Sea, it supported a peaceful resolution of the dispute and opposed the threat or use of force.[17] In May 1995, concerned about rising tensions between China and the Philippines over ownership of Mischief Reef, the U.S. Department of State issued a statement on the Spratlys which stressed that the United States "has an abiding interest in the maintenance of peace and stability in the South China Sea" and that Washington viewed "with serious concern any maritime claim, or restriction on maritime activity, in the South China Sea that was not consistent with international law, including the 1982 United Nations Convention on the Law of the Sea".[18]

In June 2010, U.S. national interests in the South China Sea were made more clearly in remarks made by then Defense Secretary Robert Gates at the Shangri-La Dialogue meeting in Singapore. Gates noted that "the South China Sea is an area of growing concern. This sea is not only vital to those directly bordering it, but to all nations with economic and security interests in Asia."[19] Due to its commitments to free and open commence, a just international order that emphasizes rights and responsibilities of nations and fidelity to the rule of law, open access by all to the global commons of sea, air, space and cyberspace, and the principle of resolving conflicts without the use of force, it is U.S. policy that stability, freedom of navigation and free and unhindered economic development in the South China Sea should be maintained. In addition, while not taking sides over competing sovereignty claims in the area, the United States opposes the use of force and actions that hinder freedom of navigation. Moreover, in response to pressure from China on Exxon-Mobil and other foreign energy companies in 2008 to suspend drilling activity off the Vietnamese coast, Secretary Gates stated that the United States objects to any effort to intimidate U.S. corporations or those of any nation engaged in legitimate economic activity.[20]

In September 2010, U.S. Assistant Secretary of State for East Asian and Pacific Affairs, Kurt Campbell, explained that U.S. policy towards the South China Sea issue has remained consistent since 1995.[21] U.S. interests in the South China Sea were further elaborated by Secretary of State Hillary Clinton at the 17th ASEAN Regional Forum (ARF) in Hanoi in

July 2010. At the ARF meeting, Clinton stated that the United States, "like every nation, has a national interest in freedom of navigation, open access to Asia's maritime commons, and respect for international law in the South China Sea".[22] In addition, she made clear that although the United States does not take sides on the sovereignty and maritime disputes in the South China Sea, "claimants should pursue their territorial claims and accompanying rights to maritime space in accordance with the UN Convention on the Law of the Sea".[23]

U.S. interests in the South China Sea were reiterated in a letter sent by then U.S. Senate Foreign Relations Committee Chairman Senator John Kerry and Senator John McCain to Chinese State Councillor Dai Bingguo on 14 July 2011, in which they wrote:

> the United States does not take a position on the overlapping territorial claims in this region, but we do maintain a deep and abiding interest in ensuring freedom of navigation, commerce, and economic exploration; maintaining US commitments to our allies and partners; and supporting peace and security in the Asia-Pacific region.[24]

The two Senators also expressed U.S. concerns over a series of naval incidents that had occurred in the South China Sea which had raised tensions in the region — on 26 May 2011, three Chinese maritime surveillance ships cut the cables of Vietnamese exploration ship *Binh Minh 2* in Vietnam's EEZ and on 9 June, it was reported that Chinese ships had cut seismic cables towed by Vietnamese research ship *Viking II* near Vanguard Bank in the South China Sea — and warned that, "[i]f appropriate steps are not taken to calm the situation, future incidents could escalate, jeopardizing the vital national interest of the United States".[25]

On 22 July 2011, at the 18th ARF in Bali, Secretary Clinton declared that "as a Pacific nation and resident power we have a national interest in freedom of navigation, open access to Asia's maritime domain, the maintenance of peace and stability and respect for international law in the South China Sea."[26] She urged all parties involved in the dispute to pursue their territorial claims and accompanying rights to maritime space in accordance with international law, particularly as reflected in UNCLOS.[27] She too expressed concern at the cable-cutting incidents because they "endanger the safety of life at sea, escalate tensions, undermine freedom of navigation, and pose risks to lawful unimpeded commerce and economic development".[28] In addition, Clinton asked the parties concerned to clarify their claims in the South China Sea in terms consistent with customary international law, particularly UNCLOS: "Consistent with international law, claims to maritime space in the South China Sea should be derived solely from legitimate claims to land features",[29] an implicit reference to China's nine-dash line map.

In October 2011, during a visit to Indonesia, then U.S. Secretary of Defense Leon Panetta asked ASEAN members to continue working towards a binding CoC. He reiterated that the United States has a national interest in freedom of navigation and overflight, in unimpeded economic development and commence and respect for international law. In addition, he said that although the United States does not take a position on competing territorial claims, it hopes that in the interest of a peaceful resolution, all parties concerned clarify their maritime claims in terms consistent with customary international law.[30] Panetta's comments were followed by remarks made by Secretary Clinton in Manila on 16 November 2011, in which she said that President Obama, when attending the 3rd U.S.–ASEAN Leaders' Meeting and the 6th EAS, would reaffirm U.S. national interests in the maintenance of peace and security in the Asia Pacific, "freedom of navigation, overflight, respect for international law, the rule of law, unimpeded lawful commerce across the region's maritime domain" and that the United States would "further seek the Law of the Sea used as the overriding framework for handling territorial disputes".[31] Secretary Clinton, in a response to a question raised by a reporter, noted that:

> the disputes … in the West Philippine Sea [South China Sea] between the Philippines and China should be resolved peacefully. The United States does not take a position on any territorial claim, because any nation with a claim has a right to assert it, but they do not have a right to pursue it through intimidation or coercion. They should be following international law, the rule of law, the UN Convention on Law of the Sea … There are mechanisms within it … for the resolution of disputes. And we stand for the rule of law and we stand for international norms and standards, which is why we support the peaceful resolution.[32]

Douglas Paal, Vice President for Studies at the Carnegie Endowment for International Peace, criticized Secretary Clinton for her "inappropriate rhetoric" during her visit to Manila, where she referred to the South China Sea as the "West Philippine Sea", a phrase adopted by the Philippines in 2011 to refer to the South China Sea. Paal commented that, "This is not official U.S. geographical terminology but appeared in China's eyes to be taking the Philippines' position in a dispute where Clinton previously said the United States would not take sides."[33]

In November 2011, at the 6th EAS in Bali, President Obama enunciated the principles-based U.S. approach to maritime security issues in the region, including freedom of navigation and overflight and other internationally lawful uses of the seas, as well as use of collaborative diplomatic processes to address the South China Sea dispute. He also stated that the United States strongly opposes the threat or use of force by any party to advance its territorial or maritime claims or interfere in legitimate economic activity. In addition, Obama reiterated U.S. support for the DoC as a responsible approach to disputed areas, and encouraged all parties concerned to accelerate efforts to reach a full code of conduct for the South China Sea.[34] On 1 June 2013, at the 12th Shangri-La Dialogue in Singapore, Secretary of Defense Chuck Hagel explained the U.S. position on the South China Sea: that the U.S. continues to call on all claimants to exercise restraint as they publicly pledged in 2002, and to seek peaceful means to resolve the dispute; the U.S. supports the recent agreement between China and ASEAN to establish crisis hotlines to help manage maritime incidents; the U.S. also welcomes efforts to start talks on a CoC for the South China Sea; and that the U.S. encourages claimants to explore all peaceful means of settling their territorial disputes and the use of the dispute adjudication resolution mechanisms provided by UNCLOS.[35]

Also in June 2013, Joseph Yun, Acting Assistant Secretary for East Asian and Pacific Affairs, delivered a speech at the third annual South China Sea Conference organized by the Center for Strategic and International Studies (CSIS), in which he elaborated the U.S. position on the South China Sea issues as follows: first, America does not take a stance on sovereignty over any specific territory whether in the South China Sea or East China Sea; second, that it supports UNCLOS and the DoC as the legitimate mechanisms for resolving and managing disputes; third that freedom of navigation is a U.S. national interest, and it must be upheld in the South China Sea; fourth, Washington supports the lawful exploitation of natural resources from the South China Sea; fifth, that it opposes the use of force or coercion by any party; sixth, that the U.S. supports all forms of negotiation, whether bilateral, mediated by a third party or international; and seventh, there can be no threat of retaliation if mediation brings an unfavourable result for one or more parties and no unilateral changes to the status quo.[36] On 2 July 2013, Secretary of State John Kerry reiterated the same position at the 20th AFR that was held in Brunei.[37]

In February 2014, in his testimony before the House Committee on Foreign Affairs' Subcommittee on Asia and the Pacific, Daniel Russel, Assistant Secretary of State, reiterated the U.S. position on the South China Sea, but called on Beijing to clarify the meaning of the nine-dash line and its legal justification:

> under international law, maritime claims in the South China Sea must be derived from land features. Any use of the "nine dash line" by China to claim maritime rights not based on claimed land features would be inconsistent with international law. The international community would welcome China to clarify or adjust its nine-dash line claim to bring it in accordance with the international law of the sea.[38]

In July 2014, in response to a further escalation of tensions in the South China Sea, Deputy Assistant Secretary Michael Fuchs proposed that the claimants agree to freeze destabilizing activities in the South China Sea by committing not to establish new outposts, not to seize features that another claimant has occupied and to clarify what types of activities are provocative and what are merely efforts to maintain a long-existing presence in accordance with the status quo since 2002.[39]

The most recent statement of U.S. interest and policy in the South China Sea was made by Secretary of State John Kerry in August 2014 at the East-West Center, Honolulu, where he said:

> The United States of America takes no position on questions of sovereignty in the South and East China Seas, but we do care about how those questions are resolved. We care about behavior. We firmly oppose the use of intimidation and coercion or force to assert a territorial claim by anyone in the region. And we firmly oppose any suggestion that freedom of navigation and overflight and other lawful uses of the sea and airspace are privileges granted by a big state to a small one. All claimants must work together to solve the claims through peaceful means, big or small. And these principles bind all nations equally, and all nations have a responsibility to uphold them.[40]

In sum, the United States has been concerned about the escalation of tensions in the South China Sea and its policy responses are aimed at enhancing the following political, economic, strategic and security interests in the area: freedom of navigation and overflight rights; military presence and security commitments to U.S. allies and partners; regional peace and stability; sea lane security; open commerce and access to maritime commons; participation in oil and gas exploration and exploitation activities; and legal order at sea. U.S. interests in the South China Sea also include the effective implementation of the DoC, the expeditious conclusion of a CoC and the settlement of disputes by peaceful means, including arbitration under UNCLOS.

THE SOUTH CHINA SEA AND RECENT DEVELOPMENTS IN U.S.–ASEAN RELATIONS 2009–14

Beijing's growing assertiveness in the South China Sea since 2007–8 has presented Washington with a convenient opportunity to reaffirm its principled position on the South China Sea issue, helped strengthen U.S.–ASEAN relations and promoted closer ties between the United States and its allies and partners in Southeast Asia. China's more assertive stance over the dispute has also heightened the security concerns of some ASEAN member states, particularly those that have overlapping claims with China. Those security concerns have pushed them to forge coalitions and develop a cooperative approach to dealing with the South China Sea dispute, such as the position they take on the legal status of the Paracel and Spratly Islands and the interpretation and application of Article 121, paragraph 3 of UNCLOS, which provides that, "Rocks which cannot sustain human habitation or economic life of their own shall have no exclusive economic zone or continental shelf." More importantly, China's belligerence in the South China Sea has pushed several ASEAN members to seek assistance from the United States in the form of capacity building support for their armed forces and coast guards. This trend of development is manifested in the joint statements or political documents issued after the conclusion of a series of U.S.–ASEAN related meetings between 2009 and 2014.

In March 2009, the U.S. Navy surveillance vessel *Impeccable* was in the South China Sea monitoring submarine activity. On 8 March, the *Impeccable* was approached by five Chinese vessels approximately 75 miles off the coast of Hainan Island. The Chinese vessels attempted to force the *Impeccable* to stop its survey activities and leave the area in question.[41] The United States lodged formal protests, stating that under international law, the U.S. military could legally conduct activities "in waters beyond the territorial sea of another state without prior notification or consent including in an exclusive economic zone of another country".[42] In response, China stated that the U.S. allegation of Chinese harassment of the *Impeccable* was "totally inaccurate".[43] China also accused the United States of violating both international and Chinese laws.[44] In May the same year, some ASEAN member states expressed concern regarding China's submission of its nine-dash line map to the United Nations Commission on the Limits of the Continental Shelf (CLCS). In its response to the Chinese note, especially the attached nine-dash line map, Indonesia argued that "those remote or very small features in the South China Sea do not deserve exclusive economic zone or continental shelf of their own", and that the map "clearly lacks international legal basis and is tantamount to upset the [UNCLOS Convention]".[45] Indonesia pointed out that,

> Allowing the use of uninhabited rocks, reefs and atolls isolated from the mainland and in the middle of the high sea as a base point to generate maritime space concerns the fundamental principles of the Convention and encroaches [upon] the legitimate interest of the global community.[46]

The Indonesian response to the Chinese maritime claim was followed by a diplomatic note sent by the Philippines to the UN Secretary General on 5 April 2011, in which the Philippines reaffirmed its sovereignty and jurisdiction over the geological features in the Kalayaan Island Group — the Philippine claim to fifty-three islands, reefs, shoals cays, rocks and atolls in the Spratlys — and challenged the legitimacy of the Chinese claim to sovereignty, sovereign rights and jurisdiction over the islands, "adjacent waters", "relevant waters" and seabed and subsoil encircled by the nine-dash lines in the South China Sea.[47] However, these developments did not prompt the United States to raise the South China Sea issue at the 16th ARF and other ASEAN-related meetings in 2009.

In May 2009, at the Shangri-La Dialogue, Defense Secretary Gates addressed major regional security issues but did not mention the South China Sea dispute specifically.[48] In July 2009, at the ASEAN Post Ministerial Conference Plus One session in Phuket, the United States and ASEAN discussed a number of issues of mutual concern, including climate change, pandemic diseases and counter terrorism. Again, there was no discussion of the South China Sea.[49] At the 16th ARF meeting, Secretary Clinton discussed the North Korean nuclear issue and moves within the ARF to enhance security in Northeast Asia, but again there was no mention of the South China Sea problem.[50]

However, renewed U.S. interest in ASEAN and Southeast Asia more generally was reflected in America's accession to the Treaty of Amity and Cooperation on 22 July 2009, the adoption of the Revised Priorities for Cooperation under the U.S.–ASEAN Enhanced Partnership, the decision to appoint a U.S. ambassador to ASEAN in Jakarta and agreement to work towards convening an ASEAN–U.S. Commemorative Summit.[51] In October 2009, the 4th EAS meeting was held in Cha-am Hua Hin, Thailand. Since the United States was not a member of the EAS, no American participants attended the meeting. The chairman's statement did not mention the South China Sea dispute.[52] On 15 November 2009, after the 1st U.S.–ASEAN Leaders' Meeting in Singapore, a joint statement was issued but it did not touch upon the South China Sea dispute.[53]

In 2009, although the United States did not raise the South China Sea issue at ASEAN-related meetings, domestically, the Departments of State and Defense, the U.S. Senate and U.S. think-tanks began to express concern regarding rising tensions in the South China Sea, the potential impact of the dispute on U.S. national interests and the need for Washington to respond. In July 2009, for example, at a hearing on maritime disputes and sovereignty issues in East Asia by the U.S. Senate Committee on Foreign Relations, Scot Marciel, Deputy Assistant Secretary of State for East Asian and ASEAN Affairs, and Robert Scher, Deputy Assistant Secretary of Defense for South and Southeast Asia, addressed the situation in the South China Sea and America's position on the issue. They both emphasized the need for the administration to protect U.S. interests in the area.[54] Scholars from U.S. think-tanks and academic institutions, such as the American Enterprise Institute, the Henry L. Stimson Center and the U.S. Navy War College also presented their views at the hearing.[55]

From mid-2010, the United States began to raise maritime security and the South China Sea issue at ASEAN-led multilateral security forums such as the ARF, U.S.–ASEAN Leaders' Meeting, ADMM-Plus and the EAS for the following reasons. First, the increasing frequency of incidents in the South China Sea involving ships belonging to the various claimants. Second, China's growing assertiveness in the area, particularly the use of the phrase "core interest" to describe the South China Sea which presumably raised it on par with Taiwan and Tibet.[56] Third, Vietnam's chairmanship of ASEAN in 2010 during which it included the South China Sea dispute on the organization's agenda with the aim of highlighting international concerns regarding China's actions in the South China Sea.

At the Shangri-La Dialogue in June 2010, Gates raised the South China Sea dispute, stating that the sea was "not only vital to those directly bordering it, but to all nations with economic and security interests in Asia".[57] At the 17th ARF Ministerial Meeting, despite China's strong opposition, eleven of the ARF's twenty-seven members joined the United States in raising maritime security and the South China Sea issues. Six of the eleven countries were ASEAN members, namely, Brunei, Indonesia, Malaysia, the Philippines, Singapore and Vietnam. Cambodia, Laos and Myanmar were silent on the dispute, while Thailand urged a non-confrontational stance towards China.[58] At this meeting, the United States reiterated its national interests in the South China Sea.[59] At the 2nd U.S.–ASEAN Leaders' Meeting in New York on 24 September 2010, the United States had wanted to include the following wording in the joint statement: that the leaders "oppose the use or threat of force by any claimant attempting to enforce disputed claims in the South China Sea". However, this line was dropped because of concerns by some ASEAN leaders that it would needlessly antagonize China and be perceived as moving too close to the United States.[60] A paragraph was included in the statement without mentioning the South China Sea, in which the two sides

> reaffirmed the importance of regional peace and stability, maritime security, unimpeded commerce, and freedom of navigation, in accordance with relevant universally agreed principles of international law, including the United Nations Convention on the Law of the Sea (UNCLOS) and other international maritime law, and the peaceful settlement of disputes.[61]

In October 2010, at the ADMM-Plus, Secretary Gates reiterated the U.S. position on the South China Sea, stressing that competing claims in the sea should be resolved peacefully, without using force or threaten to use force, through collaborative diplomatic processes, and in accordance with customary international law. In addition, while not referring specifically to U.S. maritime security in the South China Sea, Gates pointed out again that the United States has a national interest in freedom of navigation, in unimpeded economic development and commerce, and in respect for international law. According to the U.S. Defense Secretary, the United States would continue to engage in military exercises and activities with U.S. allies and partners in Southeast Asia.[62] U.S. interests *vis-à-vis* the South China Sea were also included in Secretary Clinton's intervention at the 5th EAS meeting.[63]

In May 2011, the 24th U.S.–ASEAN Dialogue was held in Washington D.C. Items on the agenda included the U.S.–ASEAN Five-year Plan of Action, the U.S.–ASEAN comprehensive partnership, U.S. participation in the EAS, as well as global and regional issues, including the South China

Sea.[64] In June 2011, Defense Secretary Gates reiterated America's position on maritime security at the Shangri-La Dialogue, but did not specifically mention the South China Sea except in the question and answer session which followed his address. He stated that maritime security remained an issue of particular importance for the Asia-Pacific region, with questions about territorial claims and the appropriate use of the maritime domain in the region presenting on-going challenges to stability and prosperity in the region.[65]

At the 18th ARF Ministerial Meeting in Bali in July 2011, Secretary Clinton repeated the U.S. position on the South China Sea, stating that the United States, a Pacific nation and resident power, has "a national interest in freedom of navigation, open access to Asia's maritime domain, the maintenance of peace and stability and respect for international law in the South China Sea".[66] Arguably, the United States and ASEAN began to move closer to the establishment of a common position on the South China Sea. For instance, at the 3rd U.S.–ASEAN Leaders' Meeting in November 2011, the joint statement recognized the need to maintain peace and stability in the South China Sea.[67] And in paragraph 18, the two sides reaffirmed their support for the DoC and welcomed the adoption of the implementation guidelines, including the eventual conclusion of a CoC for the South China Sea. They also agreed to make greater efforts to promote

> cooperation on maritime issues, including maritime security, search and rescue, and safety of navigation in the region through promotion of capacity building, information sharing and technology cooperation and explore the possibility of utilizing such venues as the ASEAN Maritime Forum.[68]

At the 6th EAS the same month, sixteen of the eighteen participating countries, including the United States and eight ASEAN members, raised the South China Sea. The only two countries that did not speak on the issue were Cambodia and Laos. Although the Chairman's Statement of the 6th EAS did not specifically refer to the South China Sea, it did include a paragraph, in which all of the EAS members recognized the importance of promoting maritime cooperation and addressing common challenges in East Asia's maritime domain, which certainly includes the South China Sea.[69]

In November 2012, at the 4th ASEAN–U.S. Leaders' Meeting held in Phnom Penh, the U.S. Secretary of State and ASEAN foreign ministers reaffirmed their shared interests on the importance of regional peace and stability, which are fundamental to growing prosperity in the region. In this context, they underscored the importance of maritime security, freedom of navigation and over flight, unimpeded lawful commerce, respect for international law, continued constructive dialogue and peaceful settlement of disputes in accordance with the universally recognized principles of international law, including UNCLOS. They welcomed deepening ASEAN–U.S. cooperation on maritime issues and the outcomes of the 3rd ASEAN Maritime Forum and inaugural Expanded ASEAN Maritime Forum, held in the Philippines in October 2012. The meeting welcomed the U.S. proposal to establish an Expanded ASEAN Seafarers Training Program.[70] In addition, the leaders recognized the importance of the DoC and welcomed its implementation. They looked forward to the early conclusion of a CoC and expressed their support for ASEAN Foreign Ministers' Statement on ASEAN's Six-Point Principles on the South China Sea, adopted on 20 July 2012.[71]

In January 2013, six visiting U.S. congressmen in Manila, led by House Foreign Affairs Committee chairman Representative Ed Royce of California, expressed support for the decision of the Philippines to seek assistance from an arbitral tribunal to be established under Annex VII of UNCLOS to resolve disputes with China over the South China Sea.[72] This was followed by a remark made by Secretary of State Kerry in support of the arbitration when he met with Philippine Foreign Affairs Secretary Albert del Rosario in Washington on 2 April 2013.[73] In May 2013, at the 26th ASEAN–U.S. Dialogue that took place in Washington D.C., U.S. Deputy Secretary of State William Burns, as well as Joseph Yun, Acting Assistant Secretary for East Asia and head of the U.S. delegation to the ASEAN–U.S. Dialogue, reaffirmed the right of any state to use mechanisms under international law for the peaceful and just settlement of disputes, including arbitration.[74] In July 2013, Kerry also pointed out at the 20th ARF that the United States strongly encourages all parties to explore the use of diplomatic, peaceful means to manage and resolve disagreements in the South China Sea. That includes the use of legal mechanisms, including arbitration. Accordingly, it is very clear that the United States gives its full support to the arbitration filed by the Philippines against China. In addition, Obama administration has increasingly moved to strengthen its relationship with ASEAN for the purpose of continuously implementing the U.S. "rebalance" strategy and deepening America's economic engagement with the region.

America's intention to strengthen its relationships with ASEAN, as well as its member states, can be found in the speech given by Secretary of Defense Chuck Hagel at the 12th Shangri La Dialogue on 1 June 2013. Hagel pointed out that with the Philippines, Washington was discussing an increased rotational presence of U.S. forces and helping the Philippine armed forces to modernize and build greater maritime capacity. With the Vietnamese, the United States is expanding cooperation in maritime security, training opportunities, search and rescue, peacekeeping, military medical exchanges and humanitarian assistance and disaster relief. The United States is also expanding maritime cooperation with Malaysia, Indonesia, Singapore, Thailand and Myanmar. The United States strongly supports the ASEAN-led regional security frameworks that include the ARF, EAS and ADMM-Plus to pursue common security objectives in the region. Secretary Hagel extended an invitation to ASEAN defence ministers to meet in Hawaii in 2014.[75] In July 2013, Secretary of State Kerry stated at the EAS Foreign Ministers' Meeting in Brunei that "the EAS can serve a key role in setting and enforcing norms and rules that will ensure we are working collectively to protect the regional peace and stability that our economic future depends on".[76]

America's policy to upgrade its bilateral relationships with the ASEAN member states to the level of "strategic partnerships" has also been observed when Vietnamese President Truong Tan Sang visited the United States in July 2013, when the 1st ASEAN–U.S. Summit was held in October 2013 in Brunei and when Secretary of State Kerry visited Vietnam and the Philippines in December 2013. During his visit to Vietnam, Kerry announced that the United States would provide an additional $32.5 million to help Southeast Asian nations enhance maritime security. Vietnam alone will receive up to $18 million, including five fast patrol-boats for the Vietnamese Coast Guard. In Manila, Kerry committed $40 million to help the Philippines to strengthen its maritime defence capabilities.[77]

In April 2014, for the first time the U.S. Defense Secretary Chuck Hagel and his counterparts from all ten ASEAN members met in Hawaii for informal discussions. During the session on regional security, Hagel revealed that,

> I told the ministers that the United States is increasingly concerned about the instability arising from territorial disputes in the South China Sea. The rights of nations must be respected. It's important that all claimants avoid the use of force or threat of force or intimidation or coercion. We urge all claimants in these disputes to clarify their claims, including their basis in international law, and to use internationally-accepted rules and standards of behaviour.[78]

On 28 April 2014, immediately prior to President Obama's arrival in Manila, Philippine Defense Secretary Voltaire Gazmin and U.S. Ambassador

Philip Goldberg signed the Enhanced Defense Cooperation Agreement (EDCA), which provides a legal framework for the increased rotational presence of U.S. forces in the Philippines.[79] During his visit to the Philippines, President Obama said, "[t]hrough our treaty alliance, the United States has an ironclad commitment to defend you, your security and your independence."[80]

In May 2014, China deployed five vessels — a survey ship, a frigate and three surveillance vessels — near Second Thomas Shoal in an attempt to prevent the resupply of Philippine Marine Corps personnel stationed on the atoll.[81] In addition, it was reported that China was conducting reclamation work at Johnson Reef South and several other atolls in the Spratlys with the aim of expanding its presence in the area.[82] In early May, Vietnam protested the deployment of the Chinese oil rig Hai Yang Shi You-981 (HYSY-981) into the disputed waters near the Paracel Islands, sparking a major crisis in Sino–Vietnamese relations.[83]

In response to China's increasing assertiveness in the South China Sea, the United States has increased its cooperation with the claimant countries, in particular, the Philippines and Vietnam, as well as ASEAN as a whole. The United States urges ASEAN member states to forge a united front on the South China Sea. The United States gives full support to the arbitration filed by the Philippines at the International Tribunal on the Law of the Sea (ITLOS) and has also made it clear that it was keen to see progress on a "substantive" CoC. The stated policy for strengthening U.S.–ASEAN relations was further elaborated by Defense Secretary Hagel at the 13th Shangri La Dialogue on 31 May 2014 in Singapore. Hagel stated that the United States would make efforts to build a cooperative regional architecture that is based on international rules and norms. In addition, the United States would enhance the capabilities of its allies and partners to provide security for themselves and the region, including arms sales. One important example is the sale of Apache helicopters to Indonesia. The United States is also providing robust assistance to the Philippine armed forces to strengthen its maritime and aviation capabilities.[84]

In August 2014, in his opening comments at the 21st ARF in Naypyitaw, Myanmar, Secretary of State Kerry said that, "The United States and ASEAN have a common responsibility to ensure the maritime security of critical sea, lands and ports" and that "we need to work together to manage tensions in the South China Sea and to manage them peacefully, and also to manage them on the basis of international law."[85] At the meeting, the United States proposed that the South China Sea claimants voluntarily freeze the sorts of activities that "would complicate or escalate disputes". This proposal was not discussed by ASEAN ministers because the DoC already proscribes such activities. The U.S. proposal was not even mentioned in the Chairman's Statement of the 21st ARF or Chairman's Statement of the 4th EAS Foreign Ministers' Meeting. However, in his speech given on 13 August 2014 at the East-West Center in Honolulu, Secretary Kerry said that, "ASEAN agreed that the time has come to seek consensus on what some of those actions to be avoided might be, based on the commitments that they've already made in the 2002 Declaration on Conduct."[86]

It is therefore clear that the United States is now committed to playing an important role in the South China Sea dialogue process. A major part of this effort is U.S. cooperation with ASEAN and individual members on a bilateral basis. Accordingly, the South China Sea dispute will remain an important issue in the future development of U.S.–ASEAN relations. The issue will also affect Sino–American relations in the years to come.

CONCLUSION

Since 2008 the escalation of tensions in the South China Sea between China and some ASEAN members, especially the Philippines and Vietnam, has presented the United States with a convenient opportunity to further its aim of upgrading relations with both ASEAN as an institution and individual Southeast Asian countries. Although up until 2009 the U.S. government had remained largely silent on the South China Sea problem at ASEAN-centred meetings, thereafter it began to play a more active role in raising the issue at the ARF, ADMM-Plus and EAS. This policy of "internationalizing" the dispute is opposed by China, but there is little Beijing can do now to reverse the trend.

In 2009 and 2010, some ASEAN members, in particular Thailand, Cambodia, Laos and Myanmar — which have traditionally maintained close economic, political and security ties with China — did not support active U.S. involvement in the South China Sea. Since 2011, however, these countries have modified their positions somewhat by joining their fellow members in ASEAN, and particularly together with the United States, to raise the South China Sea issue at ASEAN-centred meetings. Over the past three years, the South China Sea has become a major policy issue in U.S.–ASEAN relations, and the United States has benefited from rising tensions in the area, which, from the perspective of ASEAN countries, is stimulated by growing Chinese assertiveness in the maritime domain and the rapid modernization of China's armed forces, particularly the navy. For China, it is perceived that its interest and policy in the South China Sea have already been affected by the development of closer U.S.–ASEAN relations and possible cooperation between the United States and the organization to deal with the issue. If this trend continues, it will negatively impact China's national interests, not only in the South China Sea, but also in the Asia-Pacific region as a whole.

Notes

1. "U.S.–ASEAN Leaders Joint Statement", 1st ASEAN–U.S. Leaders' Meeting, Singapore, 15 November 2009, available at <http://www.whitehouse.gov/the-press-office/us-asean-leaders-joint-statement>.
2. "Joint Statement of the 3rd ASEAN–US Leaders' Meeting", Bali, Indonesia, 18 November 2011, paragraphs 17–19, available at <http://www.aseansec.org/26742.htm>.
3. Ibid., paragraph 17.
4. For the statement, see <http://www.aseansec.org/documents/19th%20summit/EAS-CS.pdf>.
5. For detailed accounts, see Yann-huei Song, "The Declaration on the Conduct of Parties and a Code of Conduct in the South China Sea: Recent Actions taken by ASEAN", *Asia-Pacific Forum* 52 (June 2011): 1–54.
6. Ibid., p. 20.
7. "The Senior Officials' Meeting for the Implementation of 'the Declaration on Conduct of Parties in the South China Sea' reaches an Agreement on the Guideline", 20 July 2011, available at <http://www.fmprc.gov.cn/eng/zxxx/t841727.htm>.
8. The text of the guidelines is available in the official website of ASEAN, <http://www.aseansec.org/documents/20185-DOC.pdf>.
9. Barry Wain, "A South China Sea Charade", *Wall Street Journal*, 22 August 2011.
10. "Deputy Foreign Minister: Chinese Side Has Been Making Efforts to Ensure Freedom of Navigation", 12 December 2011, available at <http://www.sab6.com/zcfg/picshow.asp?id=6202>.
11. For the full text, see <http://www.aseansec.org/1196.htm>.
12. See paragraphs 148–149 of the Chairman's Statement of the 19th ASEAN Summit, 17 November 2011, available at <http://www.aseansec.org/documents/19th%20summit/CS.pdf>.
13. "ASEAN's Six-Point Principles on the South China Sea", Council on Foreign Relations, 20 July 2012, available at <http://www.cfr.org/asia-and-pacific/aseans-six-point-principles-south-china-sea/p28915>.
14. "ASEAN Foreign Ministers' Statement on the Current Developments in the South China Sea", Nay Pyi Taw, Myanmar, 10 May 2014, available at

<http://www.asean.org/news/asean-statement-communiques/item/asean-foreign-ministers-statement-on-the-current-developments-in-the-south-china-sea>.

15. Song, "The Declaration on the Conduct of Parties", op. cit.

16. Jusuf Wanandi, "Insight: The South China Sea and ASEAN–China Relations", *Jakarta Post*, 10 November 2011.

17. "China's Syndrome: Ambiguity; What Seizing a Tiny Reef Says About Beijing's Soul", *Washington Post*, 19 March 1995.

18. "Dispute over Islands and China's Gunboats Roiling Asian Waters", *Washington Post*, 5 June 1995. The statement entitled, "Spratlys and the South China Sea", issued by Christine Shelly, Acting Spokesman, on 10 May 1995, can be found at "US Interests in Southeast Asia", Hearing Before the Subcommittees on International Economic Policy and Trade and Asia and the Pacific of the Committee on International Relations, House of Representatives, 104th Congress, 2nd Session, 30 May and 19 June 1996 (Washington, D.C.: GPO, 1997), p. 157.

19. Remarks by Secretary of Defense Robert M. Gates, Shangri-La Dialogue, Singapore, 5 June 2010, available at <http://www.defense.gov/speeches/speech.aspx? speechid=1483>.

20. Ibid.

21. See Kurt Campbell's remarks at the Center for Strategic and International Studies, "CSIS-Bob Schieffer School of Journalism Dialogue: South China Sea: A Key Indicator for Asian Security Cooperation for the 21st Century", 28 September 2010, available at <http://csis.org/files/attachments/100928_schieffer_transcript.pdf>.

22. For Secretary Clinton's remarks made on 23 July 2010, see the U.S. Department of State website, available at <http://www.state.gov/secretary/rm/2010/07/145095.htm>.

23. Ibid.

24. For a copy of the letter, see <http://media.ft.com/cms/4907a816-b1fd-11e0-a06c-00144feabdc0.pdf>.

25. Ibid.

26. For the remarks made on 22 July 2011, see the U.S. Department of State website, available at <http://www.state.gov/secretary/2011/07/168989.htm>.

27. Ibid.

28. Ibid.

29. Ibid.

30. U.S. Defense Secretary Leon Panetta, Statement to ASEAN Defense Ministers, Bali, Indonesia, 23 October 2011, available at <http://www.defense.gov/speeches/speech.aspx?speechid=1624>.

31. "Presentation of the Order of Lakandula, Signing of the Partnership for Growth and Joint Press Availability with Philippines Foreign Secretary Albert del Rosario", Remarks, Hillary Rodham Clinton, Secretary of State, Manila,

Philippines, 16 November 2011, available at <http://www.state.gov/secretary/rm/2011/11/177234.htm>.

32. Ibid.

33. Douglas H. Paal, "Obama in Asia: Policy and Politics", *Asia Pacific Brief* 6 (December 2011), available at <http://carnegieendowment.org/2011/12/06/obama-in-asia-policy-and-politics/8339>.

34. See "White House Fact Sheet: East Asia Summit", Office of the Press Secretary, 19 November 2011, available at <http://iipdigital.usembassy.gov/st/english/texttrans/2011/11/20111119151041su0.2769434.html#axzz1eDErWMlR>.

35. Secretary of Defense Speech, International Institute for Strategic Studies (Shangri-La Dialogue), as delivered by Secretary of Defense Chuck Hagel, Singapore, 1 June 2013, available at <http://www.defense.gov/Speeches/Speech.aspx?SpeechID=1785>.

36. "Managing Tensions in the South China Sea (June 5–6 2013)", Honors Fellows 2013, available at <http://honorsfellows.blogs.wm.edu/2013/06/12/managing-tensions-in-the-south-china-sea-june-5-6-2013/>.

37. "Secretary Kerry's Participation in the ASEAN Regional Forum Ministerial Meeting", Media Note, Office of the Spokesperson, Washington, D.C., 2 July 2013, available at <http://www.state.gov/r/pa/prs/ps/2013/07/211503.htm>.

38. "Testimony of Daniel Russel, Assistant Secretary of State, Bureau of East Asian and Pacific Affairs, U.S. Department of State, Before the House Committee on Foreign Affairs Subcommittee on Asia and the Pacific", 5 February 2014, available at <http://docs.house.gov/meetings/FA/FA05/20140205/101715/HHRG-113-FA05-Wstate-RusselD-20140205.pdf>.

39. "Fourth Annual South China Sea Conference", Remarks by Michael Fuchs, Deputy Assistant Secretary, Bureau of East Asian and Pacific Affairs, Center for Strategic and International Studies, Washington, D.C., 11 July 2014, available at <http://www.state.gov/p/eap/rls/rm/2014/07/229129.htm>.

40. "U.S. Vision for Asia-Pacific Engagement", Remarks by John Kerry, Secretary of State, East-West Center, Honolulu, Hawaii, 13 August 2014, available at <http://www.state.gov/secretary/remarks/2014/08/230597.htm>.

41. See Margaret K. Lewis, "An Analysis of State Responsibility for the Chinese–American Airplane Collision Incident", *NYU Law Review* 77, no. 5 (November 2002): 1404; W. Allan Edmiston, III, "Showdown in the South China Sea: An International Incident Analysis of the So-called Spy-Plane Crisis", *Emory International Law Review* 16 (2002): 639; Jonathan G. Odom, "The True 'Lies' of the Impeccable Incident: What Really Happened, Who Disregarded International Law, and Why Every Nations (Outside of China) Should Be Concerned", *Michigan State University College of Law Journal of International Law* 18, no. 3 (April 2010): 411; and Mark J. Valencia, "The Impeccable Incident: Truth and Consequences", *China Security* 22 (Spring 2009).

42. Ann Scott Tyson, "U.S. Protests Chinese Shadowing in International Waters", *The Washington Post*, 10 March 2009, available at <http://www.

washingtonpost.com/wp-dyn/content/article/2009/03/09/AR2009030900956. html?hpid=moreheadlines>; David Morgan, "U.S. Says Chinese Vessels Harassed Navy Ship", Reuters, 9 March 2009, available at <http://www.reuters. com/article/2009/03/09/us-usa-china-navy-idUSTRE52845A20090309>.

43. "China Hits Out at US on Navy Row", *BBC News*, 10 March 2009, available at <http://news.bbc.co.uk/2/hi/asia-pacific/7934138.stm>.

44. "China Says U.S. Naval Ship Breaks Int'l, Chinese Law", *China News*, 10 March 2009, available at <http://news.xinhuanet.com/english/2009-03/ 10/content_10983647.htm>.

45. Indonesia, Note no. 480/POL-703/VII/10, 8 July 2010, see the Commission on the Limits of the Continental Shelf website, available at <http://www.un. org/Depts/los/clcs_new/submissions_files/mysvnm33_09/idn_2010re_mys_ vnm_e.pdf>.

46. Ibid.

47. The Philippines, Note 11-00494, No. 000228, 5 April 2011, available at <http://www.un.org/Depts/los/clcs_new/submissions_files/mysvnm33_09/ phl_re_chn_2011.pdf>.

48. Defense Secretary Robert M. Gates' speech at the 2009 Shangri-La Dialogue, Singapore, 30 May 2009, available at <http://www.defense.gov/speeches/ speech.aspx?speechid=1357>.

49. See ASEAN Chairman's Statement on the ASEAN Post Ministerial Conference (PMC) + 1 Sessions, Phuket, Thailand, 22 July 2009, available at <http:// www.asean.org/PR-42AMM-Chairman-Statement-PMC+1.pdf>.

50. Remarks at the ASEAN Regional Forum, Hillary Rodham Clinton, Secretary of State, Sheraton Grande Laguna, Laguna, Phuket, Thailand, 23 July 2009, available at <http://www.state.gov/secretary/rm/2009a/july/126373.htm>.

51. See ASEAN Chairman's Statement on the ASEAN Post Ministerial Conference (PMC) + 1 Sessions, op. cit.

52. Chairman's Statement of the 4th East Asia Summit, Cha-am Hua Hin, Thailand, 25 October 2009, available at <http://www.aseansec.org/23609. htm>.

53. "US–ASEAN Leaders Joint Statement", 1st ASEAN–U.S. Leaders' Meeting, Singapore, 15 November 2009, available at <http://www.whitehouse.gov/ the-press-office/us-asean-leaders-joint-statement>.

54. "Testimony of Deputy Assistant Secretary Scot Marciel, Bureau of East Asian & Pacific Affairs, U.S. Department of State, before the Subcommittee on East Asian and Pacific Affairs, Committee on Foreign Relations, United States Senate", 15 July 2009, available at <http://www.foreign.senate.gov/ imo/media/doc/MarcielTestimony090715p1.pdf>; "Testimony of Deputy Assistant Secretary of Defense Robert Scher, Asian and Pacific Security Affairs, Office of the Secetary of Defense, before the Subcommittee on Foreign Relations, United States Senate", 15 July 2009, available at <http://www. foreign.senate.gov/imo/media/doc/ScherTestimony090715p1.pdf>.

55. For the statements, see the website of the U.S. Senate Committee on Foreign Relations, available at <http://www.foreign.senate.gov/hearings/hearing/?id= 70726788-9a47-e88b-53bb-c033438f6454>.

56. See Carlyle A. Thayer, "The South China Sea: China's 'Indisputable Sovereignty' Versus America's 'National Interest'", *China and US Focus*, 23 June 2011, available at <http://www.chinausfocus.com/peace-security/ the-south-china-sea-china%E2%80%99s-%E2%80%9Cindisputable-sovereignty%E2%80%9D-versus-america%E2%80%99s-%E2%80%9C national-interest%E2%80%9D/>.

57. Remarks by Secretary of Defense Robert M. Gates, Shangri-La Dialogue, Singapore, op. cit.

58. Carlyle A. Thayer, "Recent Developments in the South China Sea: Grounds for Cautious Optimism", in *The South China Sea: Towards a Region of Peace, Security and Cooperation*, edited by Tran Truong Thuy (Hanoi: The Gioi Publishers, 2011), p. 127.

59. For Secretary Clinton's remarks made on 23 July 2010, see the U.S. Department of State website, available at <http://www.state.gov/secretary/ rm/2010/07/145095.htm>.

60. Thayer, "Recent Developments in the South China Sea", op. cit., p. 129; "Joint Statement of the 2nd US–ASEAN Leaders Meeting", New York, 24 September 2010, available at <http://www.whitehouse.gov/the-press-office/2010/09/24/joint-statement-2nd-us-asean-leaders-meeting>.

61. "Joint Statement of the 2nd US–ASEAN Leaders Meeting", 24 September 2010, op. cit.

62. Remarks by U.S. Secretary of Defense Robert M. Gates at the ASEAN Defense Ministers Meeting Plus, 12 October 2010, available at <http://www.defense. gov/transcripts/transcript.aspx?transcriptid=4700>.

63. "Intervention at the East Asia Summit", Hillary Rodham Clinton, Secretary of State, Hanoi, Vietnam, 30 October 2010, available at <http://www.state. gov/secretary/rm/2010/10/150196.htm>.

64. Press Release, the 24th ASEAN–U.S. Dialogue, Washington D.C., 25–26 May 2011, available at <http://www.embassyofindonesia.org/press/docpdf/ PressRelease24thUS-ASEANDialogue.pdf>.

65. Speech given by Secretary of Defense Robert M. Gates, Shangri-La Dialogue, Singapore, 4 June 2011, available at <http://www.defense.gov/speeches/speech. aspx?speechid=1578>.

66. For the Secretary's remarks made on 22 July 2011, see the U.S. Department of State website, available at <http://www.state.gov/secretary/2011/07/168989. htm>.

67. "Joint Statement of the 3rd ASEAN–US Leaders' Meeting", 18 November 2011, paragraphs 17–19, op. cit.

68. Ibid., paragraph 17.

69. The statement is available at <http://www.aseansec.org/documents/19th%20 summit/EAS-CS.pdf>.
70. "Joint Statement of the 4th ASEAN–US Leaders' Meeting", 20 November 2012, paragraph 22, available at <http://www.asean.org/news/asean-statement-communiques/item/joint-statement-of-the-4th-asean-us-leaders-meeting>.
71. Ibid., paragraph 23.
72. Pia Lee-Brago, "US Lawmakers: China Should Face Phl Before UN", *Philippine Star*, 30 January 2013, available at <http://www.philstar.com/ headlines/2013/01/30/902637/us-lawmakers-china-should-face-phl-un>.
73. "US Gives Full Support to Philippine Arbitration Bid, Vows to Work with PHL in Seeking Peaceful Resolution of West Philippine Sea Row", Press Release from the Department of Foreign Affairs, the Republic of the Philippines, 3 April 2013, available at <http://www.gov.ph/2013/04/03/us-gives-full-support-to-philippine-arbitration-bid-vows-to-work-with-phl-in-seeking-peaceful-resolution-of-west-philippine-sea-row/>.
74. "U.S. Backs ASEAN on Code of Conduct and Reaffirms Support for PHL Arbitration Move", Press Release from the Department of Foreign Affairs, 6 May 2013, available at <http://www.gov.ph/2013/05/06/u-s-backs-asean-on-code-of-conduct-and-reaffirms-support-for-phl-arbitration-move/>.
75. Secretary of Defense Speech, International Institute for Strategic Studies (Shangri-La Dialogue), As Delivered by Secretary of Defense Chuck Hagel, Singapore, 1 June 2013, op. cit.
76. Jane Morse, "Cooperation is Key to Asia-Pacific Region Success, Kerry Says", *IIP Digital*, U.S. Department of State, 3 July 2013, available at <http://iipdigital.usembassy.gov/st/english/article/2013/07/20130703278115. html#axzz3CG6mObKl>.
77. See "Joint Press Availability with Vietnamese Deputy Prime Minister and Foreign Minister Pham Binh Minh", John Kerry, Secretary of State, Government Guest House, Hanoi, Vietnam, 16 December 2013, available at <http://www.state.gov/secretary/remarks/2013/12/218747.htm>; "Remarks with Philippine Foreign Secretary Albert del Rosario", Remarks, John Kerry, Secretary of State, Department of Foreign Affairs, Manila, Philippines, 17 December 2013, available at <http://www.state.gov/secretary/ remarks/2013/12/218835.htm>.
78. Carl Thayer, "US–ASEAN Defense Ministers Meet in Hawaii", *The Diplomat*, 11 April 2014, available at <http://thediplomat.com/2014/04/us-asean-defense-ministers-meet-in-hawaii/>.
79. Carl Thayer, "Analyzing the US–Philippines Enhanced Defense Cooperation Agreement", *The Diplomat*, 2 May 2014, available at <http://thediplomat. com/2014/05/analyzing-the-us-philippines-enhanced-defense-cooperation-agreement/>.
80. "Remarks by President Obama and President Aquino III of the Philippines at State Dinner", 28 April 2014, available at <http://www.whitehouse.gov/

the-press-office/2014/04/28/remarks-president-obama-and-president-aquino-iii-philippines-state-dinne>.

81. "5 Chinese Vessels Deployed Near Shoal", *The Philippine Star*, 4 May 2014, available at <http://www.philstar.com/headlines/2014/05/04/1319161/5-chinese-vessels-deployed-near-shoal>.

82. "PLA May Build Airfield on Disputed South China Sea Island", *Want China Times*, 4 May 2014, available at <http://www.wantchinatimes.com/news-subclass-cnt.aspx?id=20140504000058&cid=1101>.

83. Vu Trong Khanh, "CNOOC Oil Rig Fuels Vietnam–China Tensions", *Wall Street Journal*, 5 May 2014, available at <http://online.wsj.com/news/articles/SB10001424052702303417104579542722782830580?mg=reno64-wsj&url=http%3A%2F%2Fonline.wsj.com%2Farticle%2FSB10001424052702303417104579542722782830580.html>.

84. "Remarks by Secretary Hagel at Plenary Session at International Institute for Strategic Studies Shangri-La Dialogue", Secretary of Defense Chuck Hagel, 31 May 2014, available at <http://www.defense.gov/transcripts/transcript.aspx?transcriptid=5442>.

85. Paul Mooney and Lesley Wroughton, "U.S. call for South China Sea 'Freeze' gets Cool Response from China", Reuters, 9 August 2014, available at <http://www.reuters.com/article/2014/08/09/us-asean-southchinasea-idUSKBN0G904O20140809>.

86. "U.S. Vision for Asia-Pacific Engagement", Remarks, John Kerry, Secretary of State, East-West Center, Honolulu, Hawaii, 13 August 2014, available at <http://www.state.gov/secretary/remarks/2014/08/230597.htm>.

12

JAPAN AND THE SOUTH CHINA SEA DISPUTE: A STAKEHOLDER'S PERSPECTIVE

Yoichiro Sato

While not a party to the territorial and maritime boundary disputes in the South China Sea, Japan is an important stakeholder by virtue of its significant economic and strategic interests in Southeast Asia and especially in the region's maritime domain. As tensions have risen in the South China Sea since 2007–8, Japan has become increasingly concerned about how the dispute might undermine its national interests. Moreover, Tokyo has a bilateral dispute with Beijing centred on the Senkaku/Diaoyu Islands in the East China Sea, and it sees worrying parallels with recent developments in the South China Sea. In the minds of Japanese policymakers, the disputes in the South and East China Seas are inextricably linked. As a consequence, Japan the stakeholder is also emerging as an important diplomatic player in the South China Sea dispute.

Japan's primary economic interest in the South China Sea is to secure the free flow of maritime trade. The disputes among China, Taiwan, and the four Southeast Asian countries (Vietnam, the Philippines, Malaysia and Brunei) have thus far been confined to the political domain, and even occasional skirmishes involving their respective navies and coast guard vessels have not negatively affected Japan's economic interests in the South China Sea. However, Japan clearly has a critical interest in preventing tensions from escalating into armed conflict. Moreover, Japan keeps a close watch on possible bilateral and multilateral agreements pertaining to the territorial and maritime boundary disputes in the South China Sea. The main objective of Tokyo's diplomatic involvement is to prevent settlements among the claimants that contravene or alter the existing international legal framework and thereby restrict Japan's current rights in the maritime domain.

In terms of international law, Japan's dispute with China in the East China Sea is qualitatively different from the South China Sea disputes. Japan has exercised administrative control over the Senkaku/Diaoyu Islands since 1895, except between 1945 and 1971 when the United States administered them as part of occupied Okinawa.[1] The dispute over the Senkaku/Diaoyu Islands is not multilateral in the same sense that the South China Sea dispute is. China's claim to the islands is built upon its claim to Taiwan, and Taiwan's rhetorical acceptance of the "One China" principle binds the two claims together. Looking at broader maritime boundary disputes in the East China Sea, South Korea is also an important party. However, the Senkaku/Diaoyu Islands lie outside the area in which the continental shelf claims of Japan, China and South Korea overlap. Hence the dispute over the islands is, in reality, purely bilateral. This situation contrasts with the situation in the South China Sea, where disputes exist among the four Southeast Asian claimants and China's claims conflict with all parties. In the South China Sea, with the exception of the Sino–Vietnamese dispute over the Paracel Islands, the disputes are multilateral, notwithstanding China's stance that they are bilateral in nature and should be resolved between China and each of the Southeast Asian claimants on a one-to-one basis.

Japan's efforts to work closely with Southeast Asian countries on the South China Sea disputes since 2010 should not be taken as an indication of Tokyo's support for any of the disputants' claims. Rather, Japan's involvement was an effort to deter China from either securing international recognition of its unilateral claim of exclusive ownership of the South China Sea, or cutting bilateral deals with each of the Southeast Asian claimants at the expense of consistency with existing international maritime law.

On the issue of military activities in the maritime domain, Japan supports the position of its treaty ally, the United States. In the past, Japan did not actively exercise this right under international law, as its commercial vessels enjoyed free passage secured by the presence of the U.S. Navy in the Western Pacific, including in the South China Sea. Over the past fifteen years, however, the Japanese coast guard has gradually increased its presence in the South China Sea in response to the threat posed by maritime piracy in Southeast Asia.[2] The South China Sea has also gained significance for the Japanese Maritime Self Defense Forces (JMSDF) as it increased its naval presence in the Indian Ocean in support of U.S.-led military interventions in Afghanistan and Iraq[3] and counter-piracy operations in the Gulf of Aden. Japan's support for U.S. efforts to preserve freedom of navigation not only counters China's expansive territorial claims, but also possible infringements of international maritime law by Southeast Asian countries.

Japan's desire to play a more active diplomatic role in the conflict management process for the South China Sea is increasingly linked to its efforts to enhance U.S.–Japan security cooperation and keep the United States firmly engaged in the Asia-Pacific region. Japanese efforts to further enmesh the United States into the regional security architecture, especially the East Asian Summit (EAS), and raise the South China Sea dispute at multilateral forums are aimed not only at securing the country's interests in the South China Sea, but also upgrading America's commitment to stability in Asia's maritime domains.

CHINA'S ASSERTIVENESS AND THE END OF JAPAN'S NEUTRALITY

Japan's relevance to the South China Sea disputes has its historical origin in the Japanese military's control of the area during the Second World War. This control was based on the 1939 Japanese claim to the Spratly Islands, ownership of which was contested by France, China and Japan. Japan did not, however, officially claim the Paracel Islands, which was disputed by France and China prior to the war. The fact that Japan placed the Spratlys under the control of its then colony Taiwan lends support to Taipei's present claim to the archipelago, although Taiwan's claim is made from the stance of "One China". The 1951 San Francisco Peace Treaty was not signed by either the People's Republic of China (PRC) nor the Republic of China (ROC), nor did it bestow sovereignty of the Spratlys and the Paracels on any state. The Treaty simply nullified Japan's 1939 claim to the Spratlys and pre-empted the theoretical possibility of a Japanese claim to the Paracels at a later date. Although Japan signed a peace treaty with the ROC in 1952, as with the San Francisco Peace Treaty, it did not attribute sovereignty of the Spratlys or Paracels to either the ROC or PRC.[4]

That Japan did not take a position on the sovereignty of the Spratlys after the Second World War was a product of intensifying Cold War politics during the lead up to the San Francisco Peace Treaty negotiations, and was a reflection of the interests of the Western powers, notably the United States and France. Japan deliberately did not take a position on the sovereignty issue because it might have provided direct or even indirect support to the claims of the PRC and Vietnam.[5]

Although tensions between China and the Southeast Asian claimants began to rise in the early 1970s — primarily due to the discovery of energy resources — the nature of Beijing's claims in the South China Sea remained vague, including the nine-dash line map which the PRC inherited from the ROC but which Beijing did not, and has not, clarified. In 2009, however, a significant shift occurred when China, in response to submissions by Vietnam, Malaysia and the Philippines to the United Nations Commission on the Limits of the Continental Shelf (CLCS), attached the nine-dash line map to a protest note.[6] For Japan, this was a worrying development, as it seemed to confirm that China was claiming historic rights, if not outright sovereignty, over nearly 80 per cent of the South China Sea.

Developments in the international legal sphere over the South China Sea since 2009 should also be seen in the context of China's rising power, a phenomenon of singular importance to Japan.[7] From Tokyo's perspective, China's displacement of Japan to become the world's second largest economy, and its emergence as the number one defence spender in Asia (second only to the United States globally) have weakened Japan's power relative to that of China's. As China's power increased, Sino–Japanese relations become more fractious, especially in the maritime domain. Japan has been perturbed at increasing incursions by Chinese vessels into its waters, especially near the Senkaku/Diaoyu Islands. The ramming of two Japanese coast guard vessels by a Chinese fishing trawler in 2010 plunged bilateral relations to a new low. The Japanese government decision in September 2012 to purchase three of the Senkaku/Diaoyu Islands from their private Japanese owner for the purpose of more effectively controlling against landing attempts by both Japanese and Chinese activists was not met by understanding by the Chinese government, but by large-scale rioting against Japanese shops and businesses throughout China. Since then, Chinese civilian maritime patrol vessels have periodically entered the territorial waters around the Senkaku/Diaoyu Islands. On 13 December 2012, a Chinese military patrol aircraft flew over the islands, dangerously trying to provoke a Japanese military reaction.[8] China also flew an unmanned aerial vehicle (UAV) over the East China Sea in September 2013 and suggested using UAVs for patrolling the skies over the Senkaku/Diaoyu Islands. This was met by an announcement by the Japanese government that after appropriate warnings Japan may "shoot down" UAVs violating the territorial air space.[9] Criticism in Japan that the SDF failed to detect the UAV earlier led to the decision to install a new radar site and deploy 100 troops to Yonaguni Island and double Okinawa-based F-15 jet fighters from twenty to forty.[10] The SDF has also enhanced procurement and training for amphibious warfare over remote islands.[11] China's declaration of an Air Defence Identification Zone (ADIZ) over the East China Sea — including over the Senkaku/Diaoyu Islands — in late November 2013 was met by harsh criticism from Japan and the United States.[12] In addition to China's forceful eviction of Philippine fishing vessels from Scarborough Shoal in 2012, its unilateral declaration of a ten-week fishing ban from May to August 2013 for most of the South China Sea, China also suggested that an ADIZ would be declared over the South China Sea at a future date.[13] Increasingly, Japanese policymakers discern strong links between growing Chinese assertiveness in both the South and East China Seas.

JAPAN AND SEA LANE SECURITY

One of Japan's most tangible interests in the South China Sea is sea lane security. According to a 2009 estimate, Japan imports 4.4 million barrels of crude oil per day,[14] the bulk of which is sourced from the Middle East. Most of Japan's energy imports transit through the South China Sea. Japan's two-way trade with the European Union (13.4 trillion yen or US$152.7 billion in 2010) and the ten members of the Association of Southeast Asian Nations (ASEAN) (18.7 trillion yen or $213 billion dollars in 2010) amounts to 25.1 per cent of Japan's global trade and is dependent on the sea lanes which pass through Southeast Asia.[15] Therefore, Japan's primary interest is in the free flow of maritime trade through the South China Sea.

The passage of commercial vessels through the South China Sea under existing international law is not adversely affected by competing claims to sovereignty over the archipelagoes, for shipping transits even through territorial waters is considered innocent passage which cannot be restricted under normal circumstances. This has allowed Japan to remain largely indifferent to Southeast Asian countries' claims to the Spratlys and

Vietnam's claim to the Paracels. The occupation of islets by China, Taiwan and Southeast Asian countries beginning in the 1970s was designed to establish a physical presence rather than an attempt to control the entire area by any of the parties, and therefore did not pose a threat to Japan's sea lane security. China's occupation of atolls in the 1980s threatened Japan's interests only to the extent that it triggered a number of military incidents with Southeast Asian countries, which had the potential to escalate into major conflicts. Such conflicts, however, have been short in duration and quickly tamped down through diplomacy. Nonetheless, to warrant free passage under international legal regimes, it is important that the South China Sea does not become heavily militarized. The construction of military facilities in the South China Sea, and especially the modernization of the People's Liberation Army Navy (PLA-Navy), is a source of great concern for Japan. Therefore, Tokyo has supported Southeast Asian efforts to implement the 2002 Declaration on the Conduct of Parties in the South China Sea (DoC) and negotiate a binding Code of Conduct (CoC) with China.

Ownership of the atolls in the South China Sea, and the establishment of EEZs and extended continental shelf claims by the Southeast Asian claimants, does not seem to threaten Japan's navigational interests either. However, with China's formal submission of its nine-dash line map to the CLCS in 2009, Japan became concerned that its navigational rights in the South China Sea might be restricted if China were to claim an extended EEZ. The mid-air collision of the U.S. EP-3 surveillance plane and a Chinese F-8 fighter in April 2001 took place outside the boundary that marked China's territorial waters, but within its EEZ.[16] The incident was indicative of China's legal position that coastal states are entitled to ban foreign military surveillance activities in their EEZs. Eight years later, the harassment of the hydrographic survey vessel *USNS Impeccable* by Chinese vessels took place outside China's territorial waters but within its claimed EEZ near Hainan Island. China's actions and arguments to justify them indicated an expanded claim of coastal state's rights to restrict foreign military activities within its EEZs.[17]

Although the Impeccable Incident does not provide a direct indication of China's legal position on the free passage of commercial vessels through its EEZ, China's interpretation of the 1982 United Nations Convention on the Law of the Sea (UNCLOS) is seen in Japan as potentially undermining the principle of freedom of navigation. Moves by China to slightly clarify its claims in the South China Sea have heightened Japan's concerns. However, even if China makes EEZ claims based on its possessions of atolls in the South China Sea, for Japan to criticize China over its EEZ claims may have repercussions for Japan's claim for an extended continental shelf from Okinotori Island, which lies between Taiwan and Guam. China and South Korea have objected to Japan's claim, arguing that Okinotori is a rock, not an island, and therefore cannot be the basis for a continental shelf claim.[18] Accordingly, Japan cannot casually apply the same argument for the atolls in the South China Sea.

China's interpretation of the rights of foreign countries in EEZs could also affect other Japanese security interests. Over the past decade, the Japan Coast Guard has conducted anti-piracy patrols and combined exercises with its Southeast Asian counterparts in the South China Sea.[19] China's expanded interpretation of the coastal state's rights in the EEZ might infringe upon Japan's maritime law enforcement activities in the South China Sea. Japan's position on the various coastal states' claims in the South China Sea since 2009 has hence moved from neutrality to countering China's expansive claims and its interpretation of UNCLOS.

THE SOUTH AND EAST CHINA SEAS NEXUS

Japan and several Southeast Asian countries both have territorial disputes with China. However, commonality stops at this very general level. Southeast Asian countries' disputes with China vary (from the Sino–Vietnamese bilateral dispute over the Paracels Islands to the multilateral dispute over the Spratlys) and Japan's maritime boundary dispute with China is qualitatively different from those in the South China Sea. Given the qualitative difference between the disputes in the South and East China Seas, Japan's position towards the South China Sea dispute has not been particularly anti-China nor explicitly supportive of any particular Southeast Asian claimant country. Nonetheless, as will be described in the latter part of this chapter, the perception of an increasingly assertive China since 2009 has contributed to Japan's move away from a neutral stance towards closer cooperation with the Southeast Asian countries to promote inclusive multilateral conflict resolution mechanisms and enhance the maritime patrol capabilities of the Southeast Asian claimant states.

Japan's dispute with China in the East China Sea involves a small island group which Tokyo refers to as Senkaku and China as the Diaoyu Islands. Japan's administration of these islands through the colonial government in Taiwan and its rejection of the territorial claims by both the Taipei and Beijing governments make this dispute appear as a three-way dispute, although the "One China" principle theoretically unites the claims of the PRC and ROC into one national claim in terms of international legal debates. In this sense, the dispute over the Senkaku/Diaoyu Islands is bilateral in nature.

The real significance of the Senkaku/Diaoyu Islands dispute is not limited to Japan's EEZ claims. The islands are located on the northwestern side of the Ryukyu Trough, a deep oceanic trench that lies northwest of Okinawa and which constitutes an important part of Japan's legal defence against China's continental shelf claim in the East China Sea. Japan insists that the Ryukyu Trough does not completely separate the continental shelf on which China lies from the shallow seabed around the Japanese archipelago. As both countries share the same continental shelf, Japan believes it is only fair to adopt the equidistance line as the maritime EEZ boundary.[20] Moreover, Japanese administration of the islands (which lie inside China's claimed continental shelf boundary) challenges China's claim of exclusive continental shelf ownership. Due to the extremely important legal significance of the Senkaku/Diaoyu Islands, Japan is seriously concerned about possible military occupation of the islands by China.[21] Japanese officials have not been satisfied by a series of clarifications from their U.S. counterparts that the islands are covered by the 1960 U.S.–Japan Security Treaty. Japanese strategists suspect that the United States is unwilling to be dragged into a conflict with China over the disputed islands and believe that ambiguous language has deliberately been built into the treaty to give the U.S. diplomatic flexibility.[22]

China has not yet made a full submission to the CLCS, but has explicitly stated in its "Preliminary Information Indicative of the Outer Limits of the Continental Shelf Beyond 200 Nautical Miles of the People's Republic of China" that: "China reserves its right to make submissions on the outer limits of the continental shelf that extends beyond 200 nautical miles *in the East China Sea and in other sea areas*" [emphasis added]. The anticipated Chinese continental shelf claim in the East China Sea, as indicated in the preliminary submission, stretches all the way to the Ryukyu Trough which marks the end of shallow water less than 200 metres deep.[23]

In the South China Sea, the PRC has also left room for making a continental shelf claim from the Spratly Islands.[24] China's legal stance in the South China Sea therefore is less clear than in the East China Sea. China's preliminary submission does not include any specific ocean-geographic information pertaining to the South China Sea, thereby yielding no clues about its claims in this region. As a consequence of this ambiguity, the ongoing contentions between China and Southeast Asian countries over the South China Sea atolls has no immediate legal implication for Tokyo's dispute with Beijing in the East China Sea. However, viewed from the standpoint of Japanese interests, China's assertion of "historic rights" is incompatible with UNCLOS. China's challenge to modern international law based on its long yet highly subjective history potentially undermines Japanese maritime interests. However, as the basis of China's claim over the South China Sea can only be inferred from Beijing's limited reactions to Southeast Asian submissions to the CLCS, Japan has not yet officially commented on China's legal position.

In addition to China's preliminary submission to the CLCS, actions undertaken by the PLA-Navy and Chinese maritime law enforcement agencies offer further clues to the nature of China's claim in the South China Sea.[25] The 2009 Impeccable Incident led to a sharp exchange of words between China and the United States, but Japanese government officials remained tight-lipped.[26] Nor did Japan comment on the series of incidents between Vietnamese and Chinese maritime agencies in 2009. It was not until 2012 that the dispute was formally discussed between Japanese and Vietnamese officials.[27] That same year, China reportedly warned Japanese diplomats not to discuss the South China Sea dispute with Philippine Secretary of Foreign Affairs Albert del Rosario during his visit to Japan in June.[28] However, the two sides did discuss the issue and Japan has promised to provide capacity building support to the Philippines including the transfer of up to ten patrol boats to the Philippine Coast Guard beginning in 2015.[29] Furthermore, Japanese Foreign Minister Genba's visit to Vietnam in July 2012 resulted in an agreement to promote cooperation and exchanges on "maritime safety" and "defence".[30] This cooperation will include the transfer of six second-hand patrol boats.[31] While the governments of Yukio Hatoyama and Naoto Kan were clearly reluctant to discuss the South China Sea dispute with Southeast Asian leaders, the succeeding governments of Prime Ministers Yoshihiko Noda and Shinzo Abe have been more open to exploring bilateral cooperation with Southeast Asian countries in order to buttress Japan's national interests in the region.

As tensions have ramped up in the South China Sea, and Japanese officials have increasingly drawn parallels with the situation in the East

China Sea, Tokyo has endeavoured to have the former discussed at regional security forums where both it and Washington have a voice. Japan's support for a CoC was expressed by Foreign Minister Katsuya Okada at the ASEAN Regional Forum (ARF) meeting in July 2010. Okada countered Chinese Foreign Minister Yang Jiechi's position that the disputes be resolved bilaterally between China and each of the ASEAN claimants.[32] Okada emphasized that the maintenance of "peace and stability" and "secure maritime traffic" in the South China Sea was critical to the economic development of all countries in the Asia Pacific.[33] On the sidelines of the ARF, Okada had a meeting with U.S. Secretary of State Hillary Clinton, during which they affirmed the need for close policy coordination over the South China Sea.[34]

China's use of coercion in the South China Sea against Southeast Asian fishermen and government vessels has resulted in expressions of concern, albeit restrained, by Japanese government officials. In two separate incidents in May and June 2011, Chinese patrol boats harassed a Vietnamese oil and gas research ship and cut the submerged cables they were towing.[35] The incidents occurred within Vietnam's claimed EEZ. Prime Minister Kan avoided taking sides on the cable cutting incidents, but expressed "Japan's interests in the South China Sea problem" and "expectation for a constructive discussion at the ARF toward its peaceful resolution".[36] Sharper criticism was raised from Japanese conservatives within the political establishment. For example, former Foreign Minister Seiji Maehara, who holds the position of the director of the ruling Democratic Party of Japan's Policy Research Affairs Council, commented:

> The recent conflicts between [China and] the Philippines and Vietnam in the South China Sea might be the result of China's growing confidence toward its national power. Perhaps, the time of Deng Xiaoping's admonition "hide your capacity and bide your time" is over. China is overwhelming in its size. The rules it insists on are peculiar. When dealing with China, difference in values is a huge problem.[37]

In response to a series of Chinese actions in the South China Sea during 2012–14, including the eviction of Filipino fishermen from Scarborough Shoal, the unilateral declaration of a fishing ban and the deployment of an oil rig near the disputed Paracel Islands, Japan has more explicitly seen a parallel between the situations in the South China Sea and the East China Sea and made such understanding explicit. In a joint statement following the 2+2 meeting of foreign and defence ministers with Australia in June 2014, for instance, the Japanese ministers "reaffirmed the importance of promoting the rule of law, and confirmed the importance of regional peace and stability, unimpeded trade and freedom of navigation and overflight of the high seas" and "expressed their strong opposition to the use of force or coercion to unilaterally alter the status quo in the East China Sea and the South China Sea".[38]

Japan has actively promoted discussion of the South China Sea problem at multilateral forums, including at the EAS. In September 2011, for instance, Foreign Minister Koichiro Genba suggested to Secretary of State Clinton that the issue be raised at the EAS in November.[39] Prime Minister Noda also successfully courted the Philippines and Vietnam — the two states most actively confronting China in the South China Sea — in two separate summit meetings to support Japan's position that discussion of the South China Sea and the development of a CoC to ensure "freedom of navigation, unimpeded commerce, and compliance with established international law including the UNCLOS and the peaceful settlement of disputes" be included at the EAS.[40] Japan also attempted to pre-empt China's efforts to deal with the four ASEAN claimants on a bilateral basis and exploit divisions within ASEAN over the South China Sea by courting non-claimant members Laos, Cambodia, Myanmar and Thailand. Japan raised the dispute at the 3rd Mekong–Japan Summit Meeting — held one day prior to the EAS meeting in Bali — on 18 November 2011. The final summit statement included reference to the South China Sea and the language used closely resembled that of the earlier Japan–Philippines and Japan–Vietnam statements.[41] Japan's effort to create an East Asia Maritime Forum to forge a united front with Southeast Asian countries *vis-à-vis* China and court U.S. support resulted in an agreement at the 2011 EAS meeting to expand the ASEAN Maritime Forum to include participation by Dialogue Partners.[42] The 4th Mekong–Japan Summit Meeting in April 2012 upheld "freedom of navigation" and "peaceful settlement of disputes" based on UNCLOS, urged conclusion of a CoC for the South China Sea and "shared the view to develop an expanded ASEAN Maritime Forum (AMF) meeting as a track 1.5 format".[43]

JAPAN'S LEGAL DILEMMA ON FOREIGN MILITARY SURVEILLANCE IN EEZs

China's claim to the entire South China Sea as its "historic waters" is potentially problematic for Japan. The increasingly explicit Chinese claim to the areas inside the nine-dash line has no legal basis under UNCLOS. However, China's behaviour inside the U-shaped line suggests that it regards the area as part of its territorial waters. Most notably, China's opposition to U.S. military operations on, under and above the water as manifested in the EP-3 and Impeccable incidents challenges the principle of free passage within EEZs.

Due to its extensive military operations in the South China Sea, the United States is more concerned than Japan about the implications of China's claims. However, Japan supports the principle of freedom of navigation, which enables its principal ally to maintain its military presence in the region. Japan's effort to use the EAS to discuss the South China Sea dispute therefore serves two objectives. First, U.S. participation ensures that the EAS does not become dominated by China. Second, together with the United States, Japan endeavours to discourage Southeast Asian claimants from cutting bilateral deals with China that might conflict with U.S. and Japanese interests.

The United States has not ratified UNCLOS, yet it observes its provisions as they promote the country's national interests. China's actions during the Impeccable Incident suggest that it interprets UNCLOS to mean that foreign military surveillance activities within EEZs can only occur with the consent of the coastal state. However, Japan's support for the U.S. position that foreign military surveillance is legal in another state's EEZ creates a dilemma, as Tokyo would not be able to protest similar activities by the PLA-Navy in its own EEZ. Increasingly, China has been conducting such activities in Japan's EEZ.[44] China's surveillance activities have implications for the JMSDF's submarine operations, continental shelf claims in the East China Sea and seabed resource mining within disputed EEZs. Thus, Japan supports U.S. intelligence gathering activities in the South China Sea in practice, but does not officially articulate this support.

CONCLUSION

Japan is a country that once administered the Spratlys and briefly occupied the Paracels for military use in the South China Sea. After the Second World War, Japan was forced to relinquish any claim to these islands in the San Francisco Peace Treaty, thereby becoming a non-party to the ongoing dispute. However, Japan's interests in the area rapidly expanded after the war due to its increasing reliance on energy imports and growing economic linkages with Southeast Asia. Although tensions in the South China Sea began to rise from the 1970s onwards, Japan did not express concern until after 2007–8 when China became more assertive and submitted its nine-dash line map to the CLCS. Thereafter Japan's stance shifted from one of neutrality to a more explicit opposition to China's claim. This shift, however, has not led Japan to recognize or support any of the Southeast Asian countries claims in the South China Sea. Instead, Japan's opposition to China's claim is based on a conventional interpretation of UNCLOS and is underpinned by the U.S.–Japan alliance. Japan's efforts to multilateralize the dispute at regional forums in which both it and the United States are members is motivated by a desire to protect and promote Japanese national interests, and not at the behest of the United States. Rather, Japan's gradual emergence as a concerned player, recent shift in policy and subtle ambiguity can best be explained in the context of Japan's own maritime boundary disputes with China and the growing geopolitical rivalry between Washington and Beijing for primacy in the Asia-Pacific region.

Notes

1. Japan's current official position is that there is no international dispute over the Senkaku/Diaoyu Islands since no case has been requested to the International Court of Justice by China.
2. Yoichiro Sato, "Southeast Asian Receptiveness to Japan's Maritime Security Cooperation", Asia-Pacific Center for Security Studies, September 2007, available at <http://www.apcss.org/Publications/Maritime%20security%20 cooperation%20Japan-SE%20Asia%20Sato.pdf>; David Fouse and Yoichiro Sato, "Enhancing Basic Governance: Japan's Comprehensive Counterterrorism Assistance to Southeast Asia", Asia-Pacific Center for Security Studies, February 2006, available at <http://www.apcss.org/Publications/APSSS/ JapanCTCooperation.pdf>.
3. Yoichiro Sato, "Three Norms of Collective Defense and Japan's Overseas Troop Dispatches", in *Norms, Interests, and Power in Japanese Foreign Policy*, edited by Yoichiro Sato and Keiko Hirata (New York, NY: Palgrave-Macmillan), pp. 93–108; Yoichiro Sato, "Japan's Naval Dispatch Plans Expand the Envelope", *PacNet Newsletter*, no. 4A, Pacific Forum, Center for Strategic and International Studies, 24 January 2003; Yoichiro Sato, "The GSDF will go to Iraq Without a Blue Helmet", *PacNet Newsletter*, no. 32, Pacific Forum, Center for Strategic and International Studies, 31 July 2003; "Japan's Security Policies during the OEF and OIF: Incremental Responses Meet Great Expectations", *Asia-Pacific Security Studies* 2, no. 6 (August 2003), available at <http://www.apcss.org/Publications/APSSS/ JapansSecurityPoliciesDuringOEFandOIFSlim.pdf>.

4. Kimie Hara, *San Francisco heiwa jouyaku no mouten* [The Blind Spots of the San Francisco Peace Treaty] (Hiroshima: Keisuisha, 2005), pp. 225–48.

5. Ibid.

6. Article 4 of Annex II "Commission on the Limits of Continental Shelf" of the United Nations Convention on the Law of the Sea (p. 146) sets the submission deadline of the claim for each country "within ten years of" ratification, available at <http://www.un.org/depts/los/convention_agreements/texts/unclos/unclos_e.pdf>. China ratified the Convention on 15 May 1996 but has only submitted "Preliminary Information Indicative of the Outer Limits of the Continental Shelf Beyond 200 Nautical Miles of the People's Republic of China", available at <http://www.un.org/depts/los/clcs_new/submissions_files/preliminary/chn2009preliminaryinformation_english.pdf>. The nine-dash line resurfaced in China's official rebuttal to the joint submission of Malaysia and Vietnam. See "Reaction of China to the Joint Submission made by Malaysia and Vietnam to the UN Commission on the Limits of the Continental Shelf", CML/17/2009, 7 May 2009, available at <http://www.un.org/Depts/los/clcs_new/submissions_files/mysvnm33_09/chn_2009re_mys_vnm_e.pdf>. Furthermore, China in its rebuttal to the Philippines submission to the CLCS, stated:

> Since 1930s, the Chinese government has given publicity several times the geographical scope of China's Nansha Islands and the names of its components. China's Nansha Islands is therefore clearly defined. In addition, under the relevant provisions of the 1982 United Nations Convention on the Law of the Sea, as well as the Law of the People's Republic of China on the Territorial Sea and the Contiguous Zone (1992) and the Law on the Exclusive Economic Zone and the Continental Shelf of the People's Republic of China (1998), China's Nansha Islands is fully entitled to Territorial Sea, Exclusive Economic Zone (EEZ) and Continental Shelf.

"Reaction of China to the Submission made by the Philippines to the UN Commission on the Limits of the Continental Shelf", CML/8/2011, 14 April 2011, available at <http://www.un.org/Depts/los/clcs_new/submissions_files/mysvnm33_09/chn_2011_re_phl_e.pdf>.

7. See Kevin Cooney and Yoichiro Sato, eds., *The Rise of China and International Security: America and Asia Respond* (London: Routledge, 2008).

8. "Chinese Plane Intrusion Over Senkaku Worries U.S.", *Japan Times*, 16 December 2012.

9. "Nihon ga mujinki gekitsui sureba 'senso koui', Chugokugun ga kyocho" [Japan's Downing of UAVs would amount to "An Act of War", the Chinese Military Emphasizes], *MSN/Sankei News*, 26 October 2013, available at <http://sankei.jp.msn.com/world/news/131026/chn13102621010006-n1.htm>.

10. "Japan to build Military Site near Disputed Senkaku Islands", *BBC News Asia*, 19 April 2014, available at <http://www.bbc.com/news/world-asia-27089658>; Kyle Mizokami, "Inside Japan's New Defense Plan", *USNI News*, 20 December 2013, available at <http://news.usni.org/2013/12/20/inside-japans-new-defense-plan>.

11. Helene Cooper, "In Japan's Drill with the U.S., a Message for Beijing", *New York Times*, 22 February 2014, available at <http://www.nytimes.com/2014/02/23/world/asia/in-japans-drill-with-the-us-a-message-for-beijing.html?_r=0>.

12. Yoichiro Sato, "Chinese Announcement of the Air Defense Identification Zone — What Follows?", *PacNet*, no. 87, 4 December 2013, available at <http://csis.org/publication/pacnet-87-chinese-announcement-air-defense-identification-zone-what-follows>.

13. Zachary Keck, "PLA Officer: China Must Establish South China Sea ADIZ", *The Diplomat*, 22 February 2014, available at <http://thediplomat.com/2014/02/pla-officer-china-must-establish-south-china-sea-adiz/>.

14. CIA World Factbook, available at <http://www.cia.gov>.

15. Calculated from 2010 data collected by Japan Customs, available at <http://www.customs.go.jp>. The figure does not include other important trade partners such as India, thereby only conservatively estimating the significance of the South China Sea for Japanese trade.

16. "Who Caused the Crash?", *BBC News*, 5 April 2001, available at <http://news.bbc.co.uk/2/hi/asia-pacific/1260290.stm>.

17. Raul Pedrozo, "Close Encounters at Sea: The USNS Impeccable Incident", *Naval War College Review* 62, no. 3 (Summer 2009): 101–11.

18. "Reaction of China to the Submission made by Japan to the UN Commission on the Limits of the Continental Shelf", CML/2/2009, 6 February 2009, available at <http://www.un.org/Depts/los/clcs_new/submissions_files/jpn08/chn_6feb09_e.pdf>; "Reaction of Korea to the Submission made by Japan to the UN Commission on the Limits of the Continental Shelf", MUN/046/09, 27 February 2009, available at <http://www.un.org/Depts/los/clcs_new/submissions_files/jpn08/kor_27feb09.pdf>. The CLCS ruled on parts of the Japanese continental shelf claim on 26 April 2012, which included a favourable ruling endorsing Japan's baseline around Okinotori Island, "Okinotori-shima kaiiki no tairikudana enshin, nihon no shinsei kokusai kikan mitomeru" [An International Organization Approves Japan's Application to Extend Continental Shelf in the Okinotori Water], *Asahi Shimbun*, 28 April 2012, avaiolable at <http://www.asahi.com/politics/update/0428/TKY201204280012.html>.

19. Richard J. Samuels, "'New Fighting Power!' Japan's Growing Maritime Capabilities and East Asian Security", *International Security* 32, no. 3 (Winter 2007/8): 84–112; Sato, "Southeast Asian Receptiveness to Japan's Maritime

Security Cooperation", op. cit.; Fouse and Sato, "Enhancing Basic Governance", op. cit.

20. Akira Takeuchi, "Nihon shuhen no umi no tairikudana" [Continental Shelf Around the Japanese Seas], paper presented at "Nihonkai wo kaishita hitobito no kyouzon kyouei" [Coexistence and Co-prosperity of the Peoples Around the Sea of Japan], Japan Seaology Promotion Organization, Toyama, 26 November 2005, available at <http://www.nihonkaigaku.org/library/symposium/i051126-t1.html>.

21. Japan's 2012 defence white paper includes a Senkaku-like scenario in the section entitled, "Enhancing Capabilities to Respond to Attacks on Offshore Islands", *Defense of Japan 2012* (Tokyo: Ministry of Defense, 2012), available at <http://www.mod.go.jp/e/publ/w_paper/pdf/2012/21_Part2_Chapter2_Sec2.pdf>.

22. Ukeru Magosaki, *Nihonjin no tame no senryakuteki shikou nyumon* [Introduction to Strategic Thinking for the Japanese] (Tokyo: Shodensha, 2010), pp. 155–62. For a more expanded discussion of Japan's scepticism about U.S. commitment, see Yoichiro Sato, "Japan's U.S. Policy under DPJ and Its Domestic Background: Still Recovering from the Unarticulated 'Changes'", in *The Troubled Triangle: Economic and Security Concerns for the United States, Japan, and China*, edited by Takashi Inoguchi and G. John Ikenberry (New York: Palgrave, 2013), pp. 87–105; Yoichiro Sato, "The Senkaku Dispute and the U.S.–Japan Security Treaty", *PacNet Newsletter*, no. 57, Pacific Forum, Center for Strategic and International Studies, 10 September 2012, available at <http://csis.org/files/publication/Pac1257.pdf>; Kirk Spitzer, "Japan Frets Over U.S. Support in China Dispute", *Time*, 14 September 2012, available at <http://nation.time.com/2012/09/14/84857/>.

23. See <http://www.un.org/depts/los/clcs_new/submissions_files/preliminary/chn2009preliminaryinformation_english.pdf>. South Korea's submission of its continental shelf claim further complicates maritime boundaries in the East China Sea. South Korea's continental shelf claim overlaps with the joint development zone (previously agreed with Japan) and extends further south to the Ryukyu Trough. See Republic of Korea, "Preliminary Information Regarding the Outer Limits of the Continental Shelf", available at <http://www.un.org/depts/los/clcs_new/submissions_files/preliminary/kor_2009preliminaryinformation.pdf>.

24. See endnote 6 for the nature of China's claim in South China Sea.

25. David Shambaugh, "Coping with a Conflicted China", *Washington Quarterly* 34, no. 1 (Winter 2011): 7–28; James Holmes, "China's Maritime Strategy is More than Naval Strategy", *China Brief* XI, issue 6 (8 April 2011), available at <http://www.jamestown.org/programs/chinabrief/single/?tx_ttnews%5Btt_news%5D=37776&tx_ttnews%5BbackPid%5D=25&cHash=4f6ca6e9c397f15fd4c0e0d48ea06e1c>.

26. Officials from Japan's Ministry of Foreign Affairs continue to emphasize the importance of multilateral negotiations and rule making among all stakeholders and not limited to the claimants of the atolls in the South China Sea. Japan's Ministry of Defense became less constrained in criticizing China for its subjective interpretation of UNCLOS after the collision of a Chinese fishing boat and two Japanese Coast Guard patrol boats within the territorial water around the Senkaku Islands in 2010. See, for example, National Institute of Defense Studies (NIDS), *NIDS China Security Report* (Tokyo: NIDS, 2011), p. 19, available at <http://www.nids.go.jp/english/publication/chinareport/pdf/china_report_EN_4C_A01.pdf>.

27. The first time the phrase "South China Sea" appears as a discussion item was during Prime Minister Noda's meeting with Vietnam's Prime Minister Nguyen Tan Dung in April 2012. Ministry of Foreign Affairs (Japan), "Nichi–Vietnam shuno kaidan" [Japan–Vietnam Summit Meeting], 21 April 2012, available at <http://www.mofa.go.jp/mofaj/kaidan/s_noda/vietnam_1204.html>.

28. "Chugoku Minami-Shinakai Atsukawanu yo youkyu, Nihon Gaimusho ni" [China Demands Japanese Ministry of Foreign Affairs Not to Discuss the South China Sea], *Nishi Nippon Shimbun*, 21 July 2012, available at <http://www.nishinippon.co.jp/nnp/item/314027>.

29. Ian Storey, "Tokyo Steps Up to the South China Sea Plate", *Wall Street Journal*, 9 July 2012; Yoichiro Sato, "Japan Aid to the Philippines a Warning to China", *East Asia Forum*, 29 August 2013, available at <http://www.eastasiaforum.org/2013/08/29/japan-aid-to-the-philippines-a-warning-to-china/>; Jerry E. Esplanada, "Patrol Boats from Japan to Start Arriving in 2015", *Philippine Daily Inquirer*, 31 March 2014, available at <http://newsinfo.inquirer.net/590453/patrol-boats-from-japan-to-start-arriving-in-2015>.

30. Ministry of Foreign Affairs (Japan), "Genba gaimu daijin no Vietnam houmon (gaiyou)" [Visit to Vietnam by Foreign Minister Genba (Abstract)], 14 July 2012, available at <http://www.mofa.go.jp/mofaj/kaidan/g_genba/asean1207/vietnam.html>.

31. Shinji Muramatsu and Manabu Sasaki, "Japan to Give Patrol Boats to Vietnam to keep China in Check", *Asahi Shimbun*, 2 August 2014, available at <http://ajw.asahi.com/article/behind_news/politics/AJ201408020031>.

32. Press interview with Foreign Minister Katsuya Okada, 27 July 2010, available at <http://www.mofa.go.jp/mofaj/press/kaiken/gaisho/g_1007.html>.

33. Ministry of Foreign Affairs (Japan), "Dai 17 kai ARF (ASEAN Chiiki Forum) kakuryo kaigo no gaiyo" [Abstract of the 17th ARF (ASEAN Regional Forum) Ministerial Meeting], 23 July 2010, available at <http://www.mofa.go.jp/mofaj/area/asean/arf/arf10_kk.html>.

34. Ministry of Foreign Affairs (Japan), "Nichibei gaisho kaidan (gaiyou)" [Abstract of the Japan–U.S. Foreign Ministers Meeting], 23 July 2010, available at <http://www.mofa.go.jp/mofaj/kaidan/g_okada/asean_1007/usa_gk.html>.

35. "Vietnam Accuses China in Seas Dispute", *BBC News Asia-Pacific*, 30 May 2011, available at <http://www.bbc.co.uk/news/world-asia-pacific-13592508>. "Vietnam in Live-fire Drill Amid South China Sea Row", *BBC News Asia-Pacific*, 13 June 2011, available at <http://www.bbc.co.uk/news/world-asia-pacific-13745587>.

36. Prime Minister Naoto Kan, Response to the Questions by Diet (Lower House) Member Taro Kimura, 5 July 2011, available at <http://www.shugiin.go.jp/itdb_shitsumon.nsf/html/shitsumon/b177271.htm>.

37. Speech by Seiji Maehara, Washington, D.C., 9 September 2011, available at <http://ajw.asahi.com/article/behind_news/politics/AJ201109099829?page=2>. For conservative Maehara, the Senkaku dispute offers an opportunity to attack the government in the furtherance of his own aspirations to become prime minister. For a discussion of intra-DPJ factors in Japan's foreign policy-making, see Sato, "Japan's U.S. Policy under DPJ and Its Domestic Background: Still Recovering from the Unarticulated 'Changes'", in *The Troubled Triangle*, op. cit., pp. 87–105.

38. Ministry of Defense (Japan), "5th Japan–Australia 2+2 Foreign and Defence Ministerial Consultations", 11 June 2014, available at <http://www.mod.go.jp/j/press/youjin/2014/06/11a_jpr_e.html>.

39. Ministry of Foreign Affairs (Japan), "Nichibei gaisho kaidan (gaiyou)" [Abstract of the Japan–U.S. Foreign Ministers Meeting], 20 September 2011, available at <http://www.mofa.go.jp/mofaj/area/usa/visit/1109_gk.html>.

40. "Japan–Philippines Joint Statement on the Comprehensive Promotion of the 'Strategic Partnership' Between Neighboring Countries Connected by Special Bonds of Friendship", Ministry of Foreign Affairs of Japan, 27 September 2011, available at <http://www.mofa.go.jp/announce/pm/noda/joint_statement110927.html>; "Japan–Viet Nam Joint Statement on the Actions taken under Strategic Partnership for Peace and Prosperity in Asia", 31 October 2011, available at <http://www.mofa.go.jp/mofaj/kaidan/s_noda/vietnam1110/pdfs/1.pdf>.

41. Japan, Cambodia, Laos, Myanmar, Thailand and Vietnam declared:

> We recognized the importance of ocean as international common goods. We reaffirmed our support for the 2002 ASEAN–China Declaration on the Conduct (DOC) of Parties in the South China Sea and welcomed the adoption of Guidelines for the implementation of the DOC and look forward to the eventual conclusion of a Code of Conduct in the South China Sea. We reiterated our commitment to universally recognized principles of international law, including the 1982 United Nations Convention on the Law of the Sea (UNCLOS),

available at <http://www.mofa.go.jp/region/asia-paci/mekong/summit03/joint_statement.html>.

42. "East Asia Summit Leaders Welcome Expanded ASEAN Maritime Forum", *Kyodo News*, 23 November 2011, available at <http://www.thefreelibrary.com/East+Asia+Summit+leaders+welcome+expanded+ASEAN+Maritime+Forum. -a0273537464>; "Minami shina-kai nicchu koubou kakkoku to kyoutou saguru nippon, chugoku hanpatsu" [Japan in SCS Disputes Seeking Cooperation with Others vis-à-vis China, China Protests], *Asashi Shimbun*, 6 November 2011, available at <http://digital.asahi.com/articles/TKY201111050493. html?ref=comtop_middle_open>. All East Asia Summit members are eligible to join this forum.
43. "Tokyo Strategy 2012 for Mekong–Japan Cooperation", Ministry of Foreign Affairs of Japan, 21 April 2012, available at <http://www.mofa.go.jp/region/asia-aci/mekong/summit04/joint_statement_en.html>.
44. Japan Coast Guard, "Ryokai tou wo mamoru" [Defending the Territorial and Other Waters], *Kaijo Hoan Report, 2011* [Coast Guard Report, 2011], available at <http://www.kaiho.mlit.go.jp/info/books/report2011/html/honpen/p058_02_01.html#zh01>.

13

CONCLUSION

Ian Storey

Although the authors of this volume approached the South China Sea problem from a variety of perspectives, they each identified and explored five major themes which are key to understanding the dispute and anticipating future developments.

First, all of the contributors acknowledged that due to the South China Sea's position as a major conduit of global maritime trade, peace and stability in the area, and the uninterrupted flow of seaborne commerce, are vital for the economies of all countries in the Asia-Pacific region, and indeed all states in every part of the world. Accordingly, it is in no country's interests — least of all China's, which has enjoyed phenomenal export-led growth over the past four decades — to allow tensions to escalate to the point where sea lane security in the South China Sea is undermined. Several of the authors also stressed that freedom of navigation in the semi-enclosed sea included the right to conduct military activities in the exclusive economic zones (EEZ) of coastal states, an issue which the United States and China strongly disagree on, and which is likely to exacerbate the geopolitical dimension of the dispute in the coming years. Most of the contributors agree that the economic importance of the South China Sea mitigates the prospect of a major war in the area. However, a shared concern is that a tactical miscalculation over fishing rights or hydrocarbon extraction could spark a military clash that has major strategic consequences. As such, the negotiation of effective conflict prevention and de-escalation mechanisms between and among the claimant states and other stakeholders should be a priority.

Second, that tensions in the South China Sea have experienced a dramatic upsurge since the mid-to-late 2000s is indisputable. The experts in this volume agree on many of the triggers, including: rising nationalism over disputed atolls and waters, a phenomenon which has been promoted by several governments — China and Vietnam in particular — but which is also organic and has become more pronounced due to Internet websites and social media; competition over living and non-living resources, but especially hydrocarbons despite the recent plunge in oil and gas prices; and attempts by the various claimants to stake out extended continental shelf claims at the specialized United Nations body in 2009. Many of the contributors also identified the adoption by China of a more assertive, even aggressive, approach in disputed maritime areas as a key reason for the uptick in tensions, especially under the leadership of President Xi Jinping who seems to have centralized decision-making and imposed a greater degree of coordination among the various Chinese actors with interests in the dispute than his predecessors. The authors differ, however, on the reasons for this more assertive posture: Is China reacting to the perceived provocative and unilateral actions of the other claimants, particularly Vietnam and the Philippines? Is China being more assertive because it has larger numbers of naval and coast guard assets to do so? Or is Beijing seeking to achieve dominance within the nine-dash line because it does not anticipate a strong push back from ASEAN or the United States under President Obama? Most of the contributors do agree that the growing geopolitical competition between Beijing and Washington — and to a lesser extent between Beijing and Tokyo — is both a cause and a symptom of rising tensions in the South China Sea, and that while America's pivot/rebalance towards Asia may have been driven in large part by Chinese assertiveness in the maritime domain, it is also perceived in Beijing as a strategy to contain China and has therefore led the government to pursue a less comprising policy. The authors in this volume express mixed opinions on the merits of Washington's Asian rebalance, and the legitimate rights and interests of America in the dispute. A particular concern held by the Southeast Asian contributors is whether ASEAN can play an effective role in mitigating the competition between the PRC and America in the South China Sea, and indeed throughout Southeast Asia.

The third theme that many of the authors note is the growing power asymmetries between China and the countries of Southeast Asia. While in 2000 China's defence spending was only slightly higher than the ten ASEAN states combined ($22.2 billion vs. $19.55 billion), since then the gap has widened considerably. According to one authoritative estimate, in 2014 China's defence outlay was $216 billion — the second largest in the world (after the United States), the highest in Asia and almost six times the amount Southeast Asian countries spent ($38.2 billion).[1] China not only outspends its Southeast Asian neighbours, the military capabilities it has invested in are in many cases far superior to those fielded by ASEAN countries, many of whom still possess outdated air and naval assets. Moreover, in recent years, Beijing has greatly expanded the size and capabilities of the Chinese Coast Guard (CCG), and used it as the lead agency to respond to perceived provocations by the other disputants as well as to advance its territorial and jurisdictional claims. And while Southeast Asian states are also growing their coast guards, increases in spending and acquisitions remain far below China's. As a consequence of rising defence budgets and enhanced naval and coast guard capabilities, China has not only been able to exert a greater physical presence in the South China Sea but also use its military and paramilitary assets to coerce the Southeast Asian claimants. The 2012 Scarborough Shoal and 2014 HYSY-981 Incidents, in which the Philippines and Vietnam were left helpless, demonstrated the effect of China's overwhelming maritime power.

None of the authors believe that a resolution to the dispute, either legal or political, is in sight — indeed the prospects seem to be receding. Accordingly, the fourth major theme is the critical importance of the ASEAN–China conflict management process. Alas, here all the authors agree that the two-decade long process has been disappointing, and yielded few tangible results. The 2002 Declaration on the Conduct of Parties in the South China Sea (DoC) has failed to stem rising tensions, has yet to be even partially implemented, and few of the authors are sanguine about the prospects of an effective and binding Code of Conduct (CoC) being negotiated any time soon.

The fifth major theme that runs throughout the book is the complex legal dimension of the dispute and the importance that all parties abide by the United Nations Convention on the Law of the Sea (UNCLOS). It is in this context that a number of contributors raised the legality of the nine-dash line and the pressing need for Beijing to clarify its claims and explain how those claims comport with international law. An opportunity for China to do so was presented in January 2013 when the Philippines filed for legal arbitration at the International Tribunal on the Law of the Sea (ITLOS) — but China failed to grasp this opportunity. At the time of writing, the Permanent Court of Arbitration (PCA) is still hearing the

Philippine case, and a final ruling is expected in the second quarter of 2016 or possibly later. All agree that it will be fascinating to see what the final ruling will be, whether it will add clarity to the complex and overlapping claims, and how China will respond.

Since the authors revised their chapters, events in the South China Sea have reinforced these central themes and the overall pessimistic assessments contained in this volume. China's artificial island-building has been the most significant development. In mid-2013, China started large-scale reclamation work on seven features under its control in the Spratlys: Fiery Cross Reef, Johnson Reef South, Cuarteron Reef, Hughes Reef, Gaven Reef, Mischief Reef and Subi Reef. Even before the reclamation work was completed, China began extensive infrastructure development on the man-made islands including the construction of harbours, piers, radar and surveillance systems, large multi-storey buildings and on three of the features — Fiery, Subi and Mischief — airstrips capable of accommodating fighter jets and transport aircraft.

The reclamation projects have underscored President Xi's bold and decisive leadership when it comes to advancing the country's territorial and jurisdictional claims in the South China Sea, as many of the authors in this volume noted. It has also exacerbated the militarization of the dispute, for although Beijing has claimed that the facilities under construction are designed mainly to improve the living conditions of personnel stationed on the atolls and will enable China to provide public goods such as search-and-rescue services and marine scientific research, it is clear that the primary purpose of the reclaimed atolls is strategic. The facilities will enable the PLA-Navy and CCG to maintain a permanent presence in and around the Spratlys, without the need to return to mainland ports for reprovisioning, maintenance and crew rotations. Forward deployed PLA-Navy and CCG vessels can be used to enforce Beijing's sovereignty and sovereign rights claims in the South China Sea, and provide protection for Chinese fishing trawlers and drilling platforms operating within the nine-dash line. Radar surveillance and communication systems, together with the presence of combat aircraft on three of the features, will enable China to greatly enhance its maritime domain awareness in the South China Sea and raises the prospect that it will establish an Air Defence Identification Zone (ADIZ) as it controversially did so over parts of the East China Sea in 2013.

The reclamations have generated a great deal of concern across the region, and are likely to generate further tensions with the Philippines and Vietnam, both of whom have protested the artificial island building as violations of their sovereignty and sovereign rights. The construction work is widely seen as a gross infringement of the "self-restraint" clause in the DoC, and as an attempt by Beijing to expand and consolidate its position in the South China Sea before concluding a CoC with ASEAN. As such, China's reclamations have seriously weakened the DoC/CoC process. ASEAN itself, pushed by the Philippines, has expressed "serious concerns" that the land reclamations have "eroded trust and confidence and may undermine peace, security and stability in the South China Sea"[2] — this is ASEAN's strongest statement to date on the South China Sea, though it stopped short of blaming China directly.

China's terraforming has also inflamed tensions with the United States over the South China Sea. Washington has been highly critical of the reclamations, and senior U.S. officials have accused Beijing of altering the status quo, intensifying the militarization of the dispute, destabilizing the region, undermining international norms and rules, and violating the DoC.[3] The Obama administration is, at the time of writing, considering whether to send U.S. navy ships and aircraft to within 12 nautical miles of the artificial islands as part of "Freedom of Navigation Operations".[4] Such exercises could provoke a robust response from China, and heighten the risk of dangerous confrontations between the U.S. and Chinese militaries.

What then is the outlook for the South China Sea dispute? From the standpoint of mid-2015, the picture is less than encouraging. Although all parties desire a solution to the problem, due to a host of obstacles, a political or legal resolution to the dispute seems highly unlikely in the near to mid-term future, especially as no substantive negotiations between or among the claimants is taking place. ASEAN and China will continue their discussions on implementing the DoC and drawing up a CoC, but as China moves quickly to expand its presence in the South China Sea — now greatly facilitated by the seven man-made islands nearing completion — the DoC/CoC process appears increasingly irrelevant to events on the water. Meanwhile, the South China Sea is likely to become a greater source of discord between China and the United States, especially if Washington adopts a more hardline policy towards Beijing that challenges and imposes costs on Chinese actions in the maritime domain. While ASEAN may claim "centrality" in the regional security architecture, if present trends continue, the geopolitical manoeuvring between America and China could well determine how the South China Sea dispute develops over the next decade and beyond.

Notes

1. See SIPRI Military Expenditure Database, available at <http://www.sipri.org/research/armaments/milex/milex_database>.
2. Chairman's Statement of the 26th ASEAN Summit, Kuala Lumpur and Langkawi, 26–28 April 2015.
3. "US Defense Chief Warns Against Militarization of Territorial Rows in Asia", Reuters, 8 April 2015; "China Expands Island Construction in Disputed South China Sea", *Wall Street Journal,* 18 February 2015; Jeff Rathke, Director, Daily Press Briefings, Press Office, Washington, D.C., 20 March 2015.
4. "US Military Proposes Challenge to China Sea Claims", *Wall Street Journal,* 12 May 2015.

INDEX

Note: Page numbers followed by "n" denote notes.

www.ingramcontent.com/pod-product-compliance
Lightning Source LLC
Chambersburg PA
CBHW071353290326
41932CB00045B/1662